S0-AEU-365

INSIGHT GUIDES

Created and Directed by Hans Höfer

ICELAND

Edited by Tony Perrottet

Managing Editor: Andrew Eames

Editorial Director: Brian Bell

APA PUBLICATIONS

L

Part of the Langenscheidt Publishing Group

ABOUT THIS BOOK

Perrottet

Icelanders have always taken pleasure in curious geographical connections: it was an Icelandic farmer, for example, who compiled the world's first dictionary of the Basque language. It thus seems entirely appropriate that the *Insight Guide: Iceland* should be edited by **Tony Perrottet**, a journalist from Australia who lives in New York City and has spent much of his working life travelling in Latin America.

Although this may be one of the few encounters between Iceland and Australia since the 1840s (when the Danish adventurer Jorgen Jorgenson, who had led a failed *coup d'état* in Reykjavík, was transported by the English authorities to Tasmania), the appointment was quite logical. Perrottet first became interested in Iceland while studying medieval literature at Sydney University, neglecting his more "practical" studies in law to pore over the Old Icelandic Sagas (tragically, in English translation). Although he does not entirely credit the far-ranging Vikings for his change of heart, Perrottet took up history and became a wandering journalist.

After travelling exhaustively through India and South-East Asia, working for several years as a foreign correspondent in South America, and settling down as a writer for Australian, English and US magazines in Manhattan, Perrottet finally saw his chance to visit Iceland when Apa Publications decided to add Iceland to its series of more than 180 Insight Guides. Having already edited five difficult Insight Guides – to South America, Chile, Peru, Ecuador and Venezuela – Perrottet seemed more than qualified to tackle the equally challenging *Insight Guide: Iceland*. Soon he was packing his tent and hiking boots for a summer by the Arctic Circle. Having hired a car – not one of Iceland's cheaper luxuries – he visited the remotest corners of the country, writing many of the Places chapters and contributing a wide selection of photographs.

He also set about assembling a talented team of journalists and photographers who were either themselves Icelandic or fellow "Iceland obsessives".

The task of explaining the country's history fell to **Rowlinson Carter**, a regular Insight contributor. A widely-travelled English journalist, television documentary maker and historian, Carter believes that history is not principally about dates and events but a story about people – their glory, bravery, villainy, vanity, lechery and greed. Given such a philosophy, how could he fail to make Iceland's Sagas interesting?

Tackling the delicate task of explaining her nation to outsiders is Icelandic journalist **Birna Helgadottir**. In true Viking fashion, she left her home in Reykjavík in the late 1980s "to win renown for the old homestead" – which she has so far done from a base in London, working for, amongst others, BBC radio and *The European* newspa-

Helgadotti

Scudder

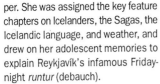

Krist

per. She was assigned the key feature chapters on Icelanders, the Sagas, the Icelandic language, and weather, and drew on her adolescent memories to explain Reykjavík's infamous Friday-night *runtur* (debauch).

Veteran journalist **Bernard Scudder** wrote the chapters on Modern Iceland, Fishing and his adopted home, Reykjavík. He was born in England but made his way to the University of Iceland, where he found himself fatally attracted. A resident of Iceland since 1977, Scudder was for many years editor of the English-language *Iceland Review* before becoming a freelance journalist and translator.

Born of an Icelandic mother and British father, **Anna Yates** returned to her roots in the mid-1970s by marrying an Icelandic naturalist and becoming a reporter for the *Iceland Review*. Now working freelance from Reykjavík, Yates took on a range of subjects from geology, wildlife and the Icelandic horse to the Reykjanes Peninsula and Snaefellsnes. US-born **Jim Wesneski**, a former *Iceland Review* journalist, explains what his compatriots are up to in the Keflavik NATO base and – one of his favourite themes – why life in Iceland is so expensive.

British travel agent and part-time photojournalist **Catherine Harlow** followed her father's obsession to specialise in Iceland, writing the chapter on the remote West Fjords for this book, while biologist and part-time photojournalist **Julian Cremona** took on the Interior and Hunafloi/Skogafjördur. Cremona has organised study trips to Iceland since 1975, and has written several guides to four-wheel-drive motoring.

Nearly a dozen photographers from

every corner of the globe have contributed to the crucial visual side of *Insight Guide: Iceland*. Best known amongst them is US-born **Bob Krist**, whose work regularly appears in a string of international publications. Krist spent more than four months in Iceland working on a feature for *National Geographic*, photographing everything from Saga manuscripts to Reykjavík discos.

Also represented are the Swedish photographer **Hasse Schröder** (who has published his own book of photographs from Iceland), Germany's **Bodo Bondzio** and Icelander **Bragi Gudmundsson**. Perrottet, Harlow and Cremona also added many images taken during their travels.

Yates

Harlow

Cremona

Eames

Thanks for helping to get this book off the ground must go to **Elnar Gustavsson** and **Ingamaria Magnusdottir** of the Icelandic-Tourist Board in New York City, and **Sigfus Erlingsson** of Icelandair. In Iceland, Director of Tourism **Birgir Thorgilsson** and the people of the Iceland Farm Holidays provided invaluable help and information.

The original book was proofread and indexed by **Gillian Delaforce** and was produced in Apa Publications' London office under the direction of **Andrew Eames**. This new edition was updated in Iceland by **Alda Sigmundsdóttir**.

CONTENTS

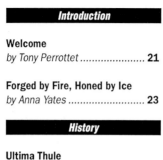

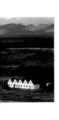

Maps

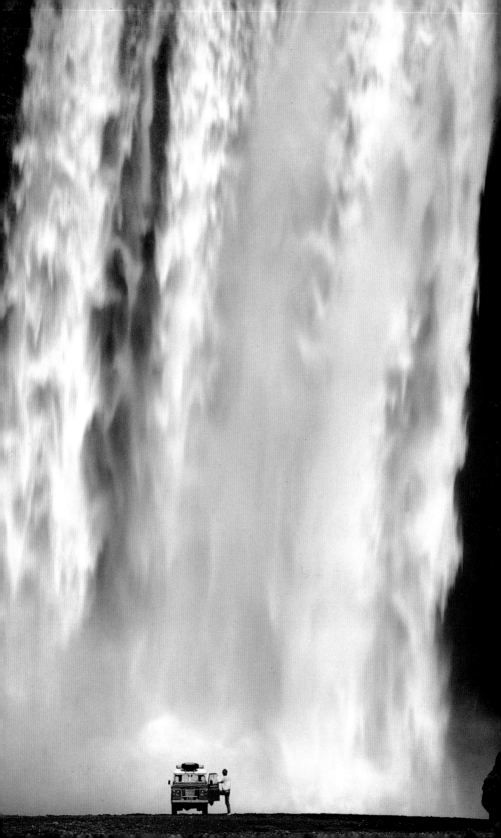

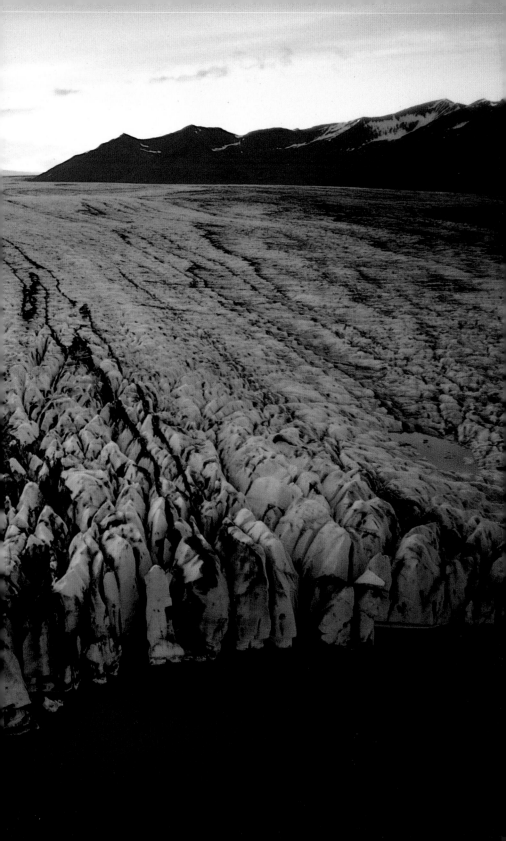

WELCOME

The reason for hereness seems beyond conjecture,
There are no trees or trains or architecture,
Fruits and greens are insufficient for health
And culture is limited by lack of wealth.
The tourist sights have nothing like Stonehenge,
The literature is all about revenge.
And yet I like it if only because this nation
Enjoys a scarcity of population...
— W.H. Auden, *Letters from Iceland*

Iceland has come a long way since the English poet Auden penned these facetious lines in 1936. From an isolated agricultural society that many people thought had scarcely progressed beyond the Middle Ages there has emerged a high-tech welfare state with one of the highest standards of living in the world. Yet at least one thing hasn't changed since Auden's visit: with only 250,000 inhabitants – the same as an average English town or suburb in a US city – Iceland still has a scarcity of population that leaves it with the greatest wilderness areas in Europe.

In fact, Iceland may be the ultimate nature trip. It has no pollution from industry (most people live, one way or another, from fishing) and all energy is either geothermal or hydro-electric. Drinking water comes from pure glaciers; fish, the staple food, is caught in unpolluted seas and rivers; even the lamb and cattle graze in fields untouched by fertilizer. The majority of Icelanders now live in and around the capital, Reykjavík, leaving huge swathes of the volcanically active island – one of the most recently formed on earth – quite deserted. Dotted by steaming lava fields, icecaps, glaciers, hot pools and geysers, the Icelandic landscape has an elemental rawness that nobody who sees it can easily forget.

Perhaps not surprisingly, the quarter of a million people who live on this extraordinary island are an eccentric breed. Speaking Europe's oldest language, little changed since the days of the Vikings, accustomed to the endless light of summer and Stygian gloom of long winters, the Icelanders can be as extreme as their homeland. Rather shy, they will rarely be the first to talk to strangers. But once their traditional reserve is broken through, they can be amongst the most friendly and hospitable people in Europe.

Which all may help explain why Iceland exerts such a powerful hold over travellers – even those who have visited for only a few days – compelling them to return again and again.

Preceding pages: 19th-century turf house at Laufás; Land-Rover and Skógafoss waterfall; Breida Merkurjökull, one of many glaciers (in the South East); snow near Akureyri; mist shrouds a natural bridge over Ofaerfoss waterfall (Eldgjá, central Iceland); early morning at the remote farm of Húsey (East Fjords). <u>Left</u>, rock hopping in the Blue Lagoon.

In geological terms, Iceland is a mere babe. No more than 20 million years have passed since volcanoes on the floor of the far northern Atlantic ocean began to spew lava, laying the foundations of what would become Iceland. Today it is still one of the most volcanically active spots on earth – giving geoscientists the invaluable chance of observing a land which is still in the making.

Movements of the earth's crust: According to the theory of plate tectonics, now widely accepted as explaining the earth's history and development, the earth's surface comprises a number of rigid plates (six major and several minor plates), which "float" on the mass of magma beneath. Geographical features like the Andes and the Himalayas are evidence of massive collisions of tectonic plates, which have folded the earth's crust up to form great mountain ranges.

Plate junctions are invariably marked by narrow zones of volcanic and earthquake activity: at "destructive" junctions, the edge of one plate is forced underneath the other and part of the earth's surface is "lost", while at "constructive" junctions, two plates pull apart, allowing magma to rise from below, reaching the surface and forming new crust. This is what is still happening in Iceland.

Iceland straddles the Mid-Atlantic Ridge, where the African and American plates are being pulled apart. Thus the island is literally being torn in two, at a rate of 2 cm (nearly an inch) a year, with lava rising up from the earth's centre to more than fill the gap.

Volcanic belt: The Mid-Atlantic Ridge, running clear across Iceland from southwest to northeast, is marked by a belt of volcanic craters, hot springs, steam springs, *solfataras* (areas of high temperature activity) and earthquakes. This belt is about 40 km (25 miles) wide in the north, and up to 60 km (40 miles) across in the south, covering about a quarter of the country.

Not surprisingly, Iceland's rocks are almost all volcanic (predominantly basalt). The sheer quantity and variety of volcanic

features, as well as their accessibility, draws geoscientists from around the world. The country's geological history falls into four clearly defined periods, evidence of each being visible from region to region. The oldest rocks, dating from the Tertiary pre-Ice Age period, are the plateau basalts of the East and West Fjords. Slightly inland are the younger grey basalts, dating from the interglacial periods. This is generally open moorland country with less evidence of glaciation. Still further in towards the present-day

volcanic zone is the palagonite formation, from sub-glacial eruptions in the last part of the Ice Age. Typical of these belts are tuff ridges and table mountains, the soft rock often extensively eroded by the forces of wind and water. Iceland's youngest rocks are found mainly in areas within and bordering the present day volcanic zone.

The northwest and the east of Iceland are no longer volcanically active. Most of the rest of the island, however, conceals a seething mass of volcanic and geothermal activity. About 25 of Iceland's volcanic systems have been active in post-glacial times (i.e. the past 10,000 years) – 18 on land and the

Left, *solfatara*, or volcanic vent, of Hverarönd, near Lake Myvatn. **Right**, on Vatnajökull, the largest icecap in Europe.

rest off-shore – and in the past few centuries Iceland has experienced an eruption every five years on average. Some are minor and short-lived, causing minimal damage, like the photogenic eruption of Mt Hekla in 1991. They are known as "tourist eruptions," because they are popular with sightseers.

The ultimate "tourist eruption" was the birth of Surtsey, which began on the ocean floor just off the Vestmannaeyjar (Westmann) islands in 1963. In addition to the familiar spectacle of lava and ash, the Surtsey eruption produced voluminous clouds of steam as cold seawater met hot lava and instantly boiled. Before the end of the eruption, the new island was 2.8 sq. km (1.7 sq. miles) in

out the sun, and led to a disastrous famine. About one-third of the population died.

In 1973, the subterranean peril was brought home with a vengeance, when a new volcano flared up on the island of Heimaey in the Westmann islands group, off the south coast. It buried one-third of the town under lava and ash (see *Crisis on Heimaey,* page 219).

Evidence of subterranean unrest has been felt since the mid-1970s around Mt Krafla near Lake Mývatn, an area free of volcanic activity for over two centuries. A massive eruption in 1724–9 laid waste three farms, before the lava flow halted at Reykjahlíd church, where the congregation was praying for deliverance. Two centuries later, the earth

area – although erosion has now reduced this to about 2 sq. km (1.2 sq. miles). The new islet was a welcome gift to scientists, a natural laboratory which offered them a chance to observe how new land develops.

In the shadow of disaster: Despite an apparently flippant attitude towards volcanoes, Icelanders do not forget the threat they live with. A catastrophic eruption of Lakagígar in the late 18th century poured out the largest lava flow ever produced by a single volcano in recorded history, with a volume of about 12 cubic km (3 cubic miles). As if that were not enough, it also emitted noxious gases which poisoned livestock and crops, blocked

began to move when construction began on the geothermal power station below Mt Krafla; many people concluded that man's interference with the forces of nature had set off a reaction in the depths of the earth. Mt Krafla has erupted several times since 1975, most recently in 1984, although the lava has never threatened the village of Reykjahlíd.

It has been estimated that fully one-third of all the lava that has erupted on earth in recorded history has come from Iceland. As any visitor will soon discover, almost all of it is of the scoria type. Loose, sharp and difficult to cross, it also creates unusual and haunting formations. A small amount is the smooth, hard "ropy" lava, known as "aa" (pronounced *aah aah*) in Hawaii.

Caps of ice: Forged by the fires of the earth, Iceland seethes with subterranean heat. Yet the surface of the island has largely been shaped by cold. Covered by glaciers during the Ice Age, the face of Iceland has been sculpted by moving ice. Glaciation has carved out its present form, gouged the plunging fjords which cut into the coastline on north, east and west, and honed mountain ridges to knife-edges. Little by little, the glaciers are grinding the mountains into sand.

Although Iceland emerged from its glacial pall about 10,000 years ago, it remains a land of glaciers and ice caps – curiously, they are

it is also bigger than all the rest put together. In 1996 a volcano, Bardhabunga, erupted beneath it, melting huge quantities of ice and scattering ash over a 100-km (60-mile) area.

Contrasts between heat and cold are nowhere so striking as in the glaciers which sit atop volcanoes. Some seem extinct: the volcanic crater on which the cone-shaped Snaefellsjökull glacier rests, for instance, has not erupted for 700 years. In Jules Verne's novel *Journey to the Centre of the Earth*, Snaefellsjökull is the entrance to the nether world.

The volcano under the glacier Mýrdalsjökull, however, is alive and kicking. Mt Katla is Iceland's largest caldera, at 80 sq. km (30 sq. miles) in size. The eruption of a

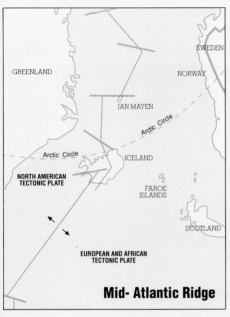

Mid- Atlantic Ridge

believed to have been formed not in the Ice Age but during a cold spell around 500 BC, reaching their largest size during the "Little Ice Age" of AD 1500–1900. From 1920 to 1965 the glaciers were actually seen to be receding, although today the process seems to have been reversed. Ice now covers 11 percent of the island's 103,000 sq. km (40,000 sq. miles); Vatnajökull, up to 1,000 m (3,200 ft) thick and 8,300 sq. km (3,200 sq. miles) in area, is not only the largest ice cap in Europe,

subglacial volcano such as this can create more devastating than those from an open-air volcano. Hot lava melts the ice triggering off sudden floods, known as *hlaups*, which may have unpredictable results.

When Katla erupts, the resulting *hlaup* can reach 200,000 cubic metres (7 million cubic feet) of water a second. In the 14th century, an eruption under Oraefajökull (part of the Vatnajökull ice cap) wiped out all the adjacent communities of Litla Hérad.

Melt water from the glaciers flows out into winding rivers, which swell whenever warm weather melts the glacial ice or when volcanic activity begins beneath the glacier.

<u>Left</u>, the 1973 eruption of Eldfell threatened to engulf the town of Heimaey. <u>Above</u>, cracked earth near Lake Myvatn.

Unlike the crystal-clear rivers fed by rain or underground streams, glacial rivers carry silt from the glacier, so they are generally brownish and murky in colour.

Unbridged rivers are one of the main dangers to travellers in the highlands, as the water can rise with alarming rapidity. (In principle, highland motorists should always travel in convoy with one or more other vehicles, and all rivers should be waded before the vehicles cross to check the depth of the water. Better to be chilly than sorry!)

With so much volcanic activity, Iceland is no stranger to earthquakes. The stretching and straining of the earth's crust at the junction of tectonic plates inevitably produces

benefit of reinforced concrete, and it is difficult to estimate just how much damage the next South Iceland Quake might wreak.

Heat from the earth: Living on a "hot spot" implies coexistence with natural risks. Yet the heat in the earth has also brought its own inestimable benefits. In a cold climate, what could be more valuable than endless natural hot water?

All spouting springs (geysers) in the world owe their name to the Daddy of them all, the Great Geysir in Iceland's southwest, which spouts to a height of up to 60 metres (196 ft). These days Geysir has given up performing, except when artificially persuaded; soap is added to the water to reduce the surface

sudden movements under pressure. Strict building regulations ensure that all man-made structures in Iceland can withstand major earthquakes.

Every 100 years or so a major earthquake hits southern Iceland – referred to, not surprisingly, as the South Iceland Quake. It is due to strike soon, and is a matter of keen interest to the population of the southern lowlands. In 1784 the South Iceland Quake, estimated at 7.5 on the Richter scale, destroyed houses, farms and a cathedral. Again in 1896, south Iceland was convulsed by violent tremors. The Icelanders of the time, though, built in turf and stone, without the

tension, which means that the spring spouts with less pressure. These induced eruptions are only carried out once or twice a year, but nearby Strokkur ("churn") erupts every few minutes to a height of about 30 metres (100 ft), and several more spouting geysers can be seen around the country.

Natural hot water bubbling irrepressibly out of the earth has, of course, been prized by the Icelanders ever since they settled the country. When Ingólfur Arnarson, the first settler, picked a place to live, he named it Reykjavík ("smoky bay") after clouds of steam he saw rising from hot springs. Those same springs, in Reykjavík's Laugardalur valley, became the community's public laundry in later centuries. Housewives would trudge the 3 km (2 miles) from Reykjavík along Laugavegur ("hot spring road") carrying their washing to the springs. The laundry springs (now dry) can still be seen in Laugardalur, adjacent to the Botanical Gardens.

In 1930, geothermal energy was first piped from the springs to the town to heat a few dozen houses and a swimming pool, and Iceland has never looked back. Developing technology has made it possible to look ever farther afield and drill ever deeper to search for hot water, and high-efficiency insulation materials mean that water can be piped long distances with little loss of heat.

fresh water for heating, and also to generate electricity. An unforeseen bonus of the Svartsengi power plant is that the hot lake formed by the run-off water has developed into a popular spa, known as Blue Lagoon. Rich in salt and other minerals, the waters of the lagoon are reputed to be beneficial for skin diseases.

Harnessing glacial rivers: Abundant geothermal energy is one of the resources which help to keep Iceland cleaner and less polluted than other countries. But another, equally valuable, gift was granted by nature in the form of its glaciated mountains and rivers: for the water that comes tumbling over precipices and flowing down steep inclines means

Reykjavík's latest source of geothermal energy is at Nesjavellir, about 30 km (18 miles) outside the city. Today 85 percent of Iceland's atmospheric heating is derived from geothermal sources, and almost every community has its own geothermally warmed open-air swimming pool.

At Svartsengi in the southwest, superheated water (two-thirds of which is brine) from far beneath the earth's surface passes through a heat-exchange process to provide

Left, warning sign at Mt Krafla, near Lake Myvatn, which is largely ignored by the thousands of tourists who pass through every year (above).

environment-friendly and constantly renewed hydro-electric power (HEP). The first small HEP plant opened in Iceland in 1904, and today giant hydro-power stations supply almost all the Icelanders' own needs, as well as providing energy to power-intensive industries which have been attracted to the country. About 13 percent of Iceland's exploitable HEP has so far been harnessed.

Whatever the changes their society is undergoing, the Icelanders still live very close to nature. They take for granted an untamed environment which is still growing, still changing, where eruptions and earthquakes are accepted as part of the tenor of life.

ISLANDIA.

29

A recent visitor to Iceland overheard two farmers talking passionately in a field; they were lamenting the premature death of a young man whom they were sure would have been a great credit to the country. This sorely-missed individual, it transpired, was a certain Skarphédinn Njálsson, a character in one of the celebrated Icelandic sagas, and he had been dead for all of 1,000 years.

Various versions of this story are told and retold by travellers to Iceland, all with the same kernel of truth: Icelanders are quite obsessed with their history, or at least a select part of it. The period they prefer to remember is mostly set between the years 930 to 1030, with little after the 13th century on which they can reflect with any pleasure. The country's current prosperity has only come about since World War II. For the 600 or so years beforehand, Iceland was a grim and depressing place, so much so that a 19th-century English visitor was moved to complain that he never once saw an Icelander smile.

This roller-coaster ride through history has tentative beginnings, with Irish monks looking for a quiet spot to meditate, and becomes substantive with Norwegian Viking settlement, traditionally dated at 874. These same sword-wielding Vikings who notoriously reduced hapless Europeans to prayers for the deliverance of their throats then performed an astonishing volte-face. Within generations, they took up intellectual pursuits – without ever quite putting down their swords – and created a literary legend which scholars talk about in the same breath as Homer and the Golden Age of Greece.

These transformed Vikings not only wrote their own history as had been passed down to them but collected and saved the oral prehistory and religion of the whole Germanic race, which includes most Europeans who are not Latin. They wrote in their own tongue rather than in the scholarly language of Latin, on manuscripts made of calf-skin, one of the

few commodities in Iceland which, bar fish, was always plentiful. A great number of these manuscripts were lost in a subsequent period of extreme hardship – turned ignominiously into makeshift clothes and footwear. Even so, those Icelandic sagas that have survived more than make up for an almost total absence of ancient monuments in the country.

The uttermost end of the earth: The cherished history of Iceland is really quite short by European standards. As far as anyone can

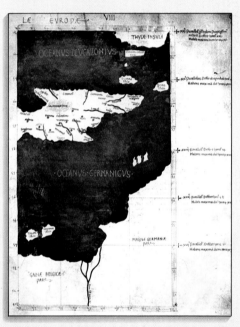

tell, no human had yet set foot in Iceland when, for example, the Parthenon in Athens was already some 800 years old and the capital of the disintegrating Roman Empire was being moved to Constantinople.

The classical Greeks and Romans were certainly interested in what existed at the northern fringe of the known world but were invariably misinformed. The most reliable information came from Pytheas, a Greek who lived in Marseilles. He explored the north personally and returned with an account of a country situated six days' sailing north of Britain and close to a frozen sea. At summer solstice, he said, the sun stayed

Preceding pages: map of Iceland by Abraham Ortelius, Antwerp c.1590. Left, Viking longship approaches the coast of Iceland. Right, the ancient Greek Pytheas included the island of Thule at the world's northern edge.

above the horizon all through the night. The place was called, he said, "Thule".

"Iceland" only came into currency much later, apparently coined by a Norwegian named Hrafna-Flóki who attempted to settle in the West Fjords area but was defeated by the bitter winter. Earlier suggestions, which obviously did not catch on, were "Snowland" and even "Butterland", the latter by a Norwegian who was thereafter known as Thórolf Butter. He said the grass was so rich that butter dripped from every blade.

Nevertheless, it was not Scandinavians who first settled on Iceland but Irish monks driven by the desire to meditate undisturbed. They set out in coracles made of hides

barbarian pressure and Irish chroniclers familiar with writers like Pytheas tended to embellish their work with borrowed, and sometimes counter-productive, erudition. Thus the story of St Brendan's discovery of "Thule" is made quite plausible by a description of a volcanic eruption which could have been Mount Hekla, but credibility suffers in more than one sense when St Brendan discovers that "Thule" is inhabited.

St Brendan and crew were bobbing about off-shore in their little boat when an inhabitant appeared: "he was all hairy and hideous, begrimed with fire and smoke". Sensing danger, St Brendan made a precautionary sign of the cross and urged the oarsmen to

stretched over a framework of branches and twigs. With hardly any seafaring experience, they "sought with great labour… a desert in the ocean". The Shetlands, Faroe Islands and ultimately Iceland were just the ticket. The monks are unlikely to have arrived before St Patrick's celebrated missionary work in Ireland, which began in 432, so evidence of an even earlier presence, like a collection of Roman copper coins, recently found at an archaeological dig, were probably booty or brought by chance visitors.

Frozen gateway to hell: Ireland was a redoubt of Graeco-Roman learning when the Western Roman Empire crumbled under

pull harder. "The savage man… rushed down to the shore, bearing in his hand a pair of tongs with a burning mass of slag of great size and intense heat, which he flung at once after the servants of Christ… 'Soldiers of Christ,' said Saint Brendan, 'be strong in faith unfeigned and in the armour of the Spirit, for we are now on the confines of Hell'." He was not the last to believe that Mount Hekla was the entrance to Hell.

Sound information about Irish activities in Iceland is contained in the works of Dicuil, author of *On Measuring the Earth*, and the Venerable Bede. Dicuil quoted priests who said that between February and August it was light enough at midnight to pick lice off one's shirt. It may be inferred from evidence elsewhere – because there is none in Iceland – that the hermits lived in beehive huts arranged around a central well, church and garden. The monks came equipped with Latin devotional literature, little bells which were used to summon the community to prayer and to exorcise evil spirits, and ceremonial regalia like the crozier, a cross which denoted an abbot.

Since the communities were exclusively male, they would not have put down roots and multiplied in the usual way. The settlements were bound to wither, but was their decline in Iceland gradual? Peace of mind

an axe in a hermit's head, scare-mongering theories about the fate of the Irish do not necessarily hold water. The surest mementoes of the Irish occupation are the "papa" (i.e. priest) place-names.

Viking Exodus: According to Snorri Sturluson, the greatest of Icelandic saga-writers, the Norwegians who chased the Irish away were themselves fugitives, in their case from the tyranny of Harald Fairhair. He became the undisputed master and first king of Norway in 872 and immediately set about mopping up the opposition, seizing the property of defeated chieftains and so forth. Of the 400 names mentioned in the *Landnámabók (Book of Settlements)*, which lists the first

would not long have survived the arrival of 9th-century Norwegians. Ari the Learned, a 13th-century Icelandic chronicler, tells the story from the Norwegian point of view. The disembarking Vikings encountered "some Christians" who shortly afterwards "went away" because they were unwilling to live among heathen. That may be putting it mildly. Nevertheless, the Vikings were usually very candid about their atrocities, and as there is no record of anyone boasting about burying

Left, episodes from St Brendan's journey from Ireland to Thule; meeting the whale and encounter with a demon. **Above**, the Norsemen arrive.

settlers, 38 are known to have been previously powerful chieftains.

Some historians prefer the less dramatic impulse of poor economic conditions in Norway; others that the majority of settlers did not come from Norway at all but were the descendants of Norwegians who had already emigrated to older colonies, particularly in the British Isles. "For the Icelanders," says one authority, "the islands west of Scotland are the cradle of their race in a much higher sense than even their motherland." This last school believes that the Norwegians may even have been outnumbered by the Irish slaves they took along, although only a small proportion of the names included in the *Landnámabók* is clearly Irish.

The best-known story about these early Norwegians concerns two foster-brothers, Ingólfur Arnarson (the official "First Settler" of Iceland) and Hjörleifur Hrodmarsson, who spent a winter in Iceland and were so impressed they returned with two ships piled high with household goods. They were accompanied by family, friends and 10 slaves procured in Ireland in what reads like a routine Viking shopping expedition. The two brothers parted company on reaching Iceland, Ingólfur going to the south coast (later to move to the site of Reykjavík) and Hjörleifur to the west, near present-day Vik.

Hjörleifur was soon faced with a rebellion by his Irish slaves because they resented having to share plough-pulling duties with his only ox. Almost all the sagas carry disparaging remarks about the character of Irish slaves, and this lot were evidently no exception. They first killed the ox, blamed it on a bear and then laid an ambush to get Hjörleifur and his companions when they came looking for the bear. As the hunters fanned out, the slaves were able to overwhelm them one by one. They abducted the women, piled into a boat and decamped to an offshore island.

The discovery of the hunters' bodies shocked Ingólfur. Death at the hands of a slave was such a shameful fate that he could only think that his brother's Christian tendencies had caused him to neglect his pagan sacrifices. The rebels were tracked down to their island refuge and surprised in the middle of a meal of roast puffin. Those who escaped being killed there and then were probably mindful of the penalties meted out to slaves who rose against their masters. Gilli Jathgudsson, an Irish slave unwilling to forgive a master for castrating him (among other grievances), tried to cut his own throat and consequently suffered the agony of a red-hot wash basin placed on his belly with gruesome results. Nevertheless, he survived – but only to be buried alive in a bog. Abandoning their roast puffin, the rebellious slaves fled to cliffs overlooking the harbour and threw themselves off. The island setting for this unpromising start to Icelandic history was Heimaey, one of the group known thereafter as the Vestmannaeyjar (Westmann or "Irish") islands.

Dividing up the island: The Age of Settlement followed these pioneering efforts and by 930 the population of Iceland was about 25,000, which was as many as could comfortably be accommodated on the arable coastline. The interior – nothing but "ice and fire" – was out of bounds and remained so for all intents and purposes until the beginning of the 20th century. The first roads were a concession to the introduction of the motor car in 1913. Before then, boats and horses were the only transport.

The first settlers laid claim to as much land as they thought they could manage, usually by throwing the wooden high seats from their longboats overboard and making their homes wherever they washed ashore – a Norse tradition that supposedly allowed the god Thor to choose the location, even if it did take several months or even years! The steady influx of new settlers meant rationing the remaining land by a process known as "carrying the fire". The owner of the ship bringing a group of immigrants was a chieftain, or at least a man of substance. The rest of the party would be made up of families and attendant slaves or "thralls". The land they were entitled to was as much as could been encircled by a ring of bonfires, with the proviso that they had to be lit with the same torch in the space of a day and that, when burning, they were visible one from another.

The criterion for women, which implies that some arrived independently, was the area a two-year-old heifer could lap in a day.

Iceland has not long been settled when the whole cycle of emigration repeated itself and for the same reasons: either land hunger, adventurism or falling foul of authority. Eirik the Red was a prime example of the last. Already banished from Norway for murder, he was banished from Iceland for more of the same. Having sailed off to the west and found somewhere else to settle, he then attempted to persuade others to join him. To succeed, he needed an attractive name for his new land, and in this he set a precedent for estate agency hyperbole ever after. It was

said, "that I am not destined to find any more lands than the one which we now inhabit." Leifur's first port of call was a place so dismally useless that there was no point in stretching his imagination beyond "Helluland", meaning "Stoneland". This seems to have been northern Labrador.

Conditions to the south improved, hence it was dubbed "Markland" or "Woodland". Further still, he came across a climate so mild that it seemed not to require winter fodder for cattle. It was clearly a worthy contender for settlement, the more so when Leifur's foster-father returned from a sortie jabbering in his native tongue, "rolling his eyes in all directions and pulling faces".

such a lush paradise, he told prospective settlers, that only one name would do: Greenland. Enough people believed him to fill 25 ships, but only 14 ships survived the voyage to the promised land.

Vikings in America: Eirik's son, Leifur, is credited with discoveries even farther afield. Old Eirik would have been a partner in this enterprise, but on his way to join the ship leaving Greenland he was thrown from his horse and injured a foot. "It appears," he

The fellow was understandably overcome by what he saw. The 10th-century Vikings were in the habit of consuming between 10 and 18 pints of powerful mead per day – man, woman and child – along with the odd beaker of sour milk. Leifur and the rest of the company might have been primarily mead-men, but the German recognised grapes and knew what could be done with them. It was thus that the prospect of a fountain of wine gave the name "Vínland" to the future America.

Leifur's observations inspired a surge of voyages to this wonderful place, including one by his dreadful half-sister Freydis in a joint venture with two Icelanders, Helgi and

Left, statue of Ingólfur Arnarson, the official First Settler, in Reykjavík. **Above**, Leifur Eiríksson sights the coast of America.

Finbogi. She seems to have inherited Old Eirik's worst characteristics, and indeed the sagas refer darkly to her "evil mind". She had married her husband Thorstein only for his money and despised him. Freydis fell out with Helgi and Finbogi when they reached Vínland and, laying the false accusation that they had insulted her, ordered Thorstein ("thou miserable wretch") to kill them and their party of 30 men and five women. Thorstein did as he was told but drew the line at killing the women. "Give me an axe," said the ghastly Freydis.

As Freydis was soon to discover, the greatest barrier to settlement in the New World was the hostility of the natives. "They were were similarly unsuccessful. "Although the land was excellent, they could never live there in safety or freedom from fear because of the native inhabitants. So they made ready to leave the place and return home." It would appear that attempts continued at least until 1347, which in turn has led to the not implausible theory that Christopher Columbus was inspired by Icelandic stories about this distant land. These stories were probably still being recounted in seafaring circles when in 1477, according to his son Fernando, Columbus called at Iceland as a crew member of an English ship.

The Icelandic commonwealth: Back in 10th-century Iceland, the displaced chieftains were

small and evil-looking, and their hair was coarse; they had large eyes and broad cheekbones." Freydis's crew retreated in bewilderment when they came under attack by these disagreeable tribesmen armed with catapults, a weapon new to the Vikings. Freydis snatched the sword of a man killed by a flying stone and faced the attackers. Yanking out a breast, she gave it a resounding thump with the flat of her sword. The Indians were as alarmed by this as the Vikings had been by their catapults. They bolted to their boats and paddled off at top speed.

The lure of the land of wine was strong, but repeated attempts to follow in Freydis's wake determined never again to be relieved of their traditional authority by a single ruler. They entrenched themselves in their respective areas, or *things*, and were called *godi*, a word derived from "god". The commonwealth Althing, created in 930, was a parliament whose history is almost continuous to the present day. Presided over by a Speaker or Law-speaker, it was an acknowledgement that certain matters required a central authority. Lesser cases were dealt with by courts in the four "Quarters" of the land.

The Althing met for two weeks every year at the Thingvellir, a point roughly in the middle of the most densely populated part of

Iceland and boasting a remarkable natural amphitheatre. The chieftains – 36 to begin with, later 39 – met in formal session, but every free man was entitled to attend and the occasion acted as a magnet for the whole population. These annual reunions were a great influence in promoting the development of a distinctive culture and help to explain, for example, why the language remained uniquely homogeneous without a trace of local dialects.

Although the Althing was the supreme spiritual and temporal authority, it was not permitted to raise a military force or to exercise police authority. Moreover, the powers of the Law-speaker were deliberately circumscribed so that the office could not be used as a springboard to monarchy; when a chieftain turned up with as many as 1,500 men to support him in a feud, there was nothing the Law-speaker could do about it.

The Althing therefore had considerable difficulty living up to its ideals. In 1012, for example, a litigant who suspected that his case was slipping away on a legal technicality unleashed his private army. The plain of Thingvellir was strewn with corpses before

proceedings could be resumed. Litigation abounded, but the law was so complicated, and the society so riddled with Sicilian-style vendettas, that the due process of the courts was forever on a knife-edge.

Settlers tried to recreate the conditions of pre-monarchical Norway as far as local conditions permitted. In Norway, farmsteads were a collection of separate wooden buildings, one for sleeping, another for cooking and so on. Timber was plentiful there; in Iceland it was always in painfully short supply. The Icelandic farmstead was therefore a single unit, a row of rooms with common walls and a turf roof. Only the framework of the walls was timber; the rest was made up of stones and sod. While the Norwegian *stofa* or living-dining quarters were often large enough to accommodate several hundred guests, the Icelanders could not heat such a space. Their buildings became progressively smaller and the windows fewer.

Life in the longhouses: Larger farmsteads able to afford the luxury of timber imported from Norway maintained the tradition of large festive halls, which also served as religious temples. In the winter a fire was lit in a hearth at the centre of the hall, the smoke being left to find its way out through shuttered apertures in the roof. The chieftain occupied a high seat at one end with the

Left and **right**, images from the recent Icelandic film *In the Shadow of the Raven*, set in the harsh early years.

guests lining benches on either side, their backs to the wall. "The flesh of the sacrificed animals, after being boiled in a large kettle over the fire," says an 18th-century study, "was served up to these rude banqueters, who frequently amused themselves by throwing the bones at one another, the manner in which they were placed on the opposite sides of the hall being very convenient for indulging in this elegant pastime."

Farmsteads were also equipped with an early version of the sauna, water being poured over a stone stove in the bath-house to produce vapour. The early settlers evidently made full use of the water from numerous hot springs to luxuriate in hot baths.

Women of the period dressed extravagantly in gold-brocaded dresses, the men in brilliant mantles and ornamented helmets. Skarphédin, the ill-fated young man whom we met at the opening of this history, made his entrance at one Althing in a blue mantle, blue striped trousers with a silver belt, and high shoes. His hair was combed back behind his ears, and round his head was a gold embroidered silk ribbon. He carried a large shield but took most pride in the battle-axe which had just despatched a certain Thrain.

Skarphédinn, like all young men, was addicted to what amounted to the national sports, horse-fighting and a kind of ball game

called *knattleikr*. Horse fights were theoretically a contest between animals, although owners and supporters could not restrain themselves. "I am tired of this noise," Skarphédinn declared at the height of a mêlée involving horses and onlookers, "it is much better that we fight with the sword."

The ball game is described in the sagas, but it is hard to work out from commentaries on play what the rules were, if there were any. "Thorgrim was unable to hold his own against Gisli, who threw him down and carried the ball away. Gisli sought again to take the ball, but Thorgrim held it fast. Then Gisli threw him down so violently that he skinned his knees and knuckles, and blood was running from his nose… Gisli took the ball in one jump, threw it between the shoulders of Thorgrim so that he fell forwards, and said: 'The ball on broad shoulders broke, which is not to be complained of'…" At the end of the game, in any case, the two players part "not as good friends as before".

Marriages were arranged by the male heads of families – young men could veto the decision, although brides had no say in the matter. Love had no part in the equation. On acceptance as a wife, the woman acquired considerable property rights and other privileges. These did not extend, however, to denying the husband his concubines. A wife could sue for divorce if she was abused; the husband could obtain one for almost any reason that entered his head. Although most marriages seem to have been successful, they could be terminated without ado, as demonstrated by one Bardi and his wife:

"It happened one morning that they were both in the bed-chamber. Bardi wanted to sleep, but his wife, wishing to keep him awake, took a small pillow and threw it in his face for fun. He threw it away, and they kept this up for a while. Finally, he threw it back in such a way that he let the fist follow the pillow. This made her so angry that she grabbed a stone and threw it at him. Later in the day, after refreshments had been served, Bardi arose and declared himself separated from Aud, stating that he would not tolerate any such treatment either from her or anyone else. It was useless to speak in opposition to it, and the matter was thus settled."

Left and right, 19th-century artists' impressions of Vikings on the warpath.

On the rung of government below the Althing, the Icelandic chieftains fought tooth and nail to preserve their individual authority. The chieftainships were in reality more like political parties than regional entities. Dissatisfied "subjects" were at liberty to switch their allegiance – and divert their taxes – to some other chieftain, even one who lived at the opposite extremity of the land. These floating constituencies acted as a slight brake on the wilder excess of ambitious chieftains; the rough and ready equilibrium, however, was severely tested by the advent of organised Christianity.

An Irish curse: The first settlement of Irish monks was at what is now known as Kirkjubaerdklaustur, or Church Farm Cloister. In going away rather than having anything to do with Norwegian heathen, the monks left a curse on any pagan who occupied the site. Otkel Skarfsson defied the curse and paid the penalty. His storehouse was burnt down by an Irish slave acting on the instructions of his scheming wife Hallgerdur Long-Legs, whose face he had slapped. The story ends in a bloodbath, like most conjugal complications in 10th-century Iceland. Another pagan settler, Hildir Eysteinsson, fared even worse. He dropped dead as soon as he laid eyes on his new home.

The Norwegian settlers arriving from the British islands must have encountered Christianity and some may even have practised it, but on reaching Iceland they reverted to paganism, or possibly paganism with a weak dash of Christianity. Icelandic paganism was a mixture of the old Norse deity, spirits who took on the likeness of men or beasts, and fetishes which made trees and waterfalls objects of veneration. A certain Eyvindur Lodinsson of Flateyjardal worshipped two large rocks on his property. Temples were built in holy places, ritual taking the form of

animal sacrifices. Only in emergencies were human sacrifices offered. Temples might have specific house rules; on the holy mountain of Helgafell at Thórsnes, for example, those wishing to enter the temple had to wash their faces thoroughly.

One of the more concerted efforts to introduce orthodox Christianity was made by Thorvaldur Kodransson the Well-Travelled. His travels included Germany, and in 981 he was baptised there by a Bishop Frederick. With the bishop in tow, Thorvaldur returned

to Iceland with the mission to convert his countrymen. The singing, ringing of bells, burning of incense and vestments involved in Christian liturgy made a favourable impression, but the number of genuine converts was disappointing. Too many merely paid lip service to avoid paying the pagan temple tolls, which did not go down at all well with the chieftains for whom the tolls were a source of income.

Matters came to a head when Thorvaldur preached at the Althing of 984. Bishop Frederick never mastered the language and was therefore merely a consultant. Hédinn of Svalbard, an arch-opponent of Christianity,

Preceding pages: a brutal conversion in the recent Icelandic film *The White Viking*. **Left**, Thorgeir, the Law-speaker at the Althing of 1000, who decided in favour of Christianity (from a stained-glass window in Akureyri church). **Right**, brawls between pagans and Christians brought Iceland to the brink of civil war.

engaged comedians to mimic and otherwise poke fun at two of them. Forgetting himself, Thorvaldur leapt on two of the comedians and killed them. Bishop Frederick "bore all with patience" but was outlawed from Iceland together with Thorvaldur. They were preparing to sail when Thorvaldur spotted Hédinn of Svalbard sawing some wood nearby. His parting shot was to kill him. "Because of this violent and unchristian act, Bishop Frederick parted from him and returned to his native country." Thorvaldur abandoned his mission to become a merchant and do yet more travelling.

Viking converts: Christianity made greater advances under the influence of Olaf

Tryggvason, the future king of Norway. Snorri describes him as "the gladdest of all men and very playful, blithe and forgiving, very heated in all things, generous and prominent amongst his fellows, bold before all in battle." His early life gave no clue to the future. He was a full-blooded Viking marauder at the age of 12, terrorising the English coast with his fleet of five longships. Resting in the Scilly Isles, off England's southwest coast, after months of strenuous atrocities, he made the acquaintance of an elderly sage who put him on the True Path. Olaf's conversion was electric and he returned to England in a different frame of mind "for England was a Christian country and he was also a Christian". Olaf applied all his former Viking energies to the conversion of his countrymen in Norway. They were, in short, given no choice. As a travelling missionary he went nowhere without a number of severed heads.

News of Olaf's missionary zeal reached Iceland: "It was rumoured that the people of Norway had changed religion, that they had discarded the old faith, and that King Olaf had Christianised the western colonies; Shetland, the Orkneys and the Faroe Islands." Olaf was clearly heading their way as if Iceland were just another Norwegian colony, an offensive presumption to those who had developed a strong sense of separate identity and pointedly referred to themselves "Icelanders".

It was one such proud Icelander, Kjartan Olafsson, who was cajoled into entering a swimming gala while on a visit to Trondheim. He found himself racing a powerful swimmer who was not content merely to beat him but ducked him repeatedly until he was on the point of losing consciousness. The graceless victor introduced himself as Olaf Tryggvason and suggested baptism. Kjartan thought it prudent to agree, as did other Icelanders who happened to be in Trondheim at the time. "When they accepted baptism," however, "it was usually for some ulterior motive, or because they regarded it as an interesting adventure."

One of these cynical converts, the *skald* Hallfred, poked out the eye of a reluctant convert and ravished a certain Kolfinna to teach her hesitant husband a lesson. The saga's verdict on Hallfred is unambiguous: "In all his conduct there is not a trace of Christian spirit."

Brutal methods: The personal history of Thangbrand, the chaplain to whom Olaf entrusted the conversion of Iceland, was not reassuring. "His knowledge of the Christian doctrine might have made him a valuable man had not his violent temper and vicious habits rendered him unfit for so sacred a calling. He not only squandered the income of his parish, but he organised piratical raids to replenish his depleted stores, an unchristian conduct for which the king finally called him to account. Due repentance saved him from banishment, but he was sent instead as a missionary to Iceland."

Relying on his patron's proven formula of exemplary terror, Thangbrand managed to win a few converts in the two years he spent in Iceland, but on returning to Norway in 999 he had to admit to Olaf that the mission had not been a total success. Olaf was furious and ordered the seizure and execution of all heathen Icelanders resident in Trondheim. The expatriate colony was then quite large and, freshly baptised, they were ordered to Iceland to spread the word. They timed their return to Iceland to coincide with the Althing of the year 1000.

Olaf was actually using Christianity as a cloak for his territorial ambitions on Iceland, and he first had to usurp the Christian party Iceland": "It seems to be advisable that at this juncture…" he intoned, before coming down on the side of the Christians. Still, his oration was a masterpiece of compromise. His advice was that all parties back down and acknowledge that the law, and not any of them, was supreme. "It will prove true that when we sunder the law we end the peace."

The adoption of Christianity as the official religion in 1000 banned the worship of heathen gods in public, but not in private. Nor were the population required to give up their practices like exposing unwanted infants and eating horseflesh. Olaf's further plans for Iceland were never revealed because he died in battle at Svolder the same year.

which had been developing in Iceland of its own accord. There had even been talk of the home-grown Christians setting up an alternative government, and the arrival of the Trondheim contingent in full battle array threatened to tip the country into civil war.

Crucial decision: Thorgeir, the current Lawspeaker, asked for time to think. He spent a day and a night with a cloak pulled over his head, eventually to throw it off and make what has been described as "perhaps the most important oration ever delivered in

It was Olaf's Christian zealotry that was his undoing. The war was the result of a grudge nursed by the wealthy Queen Sigrid of Sweden ever since Olaf first asked her to marry him and then withdrew the proposal when she declined his pre-condition, baptism as a Christian. "Why should I wed thee, thou heathen bitch?" he shouted, giving her a slap in the face to reinforce the point. "That," she replied icily, "may well be thy death." And so it proved.

Olaf Haraldsson, the future patron saint who succeeded to the Norwegian throne in 1016, appealed to Iceland's Christian leadership to tighten the loopholes which allowed

<u>Left</u>, saga figure Gisli the Outlaw in Akureyri.
<u>Above</u>, Christian torture in *The White Viking*.

pagan practices to continue, and he was so pleased with the response that he sent not only timber and a bell for a church to be constructed on the Thingvellir but also an English bishop, Bernhard the Book-wise, to speed up the conversion of the country.

One of the remaining obstacles to the establishment of orthodox Christianity was a shortage of priests. The chieftains regained a measure of authority by putting themselves or equally unqualified nominees up as candidates. As the choice of bishops had to be ratified by the Althing, the church was for a while fully integrated in the social system, and one chieftain at least "did everything in his power to strengthen Christianity".

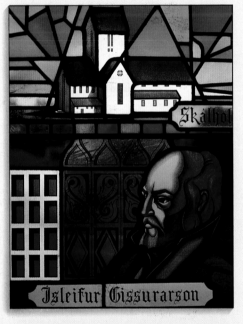

Isleifur Gissurarson

The Golden Age: Iceland enjoyed almost a century of relative peace after 1030, as if the country were quietly digesting its stormy beginnings and putting them into a narrative sequence. Long hours of darkness indoors encouraged story-telling, and the people as a whole were remarkably adept at it. An unusually large proportion of the population could read; the introduction of the Latin alphabet instead of clumsy Runic encouraged them to write as well. The Dark Ages elsewhere in Europe were characterised by clerics copying religious tracts in Latin. In Iceland people wrote in their own language – and about themselves.

Intellectual activity outstripped politics and law. The Althing of 1118 served as a reminder that government was still a hostage to the selfish machinations of chieftains. Proceedings against a notorious murderer named Mar degenerated into a bloody trial of strength between two chieftains which disrupted the Althing year after year. The general assembly passed numerous resolutions outlawing the culprits; they were laughed off.

The flaw in the legal system, as we have seen, was that the Althing could not initiate prosecutions nor force its decisions on spirited opposition. A complicated web of murder led in 1163 to violent clashes in what became known as the "Stone-Throwing Summer". The combatants were said to have been driven to such rage that they were hurling stones so big and heavy that normal men, when they tried to clean up the aftermath, could not lift them at all.

In the course of the 12th century, the country was divided between bishops aligned with the see of Trondheim and half a dozen clans in a state of perpetual internecine warfare. At the same time economic conditions deteriorated and, as the Icelanders had no timber for ship-building, they were increasingly dependent on Norwegian suppliers and shippers. Matters came to a head in the so-called Sturlung Age (1230–64), a combination of horrific violence and, ironically, an intellectual flowering which has been called the Icelandic Renaissance.

The Althing's impotence in the face of feuds tearing apart the most powerful families in the land underlined the fact that anarchy had taken over. The king of Norway was as ever ready to step in and the papal legate approved. "It was unreasonable," he said, "that (Icelanders) did not serve a king like every other country in the world."

In 1262 the Althing submitted to King Haakon by granting him the right to collect taxes. In practice, submission left the Icelandic chieftains in control of their own affairs as before except that they were forbidden to wage war on one another. The people won a respite from constant upheaval, but by the end of the 13th century it was apparent that Iceland had started an unstoppable decline.

Left, stained-glass image of Isleifur Gissurarson, the first bishop of Skálholt. **Right**, carved pulpit in Laufás church.

THE SAGA OF SNORRI

The personal life of Snorri Sturluson was made of the very same stuff which he exploited with such genius as the outstanding man of letters of medieval Scandinavia. His family were themselves descendants of the saga hero Egill Skallagrílmsson and, in Snorri's lifetime, gave their name to the so-called Sturlung Age characterised by the "Stone-Throwing Summer".

Snorri's father Sturla had a part in that episode and was repeatedly hauled up before the Althing, but "with nonchalant disregard for court deci-

sions he pursued his course of feud and contention with a certain diabolic good cheer".

Snorri, born at Hvammur in western Iceland in 1179, was the youngest of three talented legitimate sons. Following a particularly convoluted lawsuit, the family's powerful enemy Jón Loftsson offered to foster Snorri when he was three years old. In Iceland at that time an offer to foster someone's son was a compliment and honour in any circumstances. In Snorri's case it was especially fortuitous because it meant he was reared in the heady atmosphere of Oddi, the intellectual heart of the country.

Snorri's father died soon after his departure, and when he emerged from Oddi most of the

family money had been squandered by his mother. Snorri put that right by marrying, at 21, Herdis, daughter of the appropriately named Bersi the Wealthy.

It has never been suggested that Snorri married Herdis for any reason other than her money. The marriage also made him heir to Bersi's chieftainship, and he acquired another from a maternal uncle. Not yet satisfied with this, at the age of 28 Snorri moved into Reykholt, a grand estate, having reached an understanding with the elderly owner that he would eventually inherit the place in return for looking after the owner and his family.

The bath which Snorri built at Reykholt is one of Iceland's very few archaeological remains. It was "a circular basin, constructed of stones, without any cement, that nicely fitted together... about fourteen feet in diameter and about six feet deep." Hot and cold water was piped in from separate springs and could be mixed to provide the desired temperature. The hot springs were also used for remarkably efficient cooking, pots simply being lowered into them.

Snorri prospered in a number of ways. He kept a string of concubines who gave him several children, and he was elected Law-speaker of the Althing in 1215, an office he filled with distinction. Then, three years later, when 40, Snorri was sent to Norway as a kind of ambassador and walked straight into a diplomatic crisis.

The son of an Icelandic chieftain had drowned by accident in the Norwegian town of Bergen, and the father of the drowned boy held the townsfolk responsible. Seizing a number of Bergen merchants who happened to be in Iceland, he demanded the colossal ransom of 900 marks of silver. For good measure, he rounded up some Norwegians who happened to look in on their way back from Greenland and extorted money from them. As a result of this unilateral justice, Iceland and Norway found themselves on the brink of war.

Snorri handled this fiery baptism in diplomacy with considerable aplomb. He persuaded the Norwegians that a pact with Iceland's leading families was preferable to an invasion, but in Iceland this was interpreted as private collusion between Snorri and King Haakon IV. All his diplomatic skills were necessary to dispel these suspicions when he returned to Iceland, and it is a measure of his success that he was elected to a second term as Law-speaker.

Turning to family matters, he arranged good marriages for his three daughters and, for himself – he moved in with the richest woman in Iceland, the widow Hallveig Ormsdóttir. He then talked her into signing over half her property and allowing him to run the financial affairs of her two sons.

Snorri thus worked himself into the position of the richest man in Iceland which gave him the freedom to concentrate on his writing.

His solitude was disrupted by a succession of family problems, not the least of which was caused by the outrageous behaviour of Oraekja, one of his illegitimate sons. Snorri's brother and nephew captured the obnoxious youth, castrated him – the common fate of vagabonds – and applied to the court to have him exiled. Snorri nursed Oraekja during his banishment to Norway but Snorri's presence in Iceland was soon required because of another spate of killings within

treason. Snorri defied him and sailed to Iceland.

Keen to ingratiate himself with the king, Gissur volunteered to serve Snorri with a royal warrant. Gissur arrived at Reykholt in the dead of night with 70 armed men. Snorri, then 63, took to the cellar, but a servant gave him away. Of the five men who entered the cellar, three had once been sons-in-law to Snorri. One of them, Simon, gave the order to kill him. The death scene appears in a saga with typical economy:

"'Do not smite,' said Snorri.
'Smite,' said Simon.
'Do not smite,' said Snorri.
Then Arni gave him his deathblow, and Thorstein and he made an end of him."

Iceland's greatest saga-writer thus died on 22

the family. The Norwegian king Haakon, however, wished Snorri to remain in Norway because he was bent on bringing Iceland under his wing. To that end he cultivated Gissur Thorvaldsson, one of Snorri's rival chieftains and coincidentally a former son-in-law. The Norwegian bishops were also keen to help because they resented Iceland's traditional right to appoint its own bishops. The king felt that Snorri's presence in Iceland might interfere with his scheming so he warned Snorri that leaving Norway would be treated as

Left, statue of Snorri Sturluson. Above, Snorri's pool at Reykholt, one of Iceland's few archaeological remains.

September 1241 in a manner befitting his own family's *Egils Saga*, which he may well have written himself. His undisputed epitaph, however, is the *Heimskringla*, a monumental history of the kings of Norway whose breathtaking scope is reflected in the first words: "The face of the earth inhabited by man..." He worked, says the editor of a modern translation, "as if he were weaving a huge tapestry" and, indeed, the whole is spun around no fewer than 1,300 characters who are mentioned by name. Thomas Carlyle, the 19th-century Scottish historian and author of *The Early Kings of Norway*, was not alone in regarding it as "among the great history books of the world". ∎

The terms of Iceland's submission to Norway were contained in the "Ancient Covenant" and every taxpayer was obliged to pay an annual royal tribute in the native wool. Royal officials replaced the *godar*, and Gissur's reward for organising Snorri's murder was to be created the earl of Iceland. Even the weather served as a portent: it turned colder, and all over Scandinavia men dispensed with kilts and put on trousers. Temperatures continued to drop, necessitating underwear.

Gissur's "character and previous record", says Knut Gjerset, the eminent 20th-century Icelandic-American historian, "rendered him unfit to maintain peace and order, which was his principal official duty". In 1264, his enemies stormed his daughter's wedding, killing 25 guests while Gissur hid in a tub of whey. His revenge was first to lay waste the Rangarvalla district and then to invite his enemies to a peace conference. Their leader was executed, whereupon Gissur announced his retirement to a monastery. The Norwegian king decreed, and most people agreed, that Iceland would try to get along without any more earls.

Imposing the law: Iceland clearly needed a new framework of government, starting with a new legal system. The "Code of Magnús Lagaboter" proved so efficient that it served with very few amendments until the 19th century. In keeping with the contemporary view that monarchy was part of the divine order of things, the crown was made the supreme legal authority, and lawbreakers were answerable to it, not to the injured party as previously.

Murder, robbery, rape, counterfeiting, forgery and seduction became capital offences, but judges were supposed to administer the law dispassionately. "For we are to hate evil deeds," the judge's manual advised, "but love men by natural instinct as our fellow Christians, but most of all their souls."

For the first time Iceland acquired something of a national army as opposed to dozens of private armies, although it was only

240 strong and the men were posted to Norway in defence of the realm against Danish and Hanseatic threats. The power of the Church was strengthened, but it rested increasingly in the hands of foreign bishops. Church reforms required clerical celibacy, and even sub-deacons who had been married for years and had several children were obliged to give up their wives.

Public dissatisfaction in a generally peaceful era was provoked by something that would haunt Iceland for centuries to come: the control of trade. Iceland had to trade to survive, and with no merchant fleet of its own the country was at the mercy of Norwegian merchants. The king was supposed to ensure that a certain number of ships called regularly to deliver essential supplies and take away the exports which paid for them. All too often the ships never came, particularly when they were most needed because of famine and natural disasters. Even supplies of altar wine dried up and the celebration of mass had to be suspended.

Years of disaster: The 14th century presaged a run of calamities almost beyond belief. Hekla erupted repeatedly, and the cloud of volcanic dust in the atmosphere seemed to anticipate modern fears of a nuclear winter. A pall of darkness settled over southern Iceland for days on end and the following winters were unusually severe. Heavy snowfalls thawed to become devastating floods.

Hekla's 1389 eruption could be felt and heard all over the island, according to contemporary accounts: "Fire arose not only from the mountain but from the woods above Skard, the eruption being so violent that two mountains were formed with a chasm between them. In the neighbourhood hot springs welled up, forming lakes of boiling water." Smallpox and other epidemics added to the misery caused by the eruption.

The industrious Hanseatic merchants – by then well-established on Norway's west coast – undoubtedly could and would have traded with Iceland, but the Norwegian king set a precedent later to be slavishly followed by the Danes, declaring that trade with Iceland was a crown monopoly. As such, Iceland went through the extremes of either being

Left, dried fish became a staple of the Icelandic diet and a key element in trade for centuries.

completely neglected or facing demands for greater quantities of the prized codfish than the population could afford to let go.

The Scandinavian union of Norway, Denmark and Sweden effected at Kalmar in 1397 transferred the sovereignty of Iceland from Norway to Denmark, and the Danes were even more remote and less interested in Iceland than the Norwegians. Conditions deteriorated accordingly: "Our laws provide that six ships should come hither from Norway every year, which has not happened for a long time," reads a plaintive message to the Danish king, "a cause from which Your Grace and our poor country has suffered most grievous harm. Therefore, trusting in

God's grace and your help, we have traded with foreigners who have come hither peacefully on legitimate business, but we have punished those fishermen and owners of fishing-smacks who have robbed and caused disturbances."

Smugglers and pirates: The unauthorised foreign traders were mostly English and their activities would be Iceland's main access to the outside world for centuries to come. They provided essential commodities in exchange for fish, which would probably have been acceptable to the Icelanders had the English not then decided that they were better equipped to catch the fish themselves.

This fundamental conflict of interest would run and run – all the way, in fact, to the notorious "Cod Wars" between Iceland and England in the 1960s and '70s.

The activities of the English traders were therefore a mixed blessing as far as the Icelanders were concerned, but to King Eric of Denmark, who personally held the trade monopoly with Iceland, they were an unmitigated outrage. It was irrelevant to him that mainland Scandinavia was gripped by the Black Death and could barely feed itself let alone the far-flung colonies. The crisis was so grave that Greenland had to be evacuated. Still, a monopoly was a monopoly.

Eric protested to King Henry V of England over the illegal trade, and his royal commissioners in Iceland did their best to stop it, but the mainland fleets had fallen into disrepair and there was no way of enforcing the prohibition. Pirates among the English merchants – the distinction between them and merchants could not have been finer – were not slow to recognise the opportunities presented by an undefended coast, and their looting of Icelandic churches was an echo of what the Vikings had done in England.

A violent storm in 1419 revealed the extent of the illegal trade: the storm lasted only three hours, and when it was over there were no fewer than 25 English ships high and dry on Icelandic soil. King Eric made vain attempts to stop it. On one occasion a couple of royal commissioners with orders to arrest the offenders were themselves bundled into a ship and given an unplanned voyage to the dungeons of England.

Eric's successor, King Christian I, tried again by sending the chieftain Björn Thorleifsson to execute his orders. He and his wife Olof were similarly despatched to England. Thorleifsson managed to get back to Iceland for yet another attempt. On this occasion he was killed and his son captured. Olof paid a ransom to get the son back and then went to the lengths of recruiting an army to deal with the English. Some English were killed, and the affair escalated into a full-blown war between England and Denmark in 1469 although, ironically, the traders and their customers on the spot seem to have continued their prickly but profitable dealings without noticing.

Cod was Iceland's main commodity but there were a few others. Sulphur, tallow and sheepskin were in demand, as was the pure white Icelandic falcon, by far the best for the medieval sport of falconry and therefore highly valued. The English traders ran into stiff competition from the Hanseatic League, and the Danish kings at last found an effective weapon, which was to play off one against the other in what amounted to an auction for limited trading concessions.

The long decline: The auctions lined royal pockets but did nothing for Iceland. The cumulative effect of natural disaster and stifled trade was simply too much. The most conclusive evidence of national lethargy was that literary activity ceased. The only creativity, and it did not amount to much, was the

Having run wild through Grindavík, Faxaflói and the East Fjords, the pirates then descended on Heimaey on the south coast "and overran the whole island with loud yells, massacring the terror-stricken and helpless inhabitants". The youngest and strongest of the population were herded into their ships; the others into a warehouse which was then put to the torch. The local priest, a composer of hymns named Jón Thorsteinsson, was struck dead while kneeling in prayer; his wife and children and a second priest were taken to the ships, making a total of 242 captives bound for Africa.

The surviving priest was released the following spring to present the ransom demand

lightweight ballad favoured by wandering minstrels. "At wakes and other gatherings," sniffed the hymn-writer Gudbrand Thorláksson, "and likewise at weddings and parties, there is scarcely any other form of amusement or entertainment than this nonsensical poetry, which God pity!"

The extent to which Iceland became dispirited and defenceless is revealed by an invasion in 1627 by 3,000 Barbary pirates commanded by a "Rais Murad" who was actually a Dutchman named Jan Janezen.

Left, foreign traders braved both rough seas and, supposedly, monsters (**above**) to reach Iceland.

to King Christian IV. He reported that many of the captives were already dead. The girls had been sold off to harems and the young men committed to lives as galley slaves. Some of the men had exercised the option of taking the turban and becoming pirates themselves. It took five years to raise funds to secure the release of 37 captives, but in the end only 13 got back.

Heimaey never recovered from the decimation of its population, and it was set even farther back by the colossal volcanic eruption in 1783 which poured so much poisonous lava into the ocean that the fishing industry was out of action for many years. A

British traveller in the early 19th century told a sorry story of a dwindling population of 200 whose children were dying because they ate nothing but the oily flesh of seabirds. "The people are by no means respected by their neighbours on the mainland, who represent them as being remarkably indolent, and depraved in their habits... There is a church... but it does not appear to be of much use in improving the characters of those for whose benefit it was intended." Misbehaving children, however, were brought back into line – then as now – with the tale of the terrible fate which befell their predecessors at the hands of the Barbary pirates.

A dismal outpost: Iceland was so cut off by its curtain of darkness that there were few foreigners able to contradict the 16th-century writer Sebastian Münster. "In the mountain of Hecla," he wrote, "there is a great abyss which cannot be sounded and here appear often people who have recently drowned as though they were alive. Their friends beg them to come home but they reply with great sighs that they must go into Hecla and the vanish forthwith."

Münster went on to describe whales "as big as mountains... which capsize large ships and are not afraid of the sound of trumpets or of empty barrels thrown at them with which they gambol. It sometimes happens that seamen encounter a whale and if in distress cast anchor upon it thinking it to be an island... Many people in Iceland build their houses out of bones and skeletons of these whales". The whales pale in comparison with Münster's sea serpents "200 or 300 feet long" which wound themselves around ships and "a fearful beast like unto a rhinoceros with a pointed nose and back (which) eats crabs called lobsters twelve feet long". These hefty lobsters, moreover, were capable of seizing and strangling a man.

Although Iceland was not quite as removed from the real world as Münster's stories would imply, it was almost oblivious of the Reformation in Europe. The population was contentedly if somewhat forlornly Roman Catholic, and the Reformation arrived not as an intellectual awakening or rebellion against the old order but as a series of dimly understood royal decrees issued in Copenhagen and backed by military threats. It was all reminiscent of Olaf Tryggvason converting Iceland by remote control.

The Church in Iceland had slipped back into old habits. "Although priests were not allowed to marry," says one of the sagas, "holy and godfearing fathers would permit them (I know indeed not with what authority) to have concubines instead of wedded wives... It was easy for the priests to get women, so that they often got the daughters, sisters and relatives of chieftains for their helpmates. Proper and lawful agreement was entered into by both parties, so that nothing was lacking of real marriage but the name."

Feuding bishops: The old habits affected bishops too. Bishop Ogmund of Skálholt, whose sympathies were Lutheran, confronted the Roman Catholic Bishop Jón at the 1526 Althing with a force of 1,300 men against the latter's 900. Full-scale battle was averted by an agreement to let the issue be settled by a duel between champions.

The duel was fought on an island in the Oxará. Ogmund's man was declared the winner, but the following day his cathedral at Skálholt was destroyed by a mysterious fire. This calamity ironically softened his feelings towards Jón because he believed the latter could only have got away with arson with God at least a little bit on his side.

In Denmark and Norway, the Reformation was primarily a dynastic struggle with many nobles waiting anxiously for a pretext to despoil the rich estates of the Roman Catholic Church. That ambition extended to Church possessions in Iceland too, and in 1541 two warships were despatched to Iceland with orders to use force if necessary to push a new Church code through the Althing.

Bishop Ogmund, now 80 years old and blind, was still capable of mounting a spirited defence. He was dragged from bed and bundled into a Danish ship. His captors offered to release him on payment of a ransom which amounted to nothing less than his sister's money and deeds to all his property. Both were handed over but the ship sailed with Ogmund still in it. He is thought to have died on the voyage.

That left Bishop Jón, Ogmund's adversary and by now an old man himself. King Christian III, an arch-Protestant king, took grave exception to Jón's continuing defiance and in 1548 – two years after Luther's death – summoned him to Copenhagen. Jón chose instead to raise a rebellion. The geriatric bishop led 100 men down to the Protestant stronghold of Skálholt and ordered the defenders to surrender on pain of excommunication. The ultimatum brought jeers from within; Jón turned around and built himself what would be, if necessary, a last bastion at Hólar on Iceland's northern coast.

King Christian may have heard that Jón had sent a request to Charles V, Holy Roman Emperor, for military assistance. In any event, he moved decisively against the stubborn bishop. Another military force was sent to Iceland but he was not to be intimidated. On 27 June 1550 an exasperated Christian outlawed him and ordered his arrest.

Demise of the rebel: Bishop Jón's path of glory ended in his eventual incarceration.

News of the executions aroused bitter resentment. Three masked men carrying coffins presented themselves at Skálholt and asked for the bodies. The request was granted, bells were attached to the coffins, and the cortège moved through the countryside to the chiming of church bells. The bishop was buried at Hólar and remains to this day something of a national hero.

The overthrow of the Catholic party soon followed Jón's death, and the king moved in quickly on its properties. For a while he considered using the income from the confiscated lands to build schools, but on second thoughts chose to keep the money himself. Thereafter, one quarter of the tithes payable

For several days his captors debated what to do with him. A priest suggested over breakfast one morning that he knew how the prisoner could most safely be kept. Asked to elaborate, he replied that an axe and the earth would do the trick. This suggestion was at first received as a joke, but on reflection the idea commended itself. On 7 November 1550 Bishop Jón, and two sons who had been captured with him, were beheaded at Skálholt, thus providing Scandinavian Catholicism with its first and last martyrs.

<u>**Above**</u>, **an artist's impression of Iceland falling into decay.**

to the Church were to be diverted to the royal purse, as were all fines imposed in law suits. Other reforms were progressively introduced. Adultery became punishable by death, although only on the third offence: men were hanged, women drowned. The eating of horseflesh was banned, and persistent absence from Lutheran services was punished by flogging.

The crux of the matter was that the confiscation of Church property, the imposition of new taxes, and alterations to the law were all carried out without reference to the Althing or with any regard for existing Icelandic procedure. The country was, in short, feeling the draught of absolute monarchy in Denmark, and things were to get a lot worse.

Crushed by foreign rule: Trade was always Iceland's Achilles heel, and absolute rule in Denmark heralded a tyrannical monopoly worse than anything which had preceded it. Iceland was obliged not only to buy everything it needed exclusively from court-appointed Danish trading companies but also at prices fixed by the company. It was a case of paying what the company demanded or doing without. With Iceland thus held to ransom, it was no surprise that the price of imports rose by 500 percent over a period in which the prices paid for home-grown products remained static. The purchase price of

Icelandic fish was barely a fifth of what foreign buyers would readily have paid.

In 1662 matters were made worse by the division of the country into four commercial districts. These were prohibited from trading with one another; they could deal only with Danes and on the same Danish terms. Clandestine deals with foreign vessels were made more difficult by a Danish naval blockade and more dangerous by draconian penalties. A certain Páll Torfason took a couple of fishing lines from an English ship in return for some knitted goods which the Danish merchants had previously declined, and lost the entire contents of his house. Holmfast

Gudmundsson was flogged for selling fish to a near neighbour who was technically in another district.

The colonial administrators were nothing if not an extension of the arrogant court officials in Denmark. If they needed a horse, the first peasant they asked was obliged to provide one. If it was a question of crossing a fjord, the nearest farmer was required to drop everything and get his boat out. A grumble meant a sound flogging.

Unsurprisingly, the authority of the ancient Althing was completely undermined and in 1800, on royal orders, it was abolished. The new law court which took over its political functions and the surviving bishoprics were concentrated in Reykjavík, the population of which was a mere 300. The sense of separate identity was all but lost. "Up till 1800," says one of the annals, "the Icelanders, both men and women, dressed according to their national style, but after that they gradually adopted Danish styles."

Litany of wretchedness: The volcanic eruptions and earthquakes which had caused havoc in 1618, 1619, 1625, 1636, 1660 and 1693 continued practically unabated in 1727, 1732, 1755 and 1783.

The last in the series, the eruption of Laki, is still regarded as the worst in world history, scattering ash to every corner of the globe. Luckily for the inhabitants, human casualties were surprisingly light given the circumstances. However, the Icelanders kept a record of their personal losses, which were not so light: 11,461 cattle, 190,448 sheep and 28,013 horses. The people did not escape so lightly in a smallpox epidemic which followed soon afterward the eruption. Fully one-third of the population died.

There seemed to be no end to misery. Summing up the 18th century, the historian Magnús Stephensen says Iceland experienced "forty-three years of distress due to cold winters, ice-floes, failures of fisheries, shipwrecks, inundations, volcanic eruptions, earthquakes, epidemics and contagious diseases among men and animals, which often came separately, but often in connection with and as a result of one another".

Jón Jónsson brings into focus life under these conditions: "The living room of the common peasant farmstead was usually not covered with boards on the inside. One could see between rafters to the grass-covered roof, which soon looked like ordinary sod, and from which mildew and cobwebs were hanging. The floor was uncovered, consisting only of earth trampled hard. But during heavy rains when the roof was leaking water dripped down, and it soon became a pool of mud through which people waded. The walls along which the bedsteads were nailed fast were covered with a grey coat of mildew, and green slime was constantly trickling down the walls, especially in the winter. Bed clothes were very few among the poor people. Old hay, seaweed or twigs did service as a mattress, and a few blankets constituted the covering." To make life even more wretched, there was a crippling shortage of firewood.

a stranger who is not accustomed to it can scarcely endure it for an hour, as it is corrupted by the smoke of the train-oil lamps, and the respiration and perspiration of the people, of whom many are affected with scurvy and other diseases."

To make matters worse, tobacco merchants persuaded the men that smoking was good for their health. Consequently, "the men sat all day with their pipes in their mouths smoking, so that the smoke rolled out as from a factory chimney".

Other travellers remarked on the downtrodden and gloomy demeanour of the population. "Being of quiet and harmless dispositions, having nothing to rouse them into a

In some houses the family slept on a platform two or three feet above the ground while calves and lambs occupied the space underneath. The proximity of the animals at least provided some heat which was conserved by keeping windows to a minimum both in size and numbers. A thin membrane – part of an animal's insides – served as glass, but it only allowed through a little light. Life indoors was spent in a sea of perpetual darkness. "The air is so impure," a royal commission on housing reported, "that

Left, 18th-century tombstone kept at Skálholt.
Above, en route to a funeral.

state of activity, but the necessity of providing means of subsistence for the winter season; nothing to inspire emulation; no object of ambition; the Icelanders may be said merely to live… They are negligent with respect to the cleanliness of their persons and dwellings… If they give little it is because they have little to give."

The same traveller, George Stewart MacKenzie, was surprised that more use was not made of the hot springs in the home. "Their not having taken advantage of this natural source of comfort must proceed from that want of enterprise which is so conspicuous in the character of the Icelanders."

THE PUSH FOR INDEPENDENCE

Iceland, like Scandinavia in general, sat out the impact of the American War of Independence and the French Revolution. Iceland did not even feel the whiff of liberalism which passed through Denmark towards the end of the 18th century under the auspices of Dr Johann Struensee.

Struensee was a German physician who was engaged to treat the malignantly half-witted King Christian VII and contrived to run the country personally. He introduced freedom of the press and personal liberties including, significantly, the de-criminalisation of adultery. His vested interest in this particular reform was the clandestine affair he was enjoying with the young and attractive Queen Caroline Matilda, sister of King George III of England, who was also mad. The affair was discovered, the law repealed, and the unfortunate Struensee's severed head was posted on a pole to advertise that the old absolutist order was back in charge.

Denmark's misfortune, broadly speaking, was to choose the losing side in the Napoleonic Wars. The British fleet destroyed the Royal Danish Navy at the Battle of Copenhagen in 1801 and then bombarded Copenhagen itself in 1807. The entire Danish merchant fleet (some 1,400 ships) was confiscated, which of course left poor Iceland more isolated than ever. British merchants were eager to take over Icelandic trade themselves, and this provided the backdrop to the most bizarre chapter in Iceland's history, the "revolution" of 1809.

An unlikely liberator: The central figure was Jorgen Jorgensen, born in Copenhagen in 1780, a son of the royal watchmaker. A brilliant but unruly student, he found himself serving in the British Navy almost by accident as "John Johnson". His early career was chequered, to say the least, and he was actually in prison in England for gambling debts when he was taken on as an interpreter for an opportunistic and unofficial English trade mission to Iceland.

After one abortive trip, the traders landed in Reykjavík to discover that the governor, anticipating their return, had plastered the

Right, travellers stop at a village.

town with notices prohibiting any trade with foreigners under pain of beheading. The governor, Count Trampe, was not simply enforcing Copenhagen policy; he happened to own the one Danish ship which was still trading with Iceland. With a warship in the background, the English traders tried to reason with Trampe but he was adamant.

Jorgenson then came up with a bright idea: depose Trampe, reconvene the Althing (which had been abolished nine years previously), declare Iceland's independence from Denmark, and make a treaty of alliance and trade with England. Some, but not all, of the English traders thought this an excellent idea. To cries of "Traitor, you'll hang for

of Danish merchants. The Icelanders were not sure how to react. The fearsome Trampe was locked up in the ship's cabin but they could not be certain that he would remain there: the price of collaboration with the English if ever he regained office did not bear thinking about.

The new regime had been in existence for a little more than a month when a second British warship, *HMS Talbot*, hove into view under the command of Captain the Hon. Alexander Jones, the younger son of an Irish peer and not one whose sympathies would normally lie with such revolutionary activity. Jones suspected that the British government might also have certain reservations.

this", Trampe was marched out of his office and locked up in one of the English ships. Jorgenson could now properly begin.

Issuing proclamations under the self-appointed title of "His Excellency, the Protector of Iceland, Commander-in-Chief by Sea and Land", Jorgenson promised the Icelanders "peace and happiness little known in recent years" and their own national flag – three white codfish on a blue background. "You are a new Bonaparte," said one of his admirers breathlessly. His Excellency was just 30 years old.

Backed up by 12 armed sailors, Jorgenson "liberated" Iceland by seizing the property

The "revolution" squashed: The Hon. Alexander Jones's enquiries into what was going on – the flag was new to him, and he noticed that Jorgenson was building a fort at Arnárholl – brought Iceland's "independence" to an end as perfunctorily as it had been created. "All proclamations, laws and appointments made by Mr Jorgen Jorgensen, since his arrival in this country, are to be abolished and totally null and void…"

In his memoirs, Jorgensen described the manner of his departure. He stepped into a fishing-boat and was rowed out to the departing warship by a crew of Icelanders: "So I went on board quietly, many of the poor natives shedding tears at my departure. It is true, indeed, that I left the island with regret. I had established liberty and freedom there without a drop of blood being spilt, or a single person committed to prison. This revolution was brought about without mocking and insulting the Monarch, of whose saw it was deemed expedient to declare the island independent, and without inflaming the minds of the people against their former government. The thing spoke for itself; the oppressions were too great to be endured longer."

Jorgensen's subsequent career was almost beyond belief. He was jailed in a convict hulk on returning to England, released, imprisoned again for more gambling debts, did

hearted alliance with Napoleon was paid at the post-war Vienna congress. Pressure from the victors forced Denmark to grant Norway its independence, albeit in a lopsided union with Sweden, and expectations rose in Iceland of a similar concession in the near future. The mood was captured in a surge of romantic nationalism which glorified Iceland's history and language.

The Icelandic language was virtually pristine Old Norse. Ironically, the fact that it was untainted by foreign influence (unlike Norwegian, which had been heavily Danicised) was precisely what 18th-century rationalists under the forceful leadership of Magnus Stephensen railed against. They advocated

some sterling work for British Intelligence (at one point disguised as an Irish pilgrim), dashed off books on such weighty topics as the geography of Persia and Afghanistan, was sentenced to the gallows for selling the bedclothes off the bed he was using in London lodgings, was instead transported to Australia – and there served with distinction in the police force. He died in Hobart, Tasmania in 1844.

Rekindling Iceland's nationalist spirit: The real price of Denmark's ultimately half-

Left, turf houses at Laufás and, **above**, key details.

an intellectual *Aufklärung* which welcomed the best that the rest of the world could offer. To the rationalists, the old language smacked of darkness and superstition.

The rationalist movement was still alive in the early 19th century, and it clashed with new romantics who positively relished the past. The champion of these new romantics was Bjarni Thorarensen, whose *Eldgamla Isafold* was hugely popular and remains Iceland's national anthem. His poems were all about the heroic figures of the sagas. In retrospect, something was clearly stirring in Iceland, because the wheels of the ancient intellectual workshop once again turned, even if some of the best work was being done by Icelandic scholars installed at Copenhagen and Oxford universities.

Visitors noticed changes, and the foundations of Iceland's modern "cradle-to-grave" social security system particularly caught the attention of English reformers. "We have no hesitation in saying," they reported, "that in respect to the poor, an Icelandic parish was, to say the least, equally as well managed as an English one."

Care for the poor: The basic principle was that any person incapacitated by age, infirmity or "misfortune" should in the first instance be maintained by the next of kin according to their ability to pay, the criterion

marriage) failed to provide adequate support, the pauper could complain to the district Thing. The alimentor who left a parish to escape the burden was liable to the kind of house-arrest known as exclusion.

The English observers thought the Icelandic system clearly superior to the English in one respect. "The Icelanders... do not charge themselves with the support of the poor without taking especial care to keep the number of paupers within due limits; a care which we have grossly neglected, and are now enduring the fearful consequences of our want of foresight."

The number of paupers was controlled by, for example, not allowing a man to marry

being the value of their property. If circumstances required a pecking order, priority was given to a distressed mother followed by the father, children, brothers and sisters. If supporting some or all of these demonstrably exceeded a person's resources, the parish authorities stepped in.

While parishes might keep a storehouse of emergency provisions for the destitute, the responsibility for looking after them was generally passed directly to the rate-payers, the number of paupers allocated to each depending on the value of property. If the alimentor (i.e. he who paid alimony, before the term became bound up with unhappy

until he had the means to support a family. Nor was a slave to be freed unless the owner could provide him with an adequate plot of land. If a freed slave became destitute through the former owner's neglect, he retained his freedom but was entitled to alimony.

"Very stringent regulations were also passed to keep the poor within their respective parishes," noted the observers. "Clothes and shoes might be given to a pauper of another parish, but any parishioner who furnished such a pauper with victuals, except he was merely passing through the parish to go to his own, rendered himself liable to the punishment of exclusion.

"The Icelanders also took care to make able bodied paupers work for their living. Begging was not tolerated, especially at the Althing. If a beggar entered a booth on the Thingvellir plain, the booth-man might forcibly eject him, and every one who furnished such a beggar with meat, was liable to be punished with exclusion. All persons who wandered about the country for fifteen days and upwards were to be regarded as vagabonds... and punished accordingly. Besides other punishments to which they were liable, any one who thought proper might mutilate them in the manner practised in the East to qualify a man for the service of the seraglio" – in other words, castration.

next to nothing about Iceland was worthless. The romantics wanted the Althing restored. In 1840 the newly-crowned King Christian VIII agreed to reinstate an Althing consisting of 20 representatives chosen by a qualified electorate and four or six royal nominees. The assemblies were not to be held at the old Thingvellir, as the romantics wished, but at Reykjavík, which would formally become the new capital.

As usual in such circumstances, radical elements felt that these gentle reforms did not go far enough. They insisted on holding the Althing at Thingvellir, on lower franchise qualifications and on the exclusive use of the Icelandic language in government.

1979
150 ÍSLAND

JÓN SIGURDSSON 1811–1879
INGIBJÖRG EINARSDÓTTIR 1804–1879

Unsteady steps towards freedom: Some of these comments must have been out-of-date by the time they were written. Swift social progress was obviously being made, but Iceland still had to wait until 1830 before the ripples of Norway's 1814 independence reached its shores. Even then, the concession was merely two seats among 70 on an advisory body to the Danish crown. Prominent Icelanders like the jurist Baldwin Einarsson protested that such feeble representation in a body based in Copenhagen and knowing

<u>Left</u>, Reykjavík in the early 19th century. <u>Above</u>, nationalist figures are still revered by Icelanders.

The nationalist cause was championed by "the greatest figure in modern Icelandic history", the eclectic scholar Jón Sigurdsson, whose statue stands in the Old Town Square in Reykjavík, facing Parliament House. Born in Hrafnseyri in the West Fjords, he was educated at the University of Copenhagen and, curiously in view of his fame, lived in Copenhagen for the rest of his life. From 1849 he merely spent alternate summers in Iceland during which time he presided over the Althing. It was his very considerable stature in Denmark as archivist of the Royal Norse Archaeological Society and as an authority on Icelandic history and literature

ICELANDIC HOSPITALITY

A 19th-century visitor to Iceland recorded that: "No sooner had I presented myself at the door, and made known my errand than I was immediately welcomed by the whole family, and triumphantly inducted into the guest quarters: everything the house could produce was set before me, and the whole society stood by to see that I enjoyed myself. As I had but just dined, an additional repast was no longer essential to my happiness; but all explanation was useless, and I did my best to give them satisfaction." Nor did the hospitality stop there.

"Immediately on rising from the table, the young lady of the house... proposed by signs to conduct me to my apartment; I was preparing to make her a polite bow, and to wish her a very good night, when she advanced towards me, and with a winning grace difficult to resist, insisted upon helping me off with my coat, and then with my shoes and stockings.

"At this most critical part of the proceedings, I naturally imagined her share of the performance would conclude. Not a bit of it. Before I knew where I was, I found myself sitting in a chair, in my shirt, trouserless, while my fair tire-woman was engaged in neatly folding up the ravished garments on a neighbouring chair. She then, in the most simple manner in the world, helped me into bed, tucked me up, and having said a quantity of pretty things in Icelandic, gave me a hearty kiss and departed. If you see anything remarkable in my appearance, it is probably because:

This very morn I've felt the sweet surprise
Of unexpected lips on sealed eyes."

The Marquis of Dufferin and Ava, to whom this tale was recounted, went on to describe Scandinavian skoal-drinking. As a dab hand with a wine glass, Lord Dufferin was "prepared with a firm heart to respond to the friendly provocations of my host. I only wish you could have seen how his kind face beamed with approval when I clinked my first bumper against his, and having emptied it at a draught, turned it towards him bottom upwards, with the orthodox twist.

"Soon, however, things began to look more serious even that I had expected. I knew well that to refuse a toast, or to half empty your glass, was considered churlish. I had come determined to accept my host's hospitality as cordially as it was offered... Should he not be content with seeing me at his table, I was ready, if need were, to remain under it...

"After having exchanged a dozen rounds of sherry and champagne with my two neighbours, I pretended not to observe that my glass had been refilled; and, like the sea-captain, who, slipping from between his two opponents, left them to blaze away at each other the long night through, withdrew from the combat. But it would not do... So, I winked defiance left and right, and away we went at it again for another five-and-forty minutes. At last their fire slackened: I had partially quelled both the Governor and the Rector, and still survived.

"Guess my horror when the Icelandic Doctor, shouting his favourite... battle cry, gave the signal for an unexpected onslaught, and the twenty guests poured down on me in succession. I really thought I should have run away from the house... but I received them one by one."

This was not a solitary experience. Britain's future ambassador to St Petersburg recalled making a speech: "However unintelligible to myself, I must have been in some sort understood, for at the end of each sentence, cheers, faint as the roar of waters on a far-off strand, floated towards me. Then followed more speeches – a great chinking of glasses – a kind of dance round the table, where we successively gave each alternate hand, a hearty embrace from the Governor – and finally – silence, daylight, and fresh air, as we stumbled into the street." ∎

that gave his nationalist movement credibility in Danish eyes. The movement demanded a totally independent national legislature and the ending of Denmark's final say over Icelandic judicial decisions.

Progress towards more substantial independence was delayed by Denmark's preoccupation with the Schleswig Holstein nightmare, a dispute with Prussia over the sovereignty of the frontier provinces, each with a divided population whose minorities refused to give in. Moreover, the Danish royal commissioner in Iceland was obstructive. The incumbent, still, was Jorgen Jorgenson's *bête noire*, Count Trampe, and he was suspected of applying for a private army to exorcise

that the newspaper changed its tune. People were asked to postpone their departure for a year or so in case things changed, and at the same time a number of teetotal societies sprang up. The aim was not so much a campaign against alcohol as to deny Denmark the revenue from the tax on drinks.

Under this kind of pressure, the king apparently bowed to the inevitable in 1874 by giving the Althing autonomy over domestic affairs, including finance. It was not quite what it seemed because he retained an absolute veto over anything and everything the Althing did, but for the moment it was enough to celebrate, especially as the date coincided with the 1,000th anniversary of Iceland's

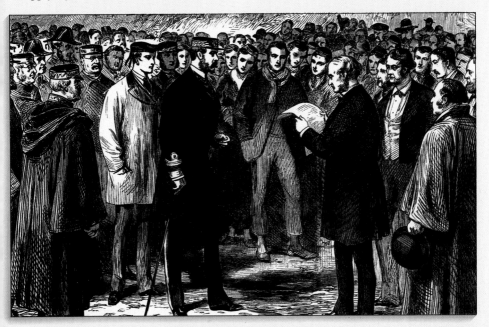

what he considered unlawful, pseudo-patriotic nonsense. While Denmark continued to turn a deaf ear to the fundamental issue of Icelandic independence, the trade monopoly was ended in 1854.

The Icelandic exodus: With true independence still apparently unattainable, the newspaper *Northanfari* suggested ironically in the 1870s that the only chance Icelanders had of tasting freedom was to emigrate en masse to Brazil or North America. As it was, Icelanders were soon leaving in such numbers

Above, poet Grímur Thomsen reads to the Danish King Christian IX at the 1874 National Festival.

settlement. King Christian IX attended the festivities and heard the first performance of *Iceland's Thousand Years* by Matthias Jochumsson, the present national anthem. Jón Sigurdsson was pointedly not invited, but it was said that in a private conversation afterwards the king asked him if Icelanders were satisfied with the new constitution. "As their chief wish had not be granted," he replied, "how could they be? Sigurdsson recognised full independence or nothing."

The first breakthrough: Full independence was a long time coming. Icelanders and Danes were generally talking at cross purposes. As far as the Danes were concerned,

Iceland was inconceivable except as an integral part of the kingdom, although they were willing to tinker with semantics. One proposal would have made Christian IX "King of Denmark and Iceland" instead of just Denmark, with Iceland taken for granted. Iceland was in no mood for cosmetic compromise, and talk turned to secession, or what in the 20th century became known as a unilateral declaration of independence.

Sigurdsson died in 1879. Every year from 1881 to 1895, his successor, Benedikt Sveinsson, submitted to the Althing a proposal calling for real self-government. It was twice passed, in 1886 and 1894, only to encounter the impenetrable stumbling block of the royal

Spain which traditionally paid for Icelandic fish imports with surplus wine.

Icelanders could not agree on their relationship with Denmark, however, and the impasse continued until the whole question of national sovereignty in Europe was brought under microscopic scrutiny in the peace negotiations after World War I. The Danish government then took the initiative and on 1 December 1918 Iceland became a sovereign state with its own flag, linked to Denmark by virtue of having a common king. The arrangements were ratified by a plebiscite with 12,040 votes in favour and only 897 against.

The "occupation" of Iceland: The end of 1940 was of course the worst imaginable

veto. The breakthrough eventually came in Denmark with the election of a liberal government in 1901. On 1 February 1904 Iceland received home rule.

The saga-writers would have felt at home in the first years of Icelandic home rule as the country fragmented into a political free-for-all, various factions feuding with seemingly no greater purpose in mind than advancing self-interests. They buried their difference long enough to open in 1911 the university at Reykvajík, a considerable achievement for a national population then numbering only 90,000. The introduction of prohibition in 1909 was not as popular, especially not in

time for Denmark and Iceland to enter delicate constitutional negotiations. There was no contact whatever between them, Denmark having been occupied by Germany and Iceland by Britain. In the latter's case, strategic considerations had taken priority over the policy of "perpetual neutrality" declared in 1915. Hitler's troops had marched into Norway and thus gained control of its immense, Atlantic-facing coastline and ports. Iceland was a logical next step, its mid-Atlantic position being of inestimable value for submarine operations and for aircraft not yet able to cross the ocean in one hop. Iceland had no defences of its own, so Britain stepped in to pre-empt any German moves in that direction, a role later taken over by the Americans.

The Allied forces, who at times amounted to one-third of the native population, were not always popular, but the war years brought unprecedented prosperity in Iceland. The national income shot up by 60 percent on the strength of construction work on American airfields and free-spending US personnel. Fish exports fetched record prices and, as they were generally paid for in dollars, Iceland had the means to import large quantities of American goods.

Not being able to negotiate with Denmark on constitutional changes, the Althing acted quired the right to a complete breaking off of the union with Denmark, since it has now had to take into its own hands the conduct of all its affairs." It added that Iceland would become a republic as soon as the union with Denmark could be formally terminated.

The termination of the union and a new constitution were submitted to plebiscite in 1944 and both were approved by overwhelming majorities. The date chosen for the formal establishment of the republic at Thingvellir was, not by accident, Jón Sigurdsson's birthday, 17 June. Denmark was then still under German occupation, and many Danes felt that what amounted to a secession had been brought to fruition while they were

unilaterally: "Seeing that the situation which has been created makes it impossible for the king of Iceland to exercise the powers assigned to him by the constitution, the Althing announces that for the present it commits the exercise of these powers to the government of Iceland."

An Althing resolution the following year went further: "The Althing resolves to declare that it considers Iceland to have ac-

Left, the arrival of British troops in Reykjavík, 1940. **Above**, a brass band greets the British, but they (and the subsequent Americans) were not always popular.

hardly in a position to do anything about it. King Christian X sent a telegram of good wishes – it was only received after a ceremony which attracted 20,000 people to Thingvellir on a cold and blustery day. The first president, elected to a four-year term, was Sveinn Björnsson.

Iceland's neutrality did not save 352 seamen from German actions at sea, but it was adhered to on principle when Iceland turned down an offer to declare for the Allies in the final months of the war. One of the first actions of independent Iceland was, on the cessation of hostilities, to demand the immediate withdrawal of the American forces.

Iceland today has all the trappings of an industrialised nation, with a sophisticated, consumer-orientated society, comprehensive welfare system and one of the highest standards of living in the world. It is almost impossible to imagine that, before World War II, many visitors thought Iceland to be barely out of the Middle Ages. The leap into the modern world has been fast and furious: greater changes have taken place in the past 50 years than in the more than 1,000 years of settlement beforehand.

Joining the modern world: Before hostilities began in Europe in 1939, Iceland was a self-governing country under crown Union with its former colonial master, Denmark. It was committed by act of parliament to "eternal neutrality" and was still a fairly poor and traditional rural society, exporting herring and saltfish. When the smoke cleared on the continent six years later, Iceland stood up as an independent republic under a native president instead of a foreign king. Although no fighting had taken place in Iceland, it now had thousands of American troops based on its soil, and was a rich exporter of frozen fish, forward-looking, energetically developing and urbanising.

The transformation occurred almost overnight. Even so, Icelandic society did not abandon the long past, but rather adapted it to the present, replanted an ancient heritage in modern soil where it has more or less flourished since. Continuity was ensured by the 19th-century nationalists, who had always looked back to the Golden Age of the Icelandic sagas for inspiration in the independence struggle. The Icelandic language has been the bridge of centuries: the history of the Old Republic had been written down in the Middle Ages using a language which modern Icelanders can and very often do read (see pages 111–115 and 116–119).

The presence of first British and then American troops in Iceland during the war, although not exactly welcome, had its brighter

sides. A frenzy of road-building and development – at times like a gold-rush frenzy – created an economic infrastructure for the postwar period. Few Icelanders can deny that the prosperity brought by the war meant that national independence, declared in 1944, could be consolidated in peacetime.

More controversial was what to do after the war. Iceland's old stand of "eternal neutrality" was abandoned in 1949 when it became a founding member of NATO. The US military left Iceland but returned in 1951

with a vengeance to set up a permanent marine air base at Keflavík – a base that is still in use today. The fact that this made Iceland a major target in the event of nuclear war hardly endeared the US presence to the majority of Icelanders; nor did Icelandic men appreciate rich American servicemen floating around the countryside. But the economic argument was powerful: Keflavík provided jobs. And strict controls on marines' movements, rarely allowing them out from behind a huge wire fence, meant that not too many ran off with Icelandic wives.

Even so, Iceland never established an army of its own and also maintained good trade

Preceding pages: the Asmundur Sveinsson Sculpture Gallery in Reykjavík. Left, new over-shadows old in a Reykjavík suburb. Right, beer was finally legalised in 1989.

relations with the Eastern bloc even during the chilliest spells of the Cold War. Anti-Keflavík feeling flared up from time to time during the Vietnam war and was a popular cause on the Left – but by the late 1970s it had become a principle which was costing rather than winning votes.

As a non-nuclear base, Keflavík kept its nose clean during the arms race against Brezhnev, and its role largely involved escorting "stray" Soviet aircraft back out of Icelandic airspace – there were up to 200 annual violations some years – and monitoring submarine movements. Always keeping a low profile, the US military effectively disappeared from view when a separate civilian passenger terminal was opened at Keflavík Airport in 1987. Until then, all visitors had to land on the base before treading Icelandic soil (including Mikhail Gorbachev when he arrived for the 1986 summit).

Riches of the sea: After World War II, the Icelandic government – with economic foresight that has probably never been matched since – channelled its wartime cash-in-hand into modernising the fishing fleet, laying the foundation for a powerful industry which has held firm right up to the present day. Soon Iceland would be producing more income per head from fishing than Saudi Arabians did from oil.

Rich on cod income, Iceland's government grew, building an impressive system of schools, public health and social security. Meanwhile, Iceland's regulation of the economy had few parallels in the developed Western world. During the 1950s and 1960s, import tariffs were thrown up to protect industry, but they gradually served to foster inefficiency and higher prices for everything from fruit to toothbrushes. It was not until the 1980s that Icelandic governments became committed, in the spirit of the day, to free market policies. The effects of loosening up the economy are still being felt – and, as travellers will attest, prices have hardly dropped from amongst the highest in Europe. The transformation in how Icelanders live may eventually be as great as the jump from the traditional to technological worlds over the period of World War II.

Throughout all of these policy changes, fishing was the mainstay of the economy (employing just a tenth of Icelanders, it provided three-quarters of the national income).

Unfortunately, no amount of government regulation could sidestep its unpredictable nature, and fluctuations in both catches and market conditions have from time to time dealt severe blows to the virtually one-track economy.

Whenever fish catches or market prices deteriorated, the government's reaction was to devalue the Icelandic króna. This triggered an inflationary spiral in the 1970s. Wages were indexed to price rises, so that Icelanders joked that no news was better than a foreign disaster: a flood in Brazil which ruined the coffee-bean harvest could push up prices in Iceland which would mean wage rises all round.

Today, wage indexation has been outlawed, although pay deals commonly include an inflation "ceiling" which grants some compensation if prices rise above a certain level. Loans, however, are still indexed, which has put paid to one of the most popular national pastimes of the 1960s and '70s: owing money. Before indexing, it was possible to take on huge debts and pray that inflation would go up enough to enable you to pay them back again. Generally it did, and whole generations bought or built the impressive apartment blocks and detached houses that decorate streets everywhere. Icelanders still live in the most spacious housing of all the Nordic countries – that is to say, when they are at home and not out working to pay for it. The average working week in Iceland of around 46-49 hours is the longest in Europe.

The affluent society: Today inflation has been brought under control and, with a fish-led recovery, Icelanders enjoy a standard of living that few other countries can boast. Despite gripes about the economy, it is still one of the most consumer-orientated countries on earth, a hangover from the high-inflation days when it paid to spend and cost a fortune to save. Icelanders are among the world's leading owners of consumer durables such as video players, cellular phones,

Icelandic society is one of the most literate in the world. Education levels are very high for both sexes: more than one-third of all 20-year-olds complete secondary grammar school, there are around 5,300 students at the University of Iceland, and another 3,000 Icelanders at foreign universities (not bad for a total national population of only 250,000). More books are published and bought per head here than anywhere else in the world.

Icelanders also have one of the longest life expectancies in the world. Traditionally, Icelandic women have vied with the Japanese for first or second place, with an average life expectancy at birth of 80.3 years. Icelandic males rank second in the world longevity

cars, personal computers, foot massagers and, basically, any other piece of wizardry that promises high-tech comfort.

But not all of Iceland's modern achievements are so disposable. The country has achieved an unemployment level that is traditionally so low as to be technically negligible (around 1 percent). Much regional work (in fish processing) is undermanned, and any recorded unemployment is generally temporary, due to fluctuations in fish catches.

Left, under-employed policeman: Iceland has very little crime. **Above**, the Icelandic coast-guard took on the British navy in the "Cod Wars".

stakes with a life expectancy of 75.7 years. Doctors say that the reasons include an unpolluted environment and the pure food which this offers; the outrageously fresh air of an Atlantic island on the rim of the Arctic Circle; a healthy fish-based diet; and exemplary public health care. Infant mortality in Iceland is the lowest in the world, and certain aspects of preventive medicine, such as early detection of female cancers, are unmatched.

Moments of glory: In recent years, Iceland has rarely hit world headlines, but some key dates stand out. In 1980, Icelanders chose Vigdís Finnbogadóttir as the world's first democratically elected woman head of state.

FOREIGN POLICY

Being the only NATO member without its own army, plus the island's strategic importance for the whole Western alliance, have naturally given a home-grown slant to Iceland's pursuit of world foreign policy issues. While broadly aligning itself with Western interests over questions of defence, Iceland has always sought good relations – largely through trade – across classical geopolitical divides, and hasn't flinched from taking a tough stand against perceived encroachments by its allies.

The classic example of Iceland "getting tough"

with an ally are the four Cod Wars with the UK which occurred intermittently between 1952 and 1976 and saw Iceland become the first NATO country to break off diplomatic relations with another member. At issue was British encroachment on Iceland's fishing grounds – then, as now, the country's lifeblood.

When a 200-mile (320-km) fishing limit was finally recognised, Iceland was generally seen as a pioneer of international marine lawmaking. In the United Nations draft convention on the law of the sea – which has not yet been internationally ratified but still carries official clout in resolving maritime disputes – there is the so-called "Icelandic clause" promising that the

concerns of coastal states with overwhelming national fishing interests should be given preferential treatment in the courts of law.

Using similar arguments, Iceland has begun campaigning for rights over the seabed up to 350 miles (560 km) from its coast – an area that extends into the Rockall-Hatton area of the North Atlantic to which the UK also lays claim. And, citing its overwhelming interests in preserving a clean sea, Iceland has also campaigned internationally for restrictions on marine pollution, toxic and nuclear dumping and planned UK shoreside nuclear recycling schemes.

One of the most explosive issues of recent years has been whaling. In 1986, Iceland agreed to the International Whaling Commission's (IWC) four-year moratorium on commercial hunting, but conducted a limited catch for research purposes – a decision that caused considerable friction with the US. Although legally valid under IWC rules, whale protection groups attacked the programme as "commercial whaling in disguise," because some of the meat was exported to Japan. One radical group even scuttled two whaling boats in Reykjavík harbour in 1986. At the 1991 IWC meeting in Reykjavík, when the whaling commission rejected a request for a limited quota as "out of order", Iceland announced it would resign from the body in 1992.

Iceland's position is that limited catches from strong whale stocks pose no ecological danger. Few foreign environmentalists agree, and Iceland's stand has won it few friends.

At the United Nations, Iceland often sides with the four continental Nordic countries, Norway, Sweden, Denmark and Finland, to form a "progressive bloc" on questions such as human rights. Nordic cooperation on all issues apart from defence has been the norm for Iceland in the post-war period, although the bonds are now loosening as continental Scandinavia looks increasingly towards the New Europe.

Iceland's own standpoint towards the European Community has been to welcome liberalisation of trade and urge for its extension towards fisheries, which are still closely regulated and protected by tariffs in the EC. Despite some fears of being dwarfed in the New Europe, Iceland has had some impact on the changing geopolitical map. It was the first nation to recognise the independence of the Baltic states, taking a lead which other NATO nations were thereby more or less obliged to follow.

When the global trend is towards peace, it is sometimes an asset not to have an army. ∎

In a neck-and-neck race, the former theatre director, French teacher and tourist guide took the Presidency – an office outside party politics whose function is to provide a figure of national unity similar to Western European monarchies and does not include involvement in day-to-day government. Vigdís has been re-elected three times to the presidency, which she is expected to hold until 1996. In the early 1980s, Icelandic women went on to produce the world's first purely feminist parliamentary party.

On a different front, Iceland was invaded by foreign journalists in 1986 when it became host to the historic Reagan-Gorbachev summit. As the mid-point between Moscow

when a longstanding ban on strong beer was finally abolished. Total prohibition had gone into effect in 1915, but wine was legalised again in 1921. A national referendum of 1935 came out in favour of legalising spirits too, but beer was not included in the vote, as a sop to the temperance lobby – which argued that because beer is cheaper than spirits, it would lead to more depravity. When the growth in international travel brought Icelanders back in touch with the forbidden drink, bills to legalise beer were regularly moved in parliament, but inevitably scuttled on technical grounds.

The absurdity of the beer ban came fully to light in 1985 when the teetotalling Minister

and New York, Reykjavík seemed a reasonable symbolic meeting place for the leaders of the superpowers to discuss nuclear disarmament and begin the eventual ending of the Cold War. The hundreds of foreign journalists, with little hard news to cover for much of the time, set about informing the rest of the world about the more eccentric aspects of this little-known fishing nation.

But an event that brought almost as much attention to Iceland was "Beer Day" 1989,

Above, President Vigdís Finnbogadóttir, the world's first woman to be democratically elected a head of state.

of Justice prohibited pubs from pepping up legal non-alcoholic beer with legal spirits to make a potent imitation of strong beer. After a couple of false starts, beer finally approached legalisation in parliament – the debate and knife-edge vote were televised live and watched by huge audiences.

Beer Day came on 1 March 1989, and was celebrated in style by crowds that thronged through –10°C (14°F) temperatures for their first taste of the true amber fluid. Contrary to predictions, the day passed without incident and now a beerless Iceland is unthinkable. This "corrupting foreign influence" has dutifully been swallowed and digested, like other banned luxuries assimilated overnight – including such sins as Thursday night TV, foreign investment, dog ownership in Reykjavík, bank accounts in foreign currencies, private broadcasting and many others.

Keeping traditions alive: The concern at maintaining tradition does not always seem so frivolous. An ancient and homogenous culture of only 250,000 people is always at risk of being swallowed up wholesale by the outside world.

Symbolic of the changes wrought in Iceland has been the growth of the capital, Reykjavík – with only 5,000 inhabitants in 1901, it now has 100,000, or 40 percent of all Icelanders. The shift from country to city has

completely altered Icelandic society: the generation of Reykjavík folk now around retirement age was largely born and brought up in the countryside, on farms or in fishing villages. Their children, now middle-aged, were born and bred in the capital, but retained some links with the outside; and the generation now at or leaving school is thoroughbred urban, most of them brought up in the "concrete lava fields" of new residential suburbs like Breidholt and Arbaer – whose populations alone outnumber those of the largest towns outside the capital area.

These are the first Icelanders to drift away from the "classical" colloquialisms of their ancient language, which is firmly rooted in the agricultural society of yesteryear. And they are the first to have no intimate, first-hand knowledge of the mainstay industries of fishing, fish processing and agriculture – hands-on experience which in the past had given Iceland's managers and technocrats a telling edge over their international competition. This lack of basic manual skills poses a threat to Iceland's few industries, a threat whose consequences few can guess.

Recognising that language is on the front line, Icelanders' defence of their ancient Norse tongue makes the French look linguistic wimps (see *The Power of Words,* page 116). The same technological advances that the Icelanders welcome so warmly also pose the biggest threats. Satellite TV, for example, comes outside the jurisdiction of Iceland's legions of subtitlers, dubbers and professional and amateur word-coiners. Linguists say that the threats are becoming more subtle: borrowed words from foreign languages stand out instantly, but "hidden" foreignisms such as Anglo-Saxon syntax and thinking patterns are easier to slip into and more difficult to detect, yet undermine the fabric of the language all the same.

And more remains of Iceland's past in today's materialistic world than the language which records it. Social scientists were astonished to find in an opinion poll that a large majority of Icelanders still claim to believe in the existence of elves (see *Icelandic Hauntings,* pages 268–269). Almost all Icelanders still believe in God. Even though only a fraction go to the Lutheran church they are all still registered at birth. At one stage in the 1960s, the Norse pagan religion was revived, although in truth it never really caught on again. Today a congregation of fewer than 100 hears the archpriest read from ancient mythological poems, and then only on special ceremonial occasions.

But perhaps the real achievement of modern Iceland has been to remain essentially democratic in a personal as well as a political sense. Iceland is at once a modern technological nation and a small village writ large – a place with little crime, few class distinctions and where everybody, thanks to the old Scandinavian patronymic system still in use, addresses one another by their first name.

Left and right, flags out on Independence Day.

Somewhere, in all these rocks and stones, is my home
> – Nationalist poet Petur Gunnarsson

Probably the first thought that occurs to many visitors as they drive through the desolate lava plain that separates Kevlavík airport from the capital, is: "Very impressive – but why would anyone want to live here?"

The inhabitants of a country often tend to reflect their environment. The Danes, for example, live in a flat, fertile country, and are by and large an easy-going, laid-back bunch. Their Icelandic cousins, however, do not really know how to relax and enjoy life. The visitor may be puzzled at how they can be brash and completely uninhibited one minute, yet stubbornly taciturn the next, and may wonder how a nation so obsessed with the benefits of good honest labour can produce so many poets and writers.

But in these tendencies towards extremes, excess and unpredictablity, the Icelanders are only reflecting their homeland. Anyone would be a little crazy after centuries of long cold winters and a struggle for survival against a hostile environment – and managing to come out at the other end with one of the highest living standards in the world.

Icelanders have a reputation for being rather dour – but this quality does not go too deep. When the country enjoys one of its very rare long hot summers, the entire nation can be seen to undergo a metamorphosis. Out come the pavement tables outside the cafés, the bottles of red wine and barbecues. Some people even stop working overtime.

Obsession with the past: Icelanders have an exceptionally strong national identity, and a cultural heritage of which they are extremely proud. However, the constant suspicion that the outside world thinks them small and insignificant, coupled with having been isolated for so many years, makes them sometimes seem insular and absurdly patriotic.

Preceding pages: a farmer and his boat in the North East; playing soccer in the midnight sun; riding the stocky Icelandic horse. **Left,** the Icelanders remain deeply proud of their genealogy and traditions.

They are prone to harp on the nation's illustrious past, "cashing cheques on deeds committed 700 years ago," as writer and scholar Sigurdur Nordal put it.

But the key to the many paradoxes that make up the Icelandic character does to a great extent lie in their ancestry. Their forebears were, according to one view, Norse aristocrats who, when King Harald Fairhair declared himself King of Norway, preferred to brave the unknown and find a new land rather than lose the liberty they loved. Or, as an Icelandic psychiatrist (who prefers to remain anonymous) put it, they were a bunch of "anti-social psychopaths who couldn't handle having an orderly system of government imposed on them." Certainly, most early settlers, when they set up their republic, chose as their national god not Odin, the esoteric, enigmatic chief of the Aesir, but the anarchic, crude, no-nonsense Thor.

These people have suffered various vicissitudes during their 1,100-year history. In its early years, Iceland was a republic with a proud record of achievements: its system of government, legal code and literature were centuries ahead of their time. Icelanders were men and women of action. They travelled to both the known and unknown worlds, gaining positions of respect at foreign courts, colonising Greenland and becoming the first Europeans to visit America.

This promising young republic did, however, have a couple of fatal weaknesses: the lack of an ultimate executive authority, and a tendency to violence. Thus, it eventually degenerated into power struggles and civil war, and lost its independence to the Norwegians in 1262. Under first the Norwegian, and then the Danish crown, Iceland became probably the poorest nation in Europe. Its already small population was devastated by plagues and famines, and at one point there was even talk of evacuating the few miserable survivors to Denmark.

Medieval to modern: Somehow, they pulled through. When the independence struggle began in the 19th century, Iceland was deep in the Dark Ages. There were no roads and very few stone-built houses. But in a single generation, around the time Iceland gained self-government in 1918, the society moved, with no apparent difficulty, straight into the 20th century.

One of the most oft-cited reasons for the speed of this transition was the high standard of education in the country. While the people were poor, they were never ignorant. Nearly all of them could read and write, and quite a few could speak foreign languages.

Another is the strong sense of national identity and community. They are a people that have had to learn to stick together through necessity and overcome impossible odds. Thus, in the fishing limits disputes with Britain in the 1960s and 1970s, the so-called Cod Wars, this country without an army had

of outsiders, at least. They are very sensitive to slights to their national pride, and react strongly to any real or imagined threats to the community.

This last can sometimes manifest itself in an unpleasant way – such as the ban on black servicemen which the Icelandic government secretly insisted on when the NATO military base was established during the 1950s. The ban is no longer in existence and the prejudice it displayed was based more on ignorance and fear than malevolence. Iceland's racial make-up was, and still is by and large, homogenously Nordic, with a dash of Celt. These days people are much more cosmopolitan, but before the 1960s a black person

the gall to take on and defeat a major world power that was threatening its interests and livelihood. A similar motivation lies behind the stubborn stand on the whaling issue. It is not so much the importance of the whale-hunt itself, but the questioning of Iceland's right to self-government – basically being ordered around by more powerful countries who hardly have spotless environmental records themselves – that really raises the national hackles.

This fierce patriotism can also give Icelanders a rather inflated view of their country's importance on the world stage. They never laugh at themselves – well not in front

walking down the streets of Reykjavík was invariably followed by a crowd of excited children. During the pre-war years Hitler and his Nazis assiduously courted the Icelanders as an example of a "pure Aryan colony", but to the country's credit few people took any notice of this dubious flattery.

In fact, Icelanders are generally free of true racism. In 1989, when 5,000 foreign citizens were already resident in the country (making up 2 percent of the population) a survey showed that a vast majority supported the idea of people of different races and colour working and settling in Iceland. A large number of Icelandic couples adopted

Vietnamese orphans during the Boat People crisis, and very few of these children have experienced anything but a warm welcome from the community.

Looking to foreign shores: It is one of the many paradoxes so typical of the Icelanders that they are, at the same time as being insular, insatiably curious and interested in the outside world, even to the most obscure detail. The world's first Basque dictionary was written by an ordinary farmer in a desolate part of North West Iceland – he had learnt the language from Basque sailors who came to fish off the nearby coasts. The only epic poem that has ever been written in honour of the medieval Balkan hero

foreign lands. They are said to be *ad gera gardinn fraegan*, "winning renown for the old homestead."

Icelanders often claim theirs is a classless society. This claim has some basis: there is certainly a lot of class mobility. But there exist, like everywhere else, disparities of income, and some families are considered older and more "aristocratic" than others. Icelanders are also obsessed with genealogy. One Reykjavík newspaper devotes a daily page to the subject and most people can trace their ancestry back at least six or seven generations. Some even have family tables going back past the age of Iceland's settlement into the realm of legend – perhaps with

Skanderbeg was composed by an otherwise unknown Icelandic clergyman in 1861.

Icelanders lay great store by being cosmopolitan and well-travelled – "sailed", as they put it. This dates back to the days of the sagas when every self-respecting Viking started off his career by going abroad, returning home laden with renown and gifts from European royalty. Modern-day young Vikings and Valkyries also have the community's blessing to quit the nation's shores and try their luck seeking fame and fortune in

Left, dressing up in Heimaey. Above, young girls in the North East.

a Norse god or two sitting proudly at the top of the family tree.

The common enquiry "who are his people?" is not just snobbery, however. It is a relevant question in a society where everyone is related to everyone else in the tenth generation.

The national inferiority complex also comes into play – and it has obviously been around for some time. The author of the 12th-century *Book of Settlements*, which charted the progress of the first pioneers who came to Iceland, stated his purpose in writing the work as follows: "so we would better be able to answer foreigners who upbraid us for our descent from slaves or scoundrels if we knew our true origins for certain."

The general use of the patronymic, in accordance with ancient Scandinavian custom, makes the genealogists' job easier. Icelandic surnames are made up from the father's first name with "son" or "daughter" tacked on; thus President Vígdis Finnbogadóttir is Vígdis, daughter of Finnbogi. Her brother would be Finnbogason. Some families do have surnames, but they are often of foreign origin: Zoega, Schram, Richter and Petersen. In the past it was also possible for surnames or "family names" to be bought for cash by up-and-coming parvenues who considered them smarter and more aristocratic.

These days, Icelanders prefer to stick to the old homespun ways – to the extent of making foreigners who wish to become Icelandic citizens take up the patronymic system. New-fangled first names must also be approved by special committee.

Small-scale society: Despite remnants of old snobberies, modern-day Iceland is on the whole an informal, egalitarian and familiar society. Everyone from the President down is addressed by their first names. Jón the doorman greets Jón the eminent politician with a cheery hello – they come from the same fishing village and are probably second cousins. As you shower after an early-morning dip in the local swimming baths there might be a famous pop-star naked in the cubicle next to you.

Icelanders do not really understand the concept of fame, with all its paraphernalia of bodyguards, electric fences and exclusiveness. They are used to everyone being accessible. The President will grant an interview to any member of the public who wishes to see her. Top sportsmen and pop-stars usually have to keep their day-jobs, as few can afford to go professional.

And of course it is very easy to be famous yourself. Anyone with a little application and talent can stand for parliament, present a television programme, get up an art exhibition or play in a football team. Anyone can be a published author – and usually is. One in 10 Icelanders will publish something during the course of his or her life and writing a book is considered almost a form of National Service. And if you fail to hit the headlines in your lifetime you will at least do so after your death. Even the lowliest and most obscure person can be sure of at least one lengthy obituary, with a photo, in the newspapers on the day of their funeral. Pillars of the community meanwhile run to several pages stretched over a period of many days.

The idea of being a member of society is very strong. As a Japanese academic who settled in the country noticed: "Everyone is equal, so everyone is important. Everyone is a participant in society, it isn't possible to opt out, to deny your responsibility." Just as being a member of the community is an honour, being excluded from it is the worst dishonour. In the Saga Age, criminals were not killed or imprisoned, but outlawed – made outcasts from society.

Every individual matters and in return is obliged to participate, to do and to consume. Iceland supports five daily newspapers, two TV channels, a national theatre and opera plus dozens of orchestras, art galleries, theatre companies, radio stations and museums. None of these could survive unless people made sure they visited the theatre at least once a year, took two newspapers, went to concerts and so on. This is perhaps why they hold the world record for theatre attendance and book ownership.

Iceland is also a highly consumerist society in the material sense. There are for example more cars per head – one for every two people – than anywhere in the world outside the United States; for video recorders per head of population, they hold the world record, bar none.

Surveys have shown that in many areas Icelanders are closer to America than to Europe. Icelanders are firm believers in market forces. In their personal tastes, they have a slight tendency towards *Dallas*-type ostentation, glamour and display of wealth. But this materialism is partly a matter of economic survival. Importers and retailers would go out of business unless every household found it a vital necessity to purchase a television, a video recorder, a compact disc player or even a foot-massager.

The spend, spend, spend mentality has been encouraged by an economy plagued through the years by soaring inflation. Today, high interest rates and inflation at last approaching single figures may dampen the spirits of some shopaholics, but most seem to carry on in their spendthrift ways regardless.

The "shopping trips" organised by Icelandair to the Scottish city of Glasgow became legendary amongst the retailers of that city, and when similar trips were organised to Newcastle in the north of England it made

Left, a baby joining in on a Lutheran service. **Above**, praying to Thor.

headline news locally. No wonder – a small but determined army of 50,000 Icelandic tourists manage to spend £23 million (US$37 million) each year in Britain.

As Nobel-prize winning author Halldór Laxness once said, "it is, in general, expensive to be an Icelander." And to finance the expense, the nation is gripped by a collective compulsion to work all the hours God sends. The Icelandic working week is one of the longest in Europe. With practically non-existent unemployment levels, moonlighting is extremely common. Many people manage to hold down two or three jobs at the same time. (As a result, they are constantly doing things at the last minute and are always late for everything. Unpunctuality is one of the country's pandemic vices.)

Even children are not exempt. They work during their three-month summer holidays and often in the evenings after school as well. Many have started saving up to buy cars, or even for a deposit for a flat, before they reach their teens.

Working hard, playing harder: It often puzzles foreigners why Icelanders put so much time, money and effort into building palatial houses with state-of-the-art furnishings when they are always at work and therefore never at home to appreciate them. But work is not just a way of getting money, it is an end in itself, a means of getting self-respect. Although the Icelandic welfare state is not as evolved as those of its Scandinavian neighbours, it is still fairly comprehensive. Nevertheless, few people would ever dream of scrounging off the state. "The comprehensive ability to work is the hallmark of the Icelander, whether a desk-bound intellectual, a farmer or a fisherman," comments anthropologist Finnur Magnússon.

This extreme devotion to the Protestant work ethic was demonstrated during the war. "British work" – employment offered by the English military forces occupying the country – was despised by the natives as fit only for layabouts and degenerates. The reason seems to have been because it was too easy and well-paid.

But at the same time the Icelanders have a secret fascination for Bohemia. Hard-nosed yuppies will occasionally hang loose philosophising with the long-hairs in one of Reykjavík's innumerable coffee-bars, and even publish a book of poems on the quiet.

Even the most vulgar nouveau-riche would never indulge in the kind of narrow Philistinism that often characterises his counterparts in other countries. In Iceland, poets and artists command begrudging respect and have a special dispensation to lead a ramshackle, layabout lifestyle. As Laxness put it ironically, "since time immemorial, the Icelandic nation has had to battle with men who call themselves poets and refuse to work for a living." However, it must be admitted that in most cases the old Protestant work ethic will out. Back in the 1960s, Icelandic hippies, although quite adept at tuning in and turning on, never really got the hang of dropping out. The real diehards had to go to Copenhagen if

tained dogs during the trial period were given special exemption licences to keep their pets.)

Icelanders may take their work seriously but they are just as single-minded about their play. An inability to do anything in moderation is in fact one of the most characteristic national traits, as is demonstrated by a trip to downtown Reykjavík on a Friday night. This excess, however, is also partly explained by the price of alcohol – it is too expensive to indulge in every day so people prefer to save up for one almighty binge at the weekend (see *Friday Night on the Town*, page 177).

They are also quick to latch onto new trends, which can sweep across the entire nation with lightning speed. Video recorders

they wanted to bum around in style – back home in Reykjavík they would be too embarrassed not to have a job.

That is not to say that Icelanders do not appreciate and often indulge in eccentricity. Until quite recently it was not possible to keep a dog in Reykjavík, watch television on Thursdays, get a drink on Wednesdays or an alcoholic beer on any day. The only one of these endearingly idiosyncratic bans still in place is the one on dogs. After it was lifted for a trial period, the citizens of Reykjavík sensibly decided that cities were no places for canines and reinstated the law. (Animal-lovers rest assured – people who had ob-

had only been in the country a couple of months before there were film rental shops on every street corner. It was the same story with aerobics, sunbeds and new-age crystals. Aerobics teacher Sóley Jóhannsdóttir began her career in Denmark, where people would come for once-a-week dancing sessions. When she opened up a studio in Reykjavík it was a different story. "Icelanders never do anything by halves – it's four times a week for most of my regulars with additional circuit training lessons as well."

Non-violent society: Although they can behave like frenzied Vikings, particularly when they are trying to get things done at the last minute or are very drunk, the Icelanders are intrinsically a gentle people. Despite having a fair share of the late-20th century social plagues – drugs, porn, latch-key kids and so on – society is essentially non-violent and Reykjavík is one of the safest capitals in the world. Even boxing is banned – Icelanders prefer the far more elegant ancient sport of *glima* (which somewhat resembles sumo wrestling.)

The lack of serious crime means that society is rather as to a loss at how to treat its more anti-social and violent elements. Even the most vicious of criminals rarely seem to get sentences of more than seven years – and then they often get to go home at weekends.

(There have been several "escapes" after the weekend furloughs but the convicts usually give themselves up after about a week. Being on the run in the Icelandic wilderness is no picnic, as many a Saga Age outlaw found.)

Icelanders are broad-minded and tolerant about most things. Single mothers, for example, are admired rather than frowned upon. Besides, everyone loves children and is happy to welcome them into the world whether they have two resident parents or one. Although a

Left, a family in Reykjavík. **Above**, Icelandic women have always played a key role in what is a matriarchal society.

few moralists have predicted imminent destruction of the social fabric from such a lax set-up, marriage, which for many years was seen as irrelevant, is coming back into fashion – even though many bridal couples have their own offspring acting as bridesmaids and pageboys.

There are fewer atheists than in any country except the US – 97 percent of Icelanders say they believe in God, although only a fraction attend church regularly. But above all, Icelanders also have a greater respect for family ties than most other societies. They take care of each other – there are few neglected grannies and grandpas left to fend for themselves in high-rise blocks. A recent survey showed that Icelanders put family as their top priority – above friends, free time and even their beloved work.

Iceland's Valkyries: A small boy in Reykjavík is watching the inauguration of President Bill Clinton on television. "How funny," says the child. "A man President!"

This sort of anecdote has been a favourite with Icelandic feminists since the election of President Vígdis Finnbogadóttir in 1980, but President Vígdis, the first woman in the world to become a democratically elected head of state, was only the beginning: in 1983, Iceland became the first – and is still the only – country to elect a women-only party to parliament. The Women's Alliance (WA), a grass-roots radical movement with no leaders and an economic model based on the concept of "the thrifty housewife," had three of its members elected only a couple of months after the party was formed – and doubled its support at the following election. It lost one seat in the early 1990s, bringing its total down to five members, but is still a political force to be reckoned with.

At the same time, Iceland got even closer to feminist Valhalla when it achieved the unique position of having three of its top four positions of office held by women: Chief Justice of the Supreme Court Gudrún Erlendsdóttir, President of the Althing (the parliament) Salome Thorkelsdóttir, and President Vígdis herself. The only man in the quartet is the Prime Minister – which unfortunately is the most powerful political position of the four.

The Viking matriarchs are not resting on their laurels. "I don't think this situation should have to require any comment," says

President Vígdis. "It should be a natural and accepted state of affairs. In fact, I am disappointed what a short way women have come in the 10 years since I was elected."

Nevertheless, the women of Iceland are veterans of mould-breaking feminist activity. They first hit the international headlines in 1975, when they marked the beginning of the United Nations Women's Decade by going on a one-day mass strike to remind their menfolk of the essential role they played in society. Secretaries downed note-pads, bank-clerks and teachers stayed at home, housewives handed babies over to bewildered husbands – and the country was brought to a standstill.

When the Women's Decade drew to a close in 1985, they staged another walk-out. President Vígdis joined the protest, causing a constitutional crisis by refusing to sign a decree that would force striking air stewardesses back to work. Male chauvinist government ministers eventually forced her to sign, but her stand was much appreciated by her female compatriots.

Then came the Women's Alliance, at first an informal slate in the municipal elections, later developing into a fully-fledged parliamentary party. It was originally formed because of wide-spread discontent at the low level of female representation in parliament and other corridors of power, and the ultimate goal of the WA is to make itself redundant. "We want society to reach a stage where there is no need of a separate feminist platform," says prominent WA member Dr Gudrún Agnarsdóttir.

They may be on their way to achieving their purpose. The Alliance's success at the polls has frightened the traditional parties into putting up more female candidates, so women MPs now hold an all-time high of 22 percent of parliamentary seats. This is not as impressive a proportion as in the other Nordic countries, but it is certainly way above the European average of 13.6 percent and completely shames the US.

The upsurge of feminism in the past 20 years may have added grist to their mill, but women have always played a forceful role in Icelandic society. The nation's symbolic figurehead is the Woman of the Mountains, a quasi-supernatural persona who plays a similar role in the national psyche to Marianne in France and John Bull in England. The sagas and old tales are full of strong, matriarchal figures – from Aud the Deep-Minded, one of the greatest of the pioneers, to the irascible Bergthora, Njáll's wife – while ancient lawbooks indicate that the medieval Icelandic woman enjoyed a great deal more emancipation than her European counterparts. She had equal rights in marriage, could own property and even hold a *godord*, or chieftainship.

Feminist advances: Iceland was one of the first countries to introduce female suffrage: women were given the right to vote in municipal elections in 1908 and general enfranchisement in 1915. The Women's Alliance also has a historical precedent. From 1908 to

1922 women-only slates were put forward for municipal and parliamentary elections, with considerable success.

What has made this remote island in the North Atlantic such a hot-bed of feminist activity? Dr Agnarsdóttir of the WA says the low population is highly relevant. "A small community expects a lot from each individual, and each individual's contributions are also more likely to be noticed and appreciated." Chief Justice Erlendsdóttir considers very important the fact that women in Iceland have always kept the old Norse tradition of retaining their natal surnames when they marry. But the factor that all eminent women in Iceland mention when asked about their emancipation is – the sea. "Icelandic women are strong because the wives of sea-farers have to be," says President Vígdis.

Former Althing President Gudrún Helga-dóttir, who is herself the daughter of a fisherman, agrees. "All through our history we have had to shoulder responsibilities," she says. "With our menfolk away at sea for months at a time, we were the ones who kept everything going at home."

Indeed, this tradition of holding the fort stretches right back to the Viking era, when women would be left in control of the farms while the men went pillaging and raiding. Today, women play a more vital role than

to the other Nordic countries: only one of Iceland's 11 cabinet ministers is female, while 40 percent of the Norwegian cabinet are women.

Professor Svanur Kristjánsson, head of Social Sciences at the University of Iceland, concurs with the view that Icelandic women need still further emancipation. "Foreigners who hear about Vígdis and the Women's Alliance assume we must live in a matriarchy, but this is not so. The very existence of the Women's Alliance is symptomatic of the weak political position women have."

On the other hand, women have benefited from the fact that those of them who have gained power have shown themselves to be

ever in the economy – as they have demonstrated through their national strikes. Nearly 90 percent of women work outside the home in either full or part-time employment. One of their main grievances is that their salaries are still on average 59 percent lower than that of men, and that like their sisters elsewhere in the world, they are still having to do most of the work in the home as well as outside it.

And, despite their advances within the male power-structure, they compare poorly

Left, enjoying a pipe on a sunny afternoon. **Above**, the younger generation dancing through the night at a Reykjavík disco.

exceptionally able. President Vígdis, for example, is enormously popular amongst Icelanders, with an approval rating of more than 90 percent.

According to Professor Kristjansson, the area where equality is closest to being attained is social and sexual behaviour. "There is very little difference in attitude here. There are very few social constraints on women, and single mothers are admired rather than frowned upon. Vígdis is a single mother, and Gudrun Helgadóttir is twice-divorced, but this has not done them any harm in the eyes of the electorate. I don't think that would happen anywhere else."

A NATION OF CHAMPIONS

Jón Páll Sigmarsson, the Strongest Man of All Time, beat all comers at international strongman championships. But then, he was starting with an unfair advantage: he comes from what is probably the world's largest race. Not only are Icelandic babies born bigger than any others in the world (except the Faroese islanders) but the adults are taller and heavier than any other nation where such surveys have been conducted.

Icelandic men reach an average height of 179.9 cm (70–71 ins), a full 7 cm (2.7 ins) taller,

than for example, Belgians. They weigh around 4 kg (9lbs) more than most other Europeans. Icelanders are not only large, but their rate of survival is also impressive – they have the lowest infant mortality rate in the world and tie with Japan as the longest lived nation.

This race of venerable giants is still growing, at a rate of a centimetre a decade. Medical opinion is split on exactly why they have got so big. But Jón Páll, four-times winner of the World's Strongest Man title and declared the Strongest Man of All Time in 1987, is in no doubt about the secret of his success. "Of course we are the strongest race – we are the descendants of the Vikings and Valkyries." Chest-thumping chau-

vinists should heed this flower of latter-day Viking manhood: "Icelandic men are so strong because we do exactly what our women-folk tell us to do," he adds. "I have always followed the advice of my mother and my wife about diet and so on." Scientific prefers to put it down to the high standard of living and the amount of fish and fish oil in the Icelandic diet.

Icelandic sportsmen manage to put up a most impressive showing on the international arena, considering that they also qualify, along with such nations as San Marino and Monaco, for the "Minnow Olympics". The sports at which they tend to do best, unsurprisingly, are those requiring strength rather than agility: shot-putting, weight-lifting and the javelin. (Icelander Einar Vilhjalmsson is among the greats of the world's javelin throwers.)

The Icelandic football team has earned a reputation as giant-killers after confounding such high-ranking opponents as France, Spain, the ex-Soviet Union and Germany. Iceland's handball team, meanwhile, is rated as one of the world's best.

Iceland has had two Miss Worlds in the past decade, as well as other, more minor titles on the beauty circuit. Needless to say, the nation is enormously proud of its beauty queens, and, along with its strong-men, almost regards them as an exportable asset. Thus, bewildered guests at international trade-fairs find stalls festooned with banners entitled "Beauty and Strength", where they are greeted by gently smiling lovelies, shortly before being thrown into swimming pools by barrel-chested young Vikings.

The Icelanders also shine at more cerebral pursuits. There are more books written and published here per head of population than anywhere else in the world: around 400–500 a year, the equivalent of 1,200 books *per day* in the United States.

In chess, the vital statistics are just as impressive. Iceland's quarter-million inhabitants can muster six chess grandmasters, a higher total than any other Nordic country and the highest per capita ratio in the world. One out of every 40,000 Icelanders is a grandmaster. In that citadel of Caissa, the ex-Soviet Union, the figure is one per more than a million.

Live satellite broadcasts of two men staring at pieces of wood on a board might not be everybody's idea of action-packed TV viewing – except in Iceland. In 1989, when Icelander Jóhann Hjartarson was beating Viktor Korchnoi to reach the qualifying series of the world chess championship , the whole nation was glued to the television. Chess had become more than a game, sport, science or art: it was a small nation's self-affirmation.

Probably brought over by the first settlers in the 9th century or shortly afterwards, chess seems to have been a common pastime in Iceland through the Middle Ages, as shown by numerous old expressions from the game which have been preserved in everyday speech. Certainly, when American academic Willard Fiske visited towards the end of the 19th century, he found eager players all over this sparsely-populated country. Fiske (who was also the patron of Grímsey island) founded Iceland's first chess magazine, providing a theoretical training ground which soon guided the game into the realms of organised sport.

A few sporadic acts of giantkilling were perpetrated during the first half of the 20th century, but Iceland was not put permanently on the international chess map until 1959. That year, Fridrik Olafsson was nominated the nation's first grandmaster, and fought through to finish seventh out of eight in the Candidates' series, the final playoff before the world championship match. The next generation of masters was inspired by the product of the "Match of the Century" in Reykjavík in 1972, when Bobby Fischer had wrested the world championship crown from Boris Spassky. Among the crowds who "caught the bug" then were Helgi Olafsson (no relation to Fridrik) and Margeir Pétursson, then in their teens and now both international grandmasters.

In their wake, slightly younger, came the country's two other grandmasters: Jón L. Arnason, who won the world under-16 title in 1977, and Jóhann Hjartarson, who reached the last eight in the world championship qualifying series in 1989, where he lost to Karpov. Not even having reached "super-grandmaster" category (an Elo rating of at least 2600), this "fearsome foursome" has been the backbone of Iceland's national team which consistently performed well at the biennial Chess Olympiads. It won fifth place in Abu Dhabi in 1986.

Today, Iceland also boasts a number of international masters who are knocking at the door of the grandmaster title, and winners of world under-12 and under-16 titles in recent years. Powerful, almost gruelling, youth work by the Icelandic Chess Federation and local clubs is part of the key to maintaining this island nation's chess profile.

Alongside the biennial Reykjavík Open, strong international tournaments with local participation were staged with considerable regularity during the 1980s, awakening public interest and giving local players the chance to win "norms" – credits towards the title of master or grandmaster. And, although big international tournaments are not so frequent nor such great crowdpullers as then, there is maybe no longer the old need. These days, the Icelandic national chess championship itself is so strong that a good performance almost counts as an international title, in a country whose entire population fits in a medium-sized city elsewhere in Europe.

Iceland also holds the world record for the number of bridge players. Bridge has been catching up with chess as the intellectual exercise of choice, especially since Iceland won the 1991 world bridge championship held in Japan. The national team, which included a video store owner and pension fund manager, went through months of training before the tournament (a punishing regime of jogging and mountain climbing was thrown in for good measure). The live satellite telecast of the final held the whole of Iceland enthralled, while a planeload of 50 Icelandic holidaymakers diverted from the Philippines to Yokahama just in time to witness the climactic last 30 minutes of play! ∎

Left, Iceland's two Miss Worlds. **Right**, Jón Páll Sigmarsson, "the strongest man of all time".

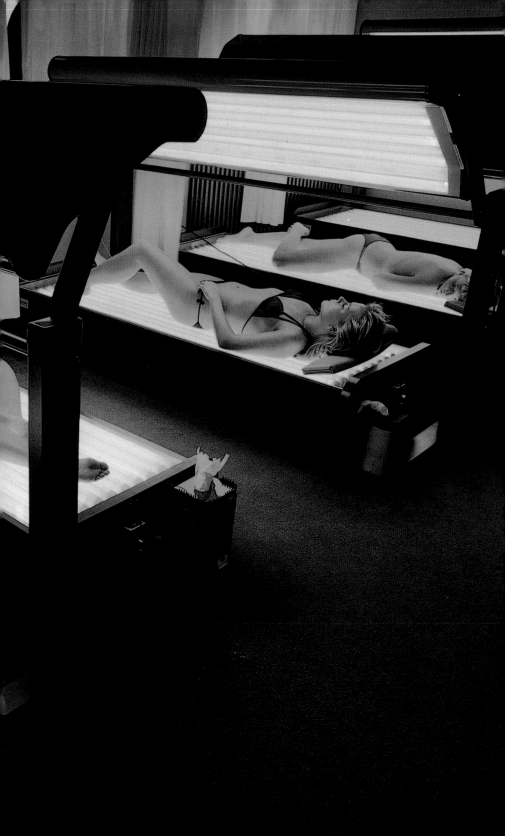

"I pitied the poor Icelanders who could not like swallows gather themselves together for a flight to a climate less hostile to the comforts of human existence. What the Icelanders can enjoy deserving the name of happiness during the long winter I cannot imagine." These were the comments of the English traveller John Stanley, who visited Iceland in 1789.

There is not so much reason to pity the poor Icelanders these days. Warm, centrally heated houses have taken the place of damp turf huts, electric light does much to compensate for the long hours of darkness, and powerful snow-ploughs mean that only the most isolated settlements are cut off during the winter months.

In fact, during winter, the inhabited areas around Iceland's coast do not experience the bitter extremes of cold that the country's name would suggest. Iceland is washed by the warm waters of the Gulf Stream and moderate south-westerly Atlantic winds, ensuring that – although summers are definitely chilly by most people's standards – the Icelandic winters are actually milder than in more southerly places like New York or Moscow. Temperatures below –10°C (14°F) in Reykjavík are unusual.

The dreaded wind and rain: Even so, as any visitor to Iceland will quickly find out, living with the climate here is still no picnic. Iceland's real plague is wind and rain. The same Gulf Stream and mild winds that bring moderate weather run up against the Icelandic mountains and the icy polar air to create some truly wretched weather. Although there are the occasional freak summers, Reykjavík normally enjoys only one completely clear day every July! In January, the average goes up to three.

The combination of gales and rain renders umbrellas completely useless, and a local joke is that Iceland is the only place where the rain falls from all directions – including horizontal. Even so, it is not uncommon to see Icelanders wandering around without any protection during quite heavy downpours. Ask them why and they might shrug: "It's rained here since I was a child. I don't even notice it any more."

The weather is worst around the southwest, Reykjavík and the West Fjords, improving markedly around Akureyri, the north and east. But luckily for travellers and Icelanders alike, the true norm for Icelandic weather is its sheer unpredictability, shifting rapidly from clear to miserably wet, then back again, several times in the course of a single day.

The polar night: Despite the blessings of the Gulf Stream, the Icelandic winter can still be a cold, long and miserable affair. At this high latitude, it is also particularly dark.

Iceland is almost completely outside the Arctic Circle (only part of the northern island of Grímsey is within its bounds), so it avoids the true extremes of month-long darkness associated with northern Greenland and the Arctic icecap. Even so, things are quite bad enough. In December and January there are no more than three or four hours of daylight anywhere in the country.

That's when Icelanders begin to suffer from skammdegisthunglyndi, or "short day depression", and the suicide rate goes up in January. Depressive patients are given "light therapy", where they sit in artificial sunlight for up to two hours a day. As some sort of compensation, winter is the best time to see the ghostly phenomenon of the aurora borealis or "northern lights" – shimmering green waves of astral electricity flickering in the starry sky.

Waiting for the sunshine: Many of the villages in the West Fjords do not see the sun at all during the long winter. Their narrow bays are surrounded by steep mountains, which effectively block out all the sunlight until February or March, when the sun finally climbs high enough in the sky for the first rays to penetrate. At the first sighting of the sun, inhabitants celebrate with a feast called "sunshine coffee."

All over the country, Icelanders wait impatiently each year for the first signs of spring. The first sightings of a bird called the

Preceding pages: getting tanned the Icelandic way at a Reykjavík solarium. **Left,** dressing up against the extreme conditions to be found in Icelandic waters.

golden plover, commonly known as the "harbinger of spring," are reported extensively in the local press.

It often seems a long time coming, but when summer truly arrives in June, the long winter wait seems almost worth it. Although temperatures can hardly be described as tropical – the mean average is between 12 and 15°C (54–60°F) – the sun shines almost throughout the night.

Strictly speaking, it is only above the Arctic Circle that the true phenomenon of "midnight sun" occurs, whereby the sun never dips below the horizon. This can be observed in the island of Grímsey, from the mountains near Ólafsfjördur or from the north-eastern

drinking ritual takes on truly gargantuan proportions in Reykjavík; and when the country's interior is criss-crossed with frantic drivers speeding around in their huge-wheeled vehicles. The *joie de vivre* is contagious and normal rules go by the board, with even very small children playing out in the street until midnight.

Foreign visitors to Iceland often find these endless days as difficult to cope with as the long winter nights: it's not easy to sleep when the sun is glistening through the window. However, there are advantages for the visitor. Photographers will find the Icelandic light at this time superb. The sun's golden rays are drawn out for hours through early

coastline just below the Arctic Circle near Raufarhöfn. But even without the true midnight sun, for the rest of Iceland real night never falls in June and July, with the sun just skimming below the horizon at midnight: a sort of extended dusk is the only sign of the passing of the day, and the stars do not come out until August.

Summer fever: Foreign visitors have often commented that Icelanders remind them of hibernating animals, sleeping in winter and letting rip in summer. June and July – and, to a lesser extent, August – are the times when Iceland's national parks are filled to overflowing on weekends; when the Friday night

morning and late night, making everything they touch appear especially gorgeous.

At any time of year, Iceland's unpolluted arctic air make visibility almost supernaturally clear. Far away objects often seem deceptively close: on a fine day in Reykjavík, for example, the distant icecap of Snaefellsnes looks as if it is only a few miles across a small bay. And a curious form of mirage called the Fata Morgana can occur along Iceland's sandy glacial deserts known as *sandur*, whereby islands or rock formations seem to appear on the horizon.

The dangers of nature: In the balmy days of summer, in the midst of civilised Reykjavík, nature seems benevolent and kindly and it is easy to be lulled into a false sense of security. But danger is always close at hand – as foolhardy travellers who set off into the highlands on a bright summer's day have discovered to their cost.

Icelandic weather is notoriously unpredictable, and a raging storm can appear out of a clear blue sky in minutes. Temperatures can plummet to –30°C (–22°F), with windchill factor, in the deserted highlands of the interior. Stranded trippers and mountaineers need not despair completely, however – as long as they had the presence of mind to notify the National Association of Rescue Groups of their journey before they set off.

This fine body of men, who work entirely on a voluntary basis, will monitor travellers and organise search-parties if they do not return to base on schedule.

They do get rather annoyed, however, at having to risk life and limb rescuing people who have got into trouble through sheer foolhardiness, so it is best to take sensible precautions, such as not attempting to climb unknown mountains except with an experienced guide.

Left, a graphic message – steer clear of the edge, Dettifoss. **Above**, keeping the roads open during an Icelandic winter is a major task.

One tragic incident in particular caused great public outcry. In the middle of winter, a young Englishman decided to climb onto the great glacier Vatnajökull alone – something the most experienced mountaineers do not attempt even in the summer months. He announced to the farmer whom he was staying with that he was not even taking victuals with him, as he intended to live off berries. His hosts attempted to forcibly prevent him from acting out his dangerous plans, but the police stopped them, informing them it was against the law. When the man did not return the entire neighbourhood searched for him for a week, at great risk to themselves, and he was eventually found dead. There is still no law to protect people against their own foolishness, so common sense must be the order of the day.

The treacherous sea: But against some natural forces even the most careful precautions are to all intents and purpose useless. The ocean is the source of Iceland's livelihood, but it can also be a killer. Despite enormous improvements in safety aboard fishing vessels, the life of the fisherman remains a dangerous one, and there are many Icelandic women who have been widowed by the treacherous seas.

Nor is one safe on Icelandic dry land, either. The South Iceland Earthquake, which appears every century or so, is long overdue, and scientists at National Civil Defence monitor each tiny seismological tremor with concern. In the absence of an army, the NCD is also responsible for conducting rescue operations in the event of other natural disasters – storms, avalanches, floods and volcanic eruptions.

Of all the natural disasters that plague Iceland, it is perhaps surprising that avalanches are the most dangerous: 16 people have died in them since 1974. But it is the threat of volcanic eruption that people find most terrifying and thrilling.

There have been 33 definite volcanic eruptions in Iceland this century, but most occurred, unseen, deep beneath the mighty glacier Vatnajökull. No-one, however failed to notice the two most celebrated eruptions – the one off the south coast in 1963, which formed a completely new island, Surtsey, and 10 years later, the Westmann Islands eruption. Suddenly, in the middle of the night, what was believed to be an extinct volcano on the inhabited island of Heimaey began to erupt. Fortunately, the fishing fleet was in the harbour, and every one of the 5,300 population was successfully evacuated to the mainland (see *Crisis on Heimaey,* page 219).

A far more devastating eruption was that of Lakagígar in 1783–84, particularly as the country's inhabitants could not call upon modern technology to aid them. The lava flow, produced by 100 craters in a volcanic fissure more than 25 km (15 miles) long, was the greatest ever recorded in human world history, and it eventually covered an area of 565 sq. km (203 sq. miles). It was Iceland's most cataclysmic natural disaster, and the

eruption, and the Haze Famine that came in its aftermath, caused the deaths of nearly one quarter of the population.

This episode, terrible though it was, is just one of many in the long saga of the Icelanders' battle with their environment. Nor are these the only environmental problems. Another old enemy is erosion. Iceland was once, according to the old chronicles, heavily forested, but now there is a startling absence of trees, and most natural vegetation is scrubby tundra. Not only is this a shame aesthetically, but the lack of trees means there is little to bind the soil, which is bad news on a such a windswept island.

Exploiting the volcanic landscape: A natural force can occasionally be tamed and made to earn its keep. Iceland's homes have been provided with cheap and environmentally friendly hot water and heating for the past 60 years by geothermal energy – water heated naturally under the earth's crust.

This water is also used to heat the 150,000 sq. metres (37 acres) of greenhouse, used for growing fruit and vegetables, in the town of Hveragerdi – the country's market-garden under glass.

And geothermal energy is also the reason Icelanders can enjoy an open-air swim on the most bitterly cold and snowy morning – and soak afterwards in a 45°C (113°F) hot pool. Swimming in Iceland is not so much a hobby as a way of life, and the geothermal pools have a total attendance of 1½ million people a year. Swimming baths serve the same purpose that bars, cafés and gentlemen's clubs do abroad – they are one of the main focuses of social life, and most of the country's most important decisions are made in lunch-time hot pool sessions.

Icelanders have been used to regarding their geothermal water as a bottomless pit – one swimming pool, for example, uses up 1.3 million tons of water a day – but there are indications that the reserves in Reykjavík may be drying up because of overuse.

One natural resource which is in no current danger of overexploitation is hydroelectricity. Provided by the country's countless waterfalls, it is estimated that over 90 percent of Iceland's hydroelectric potential has yet to be harnessed. With all this surplus energy, it seems logical to try to export some abroad. Now, with the development of ultra-low resistance wires, this scheme may soon become technologically and economically feasible, and there are already plans afoot to lay underwater cables across the ocean to Britain, and even Germany.

Some environmental exports are already a reality. Mineral water drinks such as Svali and Seltzer, which use Iceland's clean and unpolluted atmosphere as a selling point, are doing very well on foreign markets. And the environment is also of an enormous benefit to the tourist industry – clean and unpolluted, but at the same time different, exciting and slightly dangerous.

Tourism is very much on the increase in Iceland, and is one of its most important industries, bringing in 10 percent of the total foreign currency earnings. But the environment, seemingly so rugged and powerful, is extremely fragile – and the authorities are as a result not keen to see it grow out of control. "Iceland isn't open safari country," says Thíroddur Thóroddsen of the National Conservation Council. "We want tourists who are sensitive to the environment."

Keeping the roads open: Although Iceland does not fully merit its chilly name, winters are prolonged and snow can be heavy, but this does not discourage the Icelanders from travelling as much as possible all year round.

A few decades ago, the sea was the most important route for travel between Iceland's major roads. If the road network seems, to the outsider, to be a series of primitive unsurfaced tracks with the occasional stretch of tarmac, the outsider should bear in mind that it is a huge, and vastly expensive, transport network for such a small population in such a large country. The quality of the roads has advanced by leaps and bound over the past 20 years or so, and will undoubtedly continue to do so.

Policy laid down by the Ministry of Communications aims to keep all major roads passable, as far as possible, throughout the winter: the first priority is given to keeping open routes between centres of population within each region. These are generally

dispersed coastal communities. Roads hardly existed, and the coastal boats transported passengers and goods alike. Today, however, the motor vehicle is king, and overland travel has become the norm.

A vastly improved road system means that land travel is possible throughout the year, if a little difficult at times. Iceland has over 13,000 km (8,000 miles) of roads, about 8,000 km (5,000 miles) of them classified as

Left, a geothermally heated pool at Reykjavík – one of the many across Iceland. **Above**, snatching the opportunity to catch some of those rare summer rays.

cleared every working day, and more frequently in the case of unusually heavy snow. Roads out of Reykjavík, north to Borgarfjördur and east to Hvolsvöllur, for instance, are very rarely closed to traffic for more than a few hours at a time.

The second-highest priority is placed upon keeping clear roads linking one region to the next, such as the South to the East Fjords, or Akureyri to Reykjavík. These roads are cleared two or three times weekly on average, ensuring that traffic will get through at least on those days.

Minor roads are cleared less frequently, if at all. Mountain tracks across the interior, such as Kjölur and Sprengisandur, are summer-only roads and are normally closed by snow by the end of October.

Although mountain roads are largely free of snow again by May, the melt water from the same snow turns them into impassable seas of mud, and they are only re-opened once they are dry enough to sustain traffic, usually in late June or early July. The Public Roads Administration assesses the state of the highland roads, decides when to open them for traffic, and closely monitors traffic on the highlands. Unauthorised travel on the wet muddy roads in early spring can cause havoc to the road surface, and offenders are subject to heavy fines.

Alternative routes: Some major routes over highland passes – such as those into the mountainous West Fjords – are subject to such heavy snowfalls that they cannot necessarily be kept open throughout the winter, and may be closed for weeks or months. Alternative routes at lower altitudes remain open, however, and in some regions the sea route provides the main winter link between communities. In the West Fjords particularly, sea travel remains almost as important as in the past.

Although all efforts are made to keep the road network functioning, even in severe winters, the possibilities of wintertime travelling in an ordinary family car are severely limited, not least due to the unpredictable climate. The traveller may set off from home on a fine clear winter day, only to find a blinding snowstorm just over the next mountain. Ordinary saloon cars (especially without four-wheel-drive) are not happy with this kind of test. Icelanders, however, have taken enthusiastically to big four-wheel-drive vehicles which can operate in almost any road conditions, and wintertime travel has become a popular hobby.

Air travel is of unusual importance in Iceland, and even more so in winter. It takes about six or seven hours to drive the 432 km (267 miles) to Akureyri from Reykjavík, in good conditions. By air, you can get there in 45 minutes. In winter, with uncertain road conditions, the comparison becomes even more favourable. Flights are relatively rarely cancelled, although there can be delays, and Icelandic pilots attain great expertise in taking off, flying and landing in difficult, icy conditions.

The air route is also, of course, the emergency route into and out of most communities in winter. Scheduled flights operate frequently to all major centres such as Akureyri, Ísafjördur, Höfn and Egilsstadir, and less often but still regularly to a host of small centres round the country, where there may be no more than a landing strip and a windsock to indicate the "airport." For reasons of convenience and security, all airport roads are cleared regularly, and invariably in connection with scheduled flights. Road-clearing policy is decided by the Ministry of Communications and implemented by the Public Roads Administration, the actual road-clearing operations are tendered out to contractors within each region.

Hardware: Different sorts of equipment are required for various snow-clearing jobs: snow ploughs, snow graders, trucks, and snow "blowers" of various shapes and sizes. These blow the snow in a high stream away from the roadside, rather than piling it up in high, dangerous, snow-banks. One small type of snow-blower, which can be attached to the front of an ordinary tractor, is an Icelandic invention. It is designed to deal with hard, compacted snow, for instance on minor roads which are rarely cleared.

Snow is not the only hindrance to winter travel, though. Roads are often dangerously icy, mainly because of a tendency for Icelandic temperatures to hover around freezing point for much of the winter. The temperature may be 2–3°C (35–38°F) when snow falls, then warm up to reduce the snow to a smooth mush. The thermometer might then plummet to minus five or ten, and the mush freezes, smooth as a skating rink.

Winter tyres are essential from October to May, even in towns, where all roads are cleared regularly during snowy spells and salted to reduce ice. Many Icelanders opt for nailed tyres, which help give a better grip on icy road surfaces, although braking remains a problem on slippery roads. Heavy-tread snow tyres offer better braking, but may not provide enough grip for driving up slippery slopes. If you want to learn how to handle a car in a skid, Iceland is the place. With roads this slippery, you learn fast.

At work in one of Iceland's many greenhouses, a good way to maximise the growing season in a country with vast reserves of geothermal energy.

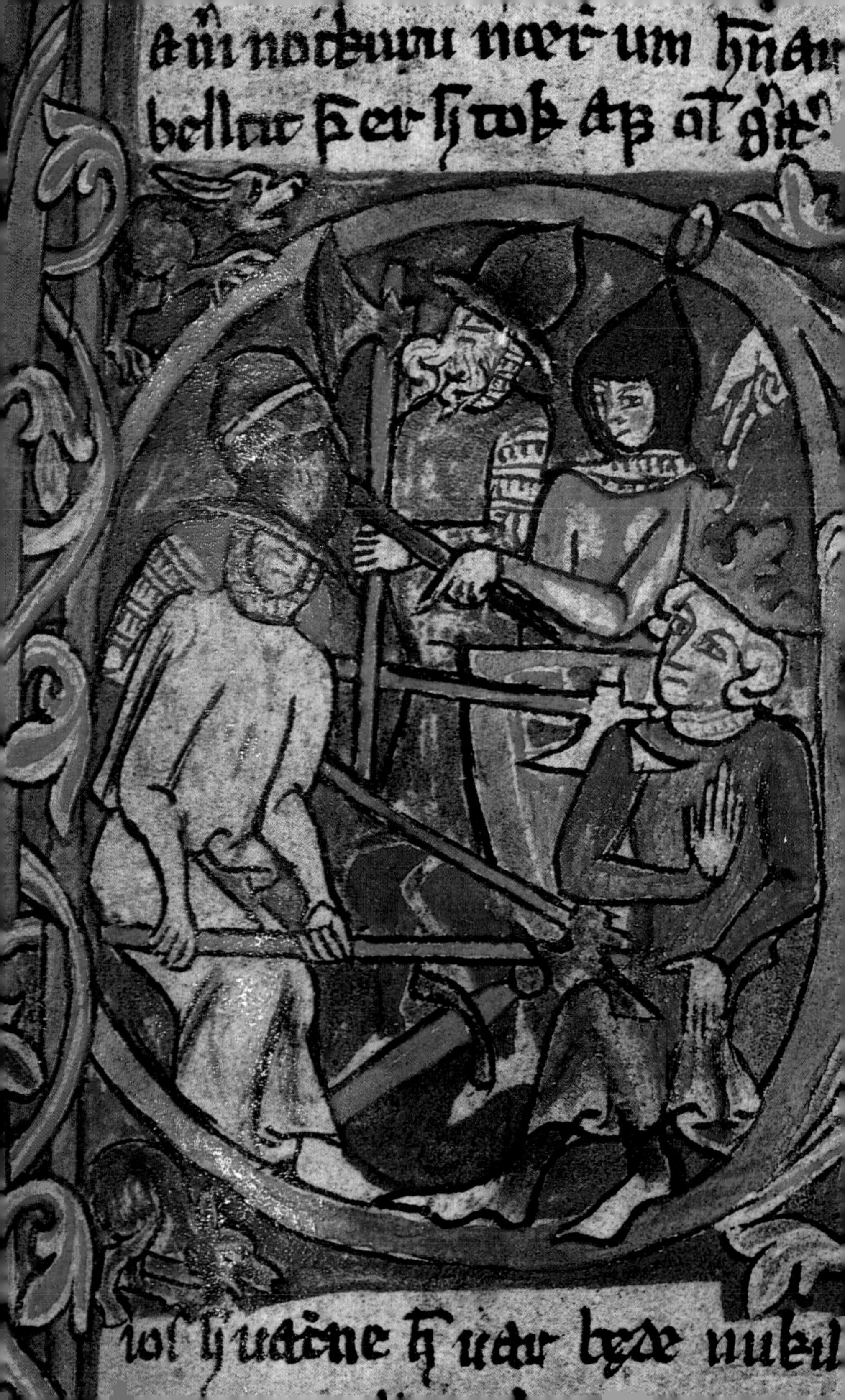

llu ē aðr lagðe huerni þa ꝩ ſa
z lꝺiꝑaðꝛa ſbꝛot ꝩ ꝉ hepꝛ
ꝺiꝑ logu oꝼ þeſ baꝛeſſtꝺꝛ ſuıı

A GAR LIOTT WAR

pta hegat bunꝺ uoꝛſ
ꞓꝛa iꞓu ẏꝓi nıu hunꝺꝛat
nıuꝺ ag’ z pirſu ar ē þa
ꝺlatı hꞃꝛ hınꞓ haꞃuꝓ ꝛl oꝼ
ẏlꝩ ar. en a þyꝺa ꝺꞃe þ
ꝛꝍgılıꝺꞓ hꝺꝛa ꝺapſ ꝩ ſı
pꝛaꝺꝺe aꝼꝺ guꝺbꝛanꝺe
ꝺoꞮꝛ ſuer barı þeꝺ eꝓꝛ
er hꝛꝺ hapꝺ ꝩ ha lꝺgu
bollat· ꝼ ꝩar ꝩ ſuꞮꝛ ſa
ſuerı ıꝛꝛ nepꝛꝺꝺ olaꝓꝛ
ꞓ ꝉ uer ueꞓıe auſıı hꝉu
꒒ulıꞓꝛ ſuo ꝺ ꞓꝛ. ꞓꝛ oꝼ·

THE SAGAS

The Icelandic saga is one of the world's most astonishing literary achievements. The anonymous 13th-century saga authors, living in a desolate northerly island in the midst of a raging civil war, were the first Europeans to write prose in their own language rather than in Latin. Why the sagas were written, whether they are history or fiction, who composed them, no-one knows. But the greatest of them – the romantic *Laxdaela Saga*; the thrilling adventures of the outlaws Gísli Súrsson and Grettir; the tale of the rogue warrior-poet Egill Skallagrímsson; and above all the magnificent epic *Njáls Saga* – can hold up their heads proudly in any literary company from Homer to Shakespeare.

Classified under the term "saga" – which in Icelandic simply means "story" – are countless historical chronicles, romances, legends, and lives of kings and holy men. But what most people have in mind are the family sagas – 40 or so chronicles about the lives of various Icelandic families in the years following the land's settlement. The events they describe therefore occur around 200 to 300 years before the sagas were written, but until the 20th century they were taken as undisputed historical fact, passed down the generations orally until being finally recorded on manuscript. More recent scholarship, however, holds that they are to all intents and purposes works of fiction. The identity of the authors remains a mystery, although the chieftain Snorri Sturluson, author of *Heimskringla*, the history of the Norwegian kings, is generally acknowledged to have written the saga of Egill Skallagrímsson.

Bloody chronicles: To summarise a saga story-line is almost impossible. They are great epic sprawls, spanning generations with dozens of characters and sub-plots. One 18th-century Icelandic scholar summed them up with the sardonic epigram "farmers at fisticuffs". He has a point – much of the action centres around blood-feuds, killings and conflict. But there is, of course, more to them

than that. They were written at a time of social chaos, when Iceland, North Europe's first republic, was being brought back under the rule of foreign monarchs because of internal power struggles and conflicts. They contain a retrospective warning to the authors' contemporaries. As Njáll, the sage-prophet hero of *Njáls Saga*, says: "with laws we shall build our land, but with lawlessness it shall be laid waste." At the same time, there is a certain nostalgia for a heroic golden age where men fought, to be sure, but for honour rather than power and politics.

Bearing in mind that Iceland was being subjugated to the Norwegian king, there is a rather wistful recurring theme of Icelanders being feted and honoured at foreign courts, and being showered with gifts by, or even getting the better of, various European monarchs. In the short saga of Halldór Snorrason, for example, the eponymous hero actually forces the Norwegian king Harald Hardrada at swordpoint to hand over his rightful bounty.

The sagas are written in a highly distinctive terse and economic style. The laconic viewpoint, both of the narrative and the characters, sometimes borders on parody. One dying Viking's words, as he has a spear thrust into his gut, were "I see the broad spears are now in fashion."

The narrator makes few moral judgements, but the sagas are not much preoccupied with good and evil in the modern sense. Most characters are mixed, and unmitigated villains are rare – the cunning lawyer in *Njáls Saga*, Mördur Valgardsson, is one of the few that spring to mind.

Despite being composed in a Christian society, the sagas portray the old pagan Viking morality. Oathbreaking, meanness and cowardice are the worst sins; open-handedness, courage and honour the greatest virtues. "Better to die honourably than to live on in shame," as *Flóamanna Saga* puts it.

Fate plays the strongest role in determining men's actions. Tragedy is usually the result of *ógaefa* – a near-untranslatable word, meaning more or less "ill luck."

The light, the dark and the ugly: The difference between the "dark hero" – the unlucky man – and the "light hero", whom fortune

Preceding pages: the old Icelandic sagas are preserved on medieval vellum manuscripts. **Left, Dr Jónas Kristjánsson, director of the Arni Magnússon Manuscript Institute.**

smiles upon, is one of the recurring themes of the Icelandic saga. The romantic Kjartan Ólafsson of *Laxdaela Saga* is the archetypal light hero – popular, handsome, accomplished and brave. In a similar mould is Gunnar of Hlidarendi in *Njáls Saga*: "his arrows never missed their mark, he could jump more than his own height in full armour, just as far backwards as forwards. He was a handsome man...extremely well-bred, fearless, generous and even-tempered, faithful to his friends but careful in his choice of them. It has been said that there has never been his equal." The peerless Gunnar contrasts sharply with Skarphédinn, son of Njáll, who was "quick to speak and scathing in his words... He had

the spectre manages to curse him with its last breath: "Your deeds shall turn to evil, and your guardian-spirit forsake you. You will be outlawed and your lot shall be to dwell ever alone." The unfortunate champion, who, thanks to the horrors of his experience with the ghost is also tormented by fear of the dark, spends 19 miserable years in exile on the isle of Drangey, and is finally killed by his enemies.

Another archetypal dark hero is Egill Skallagrímsson. Historically, Egill was one of the greatest of the early Icelandic *skalds* (poets), but unfortunately, as his saga records, also a phenomenal drinker and a murderous psychopath. The grandchild of a werewolf

a crooked nose and prominent teeth, which made him ugly round the mouth. He looked every inch a warrior."

Dark heroes are often ugly, awkward men, at odds with society, but the conventional romantic hero pales into bland insignificance in comparison with these enigmatic, tormented figures.

The outlaw Grettir the Strong, of *Grettis Saga*, is another dark hero. He is the strongest and most courageous man of his age, but "was rough in his manners and quarrelsome." Grettir meets his nemesis while helping to rid a farmstead of a troublesome ghost, Glumr. He wrestles with the fiend and lays it low, but

and a most precocious youth, he was forbidden to go to a feast when he was three years old because, as his father said, "you are difficult enough to cope with when you are sober." The toddler made his way alone across country to the feast regardless, sat at high table and composed a boastful rhyme in honour of his exploit. He committed his first killing when he was eight, and went on to cause trouble wherever he went. Never the most placid of men, he once took such umbrage at a drinking feast that he vomited vast quantities of sour milk-curds into the mouth of his host, and, waking next morning with a raging hangover, continued to act the perfect guest by storming into his host's bedchamber and gouging out his eye.

Egill was, it would seem, a poet almost by necessity – he composed his greatest poem, *Sonatorrek*, to stop himself committing suicide after the death of his two sons. Another of his most celebrated poems, *Hófudlausn* (Headransom), was to save his head after having foolishly upset King Eric Bloodaxe at York. He was to be executed in the morning, but, on reciting to the king the poem he had composed in his dungeon overnight, he was pardoned.

Inexplicably, Egill lived to a ripe and cantankerous old age. His final act, aged around 80, was to hide his treasure so others could not enjoy it, and kill the slaves that helped him do it.

The early settlers were mostly inter-related – not surprisingly in such a small community – and many of the characters pop up in more than one saga. Thus, the fearsome Egill turns up again in *Laxdaela Saga*, rather uncharacteristically, as a kindly and considerate father who refuses to marry his daughter Thorgerdur to Olafur the Peacock without her consent. This Thorgerdur is certainly her father's daughter: when her son Kjartan is slain, she presses her menfolk to avenge him, and then accompanies them to the slaughter, afraid that their bloodlust might falter unless she was present to egg them on.

Ruthless women: The saga women were certainly no less formidable than their male counterparts. Their forerunners were the terrible heroines of the ancient Eddic poems, including the Valkyrie Brynhildur, who had her former lover Sigurd Volsung put to death, and Gudrún Gjukadóttir, who burnt her husband Atli (Attila the Hun) alive after feeding him the flesh of their two sons, in order to avenge her brothers.

In the same mould as the bloodthirsty Thorgerdur is Hildigunnur, a character in *Njáls Saga*. After her husband, the saintly Höskuldur, has been killed by the sons of Njáll, she goads her uncle, the chieftain Flosi Olafsson, into avenging him. Flosi is reluctant to start yet another blood-feud, and her pleading falls on deaf ears. She then throws the cloak her husband was wearing when he was slain over Flosi's shoulders, and "the

Left and **right**, illustrated saga manuscripts dating from the 13th century.

clotted blood rained down all over him." "Monster!" cries the horrified chieftain, "Cold are the counsels of women." Nevertheless, the fate of Njáll and his sons is thereby sealed.

Njáls Saga: Gunnar of Hlídarendi makes the fatal mistake of slapping his wife, the ravishingly beautiful but wicked Hallgerdur Long-legs. Years later, the couple are besieged in their homestead by enemies. Gunnar, an excellent archer, puts up a noble defence, until one of his attackers manages to cut his bow string. He begs Hallgerdur to cut off a lock of her long, golden hair and plait him a new one. "I shall now remind you of the slap you once gave me," she says, and

refuses. Gunnar is slain shortly afterwards.

Queen of all these indomitable women is Gudrún Osvifsdóttir, heroine of *Laxdaela Saga*. Beautiful, proud and passionate, she is tricked into thinking that her lover Kjartan Olafsson has been unfaithful, and marries instead his best friend and foster brother Bolli Bollason. Kjartan responds by wedding the demure and gentle Hrefna. In a cold, jealous rage, Gudrún steals Hrefna's priceless bridal headdress, and then goads her husband, the hapless Bolli, into killing her former lover. When the news of Kjartan's death is brought to her, she casually remarks, "Hrefna will not go laughing to bed tonight."

THE ARNI MAGNÚSSON INSTITUTE

L ocated in an unassuming concrete building not far from the National Museum in Reykjavík, the Arni Magnússon Institute is home to Iceland's most valued treasures: the medieval manuscripts containing the country's oldest historical documents, its Poetic Eddas and the famous sagas.

Yet this undisputed guardian of the national heritage only assumed its present role in the early 1970s, when manuscripts began returning to Iceland after centuries of "exile" overseas. Many had been taken to Denmark, the ruling

colonial power, by researchers who combed Iceland in the 17th and 18th centuries.

The most famous and indefatigable of these researchers was Arni Magnússon, an Icelandic scholar who devoted his life to tracking down, saving and collating the vellum manuscripts. Educated in Denmark, he returned to Iceland in 1702 to conduct a census and spent the next decade obtaining every medieval document that could be bought and laboriously copying the rest. Arni's almost supernatural knack of sniffing out manuscripts has become legendary: on one occasion he found a vellum that had been made into a farmer's shoe; another time, he noticed that a document had become an Icelander's waistcoat!

Arni took back with him no fewer than 55 cases full of manuscripts. As one of the leading scholars in Scandinavia, he was able to carry on the task from his post as Secretary of the Royal Archives in the University of Copenhagen, using his influence to amass the world's best Old Icelandic collection.

Tragically, fire swept through Copenhagen in 1728 and although Arni pulled most of his manuscripts from the flames, many were lost. Modern historians believe that the best parts of the collection were probably saved, but the trauma may have been too much for the ageing scholar, who died 15 months later.

The Icelandic manuscripts remained at the University of Copenhagen – the undisputed centre of learning for Denmark, Norway and Iceland – for more than two and a half centuries. But as Iceland began to claim self-rule from Denmark in the late 1800s, so too did nationalists press for the return of its literary heritage. When the country became independent in 1944, the fate of the manuscripts was contested.

After years of wrangling and legal cases, Denmark finally agreed to return the bulk of the Icelandic manuscripts in 1961, hanging onto those relating to other Scandinavian countries. But it was not until a decade later that the first two books – the precious *Codex Regius* (containing the Poetic Eddas) and *Flateyjarbók* (the most important collection of sagas) – crossed the Atlantic in a Danish naval frigate. On 21 April 1971, thousands of spectators flocked to Reykjavík harbour to watch the manuscripts' arrival, carried ashore by naval officers in a solemn ceremony.

Since that day, some 1,500 manuscripts have been returned by the Danish Government (out of a total of 1,800 which will be returned to Iceland by the year 1996). The Icelandic Manuscript Institute, founded in 1961 to take on the responsibility of caring for the books, was renamed the Arni Magnússon Institute in 1972 after the great Icelandic researcher.

Today the Institute's library and permanent displays have become pilgrimage sites for anyone who is even vaguely interested in the literary traditions of Northern Europe. With six specialist scholars on the staff and four more on short-term projects, the Institute has become a cultural nerve centre: it looks after everything from restoring manuscripts, controlling the humidity of their storage rooms, transcribing sagas for new editions to publishing critical treatises on Icelandic folklore. ∎

Gudrún marries four times during the course of her stormy career, and ends her days as Iceland's first nun. When she is a very old woman, her son asks her which of the men in her life she had cared most about. Her enigmatic reply sticks in the mind of every reader: "I was worst to him that I loved the most."

Sagas in modern Iceland: The above quotation springs readily to the lips of any modern-day Icelander – as do numerous other phrases from the old sagas. "Fögur er hlidin" (how fair the slopes are), the first line of Gunnar of Hlídarenda's lyrical speech, when he decides not to go into foreign exile but stay in his beloved homeland and face his doom, has been a patriotic catchphrase since of the nation's heroic past and of its literary achievements, but also of its survival.

Unlike most ancient literature elsewhere, which was composed and enjoyed by a small and privileged elite, the sagas have, since their conception, been the property of the common people. Also uniquely, they remain accessible to ordinary people in their original form. Although the language is somewhat archaic, it is still readily understandable to the modern reader, as Icelandic itself is almost unchanged since the Middle Ages.

The sagas are still a living literature – numerous films and plays have been made based on the saga stories, and nearly every Icelander is familiar with the characters and

the independence struggle of the 19th century. One of Njáll's famous sayings, "med lögum skal land byggja" (with laws shall we build our land) is the punning slogan of a leading Icelandic record company – "logum" can also mean tunes. Heroes and villains live on in the language. A large boulder is called a *Grettistak* after the saga strongman's ability to lift such things, and a liar is known as a *lygamördur* from the nefarious *Njáls Saga* scoundrel Mördur Valgardsson.

The sagas themselves play a key role in the national psyche – they are symbolic not only

Above, display at the Arni Magnússon Institute.

plots of the major works. Nevertheless, there is some concern that the sagas are developing into rarefied literary relics – with the advent of television, video and paperback bestsellers, people are no longer reading the sagas as before.

Some critics feel that in all the fuss over their historical, national and academic importance, the fact that they are, above all, excellent stories has been forgotten. As Jón Bödvarsson, who runs saga study groups for the general public, says: "We should treat them like ordinary novels. That way people can carry on reading them for enjoyment – the way they were originally intended."

Land, nation and language – the
only true trinity.
— Snorri Hjartason, poet

To the Icelander, the mother tongue is far
more than just a method of communication –
it is the essence of culture, and its nurture and
preservation is inextricably tied up with the
survival of the national identity and pride.
Icelanders would never regard themselves as
bigots, but they know in their hearts that the
Icelandic language is, as the poet Einar

Preserving an ancient language: What would
be regarded in other countries as normal
linguistic developments are seen as national
disasters in Iceland. There is, for example,
"dative sickness" – a terrible and contagious
disease which causes sufferers to put nouns
which should be in the nominative or accusa-
tive case into the dative. Like most ancient
languages, Icelandic is a hideously complex
minefield of case endings, subjunctives and
inflections which can catch out many of the
native speakers, let alone foreign students.

Benediktsson said, "more noble than that of
any other nation."

Icelandic is one of the North Germanic
family of languages, its nearest relatives
being Norwegian and Faroese. Thanks to
centuries of isolation, it is still very similar to
old Norse, the language spoken by most of
Northern Europe during the 7th to 11th centuries, and is the only language to still use the
old runic symbols of ∂ (ed) and π (thorn).
Although no longer isolated, the language
continues in its unaltered state – for Icelanders will fight to the death against any influences which might corrupt or change their
beloved mother tongue.

Nevertheless, any grammatical slip-ups are
considered social solecisms of the worst
order, and if committed by a guardian of
public linguistic morals, such as a radio
show host, a sackable offence.

Foreign influences are also strictly kept in
check. The TV channel Stod 2 was banned
from showing CNN at night because the news
was broadcast without subtitles. Icelanders
have no truck with international loan-words
like "telephone", "radio" or "computer,"
which have bastardised many other languages. Academic committees are set up to
find proper, Icelandic words for these new-
fangled phenomena. Thus, the computer was

christened *tölva* – a mixture of the word *tala*, number, and *völva,* prophetess. The telephone became *sími*, from an ancient word meaning "thread". A helicopter is a *thyrla* or "whirler"; a jet aircraft is a *thota* or "zoomer". Even scientific language is firmly non-Latin. The general public joins in the fun of "word-building", and a raging debate ensues – when AIDS first reared its ugly head in Iceland, almost as much media space was devoted to what the disease should be called as to the medical and social questions it raised.

Some of these neologisms are quite creative, if not downright witty. Even such an eminently post-Freudian figure as the voyeur is cut down to size in Icelandic as a

in its literature, the ancient culture of the Norsemen. The golden age of Icelandic literature, beginning around 1100 with the historical chronicle *Book of Settlements*, was one of the most rich and diverse in medieval Europe (see *The Sagas,* pages 111–115).

But even more invaluable, for the purpose of providing a feeling of the way of life, thoughts and priorities of these people, is the poetry they have left behind them. Icelanders were, from the beginning, poets. They were so skilled at this art, in fact, that they gained a monopoly on it – between the 9th and 13th centuries there were 100 Icelandic poets working around the courts of Europe, and after the end of the 10th century the

gluggagaegir, the name of one of the 13 traditional harbingers of Christmas, who used to spy in through farm windows. And the tiny "beepers" or breast-pocket pagers used to call busy businessmen to the nearest phone are known as *Fridthjófur*, a man's name meaning literally "thief of the peace."

But Icelandic is not just known as Latin of the North because the language itself has remained unchanged – it has also preserved,

Left, reading was a popular way of passing long winter nights. **Above**, Reykjavík bookstore: more books are published per head of population in Iceland than anywhere else on earth.

position of court poet in Scandinavia was exclusively held by Icelanders.

The role of the poet: In Germanic culture, the poet or *skald* had an elevated, even mystical status. He was entrusted with preserving the deeds of the tribe in his poems, and was also in charge of raising morale with stirring heroic verse.

Like their ancient Germanic forerunners, the Icelandic *skalds* have always been very important members of society. Many writers, for example, took an active part in the independence struggle – and poetic talent has always been regarded as the hallmark of a noble personality.

The Eddic poems were composed in accordance with strict rules of internal rhyme and alliteration, but are much more accessible. These works, which deal with heroic or mythological subjects, were written down at the same time as the sagas, but most of them were probably composed much earlier. Poems such as *Hávamál* give a vivid insight into the Viking mind, revealing a people preoccupied with honour, who were sociable, generous but highly pragmatic: "Cattle die, kindred die, we ourselves also die," runs one oft-quoted line, "but the fair fame never dies, of him who well deserves it." Thus another: "A man should be a friend to his friend, and repay gift with gift. Men should meet smiles with smiles and lies with treachery."

Then there is *Völuspá*, or Sybil's prophecy, a magnificent poem composed by an unknown Icelander in the 11th century, and the best information we have today about the old pagan mythology. It tells the history of the world, its destruction at Ragnarök (the Wagnerian *Götterdämmerung* or Twilight of the Gods) and finally, its eventual rebirth.

The dark ages which followed Iceland's loss of independence proved something of a Ragnarök for literary creativity. (Although some original literature was produced, such as the much-loved Passion Psalms of 17th-century clergyman Hallgrímur Pétursson). Still, the old language and literature were carefully treasured through the years of poverty, dirt, death and disease. Since the Middle Ages, Icelanders have always been able to read and write – children could not be confirmed until they were literate – and learning has been held in high esteem. Foreign travellers write with amazement of being addressed in Latin and ancient Greek by filthy half-starved natives, and dragged into mud huts to look at priceless manuscripts.

Poetry and politics: In the 19th century, with improving social conditions and a growing independence movement, the *skald* came back into his own. The poet Jónas Hallgrímsson, born in 1807, was the poet who reached the hearts of his people as no-one else has done before or since. Known as "the nation's beloved son," he was the first Icelander to have a statue raised to his memory by his countrymen.

A Romantic in the high tradition, Jónas was at the forefront of the struggle for Icelandic independence from Danish rule, and his poetry is full of love for his native land: its language, heritage, countryside and golden-haired girls. He was a poetic radical – like Wordsworth, he wrote in the common tongue rather than high-flown poetic simile. He was also a highly-qualified botanist, and travelled round the highlands each summer, collecting material for a comprehensive account of Iceland's natural history – a Herculean task he was never to complete.

Jónas, a poor country lad from North Iceland, spent much of his adult life in Copenhagen. Here he wrote some of his best work, including *Island*, a poignant testimony to former glories and call for a better future that every Icelander knows by heart:

Iceland, happy homeland,
fortunate frost-white mother,
where is your ancient honour,
your freedom and deeds of renown...

Jónas suffered a great deal of hardship and exposure during his botanical explorations, and these, coupled with poverty and drink, took a heavy toll on his health. He put the seal on his reputation by dying a true poet's death – young, poverty-stricken and alone.

By the early 20th century, the Icelandic *skald* was taking his first tentative steps into the modern world. Einar Benediktsson (1864–1940) wrote beautiful, eminently quotable poetry but difficulties of translation means that he is not well-known outside his own country. An exceptionally urbane and cosmopolitan man, he was also somewhat eccentric and gained notoriety after allegedly trying to sell the Gullfoss waterfall and the Northern Lights abroad.

But by far the most important literary figure of modern times is Hálldór Kiljan Laxness, winner of the 1955 Nobel Prize for Literature. A truly great and innovative writer, he is one of the few Icelandic authors who can bear comparison with foreign contemporaries such as Faulkner or Hemingway.

Laxness was more or less single-handedly responsible for dragging Icelandic literature out of the pastoral mire and into the 20th century. He felt that the endless idealisation of peasant life was not doing either literature or society any favours, and called the old farming and fishing pursuits "wretched drudgery." Laxness's preoccupation with the dark underside of rural life caused much resentment among some of his countrymen, particularly the older generation, who felt he was presenting his homeland in a bad light.

But in his own way, Laxness was as fervent a patriot as any. His historical novel, *Bell of Iceland*, is set in the 18th century but contains much reference to the contemporary independence struggle: "A fat and sleek servant is not a great man," Laxness wrote. "A beaten slave is a great man, for freedom lives in his breast." The post-war *Atom Station*, written at the time of the NATO airbase controversy, contains much pointed criticism of the politicians who were ready to sign away their country's independence out of greed. His best-known creation is Bjartur of Summerhouses, the peasant crofter hero of *Independent People*. Stubborn, infuriat-

relic, he played around with it, changed spellings, used street language and colloquialisms, made up or even, worst crime of all, borrowed foreign words if it suited his literary purpose. Nevertheless, his influence has not been entirely beneficial – lesser authors are extremely conscious of the fact that they writing in the shadow of his genius.

Contemporary voices: Pétur Gunnarsson, one of the first "urban novelists," innovated the use of colloquial, humorous first person narrative. Thór Vilhjálmsson makes use of fragmented language and cultural reference to come to terms with modern life, while Gudbergur Bergsson criticises the *nouveau riche* American-worshipping culture of the

ing but ultimately "the most independent man in the country," Bjartur has come to represent the archetypal Icelander.

Break with tradition: Like all great *skalds*, Laxness took his responsibilities very seriously, and his best work, *World Light*, is a trilogy dealing with the role of the poet in society. One of his own most important contributions as a *skald* was to show other writers what could be done with the language. Unlike many of his predecessors, who treated Icelandic not as a tool but rather as a museum

Above, Hálldor Laxness, Iceland's Nobel Prize winning novelist.

post-war period through absurd humour. Amongst women writers Svava Jakobsdóttir has developed a unique brand of surreal feminism, while the lyrical narrative method of Vigdís Grimsdóttir is much admired.

There have also been great innovations in poetry. The "*atomskalds*" of the 1950s caused a storm of controversy when they broke all the rigid, old poetic rules, strictly adhered to since the country was founded, and began to write in free verse. But modernist or traditionalist, the latter-day *skalds* of Iceland still take their responsibilities seriously. They are above all keepers of the faith, guardians of the holy trinity: language, land and nation.

"Life is saltfish," wrote Iceland's Nobel Laureate Halldór Laxness in the 1930s. If he was right, Iceland now has more lives than the luckiest of cats – and, of course, more fish. These days, with the country's economy dependent on the sea more than ever before, life is still saltfish, but it's also canned fish, smoked salmon, frozen shrimps and caviar.

Fish has been an important export item from Iceland ever since the stockfish trade to Britain began in the Middle Ages. But fishing only began to outpace agriculture in economic status with the advent of motorised fishing vessels around the turn of this century. And while improvements in vessel technology soon made fisheries into Iceland's mainstay national industry, they intensified the threat of overfishing by foreign deep sea fleets, which escalated until the famous "Cod Wars" with Britain.

The first 30 years of the 20th century were a time of intense, fisheries-led economic growth. Iceland was gradually escaping from Danish colonial rule, and economic independence was an obvious prerequisite for true political independence. Iceland's fishing industry has been coloured by fierce nationalism ever since.

Salted whitefish – mainly cod, sold to Spain – and iced whitefish and herring, sold to the UK and northern Europe, were the mainstays of Icelandic fisheries right until World War II. Dependence on those few markets had its limitations: for example, Spanish wine producers threatening to ban imports of saltfish were able to "twist Iceland's arm" into lifting a six-year alcohol prohibition in 1921. Later, the collapse of the fish market in the Great Depression devastated Iceland's economy.

The fish boom begins: Unemployment ran high right up until World War II, when Iceland suddenly became the only large fish-producer in northern Europe. Icing their catches, Icelandic fishing vessels sailed directly to Britain, often suffering fatalities from U-boat attacks. Meanwhile, superior freezing technology was developed that would be the key to the postwar fisheries

The morning catch: entering Heimaey harbour.

boom targeted at both the UK and America.

Iceland made good money during the war and allocated funds for the modernisation of the trawler fleet, and an era of larger catches and more diverse markets began. Frozen block and fillets went to both sides of the Atlantic. Throughout the Cold War, Iceland retained good trading relations with Eastern Europe, and the Soviet Union became a major buyer of products such as salted herring. Meanwhile, the diversification began which remains the key to Iceland's survival as a specialist fish-producing nation today.

Situated where the Gulf Stream meets cold currents coming down from the Arctic, Iceland's fishing grounds offer choice growth pure, while the small local population and absence of large-scale manufacturing industries keep "home-grown" pollution to a bare minimum. And Iceland has even begun exporting the technology for catching and handling fish: in some specialist areas, such as the electronic weighing of fish at sea using scales that automatically compensate for the roll of the boat, Iceland is a world leader.

Surviving in a high-risk industry: But seafood is a notoriously shaky business – size of catches can never be taken for granted and prices fluctuate far more than in land-based food processing. Unstable as its economy has been, Iceland has buffered itself against some heavy market shocks by shrewdly

conditions for a wide variety of species: demersal or bottom-feeding fish led by cod, haddock, redfish (ocean perch), saithe (pollack), ocean catfish and flatfish such as Greenland halibut and plaice; shellfish such as shrimp, scallops and Norway lobster (nephrops or scampi tails); river-migrating fish such as wild salmon, trout and Arctic charr as well as pelagic (topwater) fish such as herring and capelin.

Of increasing importance in this environmentally-conscious age is the cleanness of Iceland's fish. The country's fishing grounds are far enough from the industrial centres of Europe and North America to remain very spreading its coverage and its product range.

The US was Iceland's main buyer of frozen fish from the 1970s to the mid-1980s, until a sliding dollar made Europe a more attractive proposition. Today, the two main European markets for both frozen and fresh (unprocessed) fish are the UK and Germany. Yet the two rarely compete, since the UK buys cod and haddock while the Germans prefer redfish and saithe.

A north-south split in European buying trends also exists, with Portugal, Spain and Italy (which all rank among Iceland's top 10 market countries) buying almost entirely saltfish and virtually no frozen or fresh.

Japan, the world's largest seafood market, became important for Iceland in the 1980s, yet hardly competed with established lines. The oriental taste is for flatfish, whole-frozen redfish (Europeans and Americans prefer fillets), shell-on shrimp (the British and Danes prefer peeled), and previously unexploited delicacies such as capelin roe, whole-frozen female herring, cod milt (sperm) and sea urchins. France has also shot up the market table recently, with a more catholic appetite than most other buyers.

In terms of demand, the future looks promising. Awareness of the healthiness of a protein-rich, low-cholesterol seafood diet, backed by the clean image of the waters

though only 5.2 percent of the Icelandic workforce is employed on fishing vessels and 6.7 percent in land-based processing plants. By comparison, 7.9 percent work in banks and insurance companies.

The Cod Wars: The big problem of the 1990s is supply. Major stocks are at or beyond the maximum level of safe harvesting, and with a fleet powerful enough to vacuum-clean the ocean floor in a couple of weeks if it wanted to, the industry is being forced to scale down its operations. This is not a new problem. Overfishing by foreign fleets was a strong fear in Iceland in the early postwar period. The traditional 3-mile (5-km) exclusive fishing zone around Iceland's coast was

where Iceland catches its fish, look set to keep demand buoyant well into the 21st century. An agreement negotiated in October 1991 with the EC removes most remaining tariff barriers for fish from Iceland in the 19-nation European "supermarket."

Fisheries contribute three quarters of Iceland's exports, and a seafood-led boom in 1987-88 saw the country's economy clock up one of the highest annual growth rates in Gross Domestic Product in European history, at more than 8 percent. All this, even

Left, the fishing industry goes indoors. **Above**, testing cod liver oil.

extended to 4 miles (6.5 km) in 1952, and even though this seems like a drop in the ocean now, it sparked massive protests and a temporary ban on fish imports from Iceland in the UK. The first real "Cod War" began in 1959 when Iceland upped its territorial waters to 12 miles (20 km) and Royal Navy frigates were sent in to protect, unsuccessfully, British trawlers from being evicted or arrested by Iceland's tiny coastguard force.

Eventually the dispute was resolved, only to be followed by successive extensions to 50 miles (80 km) in 1972 and 200 miles (330 km) in 1975 and renewed, more ferocious clashes, although no fatalities ever occurred.

While the British gunboats rammed coast-guard vessels and fired shots over their bows, the ultimate deterrent in the Icelandic arsenal was the dreaded "clippers" – rather like garden shears – which were used to cut trawls from British vessels, losing both their nets and catches. Some clippers are now proudly, if rather mock-heroically, on display in the National Museum in Reykjavík.

On one occasion, the world's press almost outnumbered the naval ratings when a British frigate and Icelandic gunboat had a confrontation on the high seas. Fortunately, the opposing captains had a keen sense of occasion and the ensuing exchange was not of shots but of Biblical quotations delivered

broadside by loud-hailer. Initially taken aback, journalists salvaged just enough Scripture knowledge to award the result to the Icelandic team. More formal arguments gradually swung international opinion over to Iceland's point of view and a "truce" was agreed in 1976 – by which time the UK itself had announced its own 200-mile limit. The territorial waters limit which Iceland established has since become a standard for international marine legislation.

Protecting the sea's bounty: In the wake of the Cod Wars, Iceland upgraded its fishing fleet. Part of the philosophy behind extending the fishing zone was not just to prevent foreign fishing as such, but also to be able to control how much was caught. After several years of bumper harvests, with the cod take nearing 508,000 tonnes (460,000 US tons) in 1982, the time came for holding back the nation's own fleet. Even as the Cod Wars were going on, Iceland had learned that it could overfish all by itself: the so-called "herring boom" in the North East collapsed in the late 1960s when the fish virtually disappeared from one season to the next.

A complex vessel quota system came into effect in 1984. In its present form, the system grants individual vessels tonnage quotas for individual species of fish based on recent catches, and the owners are free to swap or trade their quotas among themselves to maximize efficiency – and to make money.

Originally aimed at the all-important cod, the quota system has tended to increase diversification of catches towards other species, most of which are also close to being overfished now. Many skippers claim they have been transformed overnight from old-style heroic hunters to accountants, armed no longer with nets and maps but with cheque-books and spreadsheets. Unfortunately, years of poor spawning have forced the government to cut quotas regularly. Tradeable quotas have become a claim on a scarce resource and "paper fish" – the cod swimming unsuspectingly with a quota on its head – have grown in value at a rate that would draw looks of disbelief even from people who habitually play the money markets.

While the fleet's total quota for cod has been cut back by some 40 percent in recent years, the cost of buying the rights to catch cod has jumped. Small-boat operators say they are being priced out of business. Meanwhile, fish processors are finding that they can hardly make a profit on the highly-priced raw fish: European processing companies are ready to pay more for unprocessed fish than domestic processors could get after salting or freezing it.

Optimists say that these are just teething troubles – and that the quota system should leave Iceland's main industry leaner, meaner and more able than ever to keep Iceland one of the wealthiest nations in the world.

Left and right, only 12 percent of the Icelandic workforce is employed in the fishing industry, but it provides three-quarters of national income.

For first-time visitors, who often expect eternal winter, Iceland is a pleasant surprise. This is, in fact, a remarkably green country in high summer: the lowlands are verdant with pasture land, while mosses and shrubs give the uplands their colour. Yet the climate is cool (averaging 11°C/52°F in June, around freezing in January) and sometimes harsh, summers are short and cultivable soil is restricted to narrow coastal plains. This all adds up to a pattern of agriculture quite unlike that of countries more abundant in the riches of the earth.

Traditionally, farming in Iceland meant sheep, sheep and more sheep. Lamb was the staple diet, eaten fresh, salted and smoked, and every part of the animal was put to use. Even today, traditional fare such as blood sausage, liver sausage, pickled rams' testicles and sheep heads count among national delicacies. Nothing edible was thrown away.

While farming has diversified in the past 50 years and the rural world changed beyond all recognition, the memory of when all Icelanders lived on the land still grips the national imagination.

Iceland's rural myth: The simple life of the traditional farming family – surrounded by nature and animals, yet keenly interested in literature and history – is the background of every Icelander. It is celebrated in a thousand folktales and novels, engraved on the Icelandic consciousness. When an Icelander dons a handknitted *lopi* sweater in natural sheepskin colours, or tucks into a feast of *hangikjöt* (smoked lamb) at Christmas, he is affirming his identity as a true Icelander.

This image is a rather rose-tinted version of reality. For, if truth be told, the traditional life of the farmer in those days was usually one of unceasing toil and hardship. Many farming families scraped a bare living with the help of their sheep, which provided food, clothing, even shoes (of a kind).

In his classic novel *Independent People*, the Icelandic Nobel Prize winner Halldór Laxness depicts the farmer Bjartur and his

family, whose small turf house is little more than a dark, fetid, disease-riddled hovel. When his young wife Rósa, who has been a servant on a wealthy farm, says she longs for meat to eat and milk to drink, Bjartur concludes that she must be seriously ill. Such luxuries are only for the rich! "We eat good salted catfish, and until recently we had Danish potatoes to go with it. We've got rye bread in plenty, and loads of sugar," he says. Even less likely to supplement this dismal diet were fresh fruit and vegetables: Bjartur's

children are baffled by the Biblical tale of Adam and Eve because they cannot imagine what an apple looks like.

Bjartur's family, "independent" though they may be, have no coats to wear, nor even woollen sweaters, "because in these hard times you can't go weaving or knitting wool except for essential underwear." When the coatless and sweaterless children have worked a 16-hour day at haymaking in the pouring rain (the adults worked longer), Bjartur comments: "It's a feeble kind of person who cares whether he's wet or dry. I've been damp more than half my life, and I've never had a day's illness."

Preceding pages: at work near Akureyri. <u>Left</u>, the annual round-up, a tradition since the Middle Ages. <u>Above</u>, the hardy Icelandic sheep.

In the early 20th century, Iceland's farmers lived much as their forebears had done for 1,000 years: they kept their sheep, grazed them in summer on the highlands, cut the hay in summer, rounded up the sheep in autumn. After the autumn slaughter season, some of the livestock was foddered on hay through the winter, while the meat was salted, smoked and otherwise preserved. During the winter, wool was knitted and woven into clothes for the household. The horse, man's helpmate since the settlement, was still crucial to all farming tasks, and the main form of transport (see *The Most Useful Servant,* page 293).

Escape from the Middle Ages: The foundation of Iceland's first cooperative society, in 1882 in the north, heralded new times for the farming community. Farmers were tired of being dependent on the whims of a few (mostly Danish) merchants, to whom they sold their products in exchange for various supplies. The merchants could (and often did) undervalue what they bought, overprice what they sold, and renege on agreements. When the farmers launched their own cooperatives in competition with the Danish merchants, they cut out the middle-men and took control. The cooperative accepted products from the farmers, and with the credit they accumulated they could buy various necessities (and even luxuries).

In due course, the cooperative movement developed into a massive business empire, involved in every sector of the Icelandic economy. The many tentacles of the Federation of Iceland Cooperative Societies (Samband) included a bank, an insurance company, retail shops, agricultural suppliers, a shipping line, fish processing and exports, and more. But Samband ran into financial disaster during the 1980s: some of its divisions lost money hand over fist, bleeding the profitable sectors dry. Following mergers of some of the ailing divisions, Samband was split up in 1991 into its component parts, individual limited companies which must make it on their own.

As a result of all this, the countryside has been transformed. Iceland is no longer a nation of poor but proud farmers. Young people have left the land in droves to seek education and a better life. Some of the most rugged and hostile regions, where farming was a constant struggle with the elements have became totally depopulated in a matter of decades: Hornstrandir, for instance, in the far northwest, was simply abandoned.

Mechanisation has altered all the work of the farm, making it less labour-intensive. Roads have been pushed through and communications revolutionised, making isolation a thing of the past. The subsistence farmer has practically ceased to exist; today's farmers, essentially, produce meat, milk and crops for the market, and they themselves are consumers of purchased products like the rest of the population – though some, of course, take a certain pleasure in self-sufficiency, and grow vegetables for their own consumption.

Growing enough grass has always been

one of the farmer's main concerns. By the end of the summer, he must have sufficient hay to fodder his livestock through the winter. Today's farmers are less dependent on the vagaries of the weather than their forefathers; with modern technology they can dry hay artificially, and in a poor year they can buy fodder. Most now store their hay, not in traditional bales but wound tightly up in airtight white plastic wrapping. A good hay harvest, however, remains important. Along the south coast, forward-looking farmers have planted grass on the barren volcanic sands, thus adding to their grassland and also fighting soil erosion.

Iceland is too far north to grow cereal crops comfortably, as the climate is too cool and the growing season too short. A number of farmers, however, have started to grow the hardier cereals, like rye and barley, with the help of modern fertilisers. These grains are used in animal fodder, replacing expensive imported cereals, and barley is also being grown for human consumption.

Gone with the wind: Soil erosion is probably the single most important environmental problem facing the Icelandic farmer today.

The vegetation of the country, in delicate equilibrium before man's arrival in the 9th century, has been devastated by the impact of 1,000 years of settlement. Icelandic soils

criminately for fuel, while their livestock simply ate their way through the sensitive vegetation. As the protective layer of vegetation disappeared, topsoil was simply blown away in the wind and washed away by rivers, leading to massive desertification of a once green and pleasant land.

Probably only 1 percent of Iceland's original woods remain, and between 30 and 40 thousand square kilometres (11–15,000 sq. miles) of the country have been stripped bare since the land was first settled.

It became clear that something was wrong when sand drift from desert areas laid waste many a farm during the 19th century. In 1907 organised efforts to combat desertification

are light, lacking clay materials to bind them, with a large proportion of volatile volcanic-based loams. Nonetheless, before herbivores arrived to threaten the fragile ecology of the island, about two-thirds of Iceland's 103,000 sq. km (39,000 sq. miles) were covered by trees, shrubs, grassland and other vegetation.

The *Book of Settlements* says that Iceland was covered with trees "from the mountains to the sea" when the settlers arrived. But not for long. The settlers used the wood indis-

began. The Soil Conservation Service works to control soil erosion and reclaim waste land, as well as seeking to improve and protect existing areas of vegetation.

Spreading roots: Undoing the work of centuries of destruction and neglect is a slow task, but 80 years of effort have produced cheering results. Hardy lymegrass has been widely sown to stabilise drifting sands, while the Alaskan lupin has also proved highly successful in binding loose and volatile soil, paving the way for more vegetation.

Since 1958, the Soil Conservation Service has attacked the problem from the air, spreading grass seed and fertiliser over thousands

Left, processing *skyr*, the unique Icelandic milk-curd. **Above**, sheep corral during the round-up.

of hectares of barren land each summer. In 1990, 1,400 tons of grass seed and fertiliser were spread in this way, giving new hope of life to 4,500 hectares of land.

Since 1973, the SCS has had its own plane, donated by Icelandair after its retirement from active service. This old DC-3 workhorse dates from World War II, but is none the worse for that. Commercial pilots literally queue up to volunteer for the privilege of piloting the plane on the seeding flights and to make their contribution to the reclamation of the waste lands. As well as flying over the highlands, which are inaccessible for other means of seeding, the SCS has also seeded volcanic regions in the south and southwest,

hand. Seedling trees will take hold, even in completely barren country, provided they are protected from browsing sheep and other livestock. This has led to a new development in land reclamation through planting little trees rather than grass or lupins.

Farmers are being encouraged to turn over suitable land to forestry, and there has even been a suggestion that Iceland could have its own commercially utilisable forests within a few decades. Remote though this prospect may seem at present, it is no more absurd than visions of changing the face of Iceland – now implemented – must have seemed at the beginning of the 20th century. Land is now probably being reclaimed a little faster

as well as lending a hand in the re-cultivation of the Westmann Islands after the devastating 1973 eruption.

Campaigns for reafforestation of the once-wooded country have received enthusiastic public support over the past few decades, and the Icelanders have taken to tree-planting with a will. President Vigdís Finnbogadóttir has been an unflagging champion of the cause of afforestation, and her support has certainly boosted public interest. There is no reason why trees should not flourish once again all over Iceland.

Experiments have shown that reafforestation and land reclamation can go hand in

than it is being lost. With redoubled efforts, the Icelanders may yet redress the balance, and revive the green and pleasant land of their forebears.

Challenge to the almighty sheep: Not surprisingly, the rapid urbanisation of Icelandic society has been far from painless. For farmers, farming is not simply a matter of economics. It is a way of life. And the past few decades have turned all traditional notions of the farming life upside down. For a start, the sheep (mainstay and saviour of the Icelandic nation since the settlement) has lost its supremacy. The Icelandic sheep is a unique breed, the direct descendant of the animals brought to Iceland by the settlers in the 9th century. This sturdy and self-reliant creature has no need of rich grassland, and will graze on almost anything. Sheep have always been herded into mountain pastures for the summer months, so the typical Icelandic sheep grows strong and muscular, and the herbs and grasses it grazes on give its meat a delicate flavour.

But today's Icelanders no longer want to live exclusively on lamb (whether fresh, salted or smoked). This is a nation of indefatigable travellers, and the Icelanders have developed cosmopolitan tastes. The modern consumer demands beef, poultry, and pork. Production of these meats has been growing

fast, although lamb is still Iceland's most-eaten meat. Horsemeat was formerly very popular in certain regions of the country, though practically taboo in others. Today its consumption is plummeting, although a certain amount is exported to Japan.

Dairy farming has grown fast during this century, and the Icelanders are phenomenal consumers of dairy products, eating and drinking the equivalent of about 395 litres (103 gallons) per head each year. Any visitor to an Icelandic supermarket will be baffled

Left, man against horse. **Above**, salmon estuary on the Hvítá river.

by the range of milk (whole, semi-skimmed, skimmed and soured), cream, cheese, butter, yoghurt and, last but not least, the unique Icelandic milk-curd, *skyr*.

Growing demand for fresh fruits and vegetables (almost unheard-of in Iceland until the past 20 years or so) has also led to large-scale development of market gardening. In a good year, Iceland's potato farmers grow more than enough to see the nation through to the following year's harvest. While Iceland's climate is too cool for growing much in the way of vegetables in the open air, inexpensive geothermal energy provides the resources to grow all manner of exotic crops in greenhouses.

Market gardeners, located in geothermal areas, produce tomatoes, cucumbers, carrots, capsicums, lettuce and other salad crops, as well as various kinds of cabbage, throughout the summer months. Hothouse cultivators can even grow bananas and grapes, but this is mostly to prove it can be done, and these crops are not cultivated on a commercial scale. The bananas, grapes, apples and citrus fruits sold in Iceland are always imported from balmier climes.

An uncertain future: There are still around 4,000 working farms in Iceland. But what is the shape of things to come? Farming in Iceland moved directly from the Middle Ages to the 20th century without pausing for breath, and now farmers are plagued with problems, from desertification to over-production. While farmers proved that they were willing to adapt to new methods and new markets, they have not responded fast enough. Over-production of lamb and milk has led to the imposition of a quota system, whereby each farmer may only produce up to a certain maximum. As one set of agricultural cuts follows another, quotas have been reduced to the point where some farms have ceased to be viable.

The 21st century is certain to bring a host of new challenges, in the shape of greater competition. Protectionist legislation and heavy government subsidies have hitherto helped farmers survive, but this privileged position is likely to be threatened in the future by Iceland's participation in the European Economic Area formed by EFTA (the European Free Trade Association) and the European Union.

Radical action is clearly necessary, but

opinions are mixed on what it should be. Some extremists say that farming should simply be abandoned; instead of paying massive subsidies, the country could import the agricultural products it needs. Few would go this far, but there is a general consensus that the number of farms should be reduced. Incentives are being offered to farmers who wish to leave their farms and "cash in" their quota, and the possibility has been discussed of totally abolishing sheep farming in some areas of the country where the vegetation is particularly sensitive to grazing.

On top of all its other problems, the sheep turns out to be the main culprit in Iceland's problem with soil erosion; it may have kept

made warm, water-resistant winter garments. Today, soft half-spun *lopi* wool is used in traditionally-patterned hand- knitted sweaters, which are some of the most popular souvenirs of Iceland.

While hand-knitting and weaving never died out, large-scale industrialised woollen production developed to produce fashionwear, blankets, carpets, and so on. The textile trade is, naturally, vulnerable to fluctuations of fashion. When "ethnic" fashions were all the rage, Icelandic woollens sold like hot cakes, but the recent trend towards lighter man-made yarns and cotton knits spelled disaster for wool producers. Woollens exports have declined steadily, and in

the Icelanders alive, but it did so at the cost of destroying the vegetation of the uplands.

Icelandic wool, which was one of the country's most important exports in the Middle Ages (along with the dried fish known as stockfish), rose again to become the basis of a valuable export industry in the 20th century. Recent events in the textile industry, however, are far from encouraging.

The fleece of the Icelandic sheep, which varies in colour from white through grey and browns to near-black, is made up of two layers. The inner layer of short, fine fibres (*thel*) was used for knitting delicate laces, while the coarser, longer outer fibres (*tog*)

1991 Iceland's major textiles company, Alafoss, went broke after a long struggle. Two new small companies, Foldá and Istex, have picked up the pieces, and are re-launching on a more modest scale.

Fish, fur and "tourist farming": When it became clear, in the early 1980s, that age-old farming ways were out of sync with today's market, a number of revolutionary ideas came up for redirecting farmers into new and profitable businesses. One of these was salmon farming. This exists in various forms, from "ocean ranching" to fish farming in offshore sea pens, or in tanks on dry land, making use of geothermal resources. Most have run into problems of one kind or another, and ultimately gone out of business.

Fur farming (fox and mink) was another idea which looked very promising on paper. Commercially farmed skins fetch excellent prices at auction, and Iceland's cool climate could be expected to produce rich and luxuriant pelts. Fur breeders did not attempt to farm the native fox, but imported commercial species from abroad. In the event, however, it proved difficult to master all the skills of fur farming, and international prices have also dropped. Most of the fur farms have gone the same way as the fish farms.

Another new venture, far more bizarre on the face of it, was to prove a better bet.

Angora rabbits were imported to be farmed for their hair. This small- scale farming sideline now supplies a factory producing 100 percent angora garments, which are popular with Icelanders and tourists alike.

As farmers make a painful adjustment to changing times, the biggest success story of all has absolutely nothing to do with farming. In Iceland they call it, jokingly, "tourist farming" – offering farm holidays as an alternative to hotels or camping. Farming families started offering bed and breakfast in

Two farms with accommodation through the Farm Holiday Service: Húsey (left) and Hof (right).

their own homes, or self-catering accommodation, summerhouses, and the like. Visitors can go riding, angle for trout in some nearby lake, or even lend a hand at bringing in the hay. The idea has been a resounding success. Foreign tourists find this experience of rural Iceland truly memorable.

For the farmers, too, tourist farming made good sense. While quota restrictions limit what a farmer may produce, no quota has been imposed on tourists (yet!), and tourism offers a steadily growing market for these services. Usually, existing accommodation can be adapted for the paying guests, without major investment. The Farm Holiday Service has grown and grown, and today 131 farms all over the country offer accommodation and services of one kind or another.

Round-up ritual: The sheep is no longer the staff of life to the Icelandic nation, but there are still twice as many sheep as people, and the autumn round-up is the same ritual it has always been.

In early September, before the first snows fall on the uplands, farmers don their warm woollen sweaters and waterproofs and saddle up their horses, loading up a sleeping bag, a saddlebag of food and an indispensable hip flask. Accompanied by their dogs, they set off into the uplands. The Icelandic dog, a thick-furred, curly-tailed species with upright ears, remains a favourite with Icelandic farmers, although other types of dog also do service as sheepdogs. Directly descended from the animals brought to Iceland by Viking settlers, the dog also has a certain following abroad among breeders.

Working in teams, horsemen and dogs systematically search the highland pastures for sheep. The searchers stay overnight in mountain huts, where they pen in the sheep they have gathered so far, then hang up their damp clothes, uncork their hip flasks and swap stories and songs.

After two or three days all the sheep are accounted for, and the fat and frisky lambs, ewes and rams are herded down to the lowlands and into a corral, where they are identified by their ear-marks and sorted into the correct pens. All the local people gather to take part, and a dance is often held once the work is over. As evening falls, the farmers share a drink or two in the sheep-filled corral, and lift their voices in part-songs, just as their forefathers have done for hundreds of years.

NATURE'S BOUNTY

Traditional life in Iceland was always harsh. The population was often on the brink of starvation, and every animal, on land and sea, was seen as a resource to be used for the sake of survival. The *hlunnindi* or peripheral resources attached to a farm or community could spell the difference between life and death.

Many traditional means of making use of nature, although no longer crucial, are still upheld in various parts of the country. One of the most striking examples is eider "farming," the gathering of the soft down of the eider duck for

filling pillows, quilts and cold-weather clothing.

The eider duck is a peaceful bird, choosy about where it will nest. Eiders return year after year to certain nesting colonies. Man and the eider have learned to live together for their mutual benefit: farmers lucky enough to have eider colonies on their land will be sure to provide welcoming nesting places, and they protect these placid birds, their eggs and their young, from marauders such as gulls, foxes and mink – a round-the-clock task during the spring months. In return for this guardianship, farmers claim part of the fine down, shed from the bird's breast, which lines the nest to keep the eggs and then chicks warm.

Once the eiders and their chicks have safely waddled off to the sea, the farmers gather the down left behind in the nests. Each nest yields only a few wisps; painstakingly picked clean of all twigs, dirt and scraps of eggshell, the down is washed before being sold at a heartwarming price usually exceeding US$600 per kilogramme (a kilo will fill an average-sized quilt and last a lifetime with proper care). No man-made fibre has yet been invented to rival the insulating qualities of genuine eider down.

Seals, whales and even puffins: In the past, the Icelanders hunted seals for their meat and skins. Although they are not caught commercially today, seals are hunted on a small scale in some places, such as the remote farm of Húsey on the east coast.

In former ages, a beached whale was a welcome source of food, and even today, the Icelandic word for a "windfall" is *hvalreki* (whale beaching). Whales have been hunted through the centuries as sources of food and oil, until a few years ago when whaling was suspended. Iceland has taken a controversial stand against international pressure for a total whaling ban.

The island's steep sea cliffs, clustered with millions of sea birds, were once known as Iceland's "pantries." Icelanders would often have gone hungry had they not had the nourishment of these natural food stores. In all the areas where seabird colonies are found, men would rappel on ropes down the vertical cliff faces, gathering eggs from the nests. Today the cliff-edge "pantries" are no longer crucial for survival, and tastes in food have changed. Yet seabirds' eggs are still gathered in some quantity. *Sprang*, the art of swinging nimbly down a cliff-face at the end of a long rope, is still a much-practised skill in the Vestmannaeyjar (Westmann) islands.

Regarded as a great delicacy by many Icelanders, seabirds' eggs are commonly eaten in coastal villages in season, and are sold in supermarkets in urban areas. The eggs of the guillemot are those most often commercially sold: larger than hens' eggs, they are a mottled blue in colour. Designed by nature for narrow cliff-ledge nesting sites, they taper sharply to one end. If accidentally nudged, they will simply spin around rather than plunging off the cliff.

Some seabird species were also hunted for food, and still are today. Strange as it may seem, the charming stubby-winged puffin is regarded as a particularly mouthwatering morsel, especially in the Vestmannaeyjar islands. The islanders' affection for the puffin as Iceland's national emblem does not discourage them from seeing it as a source of food – and one which has helped them survive hard times.

Today's puffin hunters swing long-handled nets to catch the birds on the wing, avoiding the risk of accidentally catching immature birds, which could endanger the future of the puffin population. Puffin and guillemot, usually under the generic name of *svartfugl* (the Alcidae family of birds), appear on the menus of some of the more adventurous restaurants in Reykjavík. The dark gamey meat, with a slightly fishy taste, is a great favourite with many gourmets.

Other than sea birds, the goose and ptarmigan are practically the only birds hunted for human consumption. Hunters, who must hold gun licences, can shoot goose throughout the winter, while ptarmigan are hunted from September until just before Christmas, when they make a favourite festive dinner in many homes.

Duck eggs are collected by the residents of Lake Myvatn, where all Iceland's duck species can be found nesting. A traditional rule of thumb in the area protects the eggs from over-exploitation: at least four eggs are always left in the nest. A unique local way of storing the eggs is to cover them with ashes in buckets. They are kept like this through the winter to be eaten the next spring – or they may even be kept for several years in this way.

Farmers traditionally have exclusive rights to exploit the rivers and lakes on their land. If these waters are thick with salmon, this can be a real money-spinner. Iceland's salmon rivers, reputed to be some of the best in the world, attract anglers from every corner of the globe, who spend as much as US$1,300 a day for the best rivers (all-inclusive rates, admittedly, with full board). The most popular have to be booked many months in advance. A total ban on salmon fishing at sea helps to ensure that Iceland's salmon find their way back to their home waters.

Concern has been expressed, however, at the influence of "farmed" salmon on the wild stock. In "ocean ranching," young salmon are released into the sea to forage for themselves, and a certain percentage return in due course, as full-grown fish, to the place of release where they can be harvested. Some of the farmed salmon, however, wander into rivers where they do not belong, to mix with the wild salmon which are following their famed homing instincts back to

their breeding ground. Specialists fear that adding alien salmon may debase the existing stock, and ultimately confuse the homing instinct.

While salmon fishing is definitely only for free-spending enthusiasts, the humbler trout is available to anyone who can wave a rod. Farmers usually sell permits for their rivers and lakes at a reasonable cost, and many can hire out fishing gear. Fishing equipment cannot be brought into Iceland from abroad unless sterilised (a certificate is required).

Fishermen often relax at the end of the day with a feast of barbecued trout out in the open air. Both trout and salmon, however, are often preserved by smoking. In order to be absolutely authentic, the fish should be smoked over a

slow-burning fire of dung. Modern processing methods may seem more hygienic, but the end result is definitely not as tasty! Another popular way of treating salmon is to cure it in a marinade of salt, sugar and dill to make a delicious dish called *gravadlax*.

One of the most important traditional rights of farmers was the right to driftwood: whole trees can be washed ashore, carried on ocean streams from as far away as Siberia. In this near-treeless country, driftwood was the main source of building timber for centuries, and a highly valuable commodity. Even today, driftwood does not go to waste: most of it goes to make fenceposts for Iceland's farms.   ∎

Left, seal skins drying at Húsey. **Right**, puffin catcher on the cliffs of Heimaey.

Mountains, glaciers, lakes and thundering waterfalls are the very stuff of Icelandic tourism. With its wide open spaces and clear air, Iceland makes an exotic and intoxicating change, and more and more visitors want to get out and experience all that wild nature for themselves. The tourist industry presents them with plenty of opportunities.

One of the fastest-growing sectors in the industry has grown up around the glaciers, which have some mystical appeal. Lofty, almost unearthly, they are strangely inaccessible, yet they can be approached in various ways. It is generally possible, for instance, to walk to the summit of Snaefellsjökull – though this should not be attempted without a guide. On Myrdalsjökull ice cap, you can go skiing in the middle of summer.

Walking on the vast, crevassed expanse of Vatnajökull, however, is only for experienced alpinists – and even they may find it rather more than they bargained for. The ice cap is a wild place. The weather is harsh and unpredictable, and fog and snow can strike at any time. Mountain rescue teams are regularly called out to look for walkers who have gone astray on glacial expeditions, and lives have been lost.

While full-scale glacier expeditions are beyond the stamina (or even wishes) of most travellers, Vatnajökull ice cap is now accessible to the less heroic, who would still like to experience a confrontation with 8,000 sq. km (3,000 sq. miles) of ice.

Day-trippers are transported from the south-eastern town of Höfn up onto the ice cap by snowcat and/or jeep, to be shown some of the strange and spectacular sights. For those with less time to spend, it is possible to fly directly up onto the ice cap by helicopter, with the incidental advantage of breathtaking views.

The ice cap, far from being simply an expanse of snow and ice, has its own landscape (or icescape): barren, rocky peaks project up through the ice; narrow crevices

extend downwards for hundreds of metres; and at Grímsvötn, geothermal springs bubble beneath the age-old ice. After sightseeing, visitors can have a go at skimming over the vast glacial expanse on nippy little snow scooters. As a finishing touch, superb banquets can be served up on the ice cap, at a table carved from the ice. The ice in the drinks is, needless to say, ultra-pure glacier.

Winter expeditions: Glaciers are probably best left alone in winter – the very time when Iceland opens up to a whole new form of

travel. Rough-country vehicles with four-wheel drive have become a craze in Iceland in recent years, and in Reykjavík and other towns these huge-tyred customised machines tower over ordinary traffic. The fanatics of the 4x4 have developed great expertise. While off-road driving is strictly banned in summer in order to protect the delicate upland vegetation, in winter it is possible to travel almost anywhere on a blanket of snow without damaging what lies underneath.

With tyre-pressure drastically reduced, the 4x4 simply "floats" across the snow. Loran navigational equipment and radio contact help to ensure safety, even in the worst of

Preceding pages: hikers leaving Thórsmörk for Skógar. **Left**, beneath Svartifoss in Skaftafell National Park. **Right**, the Asbyrgi canyon in Jökulsárgljúfur National Park.

conditions. The 4x4 travellers always proceed in groups, ready to help each other out in case of problems. The worst that can happen is having to lie low in the vehicles for a few hours if a snowstorm blows up.

Guided 4x4 trips into the interior are now a regular feature of winter tourism in Iceland, giving a chance to see places which are normally inaccessible outside the summer season – such as the hot-spring oasis of Landmannalaugar in the southern highlands, where you can strip off on a snow-covered riverbank to take a dip in a natural hot river. For the active winter-sport enthusiast, there is also cross-country skiing into the interior (only for the very fit).

not always guaranteed. This explains the apparent paradox of Icelanders taking skiing holidays in mainland Europe. In Iceland, the main skiing season does not generally begin until after Christmas, and usually lasts until about Easter. For true skiing fanatics, Kerlingarfjöll in the central uplands operates as a summertime ski centre.

While all the major ski areas have ski lifts, they generally offer little else in the way of services, and nothing like the superstructure of an alpine ski resort. Iceland's only ski hotel is at Akureyri.

Lakes and rivers: One of the easiest Icelandic adventures is a visit to Jökulsárlón, at the southern edge of Vatnajökull ice cap, where

Skiing, both downhill and cross-country, is an enormously popular winter pastime in Iceland, and many families wait with baited breath for the first proper snow to fall. Excellent slopes can be found in the north and the West Fjords, where good snow cover can usually be guaranteed.

Farther south, however, skiing is subject to the vagaries of the weather. In a good winter (in skier's terms), the Bláfjöll ski area just outside Reykjavík swarms with skiers every weekend, yet a warm and rainy winter season will have skiers tearing their hair in frustration, cursing the bare slopes. Coverage is more regular near Akureyri, although

an icy blue-green lagoon has formed at the base of a wall of ice. With creaks and groans, great ice floes separate from the advancing outlet glacier to float eerily on the lagoon. A cruise among the ice floes, beneath the towering bulk of Europe's largest ice cap, is like nothing on earth. Don't miss it. This bizarre place of natural spectacle did not exist 50 years ago: the lagoon has formed as the ice cap has shrunk. And within another few years the lagoon may open out into the sea, adding one more fjord to Iceland's jagged southern coastline.

More excitement, again courtesy of the glaciers, can be had by white-water rafting down the Hvítá river. Very few of Iceland's rivers are navigable: fast-flowing, they are dotted with waterfalls and rapids. The Hvítá, fed by glacial melt water, is the river which thunders over Gullfoss falls, commonly regarded as Iceland's most beautiful cascade. Tons of water tumble over one ledge before turning at right angles to cascade over the second stage of the waterfall, into a deep and narrow rocky gorge. Visitors who want a more intimate experience of the Hvítá river can shoot the rapids upstream of the falls with full equipment and experienced guides.

Thrills and spills are not all that Iceland has to offer in the way of adventure. One of the many amenities of a rugged, sparsely-

populated country (about two people per sq. km) is that you can really get away from it all. You will not find too many madding crowds anywhere in Iceland (except possibly trying to gain entrance to a Reykjavík pub or night-spot on a Friday night), but if you want peace and solitude, this is where you can be sure of finding it.

Backpacking holidays are the classic way to experience faraway and roadless regions. The interior is the classic wilderness area, but there are also places like Hornstrandir; in

Left, a lone cyclist can find it hard going. **Above**, snowcatting on Vatnajökull icecap.

Iceland's far northwest, this is a totally de-populated region, reclaimed by nature after its last human residents left in the early 1960s. You can travel to Hornstrandir by sea or by road, but then you are on your own.

By foot, bike or horse: Touring clubs such as Utivist and Ferdafélag Islands offer a year-round schedule of guided walking tours, from a few hours up to a week or two in the wilderness. Since the Icelandic interior is emphatically not a place for amateurs to blunder about in, these guided tours are an excellent option for walkers who are not familiar with the country.

For those who like to walk, but not to excess, tourism companies have come up with some compromises, operating hiking tours where you avoid trudging along under the weight of a vast backpack. Your luggage is transported, so you only have to carry a small pack with your lunch and some extra clothes. A highly popular innovation has been the walking/biking bus tour, where you can sit on the bus if it rains, or ride a bike or walk when the spirit moves you.

Cycling in Iceland has become increasingly popular in recent years. To Icelanders, this development is, it has to be said, all but incomprehensible. A very large proportion of Iceland's rural roads are still gravel-surfaced, and some of them are bumpy, stony, and downright hazardous. The country is mountainous, and often very windy. If it rains, cyclists get plastered with sludge. If it is dry, they choke on clouds of dust. Cycling around Iceland is strictly for masochists.

A better way to travel, especially to places where no vehicle (even a 4x4) can comfortably take you, is to go on horseback. This also has the incidental advantage of giving invaluable insight into the Icelanders' age-old relationship with the horse. Well into this century, the horse was the only form of transport, the faithful friend without whom life would not have been liveable.

Horse farms all over the country can organise treks. Near Eyjafjördur in the north, horse treks can be made into an uninhabited region, Fjördurnar. Riding all day among deserted valleys and mountains, fording rivers, leading your second mount which carries supplies and bedroll, you will gain real insight into the way Icelanders used to live. These longer horse treks are, needless to say, only for experienced riders.

A Birdwatcher's Paradise

Any traveller to Iceland with even a vague interest in birdlife should bring along a pair of binoculars and a good ornithological guide. Around 70 species of birds breed annually in every corner of Iceland (including year-round residents and those which migrate to Iceland each spring), while a total of over 300 different species have been seen in the country at one time or another.

Some species regularly winter in Iceland before flying further north to breed in summer. Others are simply birds of passage "stopping over" on a long migratory journey. Many are accidentals – individual birds which do not belong in Iceland, but have drifted across the ocean on prevailing winds.

Seventy breeding species is not a great deal, although the actual bird population is numerically large: some of the commonest species, like the puffin, are present in millions. The Icelandic environment is particularly favourable to sea birds, which make up 23 of the country's breeding species, while it is less welcoming for passerines (perching birds). With trees in short supply, these birds have difficulty in finding places to do their perching, and their favoured food, insects, is far from plentiful. While about 60 percent of the world's birds are passerines, they only comprise 17 percent of Iceland's population.

Most of Iceland's birds are also found in the neighbouring countries of Scandinavia and Northern Europe, while some belong to the Arctic region in general. Three species, however, are specifically American: the Barrow's goldeneye, the great northern diver or common loon, and the harlequin duck, which breed practically nowhere else outside North America.

Heralds of spring: Some of Iceland's commonest birds enjoy a special place in local affections. Both the arctic tern and the golden plover are migratory birds commonly regarded as harbingers of spring. The golden plover, which generally arrives in early April, is a particular favourite with Icelandic poets:

Lóan er komin ad kveda burt snjóinn,
ad kveda burt leidindin, thad getur hún.

<u>Right</u>: a photographer homes in on circling birds at Jökulsárlón.

146

Hún hefur sagt mér ad senn komi spóinn,
sólskin í dali og blómstur í tún.

"The plover has come and she'll sing away winter / Drive off all sorrow as only she can / She says that the whimbrel soon will be coming / Sun on the valley and hayfields in bloom."

The arctic tern, which usually appears in early May, is one of the wonders of the ornithological world. It migrates each spring from Antarctica, 17,000 km (10,000 miles) away. The arctic tern is a graceful flyer, often seen hovering over water. It also makes unnerving "dive-bombing" attacks on humans who venture into its nesting colonies during June and July, screeching "kría!" (which is also the bird's name in Icelandic).

sea cliff, puffins are usually found nesting at the top, where a little soil and vegetation provides the space to dig. Puffin pairs will return year after year to the same burrow. After the Vestmannaeyjar (Westmann) Islands eruption in 1973, many returned to find their burrows buried under a thick layer of lava. Rather than nest elsewhere, they tried to burrow down to their old nesting places, and even died in the attempt.

Special importance has been attributed to the raven, known by the affectionate nickname "Krummi," ever since pre-Christian days. This was the chosen bird of Odin, the one-eyed High God of Norse mythology, and as such enjoyed respect. In more recent

The puffin is Iceland's commonest bird, with a population of eight to 10 million. The comically dignified stance of this decorative bird has earned it the nickname of *Prófastur* (The Dean). Around 20 May each year, the puffins start flying ashore for the breeding season, after spending the winter out on the North Atlantic. Their main breeding grounds are on sea cliffs (particularly in the Vestmannaeyjar/Westmann islands and the West Fjords), and they are also found on low-lying off-shore islands such as Grímsey.

These unusual birds do not simply build a nest – they dig a burrow, up to 1.5 metres (5 feet) deep, where a single egg is laid. On the

times, Icelanders believed that ravens could prophesy the future: a raven cawing at the window presages a death, while if the bird jumps around in an agitated manner, limps, ruffles its feathers and caws into the air, it is a portent of danger at sea. Most Icelandic farms have a resident pair of ravens, which may even be fed with scraps of food. The popularity of the bird is such that *Hrafn* (Raven) is a common personal name. The raven features in many verses and rhymes, sometimes sinister, sometimes humorous:

Krummi krunkar úti,
Kallar á nafna sinn.
Ég fann höfud af hrúti,

Hrygg og gaeruskinn.
Komdu nú og kroppadu med mér,
Krummi nafni minn.
"The Raven caws outside / Calls to his namesake / I found a ram's head / With bones and fleece / Come and have a snack with me / Krummi, my namesake!"

Last of the Great Auks: One of the most famous of the island's bird species is, sadly, extinct. The great auk (*Pinguinus impennis*) was a big, awkward, flightless seabird, about 70 cm (27 in) high, and very tasty, according to the fishermen who hunted it for food. A timid and defenceless, the great auk was easy prey. Once found all around the north Atlantic, it gradually disappeared from mainland

originally part of the taxidermic collection of a Danish nobleman, which was bought at auction in London in 1971.

Today all rare and endangered species are especially protected by law. An endangered species native to Iceland is the gyrfalcon, the largest of all falcons, 51–60 cm (20–23 in.) long. About 200 pairs are estimated to breed each year. The gyrfalcon has a colourful history as one of Iceland's most prestigious and valuable exports. Due to their skill and manoeuvrability in the air, gyrfalcons were prized as hunting birds and made gifts fit for kings and princes. In the Middle Ages, up to 200 trained birds were exported each year, and in the 16th century the king of Denmark

coasts, retreating to island habitats.

By the early 19th century the great auk had disappeared from North America, Greenland, the Faroe and Orkney Islands. Off the coast of Iceland, great auks were hunted in large numbers on their favoured breeding grounds, the skerries around Eldey island, 14 km (9 miles) off the Reykjanes peninsula. The last two great auks were clubbed to death on Eldey in 1844, making the species extinct. The Institute of Natural History in Reykjavík has on display a stuffed great auk,

Left, Barrow's goldeneyes, normally found only in North America. **Above**, a pair of puffins.

(who also ruled over Iceland) claimed a monopoly on the trade, which made a significant contribution to the royal coffers.

Although falconry largely died out in Europe by the 18th century, it continues in other parts of the world. Even today, an illicit trade in hunting falcons exists, and isolated attempts have been made in recent years to steal falcon eggs and chicks and smuggle them out of the country. The smugglers (including, on one occasion, a German "tourist" with two chicks hidden in his luggage) have been apprehended and heavily fined. Iceland's gyrfalcons enjoy special protection: their nesting places are kept secret, and carefully monitored. No one may approach the nests, or photograph them, except by permission of the Ministry of Culture.

The gyrfalcon lives in close community with its preferred prey, the ptarmigan, although it also hunts down other birds when ptarmigans are unavailable. Humans share the falcon's taste for ptarmigan (*Lagopus mutus*), a species of grouse. Considerably smaller at 35 cm (13 in) than its European relatives, the red and black grouse and the capercaillie, the ptarmigan adopts protective white colouring in winter. This does not stop hunters shooting it in considerable numbers during the winter hunting season, as ptarmigan is a favourite Christmas dinner.

The gyrfalcon may be spotted in most parts of the country, but Iceland's most numerous bird of prey is the merlin. Smaller than the gyrfalcon at 27 to 32 cm (10 to 12 in) long, the Icelandic merlin is a unique subspecies, *Falco columbarius subaesalon*. It lives mostly on passerines such as redwings, wheatears and meadow pipits.

Lord of the skies: The monarch of Iceland's birds of prey is the white-tailed eagle, up to 90 cm (3 ft) long, with a wingspan of up to 2.5 metres (8 ft). This is a close relative of the bald eagle, the US national bird. It is a rare sight today, following determined at extermination. During the early 19th century, there were 200–300 breeding pairs in Iceland. The bird was accused, however, of carrying off lambs, and it certainly disturbed eider colonies by taking eggs and chicks. A bounty was offered for eagles. They were shot and poisoned by farmers and eider breeders until, in 1920, only 10 pairs remained. Since 1913 the eagle has been protected by law, and is making a slow recovery. Today breeding pairs number 35 to 40, so prospects for the future seem promising.

Town and country: Wherever you go in Iceland, expect to run across interesting birds. Even the lake (Tjörn) in downtown Reykjavík reinforces this point. While visitors may take this for an artificial pond with decorative birdlife, the lake is in fact a natural habitat for wild birds. In addition to ducks, geese and swans, it is also the location of a breeding colony of arctic terns, and one may even glimpse a red-necked phalarope. In spring, the water rings with the calls of web-footed mothers and their rows of ducklings.

Anyone with a liking for ducks should not miss out on seeing Lake Mývatn, in the north. Mývatn is a unique natural phenomenon, a large lake, 37 sq. km (14 sq. miles) in area, yet shallow – one to four metres (3-13 ft) deep. It is also fed by underground hot streams from the adjacent active geothermal and volcanic area, which raise the temperature higher than one would expect both at this northerly latitude and at its altitude of 277 metres (908 ft) above sea level. Even in severe winters, the lake never freezes completely, thanks to this input of warm water. Mývatn is a paradise for ducks, providing lavish feeding whether for divers or dabblers, and all of Iceland's duck species save the eider (which prefers life on the ocean wave) are found breeding here.

Most common is the tufted duck (3,000 pairs), then the scaup (1,700 pairs) and Barrow's goldeneye (700 pairs). Other common species include the common scoter, red-breasted merganser, long-tailed duck, gadwall and teal, while the mallard and pintail are less common. The goosander, shoveller and pochard are rare. The harlequin, which invariably chooses fast-flowing waters, is found on the adjacent Laxá river.

Many other bird species are also found in the Mývatn area: the slavonian grebe nests at Mývatn, and the short-eared owl on nearby marshes, along with snipe and red-necked phalarope. Both merlins and gyrfalcons nest in the nearby mountains.

By the sea: Iceland's coasts and offshore islands provide marvellous opportunities to see sea birds at close quarters. The islands of Breidafjördur, for instance, teem with shag and cormorant, and the occasional white-tailed eagle may be seen. The grey phalarope (which is much rarer than its red-necked cousin) also breeds on the islands. On sightseeing cruises from Stykkishólmur, birdwatchers can sail in close to see the birds.

Birdcliffs are found in many places around the country, although the mixture of species nesting on the cliffs varies from region to region. The common guillemot, for instance, prefers the north, while the Brunnich's guillemot is found most commonly in the south. Along with the puffin, sea cliffs provide ledges and hollows for fulmars, kittiwakes, guillemots and razorbills.

Látrabjarg, at Iceland's westernmost point, is one of the world's great birdcliffs. Sixteen km (10 miles) long, the cliffs soar 500 metres

(1,600 ft) up from the sea. Haelavíkurbjarg and Hornbjarg, in the far northwest, are less accessible, but certainly no less spectacular. Other birdcliffs can be seen on the Vestmannaeyjar islands (accessible by sightseeing cruises from the main island, Heimaey), plus Krísuvíkurbjarg on the southwestern peninsula, Reykjanes. The Snaefellsnes peninsula is also an excellent area for viewing cliff birds and other seabird species.

Grímsey island, 40 km (25 miles) off the north coast, is a must for birdwatchers, with dramatic birdcliffs. It is also the only Icelandic habitat of the very rare little auk. The little auk is so well protected by law that you need a permit simply to approach the nesting

geese, winter residents in England and Scotland, breed here each year.

The southeast corner of Iceland is a particular favourite with birdwatchers on the lookout for exotic "accidentals", as this is the first landfall of lost birds from mainland Europe. At Skaftafell National Park, an excellent location for birdwatching, the wren is particularly common. Though the smallest of Icelandic birds at 12–13 cm (5 in), it is larger than wrens in nearby countries, and is defined as a special subspecies, *Troglodytes troglodytes islandicus*.

One Icelandic bird you cannot expect to see is the water rail. This extremely shy bird is so wary and elusive that it has hardly ever

area. About 16,000 pairs of gannets nest on Eldey island, the fourth-largest gannet colony in the world. Casual birdwatchers, however, are not welcome, as Eldey is a closely-protected bird sanctuary.

Bogs, marshes and wetlands also provide important habitats for many species of birds, including the whooper swan, the greylag goose, and waders like the whimbrel and golden plover. In Thjórsárver, in the depths of the highlands, Iceland boasts one of the largest breeding sites of the pink-footed goose. About 10,000 pairs of pink-footed

Above, the great skua.

been photographed, although its call may be heard in its typical habitat, reedbanks edging marshy lowlands. Wholesale draining of marshland has gradually been destroying the water rail's habitat, and it is also an easy prey for the fast-moving and bloodthirsty mink, so its call may not be heard for much longer.

From common-or-garden sparrows, starlings (Icelandic residents only since 1912) and redwings to the rarely-glimpsed eagle or little auk, Iceland promises the birdwatcher endless pleasure. Even those who cannot tell a hawk from a handsaw may find themselves flicking through ornithological guides in search of identifying features.

Because Iceland was never connected to any of the ancient land masses, it's hardly surprising that it has few native animals – although a variety of marine mammals have been established on its coasts for millennia.

The only land-based Icelandic mammal which pre-dates the arrival of man in the 9th century is the arctic fox (*Alopex lagopus*), a small breed found throughout the Arctic region. Two variants of fox exist: the "blue," relatively rare in other Arctic areas, comprises about two-thirds of Iceland's fox population; it is actually dark brown in summer, and turns a lighter brown in winter, with a bluish sheen. The "white" variety only lives up to its name when in winter camouflage; its summer coat is greyish-brown with grey or white belly. Exceptionally well insulated from the cold, the arctic fox grows a thick and furry winter coat, including fur on the soles of its paws.

Icelandic farmers have always believed that foxes killed lambs, and retaliated by trying to exterminate them. Icelandic fox-hunting has no ruling-class overtones of a "blood-sport" as it does, say, in England. The hunters simply go out with their shotguns, shooting to kill. Research has, however, shown that Iceland's foxes pose little threat to livestock. They prey on small rodents, birds like eider or ptarmigan, chicks and eggs, as well as catching fish and shellfish, but they are also unfussy scavengers, feeding on a sheep's carcass or a dead seabird, or perhaps finishing off an injured lamb. Today, the fox is no longer regarded as an unmitigated pest: elimination has itself been eliminated from the agenda, and fox-hunting aims only to control numbers.

In recent years, farming of foxes for their pelts has been initiated in Iceland, but the native fox has not been used in these enterprises. Instead, specimens of established commercial species have been imported, and held in quarantine before being placed on farms. Some inmates of the fox farms have, however, escaped to the wild and mated with native arctic foxes, producing hybrids. In addition to the first-comer, the fox, Iceland

Left, baby seal in the East Fjords.

has several other naturalised mammals. They have all been introduced, whether deliberately or inadvertently, over the centuries.

Rodent residents: Four species of rodents have settled here, presumably arriving with man as stowaways on ships. These are the long-tailed field mouse or wood mouse (*Apodemus sylvaticus*), house mouse (*Mus musculus*), brown rat (*Rattus norvegicus*) and black rat (*Rattus rattus*). The house mouse, brown rat and black rat are only found in and around urban areas, and of them only the brown rat is common.

The long-tailed field mouse (a uniquely Icelandic sub-species, *Apodemus sylvaticus grandiculus*) certainly deserves its name, with a tail as long as its body (8–10 cm, 3–4 inches). It is found all over the country, both near human habitation and in remote areas. The mouse lives mostly off the land, eating plants, berries and fungi, as well as small insects. It does not hibernate, and sometimes takes shelter in houses and outbuildings in cold weather. In the past, it is said that mice sometimes burrowed into the thick fleece of sheep, kept indoors over the winter, where they kept comfortably warm and gnawed the sheep's flesh occasionally by way of winter nourishment.

Both the house mouse and long-tailed mouse are long-established residents in Iceland, probably dating back to the original settlement. Some zoologists believe that the long-tailed mouse must, like the fox, pre-date human habitation, as 1,000 years would not account for the development of this sub-species' differences from its mainland cousins. The brown rat is believed to have arrived in 1840, and spread with lightning speed to every region of the country. The black rat has been sighted from time to time since 1919, but is not a firmly established resident.

Another addition to Icelandic fauna was accidentally introduced into the wild. The American mink (*Mustela vison*) was brought to Iceland in the 1930s for the first attempts at fur farming, but cages tended to be inadequate and a number of animals escaped. Within 35 years, the species had spread all over the country. Only the central highlands, a localised area of the southeast and some islands have totally escaped colonisation.

These blood-thirsty predators cause havoc among nesting birds by taking eggs and chicks, whether from cliff-dwellers like the puffin and guillemot, or from duck and eider colonies. They also feed on fish and small birds and mammals. Like the fox, they are hunted by farmers, although their numbers remain high.

Imports from Lapland: Another of Iceland's wild mammals is a reminder of a well-meaning but misguided attempt to alter the Icelandic way of life. Several dozen reindeer (*Rangifer tarandus*) were introduced from northern Scandinavia in the period 1771–87, at a time when the Icelanders lived in penury, on the verge of starvation. The beasts were imported on the grounds that some Icelanders could adopt the nomadic herders' existence of the Samish people, also known as Lapps, in northern Norway and Finland. The upland environment was, after all, roughly similar to the north Scandinavian tundra. But the people were not at all the same, and Icelanders did not take kindly to the idea of living as reindeer herders. The reindeer reverted to the wild, to add an exotic touch to the uplands, and bring some meat to the tables of hunters.

By 1817, reindeer were widely distributed in many areas of the country, and their growing numbers gave rise to fears that they were overgrazing the upland pastures, traditionally sacrosanct to the sheep, the mainstay of the Icelandic economy. A royal charter of 1817 permitted unlimited hunting of the animals, except for juveniles under a year old. Half a century of indiscriminate slaughter left the reindeer stocks in a poor state by 1882, when hunting was restricted.

Thanks to a total hunting ban from 1901 to 1940, the herds made an excellent recovery, and the population is now estimated at around 3,000. The reindeer is a protected species, but in most years a limited cull is allowed in order to control the population, so steaks remain an occasional treat.

Herds of deer are now found only in the mountains and valleys in the east of Iceland. They graze on mosses, fungi, lichens and grasses, but will also nibble on shoots of shrubs and young trees. The shy creatures can rarely be spotted in summer, when they keep well clear of curious humans. In the depths of winter, however, they sometimes descend to lowland farms and villages in search of adequate grazing.

Attempts have been made to introduce the musk ox (*Ovibos moschatus*) and the snow-shoe or mountain hare (*Lepus timidus*) into Iceland, but with no success. In the early years of the 20th century, two ferrets (*Mustela putorius furo*) were released into the wild, with the idea that they would kill rats. They did not breed, and survived only a year.

Examples of Iceland's wild mammals, which are at times difficult to spot in the wild, can be seen at Reykjavík's small zoo: fox, mink and reindeer can be viewed in semi-wild open-air pens.

Visitor from Greenland: The polar bear is not actually an Icelandic animal, and is no more than an occasional visitor to Icelandic shores. Bears sometimes do drift across the ocean from Greenland on ice floes, or even walk the 400 km (250 miles) or so across the Arctic pack-ice when it temporarily bridges the gap between the two countries.

Most sightings of polar bears occur in the North and North West, the regions nearest to Greenland. Folklore abounds with bizarre and colourful beliefs about these powerful carnivores, which clearly had a remarkable hold on the Icelandic imagination. The polar bear was thought to be a human being under a spell, and folk tales assert that the bear gives birth to human young, which are then transformed into cubs.

According to one tale, a female polar bear came ashore on the northern island of Grímsey, where the farmer saw her whelp several human babies. He took one of them, a girl, and brought the child up for some time, but she always a had a hankering for the sea, and one day she got out onto the drift ice in the bay, where her mother was waiting. The bear covered the child with her paw, and she was metamorphosed into a cub.

An attribute much envied by humans was the bear's resistance to cold, known as "bear-warmth." Icelanders believed that if a child were born on a polar-bear skin, he or she would acquire this sought-after quality of never feeling the cold.

Polar bears enjoyed a heyday of popularity in the Middle Ages, when they became a priceless status symbol to the kings and princes of Europe. The difficulty of capturing such a fierce beast alive in distant Greenland or Iceland, then transporting it across the ocean, ensured its novelty value. The tale of Audunn, one of the short stories of the Saga Age, illustrates the extraordinary desirability of a polar bear to a medieval potentate. Audunn, an Icelander, pays with all his wordly goods for a polar bear in Greenland, then sets off to present the bear to King Sveinn of Denmark. Once he has (not without difficulty) reached the king, the monarch is so thrilled with the gift that he invites Audunn to join his court, finances him on a lengthy pilgrimage to Rome, then presents him with a fine new ship, a bag of silver and a gold ring when he sets off home to Iceland.

In all probability, far more polar bears used to reach Iceland a few centuries ago,

marine mammal species have been long established around its rugged coast.

Seals are most likely to be spotted by visitors. Breeding in Iceland are two species, the common or harbour seal and the grey seal. The former is by far the most common – in fact, Iceland boasts about half the world population of harbour seals, which often can be seen sunning themselves on the black sands of remote fjords. Five other species breed on the coast of Greenland and the polar ice floes but make occasional visits to northern Iceland: they include the ringed, bearded, harp and hooded seals, as well as the Atlantic walrus. The walrus is probably the least frequent visitor, the last example dating from

when the climate was cooler and the pack-ice consequently reached farther south than it does now. This would explain their apparently exaggerated influence in folklore. Today the great white bears are only rarely seen ambling ashore – perhaps one every decade or so. Since such arrivals are invariably ravenously hungry after their long journey across the ocean, they are rather dangerous and so are always shot on sight.

Mammals of the sea: Although almost all of Iceland's terrestrial mammals are either recent arrivals or occasional visitors, a range of

Above, horses run wild in the countryside.

1983 on the Snaefellsnes peninsula.

Although Iceland was famous in the Middle Ages for the whales off its coast, these days it is difficult to spot one. The most common by far is the killer whale, or orca, which hunts in shallow waters. Its black and white back and tail fins – so smooth and shiny that they seem to be made of porcelain – can sometimes be seen arching through the waves on boat trips in places like the Vestmannaeyjar (Westmann) islands. Of the larger whale species, the sperm whale, fin whale, humpback and minke whales are probably the most common, with late spring and summer the best times for sighting.

PLACES

Iceland is one of the world's most expensive countries, and this basic fact helps shape every Icelandic itinerary. Renting a car gives the most freedom in a visit, but can cost an arm and a leg (and five minutes on most Icelandic roads, which can seem little more than rutted dirt tracks, will explain why). Luckily, a range of bus and air tours operates to all major destinations throughout the summer season, early June to mid-August – which is also the only time that many museums and hotels are open, and when the vast majority of people come to Iceland.

Most visitors first arrive at Keflavík airport and stay in the capital, Reykjavík – a city that is almost painfully quiet except on Friday and Saturday nights, when Icelanders let loose in the bars and discos in true Viking fashion. But nobody comes to Iceland for its urban life. The real star is Nature, and you don't have to go far to find it.

Each region has its own attractions. A few hours' drive from Reykjavík in the South West is the so-called "Golden Circle" of Iceland's best-known natural spectacles, including the waterfall Gullfoss, the eponymous Geysir and Iceland's great historical centre, Thingvellir. Just off the south coast are the Vestmannaeyjar (Westmann) islands, still scarred by the effects of a 1973 volcanic eruption. The South East offers Iceland's most accessible glaciers and Skaftafell National Park, a favourite hiking spot amongst Icelanders.

North of Reykjavík is the historic Snaefellsnes Peninsula, setting for many Icelandic sagas and Jules Verne's *Journey to the Centre of the Earth*. Beyond Snaefellsnes, the remote, windswept West Fjords region offers some of the wildest (and wettest) landscapes in Iceland. Akureyri, arguably Iceland's most pleasant town, is the jumping-off point for exploring the North. Nearby Lake Mývatn is Iceland's most popular tourist spot outside the "Golden Circle", where dramatic volcanic activity can be seen at close range. In the North East is Jokulsglufir National Park, an awe-inspiring series of canyons leading to Dettifoss, Europe's most powerful waterfall. The East Fjords region is the warmest in Iceland, where quiet fishing villages are surrounded by rugged scenery.

Finally, there is the interior – an area quite different from the rest of Iceland. Almost all coastal roads, including the "Ring Road" that circles the country, are passable in normal, two-wheel drive cars; the interior demands four-wheel drive or a specially designed touring bus. The coast has hundreds of villages and farms offering accommodation; in the interior, camping is the only option. And weather around the coast is relatively warm, if often wet; temperatures in the interior can plunge to dangerous levels without warning.

Preceding pages: a winter drive through Landmannalaugar in central Iceland; Jökulsárlón (the South East); Dettifoss, Europe's most powerful waterfall (the North East); a farmer rounds up horses. **Left**, hiking to the sea in the West Fjords.

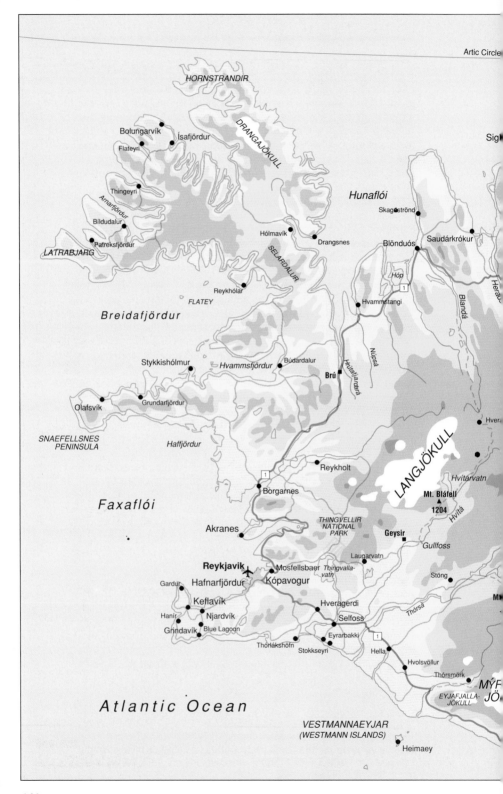

HORNSTRANDIR

Bolungarvík
Flateyri
Ísafjördur

DRANGAJÖKULL

Sig

Thingeyri

Arnarfjördur

Bíldudalur

Patreksfjördur

LATRABJARG

Hólmavík

Drangsnes

SELARDALUR

Reykhólar

FLATEY

Breidafjördur

Hunaflói

Skagaströnd

Blönduós

Saudárkrókur

Hóp

Hvammstangi

Blanda

Herad

Stykkishólmur

Hvammsfjördur

Búdardalur

Brú

Nupsá

Hrútafjardará

Olafsvík

Grundarfjördur

SNAEFELLSNES
PENINSULA

Haffjördur

Reykholt

LANGJÖKULL

Hver

Hvítárvatn

Borgarnes

Mt. Bláfell
▲
1204

Hvíta

Faxaflói

Akranes

THINGVELLIR
NATIONAL
PARK

Geysir

Gullfoss

Laugarvatn

Reykjavik

Gardur
Hafnarfjördur
Keflavík
Hanir   Njardvík
Grindavík   Blue Lagoon

Mosfellsbaer
Kópavogur

Thingvalla-
vatn

Stöng

Hveragerdi

Thórsá

M

Selfoss

Eyrarbakki

Thórlákshöfn   Stokkseyri

Hella

Hvolsvöllur

Thórsmörk

MÝF

EYJAFJALLA-
JÖKULL

JÖ

Atlantic Ocean

VESTMANNAEYJAR
(WESTMANN ISLANDS)

Heimaey

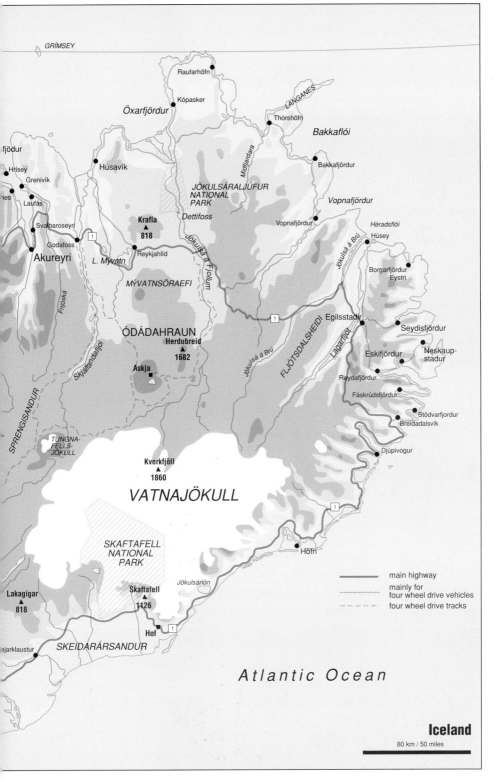

GRÍMSEY

Raufarhöfn

Kópasker

Öxarfjördur

Thórshöfn

Bakkaflói

fjödur

Hrísey

Grenivík

Húsavík

Bakkafjördur

nes   Laufás

Midjardara

JÖKULSÁRALJÚFUR
NATIONAL
PARK

Vopnafjördur

Svalbaroseyri

Krafla
▲
818

Dettifoss

Vopnafjördur

Héradsflói

Húsey

Godafoss

Akureyri   L. Mývatn

Reykjahlíd

Jökulsá á Fjöllum

Jökulsá á Brú

Borgarfjördur
Eystri

MÝVATNSÖRAEFI

Frjóská

Skjálfandafljót

ÓDÁDAHRAUN
Herdubreid
▲
1682

Egilsstadir

FLJÓTSDALSHEIDI

Seydisfjördur

Askja
■

Jökulsá á Brú

Lagarfljót

Eskifjördur

Neskaup-
stadur

Reydafjördur

Fáskrúdsfjördur

SPRENGISANDUR

TUNGNA-
FELLS-
JÖKULL

Stödvarfjordur
Breidadalsvík

Kverkfjöll
▲
1860

Djúpivogur

VATNAJÖKULL

SKAFTAFELL
NATIONAL
PARK

Höfn

main highway

Lakagígar
▲
818

Skaftafell
▲
1126

Jökulsárlón

mainly for
four wheel drive vehicles

four wheel drive tracks

Hof

ejarklaustur   SKEIDARÁRSANDUR

Atlantic Ocean

Iceland

80 km / 50 miles

167

REYKJAVÍK

Visitors are often unsure whether Reykjavík is a scaled-down city or scaled-up village. Probably it is both. Housing fully two-fifths of Iceland's population, it is the undisputed political, business, cultural and intellectual centre of the country. Yet it retains a certain slow pace and almost rustic charm that makes it unique amongst the world's capitals.

It was here that the "official" settlement of Iceland began, after a few false starts, in the late 9th century AD. For centuries there was little to distinguish it from any other cluster of farms elsewhere in the country, although the strands of its noble fate had already been woven: while the practical details of settlement and development were entrusted to man, the site itself was originally chosen by the pagan gods.

Ingólfur Arnarson, who has won the title First Settler of Iceland, brought with him from Norway not only his family and cattle but also the high seat which was the symbol of the homestead. Following established Viking custom, Ingólfur dutifully tossed overboard the pillars on which the high seat was mounted – wherever they washed ashore, that was where the gods willed him to live.

It took over three years for Ingólfur's slaves to find the pillars, while the Viking himself stayed temporarily in the south, but eventually they turned up on the shores of what is now Iceland's capital. One of the slaves, less than impressed with the gods' choice, snapped that "to no avail we have crossed fine districts to live on this outlying wilderness," and ran off with one of Ingólfur's maidservants. But the other slave, Vífill, was given his freedom; he lived at Vífilsstadir, now the site of a sanitorium between Reykjavík and neighbouring Gardabaer. Ingólfur himself submitted to the gods' judgement and probably built his house in the old city centre, with a view of the duck-filled *tjörn* – literally, the lake.

In the shadow of steam: The First Settler Ingólfur named his new home Reykjavík, (Smoky Bay) after clouds he saw rising from the ground, probably in what is now the Laugardalur area. The "smoke" was steam from geothermal springs – ironically, the same "smoke" that today makes Reykjavík an almost completely pollution-free city. The first pipes bringing hot water to the city were laid in 1930. Today all houses are heated from natural geothermal sources, removing the need for fossil fuels.

As for Ingólfur, he still has a presence in the shape of one of the statues so characteristic of the capital (by Einar Jónsson, 1874–1954, a master of symbolism and epic, whose studio home next to Hallgrímskirja church is now a museum housing his works). The First Settler is now perched atop **Arnahóll** hill, at the virtual central point of the city: next to Government House, his back turned upon the Judicial Building and the National Theatre, with the Central Bank and several government ministries to his right, Ingólfur gazes across

1 Parliament Building (Althing)
2 National Theatre
3 Government House
4 Tourist Information
5 National Library - National Theatre
6 Landakotskirkja (Church)
7 White Nights Show
8 National Museum, University
9 Nordic House
10 Umferdarmidstödin BSI
   (Coach terminal)
11 Landspítalinn (Hospital)

12 Hallgrímskirkja (Church)
13 Hótel Loftleidir
   (Bus to Kfelavík, Airport)
14 Kjarvalsstadir (Gallery)
15 Háteigskirkja (Church)
16 Sjómannaskólinn (School)
17 Flugleidir (Domestic Airport)
18 Öskjulid hot water tanks and restaurant
19 Asmundur Sveinsson Museum and Sculpture G
20 Laugardalshöll (Sports)
21 Stadium
22 Hús verslunarinnar (House of Commerce)
23 Borgarleikhúsid (City Theatre)
24 Höfdi House
25 Museum of Natural History

Reykjavík

400 m / 0.25 miles

172

Saetún
Borgartún
Hofteigur
Gullteigur
Sigtún
Höfdatún
Samtún
Hátún
gata
Mjólnisholt
Stangarholt
Medalholt
Raudarárstigur
Hjartansg
Bollagata
Laugavegur
Bolholt
Nóatún
Háteigsvegur
Uthlíd
Langaheio
Reykjahlíd
Máhlíd
Eskiheid
Skógarhlíd
Blönduhlíd
Flugskálavegur
Hlídarfótur

Holiday Inn
Hotel

Sudurlandsbraut
Kringlumyrarbraut
Ármúli

Hotel Ísland

Esta Hotel

Starmyri
Safamyri

Skaftahlíd
Miklabraut
Hvassaleiti

Stakkahlíd

Hamrahlíd
Sigahlíd
Háaleiti
Ofanleiti

Háahlíd

Bústadavegur
Kringlumyrarbraut

Skógarhlíd

26 Gaukur á Stöng pub
27 Kolaportid Flea Market 4
28 Central Post Office
29 Icelandair Office
30 Cinema
31 Hlemmur Bus Terminal
32 National Museum of Art
33 Volcano Show
34 Einar Jónsson Museum
35 University
36 Árni Magnússon
    Manuscript Institute

the harbour to where the glacial cap of Snaefellsjökull twinkles mystically on the horizon on clear days, almost 100 km (60 miles) away.

For centuries after settlement, Reykjavík remained little more than a few farmhouses. In a census taken in 1801 its population was a mere 301 souls, mainly spread between the lake and the Old Harbour where the shops and offices of the old city centre now lie. The population was presumably even less in 1786, when Reykjavík was first granted a municipal charter as an official trading post. In 1901, Reykjavík still only had 5,000 inhabitants. The sudden leap to today's 100,000 has occurred mostly since World War II.

Sadly, many newer suburbs have the soulless, antiseptic feel of planned cities elsewhere in the world. For a visitor, the old city centre is definitely the most charming part of the capital, and so compact that it can be walked around easily. Yet even here atmosphere is sometimes thin on the ground: it is very often the stories associated with places, rather than the places themselves, that give Reykjavík its distinctive character.

Exploring the old city: Street names give some hint of the way Reykjavík looked in the 19th century and before. The traffic artery of **Laekjargata** ("brook street"), for example, followed a stream between the shore and the lake; eels were caught there once, but it is now buried beneath asphalt and flagstones. Today's main shopping street of **Laugavegur** ("pools road") points the way that women followed on foot or horseback to the Laugardalur hot springs to do their washing.

The pedestrian shopping mall of **Austurstraeti** was until recently the city's most easterly point – the street's maidens were immortalised, like distant cousins of Heine's Daughters of the Rhine, by Tómas Gudmundsson (1901-1983), Iceland's first urban poet. The town plaza **Austurvöllur** ("eastern field") is today a relaxing park laid out around a statue of the nationalist hero Jón Sigurdsson. It is said that Ingólfur Arnarson actually grew his hay here.

Flowers bloom in downtown Reykjavík.

Adjacent to Austurstraeti, **Hafnarstraeti** ("harbour street") is no longer on the harbourfront – that honour goes to **Tryggvata**, built during World War I on gravel and sand dumped to extend the waterfront. It now houses the customs office, tax office and a couple of pubs, but the houses on the southern side of Hafnarstraeti date back to the 19th century. This is a good place to go souvenir-shopping.

On Saturdays, across from the harbour, the **Kolaportid flea market** is a cheerful occasion, selling plenty of clothes and assorted odds and ends.

Adalstraeti ("main street") is the site of Reykjavík's oldest buildings. In the 18th century, Adalstraeti was earmarked by High Sheriff Skúli Magnússon (who was nicknamed "the Father of Reykjavík") for a crafts and trades development project. An unusual effort to catch up with the outside world, it was a scheme for creating cottage industries – wool dyeing, knitting, weaving and the like. Although it folded, the project left not only inspiration, ambition and skills,

but also the capital's earliest surviving architecture.

Parts of the workshops are renovated. **Adalstraeti 10** is the oldest surviving building in the city, built in 1764 to replace a 1752 weaver's shop which had burned down.

Its history is dotted with larger-than-life characters, including one-time owner Bishop Geir Vídalín (1761–1823). A cleric famed for his hospitality, Bishop Vídalín left an immortal dedication to the city's nightlife: "There are two places where the fires never die down – Hell and my house." Burning a hole through his wallet in the process, Vídalín won the dubious honour of becoming the only bishop in ecclesiastical history to be declared bankrupt.

Later, the building took a different biblical slant. As the first shop to import fruit to Iceland, it sported Iceland's first advertising slogan in its window, a quote from St Matthew: "By their fruits ye shall know them." Today Adalstraeti 10 is a pub, named **Fógetinn** (The Sheriff) in honour of the Father of Reykjavík.

ow, view of city from spire of Hallgrímskirkja. ht, a sunny summer ernoon by rn (the e).

Humble beginnings: Iceland's **Government House** (Stjórnarrádid) stands on a small grassy bank overlooking Laekjartorg Square, a stone's throw downhill from Ingólfur's statue on Arnarhöll ("eagle hill"). Built in 1765–70, this unassuming whitewashed building now houses the offices of the Prime Minister, yet it began its days less gloriously, as a prison workhouse. (The President of the Republic used to work here too, but has now moved to premises at Sóleyjargata.)

The **National Gallery**, overlooking the lake, has also had its ups and downs. It was originally built as a cold store in which to keep ice cut from the lake which was then used for preserving fish. Later it served as a fish-freezing plant and a hot dance spot – so hot, in fact, that it once caught fire. Now renovated in a light-filled modern style, the small gallery has a fine permanent collection of Icelandic artists that is supplemented by a changing exhibition.

Not all of the capital's most noteworthy buildings are conversions, however.

The grey basalt **Althing** or parliament building on Austurvöllur Square was custom-built in 1880–01 to house the ancient assembly. After more or less continuous operation in nearby Thingvellir since the year 930 (albeit mostly as a court, because Iceland lost its independence in 1262), the Althing moved to Reykjavík in 1798, and this building was built to house it during the tide of the 19th-century nationalist awakening.

On a clear day, it is worth taking some time to stroll around **Tjörn** ("the lake") itself. Extraordinarily, this is still a natural breeding habitat for over 40 species of bird – most noticeably ducks. There are seats and a pleasant walkway along its eastern side (below Fríkirkjuvegur), giving views of a splendid row of houses on the opposite bank. Within a short distance of the lake are two of Reykjavík's most unusual night entertainments: **Light Nights** is a summer show for tourists based on the sagas and Viking tales. The atmosphere is rather like a high school play, making a pleasant introduction to Iceland's rich folklore.

A building the old city

FRIDAY NIGHT ON THE TOWN

The innocent stranger to Reykjavík, emerging from a pub at 2am on a sunny Friday night in June, might be excused for assuming that he has walked straight into adolescent anarchy.

Reykjavík is one of the world's cleanest, most civilised and sedate cities, where traffic jams are unheard of and violence is rare. Or at least that's what it is like when the adults are in charge. But on Fridays between the hours of 11pm and 3am the teenagers take over, and downtown Reykjavík looks more like one of Hieronymus Bosch's wilder flights of fantasy. Thousands throng the streets, on foot or in cars, a tangled, drunken, exuberant mass of teenage *joie de vivre*. Groups of girls, most of them exceptionally pretty, run around shrieking in mini-skirts. Occasionally one bursts into tears for no apparent reason. Boys shout, sing and stalk each other like fighting cocks. Drunken couples scuffle in doorways and then make up in tearful embrace. There is the ominous sound of a shop-window shattering. Cars sit bumper to bumper, horns and music at full blast.

This is the *runtur*, or circuit, the Arctic Circle's answer to the *corso* of Italy and the *paseo* of Spain. On a Friday night around 4,000 teenagers – more or less the city's entire population of 14 and 15-year-olds – flood the streets. At age 17, the long-awaited driving licence allows the added cachet of doing the *runtur* by car. Cruising is not really the operative word – once stuck in the circuit you will be lucky to do more than one lap in a night.

Reykjavík youth does not confine its nocturnal bacchanalia to the balmy heights of summer; it braves the bitterest December storms with equal panache. But what is a teenager's duty in winter becomes a pleasure in June,. when the midnight sun warms the crowds. Some are filled with youthful high spirits, others with spirits purchased from the state liquor stores by obliging elder siblings. Plastic litre bottles of Coca-Cola are spiked with *klaravin* or vodka. You can spot the odd trend-setter wielding a bottle of white wine, but by and large this lot are still at the age where one

drinks for maximum effect and minor points such as taste go by the board.

The *runtur* is a time-honoured tradition – many of the present generation's great-grandparents first met on a romantic 1920s summer's evening downtown. Even so, things have changed with the years. Dress has become much more stylish, with most of the kids looking straight out of the pages of *Vogue*. The crowds get bigger every year, and sex and drugs and rock 'n' roll play a larger part in the night's events.

As you squeeze your way through the crowds, stepping over broken bottles and unconscious youngsters, it is difficult to see any rhyme or reason in what is going on. But like any self-respecting ritual, strict etiquette governs the *runtur*. It is, for example, quite *outré* to arrive downtown before 11.30pm, and Friday is the in night – Saturday is fairly quiet by comparison.

The night reaches its zenith at around 3am, as the older people spill out of pubs and clubs to join the queues for hotdogs and taxis. As they do so, they try to avoid their embarrassingly drunk younger brothers and sisters. ∎

day night when ykjavík mes alive.

The **Volcano Show**, presented by noted film-maker Vilhalmer Knudser, is a series of documentaries and talks on Iceland's unstable geology.

A bridge across the Lake leads to some grassy park areas with a series of public sculptures, followed by the **National University**, which was founded in 1911 – although its ponderous Third Reich-style main building dates from the 1930s.

On the outskirts of the university is the **National Museum**, which is a must for anyone interested in Icelandic history. Most of the archaeological finds around Iceland in the past few hundred years have ended up in its halls – including the famous wooden church door from Valthjófsstadur in the east, carved in the 13th century with the story of a knight who slays a dragon. This is really the only place in Iceland to see any relics from the Viking period.

Heading east from the lake, all roads climb to the imposing **Hallgrímskirkja** church, a modern basalt structure that most visitors find profoundly ugly. You can, however, climb the tower for the best views of Reykjavík and the deceptively close Snaefellsnes peninsula. On a clear day, as they say, you can see forever. (The tower opens daily 11am–6pm, except Monday, and there's an elevator for those disinclined to climb.)

In front of the church is an impressive **statue of Leif Eiríksson**, "Discoverer of America", a gift from the US on Iceland's 1,100th anniversary of settlement in 1974.

Located back down near the shoreline is Reykjavík's best-known building internationally, **Höfdi House**, the municipal reception hall behind whose clapperboard exterior presidents Ronald Reagan and Mikhail Gorbachev met in October 1986 to take their first bows before the *pas-de-deux* towards global disarmament. At the time of its completion in 1909 to house the French consulate, Höfdi was on the outskirts of the capital, and became the exclusive residence of poet and businessman Einar Benediktsson (1864–1940). This famous figure brought to the house not only his

The city fro the banks o Tjörn.

family but also a ghost. Reportedly, the ghost stayed on rent-free when the poet's family sold it to the British consulate, which grew in turn so tired of being haunted that the building was eventually sold to the city.

The New Reykjavík: Since World War II the capital has been expanding to the east, leaving its past behind. In the 1980s, as it approached a six-digit population, more modern and grandiose architecture appeared on its skyline. A new city centre was built entirely from scratch, including not only two shopping malls but also a complex to house the Municipal Theatre company, which was founded in 1896.

As new residential suburbs sprang up – tasteless "concrete lava fields" like Breidholt and Arbaer, each many times more populous than the largest of rural Icelandic towns – so this new part of Reykjavík has become the geographical as well as the business and commercial centre. This expansion is perhaps the most instantly visible result of Iceland's rapid shift from a traditional, rural country to a modern technological society.

And building in Reykjavík is still taking place on a grand scale. The literally outstanding feature of the Reykjavík skyline these days is the glass-domed "Pearl" – a revolving restaurant that sits on top of the glistening silver hot water tanks on **Oskjulid** hill, offering a breathtaking view of the city on clear days. The tanks can take 24 million litres of hot water and cater for almost half of Reykjavík's water consumption. Meanwhile, a controversial new **Town Hall** has been built on the edge of the lake – an impressive postmodern edifice in its own right, but attacked by many Reykjavík residents for clashing with its serene environs. However, you should still have a look at the huge relief map of Iceland in the entrance hall.

Although the old centre has diminished in importance by day, once night falls it regains something of what it has lost. A plethora of pubs and restaurants lends a boisterous – but entirely safe – atmosphere to downtown Reykjavík by night, creating a beehive of activity more

The "pearl": hot water tanks on Oskjulid capped by a revolving restaurant.

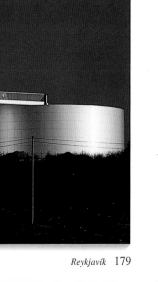

WHY DOES EVERYTHING COST SO MUCH?

Visitors to Iceland are often shocked by the high price of everything. It's not at all uncommon to discover that one has just paid two, three, or even four times as much as one would expect to part with back home for the same item of comparable quality.

Why is everything so expensive? For starters, Iceland's geographical isolation and harsh climate make it virtually 100 percent dependent on imports for everything except meat, potatoes, fish and dairy products. As a result, a web of importers, wholesalers and other middlemen has developed, supplying every corner of the land. While virtually every conceivable item is available, import tariffs and multiple layers of price markup can, and do, drive retail prices sky-high.

Imports of agricultural products are, with few exceptions, banned; at the same time, an overproducing farming sector is propped up by government subsidies which allow lamb, beef, milk, potatoes and other products to be produced at a huge loss in this highly inefficient sector. Although these subsidies should help to keep prices down, due to the lack of economies of scale to fall back on, supermarkets and other food retailers must count on huge markups to make up for the lack of volume. Throw in a 24.5 percent value-added tax on already-expensive farm supplies, equipment, and fuel – plus the VAT at the supermarket checkout – and you have a recipe for some of the highest priced victuals that money can buy.

How Icelanders can afford to live here? The answer is relatively simple: almost everyone who is able to, works. Eighty percent of persons between the ages of 15 and 74 are employed outside the home, including seven out of 10 women; unemployment is less than 2 percent. Generally low wages are compensated for by working weeks of 50, 60 or even 80 hours in some instances. In many instances, even this isn't enough to make ends meet. Thousands of families are heavily in debt and struggle to pay off mortgage, car, and appliance loans, a situation compounded by Icelanders' exclusive tastes.

The dilemma is not limited to domestic households. Over the past few decades, government borrowing abroad has helped create a highly developed and costly system of social services. A seeming inability to halt the taking of such loans overseas has earned Iceland the dubious distinction of having the world's highest level of foreign debt per capita. To help meet repayment obligations, which consume one-fifth of the country's export revenues annually, the government has resorted to a three-pronged strategy of tax, tax and tax.

Of course, with nearly everyone working, taxes shouldn't really need to be so high. However, roughly one-quarter of the population are civil servants and as such do not contribute to the national wealth in the same way as, say, fish exporters do. The nine Icelandic embassies in Europe, Scandinavia, Russia and North America – a lot for a nation barely the size of an American suburb – also cost a lot to run.

It all adds up. A tiny, isolated population with one of the highest living standards in the world is an expensive proposition. ■

The high price of alcohol would driv[e] anyone to drink in Iceland.

in keeping with a city many times the size. Nightlife begins late and lasts until early morning (*see panel, page 177*). Bar prices are outrageous and most nightlifers "warm up" with a few drinks at home before taking the plunge.

Nature and high art: For all Reykjavík's modern expansion, the city's natural treasures remain as precious as ever. The **Laugardalur** area, a green belt by the side of one of the main roads through town, has been largely preserved from development and until very recently still had sheep and horses on it. It serves as the capital's main sports area with a large open-air, geothermally-heated swimming pool, soccer stadium, sports hall and artificially-frozen ice-skating rink. There is also a leisure park with botanical gardens and a children's zoo.

Over the road from the soccer stadium is the **Asmundur Sveinsson Sculpture Gallery.** Sveinsson lived 1893–1982. His works are set in and around his bizarre dome and pyramid studio/home. The outdoor sculpture garden is impressive, and open at all

hours – many travellers will pass it regularly, as several new hotels, including the Grand Hotel Reykjavík and Hotel Island, have been built nearby.

Not far away on the shoreline is the **Sigurjón Olafsson Museum,** dedicated to an Icelandic painter who lived from 1908 to 1982.

And visitors interested in culture won't want to miss the **Kjarvalsstadir Municipal Gallery** in Miklatún park, dedicated to Iceland's most famous modern artist, Johannes Kjarval. Born in 1885, Kjarval worked on a fishing trawler until his artistically-minded fellow workers ran a lottery to raise money for him to study in Copenhagen. The collection of his landscapes here are well worth seeing.

Between the large suburbs of Breidholt and Arbaer, and well within the city limits, runs the idyllic **Ellidaár river,** which pays handsome tribute to the lack of pollution in Reykjavík as one of the best salmon rivers in Iceland, with annual catches of around 1,600 fish. This is why the city's burgermaster is always

king out in wntown ykjavík.

keen to attend the traditional opening of the fishing season on 1 May.

Angling permits, being carefully shared out, are difficult for visitors to come by, but there is no problem in buying permits during the summer season for nearby **Lake Ellidavatn**, where there is good local trout in wonderfully calm and picturesque surroundings.

Ellidavatn borders the capital's **Heidmork nature reserve**, a popular spot for picnics and strolls, where wild patches merge harmoniously with areas reclaimed from wind erosion by the planting of trees and lupins.

One other natural landmark is on the city leisure map, although not part of Reykjavík as such. The **Bláfjöll** ("blue mountains") skiing area, only 15 minutes' drive from town, has both slopes (with ski lifts) and cross-country tracks – and, when the weather is right, a good layer of that vital ingredient, snow, for the greater part of the year.

Boat excursions: The island of **Videy**, five minutes by motorboat off the north shore from the new Sundahöfn harbour,

was given to the Reykjavík authorities as a birthday present in 1987 when the capital celebrated the 200th anniversary of its municipal charter. Today it provides a haven for Reykjavík's inhabitants to "get away from it all," with a curious historical twist. Before the Reformation it housed the richest monastery in Iceland – which, in fact, owned a good part of Reykjavík and the land beyond, until it was torn down by Lutheran zealots.

High Sheriff Skúli Magnússon moved to Videy in 1751 and had a residence built there, completed in 1755. It has recently been restored and now houses a splendid, if somewhat pricey, restaurant. The church on the island dates from 1794 and is also one of the oldest in the country. An ambitious scheme for a fisheries operation here was launched earlier this century but eventually went bankrupt; remains of the "ghost town" can still be visited on a pleasant walk around the eastern part of the island, which takes about an hour.

Another short boat trip used to leave from Sundahöfn docks to **Lundy** ("puffin island"). It was popular with travellers who weren't going far into Iceland but wanted to see puffins, and there are hopes the service may be revived.

Reykjavík and the towns surrounding it have been growing so fast that they now form an almost continuous conurbation, known as the **Greater Reykjavík Area** and home to some 155,000 people – almost three-fifths of Iceland's total population.

Most of these towns are very new and quite colourless, including **Kópavogur**, which has swollen in recent years to accommodate 16,000 people and is thus the second largest community in Iceland. But a couple are included on sightseeing tours of the southwest peninsula: **Bessastadir**, the old colonial governor's seat and now the official residence of the President; and the 15,000-strong fishing town of **Hafnafjördur**, much of which nests picturesquely inside the Burfell lava field covering much of the peninsula. (For more on Bessastadir and Hafnafjördur, see the following chapter on the Reykjanes Peninsula).

Left, Americana makes it to Reykjavík. Right, the Asmundur Sveinsson Sculpture Gallery.

THE REYKJANES PENINSULA

The Reykjanes peninsula is easy to ignore – a smallish promontory south of Reykjavík, it is undeniably overshadowed by the capital's greater pulling power. Yet most people's first glimpse of Iceland is actually of Reykjanes – Keflavík international airport is situated right in its heart.

Almost all arriving tourists simply jump aboard the bus or hire a car, and head for the mountains or the city without a backward glance. But one really should give the region a little time. Reykjanes offers accommodation, restaurants, sports, sightseeing and birdwatching, as well as the unique Blue Lagoon. Many of the principal sights of the area can be seen on a day tour, but hikers, birdwatchers and devotees of the Blue Lagoon may find it difficult to tear themselves away.

Lashed by the Atlantic: Reykjanes is a wind-blown area, lying open to the violent North Atlantic ocean – which supplies a large proportion of the population with their livelihood. Small, nondescript fishing villages dot the peninsula's coastline.

Much of this low-lying promontory consists of lava fields, some of which flowed as recently as the 14th century. While the broad expanses of volcanic rock may seem grey and barren at first glance, in fact they have donned a coat of Iceland's typical grey-green moss, soft and springy under the feet. And the tenacious moss has paved the way for higher plants, which thrive in the more sheltered areas. Two hundred species of grasses, mosses and flowering plants have been identified, along with the occasional birch or other tree.

The gateway to Reykjanes, only 15 minutes by bus south of central Reykjavík, is the old town of **Hafnarfjördur**. This was one of Iceland's most important ports long before Reykjavík had even grown into a village: in the

Left, the Peninsula suffers some of the country's worst weather.

15th century it was run by English traders and in the 16th century by Germans, before the Danes imposed their trade monopoly of 1602.

Picturesquely situated among craggy lava fields, Hafnarfjördur is now a part of the Greater Reykjavik Area but is by no means a satellite town of the capital. It has a thriving port and fishing industry, and a broadly-based local economy. A pleasant public park, **Hellisgerdi**, is situated in the middle of the town, in among the lava. The **Hafnarborg Arts Centre** by the harbourside offers a variety of art shows and musical events, as well as a cosy coffee-shop. The Hafnarfjördur **Maritime Museum** is considered one of the best in the country, and many Reykjavík dwellers make the short trip here to visit the several upmarket restaurants on the waterfront.

At **Bessastadir**, north of Hafnarfjördur, is the presidential residence. Dating from the colonial period, it was originally built as a governor's residence in 1763. The adjacent church was built in the period 1780 to 1823. The president's residence has recently been renovated, giving the opportunity for archaeological excavations on the site which have yielded a range of artefacts dating back to the Middle Ages.

Wilderness area: A large sector of the Reykjanes area, 300 sq. km (115 sq. miles) in area, is a nature reserve, **Reykjanesfólkvangur**. Stretching from the outskirts of Hafnarfjördur down to the south coast, the area is criss-crossed with pleasant walking routes and bridle paths. The Reykjanes nature reserve is contiguous with two others, the **Bláfjöll** area which is a popular ski centre in winter, and **Heidmörk**, a stretch of hilly lava country covered with birches and other vegetation which stretches from the Reykjavík city limits down to Hafnarfjördur.

Route 41 along the north coast of Reykjanes leads to the twin towns of **Njardvík** (population 2,500) and **Keflavík** (population 7,300). Both trading centres since the Middle Ages, they have virtually joined together in recent years. Fishing and other commercial **In the Blue Lagoon.**

enterprises are strong here, but the big employer of local labour is the nearby Keflavík naval and air base.

Beyond Keflavík is the outcrop known as **Midnes**, with the tiny fishing outposts of **Gardur** and **Sandgerdi**. The ruins of the village **Batsendar** are nearby, destroyed by a freak tide at the end of the 18th century.

The dirt road Route 425 follows the coast to the peninsula's southeastern tip. There is a lighthouse and view out to a 50-metre (165-ft) rock pinnacle **Karl** ("man"), while pillars of steam spray from the lava fields on the horizon.

Grindavík, now a typical fishing community of about 2,000 people, can look back on a long and eventful history. It was a major trading centre during the Middle Ages, and in 1532 a business rivalry between English and Hanseatic merchants led to the murder of an Englishman, John "the Broad". Barbary pirates raided Grindavík in 1627, capturing a number of Danes and Icelanders, as well as two merchant ships. The creeping thistle (*Cirsium arvense*), otherwise rare in Iceland, grows in Grindavík, and a local tradition claims it grew up on the spot where Christian and heathen blood was spilt. Today Grindavík is a quiet and unassuming town, with a statue to the families of local fishermen lost at sea.

Surreal spa: Just outside Grindavík, and a convenient 15 km (10 miles) from the airport (for those just passing through) is the **Blue Lagoon**. The evocative and more than slightly derivative name notwithstanding, this is not a natural phenomenon, but a recent by-product of geothermal-energy usage.

The Svartsengi power plant pumps mineral-laden water from up to 2 km (1¼ miles) beneath the earth's surface, at a temperature of 240°C (470°F). The superheated water passes through a dual process, on the one hand to generate electricity, and on the other to heat fresh water. The run-off water, rich is silica, salt and other elements, flows out at a temperature of about 70°C (158°F), to collect in the Blue Lagoon. Psoriasis and eczema sufferers noticed some years

ago that bathing in the lagoon seemed to ease their symptoms, and, once the word was out, the place started developing a reputation as a health spa.

Bathing is permitted only in about one hectare of the lagoon, where the temperature is around 40°C (104°F). Facilities are basic (communal changing rooms and showers, no lockable closets) but clean, and further developments are planned. Car parking is adequate, and the Blue Lagoon has a restaurant and a guesthouse. Bus services are regular during the summer, less frequent in winter, but the lagoon is on the itinerary of many sightseeing tours, and can even be included as a first stop after landing or a last stop before departure from Keflavík airport. Cocktails and dinners can be served to guests in the lagoon, at floating tables.

Hot spot: Geothermal power in a more natural setting can be seen east of Grindavík at **Krísuvík**, where *solfataras* and boiling mud springs surround the world's largest blowing steam vent. While the intention has always been to harness the geothermal energy at Krísuvík for heating purposes, nothing has yet come of this. The whole area seethes with subterranean heat, so tread carefully and keep to the marked paths to avoid being scalded.

Near Krísuvík is the dramatic and somewhat spooky **Lake Kleifarvatn**, reputed to be the home of an aquatic monster; if you are not put off by this reputation, you can also fish for trout in the lake. Permits are available in Reykjavík, Hafnarfjördur and Keflavík.

On the coast beyond Krísuvík is **Krísuvíkurbjarg**, one of Iceland's best-known birdcliffs: most numerous are kittiwakes, while fulmar, razorbill, common guillemot and Brunnich's guillemot are also plentiful. Puffin, shag, herring gull and black guillemot, though less common, can be observed at Krísuvíkurbjarg, while seals can often be seen basking on the shore. Farther offshore, one may occasionally glimpse schools of whales.

About 14 km (9 miles) off the Reykjanes shore lies the island of **Eldey**, a high rocky pillar standing 77 metres (250 ft) out of the sea. Eldey is home to the world's largest gannet colony – around 70,000 birds nest on the island each year. The island is a nature reserve, and public access is prohibited without a special permit. It was on Eldey island that the last of the great auks was clubbed to death in 1844 (see *A Birdwatcher's Paradise,* pages 146–151).

Church of miracles: The little **Strandarkirkja** church on the south coast between Krísuvík and Thorlákshöfn has a bizarre history. Tradition says that a ship on its way to Iceland ran into a storm; the crew prayed for deliverance, and promised to build a church if they were saved. An angel appeared on the shore and guided them to safety; they landed at the spot where Strandarkirkja stands today. A tradition arose that the church could work miracles: through the centuries seamen in peril have prayed and promised donations to Strandarkirkja, and they still do so today. As a result, this little church, which no longer has any parish to serve, is reputed to be one of the wealthiest in Iceland.

Stunning spring colours.

Keflavík Nato Base

The midnight sun bounces off myriad shiny surfaces on the barren earth. A scene on nocturnal Mars? Not quite, but to many of the 5,000 Americans stationed at the Naval Air Station in Keflavík, southwest Iceland, it's just about the closest thing to it.

Surrounded by a vast lava field, military personnel at the base are famous for taping aluminium foil on windows during summer months in an attempt to keep out the all-night, sleep-robbing light.

Foil and celestial bodies aside, the United States military personnel haven't always been able to sleep easy in Keflavík. This Naval Air Station – comprised mostly of Navy and Air Force personnel together with family members, plus a small contingent of Marines assigned to guard the US embassy in Reykjavík – has been the centre of controversy in Iceland ever since it was established in 1951. The prospect of hosting a foreign army on home soil – Iceland has never fielded an army in its 1,100-year history – disturbed a population which had ended centuries-long status as a colony of Denmark only in 1944.

Following independence, a strong left-wing movement amongst Icelandic workers pushed for the country to remain neutral. When the government voted to join NATO in 1949, the issue even provoked a riot outside the Althing in Reykjavík – Iceland's only civil disturbance to date. Regular marches against the base have taken place virtually ever since.

Without a doubt, opposition to the present *kanar* (short for *Amerikanar*, or Americans) was also due to Icelanders' experience with Allied soldiers during World War II. Fear of a German invasion brought a flood of first British and later American soldiers, eventually outnumbering Icelanders themselves. Although engagement with enemy forces was virtually zero, Icelandic males lost many a battle for love to uniformed Brits and Americans, and were forced to watch despondently as hundreds of war brides departed for foreign shores.

But back to the 1990s. The Cold War having thawed, anti-base sentiment has fizzled out (mostly) and has given way to a pragmatic viewpoint, with the Keflavík installation seen more as a source of revenue than anything else.

Marches are still held every few years in protest at the foreign presence, but xenophobic zeal has dwindled since the National Economic Institute revealed that the base has provided 10 percent of Iceland's annual net export revenue since 1951.

Over 1,000 Icelanders are employed directly by the US forces, that's 1–1.5 percent of the total labour force, and close to 2,000 families in the southwest derive their income entirely from the *útlendingar* (foreigners). Troops remain isolated from Icelandic life. Strict rules imposed by both the US and Iceland authorities govern behaviour and limit mobility for off duty troops.

Until a handful of years ago, Keflavík Naval Air Station was the country's only international airport. However, the completion of the nearby Leifsstod terminal in 1987 has given the country a surprisingly modern facility without the drawbacks of big-city bustle. The base now has an exclusively military role. ∎

A protest march against the US military presence.

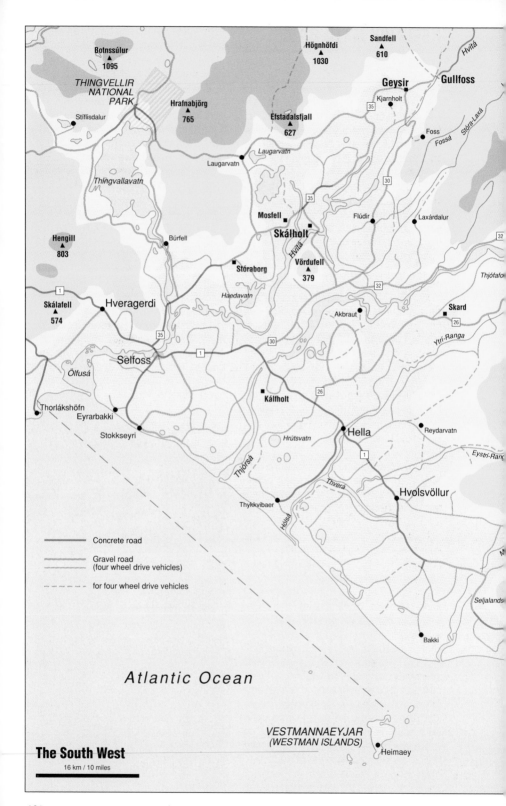

Botnssúlur ▲ 1095

THINGVELLIR NATIONAL PARK

Stíflisdalur

Hrafnabjörg ▲ 765

Högnhöfdi ▲ 1030

Sandfell ▲ 610

Hvítá

Geysir   Gullfoss

Kjarnholt
35

Efstadalsfjall ▲ 627

Foss
Fossá   Stóra-Laxá

Laugarvatn
Laugarvatn

Thingvallavatn

30

35

Mosfell ■

Skálholt ■

Flúdir ●   Laxárdalur ●

32

Hengill ▲ 803

Búrfell

Hvítá

Stóraborg ■   Vördufell ▲ 379

Thjófafo

32

Haedavatn

1

Skálafell ▲ 574

Hveragerdi

Akbraut ●

Skard
26

Ytri-Ranga

35

30

Selfoss

1

Ölfusá

Kálfholt ■
26

Thorlákshöfn ●
Eyrarbakki ●

Stokkseyri ●

Hrútsvatn

Hella ●   Reydarvatn ●

Þjórsá

1

Eystri-Ranc

Thverá

Hvolsvöllur ●

Thykkvibaer ●

Hólsá

Concrete road

Gravel road
(four wheel drive vehicles)

for four wheel drive vehicles

Seljalands

Bakki ●

Atlantic Ocean

VESTMANNAEYJAR
(WESTMAN ISLANDS)
Heimaey ●

The South West

16 km / 10 miles

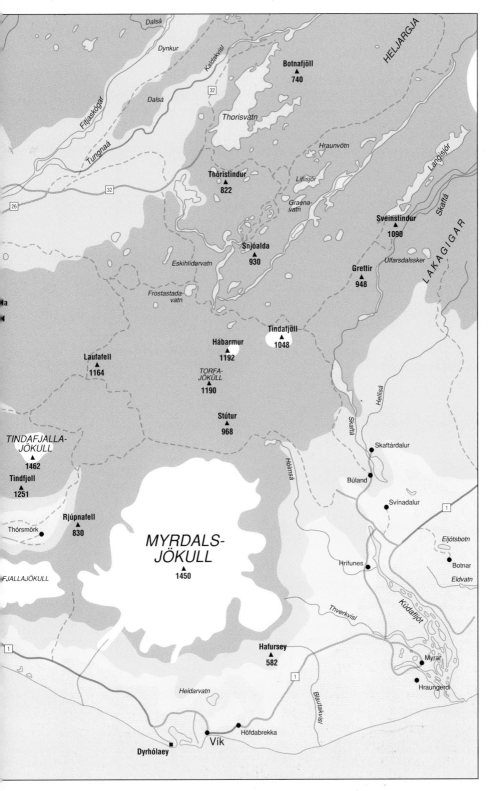

191

THE SOUTH WEST

The rich farming land of the South West has made it one of the most densely populated parts of Iceland since the Saga Age. Today it is also the most heavily visited: Iceland's most famous attractions are all within striking distance of Reykjavík, tied together under the snappy label of "the Golden Circle."

Every day, hundreds of travellers are bussed from one natural marvel to another, with scarcely enough time to draw breath between snapshots. This may be fine for anyone on a short stopover in Iceland and is probably an unfortunate necessity for those without their own transport. But others will prefer to take a more leisurely pace around the whole region, stopping in the more obscure valleys and farmhouses to appreciate Iceland's mellow rural atmosphere.

Christian lava field: The Ring Road east of Reykjavík quickly ascends to a volcanically-scarred mountain pass. The moss-covered scoria lava field here, known as **Kristnitökuhraun**, was spewed up from the earth while the first settlers were discussing whether to convert to Christianity at the AD 1000 Althing in nearby Thingvellir. The eruption destroyed a Christian's farm, which the pagans naturally took as an omen – mistakenly, as it turned out, since they lost the vote in Thingvellir.

Steaming crevasses and yellow sulphur markings on the surrounding hills announce **Hveragerdi**, a town of 1,500 people that has made a living from harnessing geothermal activity. Greenhouses provide the bulk of Iceland's home-grown produce, including bananas and tropical fruit (which are grown less for commercial use than to prove that it can actually be done). Although an unashamed tourist trap, the **Eden** greenhouse is open to visitors, while the Naturopathic Health Association of Iceland operates a clinic here for spa and mud cures. Lying just to the north of town are the hot springs of **Grýla**, named after a hungry local she-troll with a penchant for devouring small children.

While Hveragerdi itself is unlikely to hold travellers' attention for more than a couple of hours, it can be a base for hikes into the surrounding countryside – the nearby mountain **Selfjall** and the lava tube **Raufarhólshellir** are popular destinations.

The next town along the Ring Road is **Selfoss** (population 4,000), the centre of Iceland's thriving dairy industry and a major road intersection. On the highway just before town, **Hjardarbol** offers farmhouse accommodation and comprehensive tours to every corner of the South West.

To the south of Selfoss lie a trio of fishing towns, including **Stokkseyri**, where a maritime museum has been set up in the house of Thuridur Einarsdóttir, a well-known woman captain of a local fishing boat. More atmospheric is **Eyrarbakki**, by the shores of a driftwood-strewn black sand beach: it has several 18th-century buildings still intact and a new maritime museum. A modern sculpture, Krían ("the arctic tern") stands on the outskirts of town.

Across a bridge on the Reykjanes peninsula lies **Thorlákshöfn**, the only decent harbour on the whole south coast between Grindavík and Höfn. It is also the departure point for the twice-daily ferry to the Vestmannaeyjar (Westmann) islands, a journey that can be very pleasant in mild weather but truly wretched when seas are rough (which is often).

The paved Route 35 turns off north of Selfoss at the hillock of **Ingólfsjall**, where the First Settler, Ingólfur Arnarsson, is held to be buried. Amongst a group of smaller craters is the 55-metre (180-ft) deep **Kerid**, blasted out 3,000 years ago and now containing a small lake. Postcards are still sold of a concert held here in 1988, when local rock bands strutted about on a raft in the lake.

Across the bishop's tongue: Route 35 now enters an area which is known poetically as **Biskupstungur** ("bishop's tongue"), lying between the rivers Bruará and Hvítá. The main attraction is **Skálholt**, Iceland's first Christian bishopric and for over 700 years the country's theological powerhouse.

Skálholt's power was built by a powerful dynasty of chieftain-priests (in the days when Icelandic priests did not take vows of celibacy). First it was the farm of Gissur the White, the browbeating holy man who had led the pro-Christian faction at the AD1000 Althing. His multi-talented son, Isleifur, was educated in Germany to become the first properly trained Icelandic priest and, in 1056, Iceland's first bishop. Able to perform miracles like making stale beer drinkable, Isleifur put Iceland on the map by travelling to meet the Pope in Rome and giving a polar bear from Greenland to the Holy Roman Emperor.

Finally, Isleifur's eldest son, Gissur, took up where his father left off and made Skálholt the undisputed Church centre of Iceland, its many schools financed by the first tithe to be imposed in northern Europe.

Skálholt maintained its position of power even through the Reformation, but in 1797 the holy see was moved to Reykjavík and Skálholt all but disappeared. In 1953 – precisely 900 years

Pottery for sale at the Eden greenhouse, Hveragerdi.

after the ordination of Bishop Ísleifur – the foundations were laid for the new church that now stands on the site. In the process, archaeologists found the remains of one of Skálholt's many cathedrals that had burned down in 1309. At 50 metres (165 ft) in length, it was more than twice the size of the current church.

Even more bizarrely, excavators found the carved stone coffin of Páll Jónsson, another of the learned, hard-as-nails early bishops. According to *Pals Saga*, the bishop's death in 1211 was greeted by an earth tremor and deluge. When the excavators opened the coffin in 1953 – revealing the skeleton and walrus bone bishop's crook – the heavens opened up with one of the biggest downpours that Skálholt had seen in years.

Today Páll's coffin is kept in a crypt in the basement of the church, along with some grave plates. Enter through the main church doors, have a look at the modern stained glass and mosaics, then take the spiral staircase down. The best exit from the crypt is out of the wooden door, through a damp underground passage that was once part of the medieval cathedral. Turn off the lights and lock the door behind you – even though it may make your skin crawl.

The land of boiling waters: Within sight of Skálholt, 3 km (2 miles) away, the idyllic working farm of **Sel** offers accommodation amongst sheep-filled fields. Slightly further on is the village of **Reykholt**, which has a geyser that erupts several times an hour and a pleasant, thermally-heated swimming pool. Lying south of Skálholt is **Laugarás**, a verdant, geothermally active area with a camping ground.

The paved Route 37 turns off directly north of Route 35 to **Laugarvatn**, perhaps Iceland's premier spa village, by the shores of the lake of the same name. Summer brings hundreds from Reykjavík to enjoy its pleasures, including the hot spring **Vigdalaug** which was used as an all-weather baptism spot by the first bishops of Skálholt.

Both Routes 35 and 37 finally lead to **Geysir**, which has given its name to all such water spouts around the world. Sadly, the Great Geysir, which started

erupting in 1294, hasn't performed well for decades: earlier this century, eager tourists poured gravel into its mouth to lower the water level and force an explosion, but the process seems to have only made it more and more difficult. The English poet W.H. Auden noted in the 1930s that Icelanders were already using liquid Sunlight soap for the same purpose – it had to be the imported brand, since the thinner local type would not work. Nowadays soap is still used, but only used on special occasions like Independence Day. Even then, there are no guarantees that the geyser will perform. If it does, however, the spume can hit 60 metres (200 ft) in height.

For the rest of the time, visitors will have to be content with the smaller but more reliable geyser, **Strokkur** ("the churn"), which spits its column of water up every five minutes or so to a height of around 20 metres (66 ft). Not exactly Old Faithful, but still impressive. The spout lasts less time than you'd think, so keep your camera poised if you want a photo. Meanwhile, the whole Geysir

emorial to
gridur
masdóttir,
ose efforts
ved
Ilfoss.

area is geothermically active, with walking trails marked out amongst steaming vents and glistening, multi-coloured mud formations. Obey the signs and never stand too near to Strokkur – an average of seven tourists are scalded every week in summer, mostly from putting their hands in water pools to test their temperatures.

Although there's nothing to suggest it now, the surrounding **Haukadalur** ("hawk valley") housed a school that was ranked with Skálholt and Oddi as one of the three great seats of learning in the Saga Age – with none other than Ari the Learned, author of the *Book of Settlements*, amongst its alumni.

The greatest waterfall: Nine km (6 miles) further along Route 35 is the big attraction of the Golden Circle tour and possibly Iceland's best-known natural wonder: the waterfall **Gullfoss** ("golden falls"). A path from the parking area leads alongside the deafening double falls, where the River Hvítá tumbles 32 metres (105 ft) into a 2.5-km (1½-mile) ravine. Trails climb past the waterfall's northern face, allowing you to get within an arm's length of the awesome flow. But you should wear a raincoat, or the clouds of spray that create photogenic rainbows on sunny days will douse you from head to foot.

A stone plaque near the parking area remembers Sigridur Tómasdóttir, a farmer's daughter who lived on the nearby farm Brattholt. Private plans had been drawn up to dam the Hvítá River at Gullfoss for a hydroelectric project, but Sigridur walked to Reykjavík to protest to the government and even announced that she would fling herself into the waterfalls if construction went ahead. The government instead bought the falls and made it a national monument.

Another path leaving from the parking area climbs to the top of the surrounding cliffs for a panoramic view of the falls. From Gullfoss, the road stretches ahead into the uninhabited deserts of central Iceland, and on a clear day you can see the icecap Langjökull.

Viking relics: For anyone even vaguely interested in Saga Age history, it is

The serene farmland of the South West.

worth making the tortuous detour to the excavated Viking longhouse of **Stöng** and its recreated twin, **Thjódveldisbaer** ("the Commonwealth farm").

Both lie in **Thjórsárdalur** ("bull river valley"), formed 8,000 years ago by the biggest lava outpouring since the Ice Age. The valley is overshadowed by the snow-capped form of **Mt Hekla**. Instead of a classic volcano cone, Hekla is part of a rather squat series of ridges – although even this is usually hidden behind the thick bank of clouds that earned Hekla its menacing name, which means "hooded." The seafaring Irish monk St Brendan might have been the first to see Hekla's volcanic pyrotechnics as he sailed past Iceland in the 8th century, and soon after settlement Hekla showed that it was a presence to be feared. Indeed, the volcano's notoriety grew such that, in medieval Europe, Hekla was widely known to be one of the twin mouths of hell. It has remained active, with the last eruption occurring in February 1991 – the same day, coincidentally, that US forces attacked Iraq.

Stöng was the farm of the warrior-farmer Gaukur Trandilsson, whose saga, sadly, has been lost. He moved there some time at the end of the 11th century, but in 1104 Mt Hekla erupted without warning, soon covering the once-lush valley with a thick layer of white ash. Stöng and 20 other nearby farms had to be abandoned, and Thjórsárdalur was never resettled. According to *Njals Saga*, Gaukur escaped Hekla's wrath only to be slain in single combat by his foster-brother Asgrímur Ellida-Grímsson, probably for having an affair with one of his kinsmen.

In 1939, archaeologists uncovered Gaukur's house: it was in the form of two long rooms built end to end, with two annexes for the dairy and lavatory. As Iceland's best example of an early medieval home, it became the model for the nearby reconstruction of Thjódveldisbaer, begun in 1974 to celebrate the 1,100th anniversary of the country's settlement. (The unlucky Viking Gaukur, meanwhile, earned a measure of immortality by giving his name to

e Icelandic rse has a iquely ooth gait.

Reykjavík's famed pub, Gaukur á Stöng – Gaukur from Stöng).

It's worth visiting the turf-covered reconstruction first, designed by Icelandic architect Hördur Agústsson using the Stöng floorplan and built using traditional methods (note the irregular shaped planks of wood for the roof, fitted together so as not to waste an inch of precious wood, and the marks of axes used to plane them). The interior details were provided by artists and historians using information gleaned from digs in Iceland and Greenland, as well as descriptions of living conditions in the sagas: they include a carved wooden "bed closet" for the farmer and his wife, large *skyr* vats in the dairy and furs for the communal sleeping hall.

The original Stöng is hidden away several kilometres further along a very poor dirt road. A large wooden shed has been built over the ruins to protect them from the elements, but it is never locked. Although only the stone foundations remain, this damp, slightly overgrown set of stones is the best place in Iceland to get the historical imagination working.

On a fine day, those with spare time might want to take the two-hour walk beyond Stöng to Iceland's second highest waterfall, **Háifoss**.

Following the south coast: Back on the Ring Road, the unassuming towns of **Hella** and **Hvolsvöllur**, both with around 500 inhabitants, mark the beginning of the countryside where perhaps the most famous of the Icelandic Sagas, *Njáls Saga*, took place.

Between the two towns, Route 266 heads south to **Oddi**. Legend has it that Oddi's first church was built on the strength of a vision: a giant spear flew from the heavens and landed here. Whatever the truth, Oddi quickly became home to Iceland's most learned saga writers, including Snorri Sturluson.

Even more colourful was Oddi's first inhabitant, Saemundur the Learned, who was well known to be a wizard: the man had no shadow, since it had been stolen by the devil while he was studying at the "Black School" for satanists in Paris. Saemundur offered his soul if Satan

A glacier burrows into Thórsmörk.

could take him back to Iceland without getting him wet. In the shape of a giant seal, the devil swam the North Atlantic with Saemundur on his back, but as soon as they got near the coast, Saemundur whacked him on the head with a big book. The wily wizard swam the rest of the way, and, since he was soaked, kept his soul.

The church at Oddi today was built in the 1920s, but has a number of curious artefacts on display, including a silver chalice dating from the 14th century.

Thunder god's forest: Lying east of the Ring Road along Route 294 is the valley of **Thórsmörk** – literally, "Thor's forest", one of Iceland's most spectacular but inaccessible wilderness areas. Sealed off from the outside world by three glaciers, two deep rivers and a string of mountains, Thórsmörk has received added protection since the 1920s as a nature reserve operated by the Icelandic Forestry Commission. The single dirt road into the park is impassable to everything but the specially designed high-carriage buses – some of the oversized

Icelandic four-wheel drives can make it in when the glacial rivers are low, which is usually in the early morning.

Despite the difficulties, Thórsmörk attracts around 1,000 Icelandic campers every summer weekend and a growing number of foreigners on day trips (there are no hotels or guesthouses here). Those who make the effort are rewarded with spectacular glacier views, fields full of wildflowers, pure glacial streams and forests of birch and willow full of black-birds, ravens and white wagtails.

The Ring Road continues south along a narrow plain of farmland between the black sand coast and rugged cliffs that lead to the ice cap **Eyjafjallajökull**, riddled with caves and marked by thin waterfalls. Ruins of indeterminate age crop up at regular intervals here, giving the area considerable atmosphere. Beside the driveway to the farm **Drangshlid** are collapsed turf houses built into caves. You can climb inside and get an idea of how they were constructed – as well as how damp they must have been to live in. There are more caves in the

ugh trial cyclists, rsmörk.

cliffs behind the farm, some of which were supposedly inhabited during saga times.

Three km (2 miles) further east, **Skógar** is home to a meticulously managed **Folk Museum**, the most visited of its kind in Iceland, run since 1959 by a local character Thórdur Tómasson. Apart from a 6,000-piece collection, the museum has examples of different types of Icelandic housing down through the ages. There is a summer Edda Hotel at Skógar, as well as the splendid waterfall **Skógafoss**, whose sheer fall offers one of south Iceland's best photo opportunities. The trek from here to Thórsmörk, passing between the icecaps of Eyjafjallajökull and **Mýrdalsjökull**, is becoming popular with the hardy during July and August, so much so that it can get quite crowded.

Six km (4 miles) east of Skógar, **Fúlilaekur** ("foul river") announces itself with the overpowering rotten-egg stench of sulphur. The river emerges from beneath the **Sólheimajökull** glacier, which can be seen from the road, and originates near the volcano **Katla**, whose subterranean activities beneath the Mýrdalsjökull icecap have often sent glacial tides to devastate this area. Further on, Route 218 cuts south to **Dyrhólaey**, a protected nature area with a steep cliff and a much photographed natural rock arch out to sea. This was where saga hero Njáll's son-in-law Kári had his farm.

Vík (sometimes referred to as Vík i Mýrdal to distinguish it from other Víks), is a small town of around 400 people set along a dramatic stretch of coastline: here the dark North Atlantic hits the land with surprising violence, its waves crashing dramatically on a long beach of black sand. At the end of the beach are the **Reynisdrangur**, towering fingers of black rock standing out to sea and inhabited by colonies of arctic terns. The relentless, battering wind adds to the Gothic scene – helping make this the only non-tropical beach to be rated by *Islands,* a US magazine, as one of the top 10 beaches in the world.

Right, the black-sanded beach at Vik.

IN PURSUIT OF NJALL

For a country with such a rich history, Iceland has very few monuments. Instead, the old Icelandic sagas give vivid historical resonance to every river, mountain, plain and hillock. It is possible to structure a visit to several parts of Iceland just by following a single saga's colourful and bloody course.

The action of *Njáls Saga* – most often read today and considered the greatest of the sagas – takes place in a small stretch of the south-western coastal plains between the rivers Rangá and Markarfljót. Written by an unknown scholar in the 13th century, *Njáls Saga* is the rip-roaring tale of a 50-year blood feud. Unlike many medieval works from the rest of Europe, which are eye-glazingly dull to the average modern reader, *Njáls Saga* is brought to life by a host of fully-drawn characters, using crackling dialogue and vivid descriptions. It's classic plot is an example of what led the Argentine writer and Old Icelandic buff Jorge Luis Borges to believe the sagas were forerunners of modern "westerns."

Njáls Saga is divided into three parts. The title character, Njáll Thorgeirsson, is the most skilled lawyer in Iceland, blessed with second sight and universally respected for his fairness and integrity. A farmer who never raises his sword in anger, he is nevertheless bound by the strict codes of family loyalty and honour. Oddly, Njáll plays a small role in much of the saga, reacting to rather than shaping events.

The first part of the saga concerns Njáll's friendship with the greatest champion of the land, Gunnar. So, the best place to start a saga tour is at Gunnar's farm, Hlídarendi. Set above the marshy Rangá plains on Route 261 (turning south from the Ring Road east of Hvolsvollur), the farm now consists of a few white buildings and pretty little church set among some trees in a mellow and peaceful landscape.

The veteran of many a Viking tour of duty, Gunnar could fight so skilfully that "he seemed to be brandishing three swords at once," and often used a magic halberd that sang when it was about to draw blood. Despite his prowess, he was a fair-minded fellow (by Icelandic standards), slow to anger and keen to avoid trouble. But the problems began when he married the beautiful, manipulative Hallgerdur Longlegs, who had arranged the demise of two previous husbands for slapping her face.

Hallgerdur started up a feud with Njáll's equally shrewish wife, Bergthora. Each of the women ordered the murder of the other's slaves in an escalating feud that the friends Njáll and Gunnar refused to be drawn into yet seemed unable to stop. Relatives of the victims became involved, until Gunnar was prosecuted at the Althing for butchering some assailants in self-defence. Sentenced to outlawry for three years, the hero was riding away from Híldarendi when his horse stumbled and he looked back on his home. "How lovely these slopes are," he said, "more lovely than they ever seemed to me before, golden cornfields and new-mown hay. I am going back home, and I will not go away."

The decision was a fatal one. Gunnar's enemies soon surrounded the farm, although he was able to keep them at bay using his bow and arrow. Unfortunately, his

41. Skarpheðinn á Markarfljóti

string broke. Gunnar then asked his wife for two locks of her hair to plait a new bowstring, but the treacherous Hallgerdur – who had once been slapped by Gunnar – refused. Gunnar's reply to this death-sentence is one of the most famous lines in the sagas: "To each his own way of earning fame... You will not be asked again." Although Gunnar took many of his enemies with him, he was finally slaughtered.

The bloodshed was far from over. Njáll's three sons – Helgi, Grimur and the almost psychotic eldest, Skarphédinn – helped take vengeance on the killers of Gunnar. But they also wanted to kill Thráin Sigfússon, a vain relative of Gunnar's who had been present at an earlier ambush.

Directly south of Hildarendi, half way between Gunnar's home and Njáll's on the rough but passable Route 250 is a rounded hill in the middle of the plain. Today called Stóra-Dímon, it was in Njáll's time called Raudaskridur, or "Red Skree." Thickly forested in those days, it is where the three Njálssons lay in wait one winter's morning in 995 for Thráin Sigfússon and his surly friends.

...rphédinn ...es away ...frozen ...after ...tting ...in ...usson's ...

The ambush was spotted, and it looked as if Thráin would get away, but Skarphédinn leapt onto the glassy ice of the Markarfljót, skidded downstream on his smooth leather boots and sliced Thráin over the head with his axe – "spilling his back teeth onto the ice." The gymnastic Skarphédinn had swooped off to safety before anyone knew what had happened.

Njáll was horrified when he heard of the killing, but organised a settlement at the Althing. To smooth things over, Njáll even adopted Thráin's orphaned son, the cherubic Höskuldur. Höskuldur grew up to take over the farm Ossabaer, which is now a ruined site on Route 252 heading south, but the Njálssons grew jealous of him. One day the three sprung upon him without warning in a corn field and cut him down.

Putting the Njálssons up to this butchery was the diabolical Mördur Valgardsson. Often compared to Shakespeare's Iago as a study in motiveless, twin-faced evil, Mördur loathed Gunnar and plotted to destroy Njáll's family. His chance came when arrangements for a money settlement over Höskuldur's murder fell through at the Althing. Höskuldur's kinsman, Flosi Thórdarson from the Skaftafell area, was about to accept a deal from Njáll when Skarphédinn insulted him, suggesting that he was regularly sodomised by a troll.

Route 252 should now be followed to the site of Njáll's farm, Bergthórshvoll. The modern farmhouse is uninspiring, but you can still see the three hills of the saga. On a clear day, the snow-covered mountains on the horizon make a spectacular sight.

Njáll's actions here are amongst the most hotly debated in the sagas. Having stuck by his bloodthirsty sons, Njáll spotted Flosi with 100 men bearing down on the farm. But instead of fighting, he ordered them to all retire into the house – thereby effectively committing suicide, since Flosi promptly set the place on fire. Njáll and his wife refused an offer of mercy, preferring to die with their three sons. Only Kári Sólmundarson escaped, disappearing through the smoke to a nearby creek.

Interestingly, archaeological digs at Bergthórshvoll in the 1920s and 1950s have found evidence of a Saga Age burning (the accepted date is 1011), suggesting that the dramatic story may be true. ∎

THINGVELLIR

When Iceland's unruly early settlers decided to form a commonwealth in AD 930 – optimistically hoping to cut their losses after six decades of blood feuds – the site they chose for their new national assembly, the Althing, was the spectacular natural amphitheatre of Thingvellir ("parliament plains"). It was a grand experiment in republicanism at a time when the rest of Europe wallowed in rigid feudal monarchies, and it lasted, despite occasional lapses into chaos, for more than three centuries.

Almost every important moment in Icelandic history has taken place at Thingvellir. Here the decision was made for Iceland to convert to Christianity in AD 1000. This was the place for Byzantine legal cases to be argued and voted on, although they were often finally resolved by the Viking recourse to arms and the field of Thingvellir would be soaked in blood (*see panel on page 213*). In time, this violence would grow out of control, and it was at Thingvellir in 1271 that Icelanders would vote away their independence.

The Althing at Thingvellir kept operating as a court until the 1760s, although with less and less relevance as first Norway and then Denmark asserted colonial control. Even so, Icelanders kept a special affection for Thingvellir, as a place where, no matter how imperfectly, the country had managed its own affairs. Poets and agitators would appeal to the saga past when they pushed for independence and, when Iceland finally did declare its nationhood again in 1944, the field of Thingvellir was the obvious place for the ceremony.

Nature and history meet: Today Thingvellir is still regarded with reverence by Icelanders, its historical weight reinforced by a serene natural beauty. Declared part of a national park in 1928, the historical section is set along the north of Thingvallavatn – at 84 sq. km (30 sq. miles) Iceland's largest lake – and by the banks of the **River Oxará** ("axe river"). On the horizon in every direction lie low, snow-capped mountains: to the north lies the volcano of **Skjaldbreidur** ("broad-shield") whose lavas created Thingvellir, flanked by the mountains **Botnssulur, Hrafnabjörg** and **Armannsfell** (home, it's said, to Armann, a spirit who is the guardian of Thingvellir). To the south lies the geothermally active **Hengill.**

The lava plain of Thingvellir itself is covered in gnarled plant life with wildflowers in summer and sumptuous shades of red in the autumn. This is also a spot where the two halves of Iceland – the European and American tectonic plates – are obviously coming apart. Aerial photographs show that the great crack of Almannagjá ("everyman's chasm"), on whose flanks the Althing was held, is just one fissure in an enormous series running northeast like an ancient wound through the plains. Occasional earthquakes have reshaped the site: during one such in the 1780s, the plain dropped about 1 metre (3 ft).

When the Althing was first held here, this was the fringe of the farm Reykjavík,

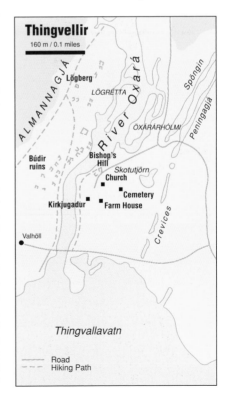

Thingvellir
160 m / 0.1 miles

ALMANNAGJÁ
Lögberg
LÖGRÉTTA
River Oxará
Spöngin
Peningagjá
ÖXARÁRHÓLMI
Búdir ruins
Bishop's Hill
Skotutjörn
Church
Kirkjugadur
Cemetery
Farm House
Valhöll
Crevices
Thingvallavatn
———— Road
– – – Hiking Path

which was owned by the descendants of the First Settler, Ingólfur Arnason. It was, and remains, in the centre of the densely populated farming areas of the land. Now within an hour's drive from the capital, a visit to Thingvellir is included at the end of the popular "Golden Circle" tour, although only a short time is allotted.

While there are surprisingly few man-made monuments here (and those not well marked), it is worth taking a little longer to soak up the atmosphere of what is, as far as Icelanders are concerned, the heart of the country.

Journey into the past: Thingvellir's historical district can be reached from two separate parking lots. The path through the Almannagjá fissure crosses a bridge over to the west side of the Oxará. Below the bridge is **Drekkingarhylur**, the famed "drowning pool" that came into use in the 16th century. Men condemned to death were beheaded, but women who committed adultery, infanticide or perjury were tied up in a sack and then flung into the pool –

which was rather deeper and more turbulent than it is today.

The path continues over the Almannagjá fissure to what was the focal point of every Viking Althing: **Lögberg**, the "Law Rock", today marked by a stone and a flapping Icelandic flag. This was the volcanic podium for every speaker. The crowds of onlookers stood below, in between Almannagjá and the River Oxará – although it should be noted that, according to the *Sturlung Saga*, the river was actually diverted by settlers to run through here some time in the 12th century.

On the smoother ground below, the Lögrétta (Legislature) took place, attended by the 36 (later increased to 39) *godar* or chieftains who would debate new laws. All free men were welcome to listen or comment, but only the *godar* could vote (actual democracy was still a little beyond the pale, even for the Icelanders). It was also the site of the Quarter Courts, one for each section of the country. This is the place to take a break and try to imagine the medieval scene.

The rich colours of autumn in National Park.

The proceedings were considered so important that farmer-warriors rode in from every corner of Iceland, even taking as long as 17 days to arrive from the East Fjords. The Lögrétta was part parliament, part carnival. Great issues were debated amongst a babble of food vendors, swordsmiths, beer drinkers and hangers-on, while saga heroes forged their new allegiances and met their future brides.

Most famous of the Althing romances must be the champion Gunnar's whirlwind courtship with Hallgerdur the Long Legged in *Njáls Saga* – a coupling that would have disastrous consequences for all of Iceland (*see pages 204–205*).

The whole business was run by the Law-Speaker, who was elected from amongst the chieftans. His was a difficult job: apart from keeping the proceedings orderly, he had to recite from memory all of the Icelandic laws, one third every year, from the Lögberg. The acoustics here are still excellent.

Scattered amongst the grass and lava on either side of the Lögberg are the few remains of various *búdir*, or **booths** – although, frustratingly, none are signposted. Every chieftain set up his own personal booth for the two weeks that the Althing lasted (usually from the Thursday after 18 June each year), a canvas-covered place to sleep, eat, drink and meet. The stones that can be seen today all probably belong to booths from the 18th century, although one, called Njálls booth (unmarked, but it's the one furthest south, on the banks of the Oxará), is held to have belonged to the ill-fated saga figure. The **Hotel Valhöll**, built in 1898, is on the site of Snorri Sturluson's booth, Valhöll.

Water and wine: From Valhöll, a bridge crosses the Oxará to the eastern bank. Folklore has it that this shallow river turns to wine for one hour every year on New Year's Eve. Many years ago, two priests visited Thingvellir and happened to fill their bottles during that hour. After an unusually merry night, they tried to repeat the experience next year, only to find their bottle full of blood. The elder priest predicted that this was

rior of the
ngvalla-
ja
urch),
ing from
9.

an omen, and, indeed, at the next Viking Althing, a legal case ended up in a pitched battle that left dozens dead.

On the east bank of the river is the glistening white Thingvellir **farmhouse** and **church**. A church at Thingvellir was the first in Iceland to be consecrated, probably soon after the conversion of 1000, although not on this location. The present version dates from 1859. To enter, ask at the farmhouse – the older part, built in 1930, is occupied by the park warden, who also happens to be the priest; the newer section, dating from 1974, is the summer residence of the Prime Minister. Visitors are loaned the huge, gilded church key, almost more impressive than the church itself.

Inside, there is a pulpit dating from 1683 and a treasured altarpiece, painted by Ofeigur Jónsson of Heidarbaer in 1834, that had been taken from Iceland and wound up in a church on the Isle of Wight. It was rediscovered only in 1974, and returned to Iceland in time for the 1,100th anniversary of the settlement, which was celebrated at Thingvellir.

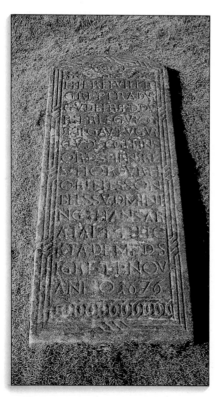

There are three bells in the church steeple: one dating from the Middle Ages, one from 1698, and the third called Íslandsklukkan – "Iceland's bell" – moulded to ring out for Iceland's independence in 1944.

There are two cemetries at the church, the higher one a circular plot of ground with only two graves in it: both of poets, the illustrious nationalists Jónas Hallgrímsson (1807–45) and Einar Benediktsson (1864–1940). Offers have been made, but no contemporary Icelander has agreed to be buried in their company. Just to the north of the church is **Biskupabud**, the "Bishops' booth", which is the largest ruined booth in Thingvellir and one that dates back to its earliest Viking times.

It is possible to walk back to the parking areas from here, with a short detour to a strip of land, **Spöngin**, caught between two fissures. Some historians believe that the Lögrétta was initially held on the flat land near here, but had to be moved closer to the Lögberg when the River Oxará was diverted. On the opposite side of the bridge here is **Peningagjá** ("coin rift"), a natural wishing well. Toss in a coin and ask a yes-no question: if you can follow the coin with your eyes right to the bottom, the answer is Yes; if not, it's No.

Around the lake: After visiting the historical sites, it is possible to take day hikes into the surrounding countryside. Almost all paths lead to the old sheep farm of **Skógarkot**, abandoned in 1936, to the west of Thingvellir. About a kilometre south is **Skógarkotshellir**, a long cave that has never been fully explored.

The less energetic can enjoy a drive around Lake Thingvallavatn on the narrow dirt roads – although this can get a little hectic on summer weekends and might best be avoided. Luxurious summer houses line the whole lakeside, retreats for Reykjavík inhabitants.

From Thingvallavatn, roads cut off in every direction – west to Reykjavík, north to the deserts, east to Geysir and south to Selfoss – following the ancient routes that were once ridden by Viking farmers, every June, to their unique, quixotic assembly.

Seventeen**
century gra**
in Thingvel**
cemetery.

LAYING DOWN THE LAW

By their own admission, Icelanders have always been rather quarrel some, and much of their history concerns aggrieved characters making the difficult choice between taking up the sword and going to court. The annual Althing set up in 930 provided the best of both worlds: legal proceedings punctuated by an unauthorised adjournment while the litigants fought pitched battles. They could then apologise to the court, sit down, and allow the proceedings to continue.

"Icelanders," wrote an 18th-century English commentator, "have surpassed all other nations, ancient or modern, in legal chicanery. Jurisprudence was the favourite study of the rich. A wealthy Icelander was always ambitious to plead a cause before the Althing, and the greater proficiency he showed in the art of prolonging… the greater was his celebrity. A man, in fact, gained as much reputation for defeating his adversary in a lawsuit as for killing him in a duel."

Law covered every contingency imaginable. Thus: "If a man holds his weapons in a peaceable manner, as a person ordinarily does when he is not going to use them, and when they are in this position another man runs against them and wounds himself, he who held the weapons is liable to the punishment of banishment if competent witnesses can prove that he held them in this apparently quiet manner, in order that the other might run against them and be wounded thereby."

This law – and a hundred like it – reflected the fine calculation that made punishment fit the crime. The case of a man who seduced a girl and was then wounded by the girl's father was considered all square. Punishment, when required, fell into three categories: death and two types of "banishment", exile or house arrest. The last normally carried the option of a fine, which was just as well because it was almost impossible not to break laws and most people would have spent a large part of their lives indoors.

Witchcraft and theft commonly carried the death penalty, murder or manslaughter rarely so. Thieves were beheaded; those convicted of witchcraft, usually men, were burnt or drowned to reduce the risk of trouble with their ghosts. Killing was shameful only if it was done in an underhand manner, like killing someone asleep. In other circumstances, which drew no distinction between self-defence and mindless butchery, it could be sorted out by the payment of a fixed penalty determined by the social status of the victim.

In retaliation for effrontery or insult, killing was absolutely honourable, merely requiring a frank public announcement of the deed, which had to be made on the same day. After the event, care had to be taken not to conceal the body beyond a covering to protect it from scavengers. If insults were not immediately dealt with by the offended party, offenders were liable to exile. Indictable insults included throwing sand at someone, a punch, and attempting to throw a man into a mire "though he may actually not fall therein".

Exile lasted 20 years and in practice was not far short of the death penalty. Anyone exiled had a price on their head and could be killed with impunity. ∎

Vikings in discussion.

VESTMANNAEYJAR (WESTMANN ISLES)

In the earliest years of Iceland's settlement, five Irish slaves ambushed and butchered their master Hjörleifur Hrodmarsson, brother of the first successful settler, Ingólfur Arnarson. Dragging along a handful of slave women, they commandeered a rowing boat and – according to the ancient *Landnámabók* – escaped from their farm near Vík to one of the small green islands visible from the country's south coast.

Not surprisingly, the slaves' newfound freedom was short-lived. Two weeks later, the other Viking settlers tracked them down, stormed their camp and mercilessly put the escapees to death.

Even so, the whole archipelago has since been known in the slaves honour as the Vestmannaeyjar – the Westmanns, or islands of the western men.

Today the Vestmannaeyjar (pronounced, roughly, *vestman-air*) have become one of Iceland's most popular destinations. Comprising 13 small islands and some 30 rocks or skerries, they combine a seductive serenity with raw natural beauty: the archipelago is amongst the world's newest volcanic creations, and one of its islands, Surtsey, only emerged from the ocean in 1963.

Even Heimaey – the largest of the Westmanns and the only one with a permanent human population – is scarred black with fresh volcanic flow from the 1973 eruption that nearly caused it to be permanently abandoned (*see panel on page 219*). The eruption changed the shape of the island forever, adding 15 percent to its area and introducing a new volcanic peak, Eldfell. In parts of Heimaey the ground still steams and is warm to the touch, and one can easily imagine that this is how the earth looked at the time of its formation.

Violent birth: Although this area off Iceland's southern coast had been the scene of underwater volcanic activity for hundreds of thousands of years, scientists estimate that the first land did not emerge from the sea here until 10,000 years ago, and most islands were not formed until 5,000 years ago – the blink of an eyelid, in geological terms.

As a result, most of the Westmanns are tiny, rugged and inhospitable. Each is ringed by sheer cliffs, topped with lush vegetation and crowded with sea birds: more species gather here than anywhere else in Iceland. Most are populated only by seasonal puffin catchers, whose huts can be seen from the sea.

For the vast majority of visitors, the point of arrival will be **Heimaey** (pronounced *hay-may*). The name of both the largest island and its township, Heimaey can be reached by a 25-minute flight from Reykjavík or a three-and-a-quarter-hour ferry trip from Thorlákshöfn on the coast (a glorious journey when it is sunny, but when the sea is rough, one of the most dismal in Iceland). Many travellers make only a day trip to the island, although it is worth staying overnight.

Heimaey's 5,300 inhabitants are a hardy and independent breed, steeled by generations of isolation, brutal living conditions and an extensive history of

of
aey from
lanks of
ll, a
no
ed in the
eruption.

Heimaey

2,4 km / 1.5 miles

FAXASKER
SKELLER
Faxasund
Skerssund
Midklettur
STORI ÖRN   YSTIKKLETTUR
LITLI ÖRN   Stóraklif
ASLEYSA   Litlaklif HEIMAKLETTUR   Klettsnef
Camping
RUNEY   Dalfjall   Ground   Harbour
HANI   Golf
KAFHELLIR   Course   Há Flatir
HAENA   Vidlagafjara
Hundradsmannahellir
NEW LAND
CREATED BY
Heimaey   Eldfell 1973 ERUPTION
Teistuhellir   Agdahellir ▲
Helgafell ■
Djúpidalur
Airport ■ Terminal
Skarfatngi
Seafall   LITLISTAKKUR
STÓRISTAKKUR
LANDSTAKKUR
Litlhöfdi Litlhöfdahellir
Brimurd
(Boulder Beach)
Stórhöfdi
Höfdahellir
Ketilssker

OFANLEITSHAMER
OFANLEITISHAMER

disasters. After the Irish slaves' abortive attempt to hide out here, the island was first occupied by a certain Herjólfur Baldursson, a reclusive farmer who had tired of the constant strife on mainland Iceland. Life was relatively peaceful – if not particularly easy – on the island for several centuries, until it became a target for pirate raids.

As if to repay the islanders for the depredations of their Viking ancestors, a series of cut-throats descended on the Westmanns: British pirates ran the place for almost a century, and then, in 1627, the Turks arrived. Well into the 20th century, island children were terrified by the tale of the bloodthirsty heathens who put 34 men and women to the sword and carried off more than 200 as slaves. Those who tried to hide in the cliffs were shot down like birds.

Epidemics wracked Heimaey for the next couple of centuries, while the 1783 eruption of Laki on the mainland killed off all the fish around the islands, reducing its inhabitants to living on sea birds and an edible root called *hvönn* (with plenty falling to their deaths from cliffs in pursuit of both).

Later, fishing accidents would take a dreadful toll: twice, when the island's population was less than 350, storms would send more than 50 men to the bottom of the sea on a single day. In the 19th century, some 100 fishermen drowned from Heimaey, a fact of life which may have accounted for the population's famous *sangfroid* in the face of the 1973 volcanic eruption.

Fishing capital: Today Heimaey is the most important fishing centre in the whole of Iceland – with only 2 percent of the country's population, it supplies some 12 percent of its exports. A large part of the catch is processed on the island, giving locals a healthy slice of Iceland's modern prosperity.

The town itself is spread out around the **harbour**, where over 100 colourful trawlers can dock in the natural windbreak of the lava wall created by the 1973 eruption. The setting is spectacular, with rugged brown bluffs on one side and the two volcanic peaks, Eldfell

The entran to Heimaey harbour, se from the w of lava that threatened in 1973.

and Helgafell on the other. Keep an eye out for the colourful **mural** painted by school children on the side of a building near the harbour, depicting the fateful morning of the eruption.

Walking away from the harbour into town along Kirkjuvegar (to the left of the harbour, with the water at your back), the streets run along the base of the lava wall where it was stopped in 1973 – literally, in some people's backyards. The ruins of one house still haven't been removed, as a reminder of the destruction. Steps have been built up onto the convoluted lava fields, here covered with a thin film of green moss, through which the wind whistles eerily.

With few cars in Heimaey, the streets are empty and peaceful – in fact, their utter desolation on Sundays gives them the haunting feel of a Bergman film. Points of interest include the picturesque white **church**, with a statue commemorating the island's fishermen lost at sea, and the **Folk Museum**, above the library, with a well-organised set of relics, model ships and photographs.

Well worth a visit to see its extraordinary live collection of Icelandic fish is the **Aquarium and Natural History Museum**. Particularly odd are the Icelandic cod, which appears to be made of white plastic, and the horrifying Icelandic catfish, a fish that boasts piranha teeth and a bad-tempered, strangely human expression.

Exploring the island: Unless you have brought a car over by ferry from the island, or have the time and energy to walk, the easiest way to visit Heimaey's attractions is on one of the twice-daily bus tours run by Páll Helgason (the ubiquitous islander who owns hotels, boats and a good deal more on Heimaey). The tour meets most flights at the airport, or you can arrange to be picked up at your hotel.

A rough dirt road has been cut to **Eldfell**, the 220-metre (720-ft) high peak formed during the 1973 eruption. The spectacular view from the base clearly shows how a sixth of the island is now fresh lava flow. The vista stretches across the brightly painted corrugated iron roofs

maey
bour.

of Heimaey to the harbour and, on a clear day, over to the looming Vatnajökull glacier and Mt Hekla on mainland Iceland. A short walk up also leads to barren, steaming tephra fields. If the ground seems warm to the touch, dig a few inches down – it's hot enough to bake bread, and Heimaey housewives, in their more whimsical moments, can still use the earth for that purpose.

Although the bus tour doesn't allow time, there is a path running up to the peak of Eldfell. Only about half an hour is needed for the return journey, but wear strong boots: the tephra is treacherous and increasingly hot as you climb, warming your toes almost uncomfortably (during the 1973 eruption, rescuers' boots actually burst into flames). Having no fear of heights is also a plus, since the path runs along some steep slopes and winds can quite powerful. Eldfell's half-eroded crater turns out to be only filled with sand, but the summit is impressive, with steaming, multi-coloured clay and a heavy stench of sulphur in the air. A track also leads to the summit of **Helgafell**, the older of the island's two peaks.

Roads have also been cut into **Kirkjubaejarhraun**, the 3-sq. km (7.4-acre) lava field spat up in 1973. Apart from a pillar marking where the oldest settlement on the island once was (now 300 metres/980 ft below ground), little disturbs the dark lava's contorted expanse besides geothermal units, heating the town's water and houses.

Down on the other side of the town, a road leads past a surreal monument in the shape of a giant football, to the lush natural amphitheatre of **Herjólfsdalur**. Archaeologists found the ruins of a Saga Age home here, assumed to be that of the island's first settler, Herjólfur Bardursson. These days, however, it is more famous as the camping ground where thousands of Icelanders gather around a giant bonfire for three days to celebrate the Thjódhátíd festival in early August. The prodigious feats of drinking make this long weekend a must for many Icelanders, but most foreigners find it a good time to avoid the island.

Church and memorial t lost fisherm (with Eldfel in the background

CRISIS ON HEIMAEY

Early on the morning of 23 January 1973, a mile-long fissure cracked open without warning on the eastern side of Heimaey, and a wall of molten lava poured out towards the fringe of the town.

Icelanders were woken by a red glow, and were told they should abandon their houses and head down to the harbour. By extraordinary good fortune, the entire Heimaey fishing fleet was in dock that night: foul winter weather the day before had cancelled all fishing trips. Some 5,300 people left the island on trawlers. The evacuation was carried out with almost uncanny calm, as if nobody could believe the pyrotechnics before their eyes, or the din of the now constant volcanic belchings. Not a life was lost.

But the battle with nature had only just begun. Over the next five months, some 33 million tons of lava and debris would spew from the fissure, threatening to devastate the island completely.

Hundreds of tonnes of *tephra* (volcanic debris) hailed down on the town, smashing windows and igniting houses. Volunteer teams worked furiously to cover 14,000 windows with corrugated iron and shovel "black snow" from rooftops to save houses from caving in. All the while they dodged flying lava bombs that could crack their skulls like eggshells.

By early February it was obvious that the greatest danger was from the wall of lava some 165 metres (500 ft) tall moving towards the harbour, which was the best in southern Iceland and the lifeline of the local community. Without the harbour Heimaey would be abandoned.

It was then that the physicist Thorbjörn Sigurgeirsson thought of using jets of water to cool the lava. Such a plan had never been tested, but Thorbjörn reasoned that a wall of chilled lava could dam the flow. An initial experiment showed that, even with lava at 800°C (2,000°F), a cubic metre of sprayed water, dissipating into steam, could change three-quarters of a cubic metre of lava into solid rock.

Even so, a massive effort would be needed to halt the lava tide, which lurched forward at a rate of 30 metres (100 ft) a day with the sound of breaking glass. Fire hoses looked as if they were just "pissing on the lava," as Icelanders described it. Larger pumps were brought in, and then two commercial dredging ships with water cannons pumped a total volume of over 43 million litres (11½ million gallons) of water a day. Heimaey was covered in a blanket of steam, but the effort was worth while: the lava flow was stopped before it blocked the harbour entrance.

After this initial success, the Keflavík NATO base provided extra military pumps, which worked around the clock for the next three months to help cool over 5 million cubic metres of lava.

Scientists pronounced the eruption over in July, and the residents of Heimaey began returning to their homes. One-third of the town had disappeared under the lava and the harbour entrance was a fraction of its former size. But even with the smaller harbour mouth the rescuers scored a victory. The new harbour is completely protected from the wind and thus a great improvement on the old. ■

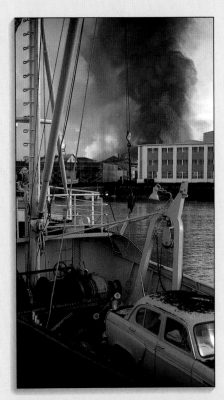

Evacuating Heimaey in 1973.

Puffin catching: A path across the golf course near here leads to a splendid view of several block-shaped islands including **Haena, Kafhellir** and **Hani**. The cliffs here house the island's most accessible puffin colony. High above, puffin catchers can be spotted at work with their 3-metre (10-ft) nets – some 16,000 are caught on the island every summer to make up Iceland's national dinner, without apparently endangering the colony's numbers. The record for a single puffin-catcher is 1,202 in a day.

The island attitude towards these ungainly birds is not always so mercenary. Late in August every year, thousands of baby puffins waddle into the township of Heimaey – lured by the bright lights in their search of food, since their parents cease feeding them in late summer. To save the puffins from a grisly end from cats, dogs and cars, Heimaey's children flock to the streets and collect them in cardboard boxes. Next day, the baby puffins are taken to the coast and ritualistically flung out to sea – and, hopefully, a successful puffin career. At least, they will not end up on island dinner tables until they reach adulthood, since an unwritten law holds that the young should not be eaten. As a somewhat crass Westmann saying has it: "Wine, women and puffins – the older they get, the better they taste."

From Herjólfsdalur, precarious trails requiring mountain equipment can be taken along the cliffs to the northern promontory of **Ystiklettur**, above the harbour. An easier trail also follows the road south to **Stórhöfdi**, where a lighthouse looks out over the island's most exposed coastline. Winds of 250 kph (150 mph) and waves as high as 23 metres (75 ft) have been recorded here during storms.

Boat cruise: A visit to Heimaey would not be complete without an excursion on the waves. Regular departures in small boats leave from the harbour docks, weaving out past the salmon farm (the huge salmon can actually be seen leaping from the water) and around the island. The trip gives views of Heimaey's steep cliffs crowded with

The three-d Thjódhátíd party in ear August.

sea birds (gannets, five species of auk, storm petrels, guillemots and puffins) and usually several sure-footed sheep perched on what appear to be almost vertical green fields.

If you're lucky, orcas (killer whales) can be spotted amongst the smaller islands, their glistening black and white flanks clearly visible as they leap from the waves.

Boats also pull in to several of the natural caves on the coast. In **Klattsvík**, near the harbour, the waves are so calm and acoustics so good that the captain usually climbs out on the bow and gives a short flute concert.

The final summer attraction in Heimaey is the local **Volcano Show** (different from Reykjavík's) – including a documented story that has become emblematic of the Westmann islanders' constant battle with Nature.

Half man, half seal: One night in March 1983, a fishing vessel capsized 5 km (3 miles) off Heimaey's coast. All of the crew quickly perished in the freezing winter seas, except for a fisherman named Gudlaugur Fridthórsson. He staved off the confusion of hypothermia by talking to hovering sea birds, and set off swimming for shore. It took him six hours – about five hours longer than anyone else has ever survived in water that temperature.

As if that wasn't enough, Gudlaugur swam ashore onto some of the sharpest lava on the island, cutting his feet to ribbons and losing considerable blood as he stumbled to the town. Doctors could not find his pulse, but the fisherman survived. Later, when the London Hospital Medical College performed tests, Gudlaugur's body fat proved to closely resemble a seal's.

It's a story that islanders recount fondly, as if to steel themselves for the next skirmish with the sea, the winds or the volcanic peaks that threaten them every day.

The birth of an island: The youngest of the Westmann islands, **Surtsey**, burst from the North Atlantic in a dramatic eruption in 1963. Captured on film by airborne camera crews, highlights of its

e smaller
estmann
ands are
habited
ly by puffin
tchers.

fiery, four-year-long birth were seen around the world, providing a unique glimpse of how Iceland was formed and still giving scientists invaluable data on how virgin habitats are first colonised by plant and animal life.

The eruption began below the waves in the Mid Atlantic Ridge, the submarine mountain chain that runs into the south coast of Iceland. Island fishermen were the first to notice smoke rising from the sea in November 1963. Molten lava spewing onto the sea floor was cooling on contact with the icy waters, but soon a pile of volcanic debris had risen the 130 metres (430 ft) to the surface to create a burning, burping mass above sea level.

A pillar of black ash, intertwined with a white stream of steam, was sent some 10 km (6 miles) into the air – looking menacing from nearby Heimaey and visible even as far away as Reykjavík. The first flights over the site confirmed that the Westmanns now had a 16th island, and that eruption was still continuing: fluid lava was piling up over the

mound of tephra and solidifying, turning it from a giant volcanic refuse heap into a permanent presence.

The new island was named after the fiery Norse giant Surtur, who sets the world alight at Ragnarok, the end of the world. For the next four years, until June 1967, Surtsey provided the world's scientific community with the spectacle of its ongoing formation, before finally settling down to an area of 2.6 sq. km (1 sq. mile) and 173 metres (567 ft) in height. During the same period, two smaller islands emerged from the eruption but have since eroded away and disappeared below the waves.

Fascinating as Surtsey's formation had been, its greatest scientific value began when the eruption ended. Its 1,000°C (1,830°F) surface temperatures during the eruption had left it completely free of any living organism: the island became a sort of natural laboratory approximating how Iceland must have been when its first segments emerged from the sea some 20 million years ago.

Seeds arrived on the island in its first summer, carried by the wind, sea and passing sea birds. The first sprouting plants were noticed in the next year, 1965, even before the island's eruption had fully finished. By the end of 1967, four species of plants had established themselves around the coast.

Midges and flies were the first animals to settle the island, with seals making an appearance after the surrounding seas became restocked with fish. In 1970, black-backed gulls became the first birds to nest on Surtsey. Since then, scientists have observed 60 bird species on the island – some just stopping in en route to other shores, others making this their new home.

Surtsey is still a scientific station and off-limits to casual visitors. Any uncontrolled intrusion might upset the island's development, either by damaging fragile plant life or accidentally bringing in new presences (a seed caught on a visitor's shoe, for example, might sprout into a plant). Fly-overs in light aircraft, taking about two hours, however, can be organised in Reykjavík.

Left, a boat tour around Heimaey. Right, scientists record plant life on the new island Surtsey.

THE SOUTH EAST

Icelanders often say that their country was unfairly named, since it is, after all, strikingly green for much of the year. But anyone paying a visit to the South East will have ice on their minds, no matter the season. The whole area is dominated by Europe's largest icecap, Vatnajökull, whose enormous glaciers creep down through every crack in the coastal mountains like oozing blue putty.

Volcanoes regularly erupt beneath it, devastating farmland with flows of melted ice and debris as large in volume as the Amazon river. Little wonder then if the Viking explorers – including the First Settler, Ingólfur Arnarson, who spent three years here – thought the name "Iceland" appropriate.

The damage caused by Vatnajökull's glacial flows (called *hlaups*) made much of the coast next to impassable for centuries. Until the Ring Road was finally driven through in 1974, parts of the South East were amongst the remotest in Iceland. To reach Skaftafell or Höfn by land, for example, one had to drive the entire 1,100 km (680 miles) around the north of the country.

Today the highway from Reykjavík to the South East is fully paved, and the glacier-riddled Skaftafell National Park has become the most popular wilderness area in the country. (In fact, on June and July weekends, it becomes so crowded that it is probably best avoided by travellers.) Meanwhile, the drive along the coast passes a luxuriant, haunting landscape dotted with tiny farms and historic settlements.

Curse of the Irish monks: The gateway to the South East is **Kirkjubaejarklaustur** village (call it "Keerk-ya" and you will be understood), a green oasis town in the volcanic desert formed by the eruptions of the Laki craters in 1783 – an event that devastated Iceland and is still considered to be one of the worst natural disasters in recorded history.

Kirkjubaejarklaustur was first settled by Irish monks, who fled the Vikings

Preceding pages: hik[...] near Höfn. Below, a fa[...] is overshad[...]owed by Myrdalsjök[...] icecap.

but left a curse that no pagan would ever live here. A Christian Norseman named Ketill the Foolish (so named by his peers for converting from the worship of Thor) lived on the site quite happily for many years. But when another Viking, Hildir Eysteinsson, decided to move in, he no sooner clapped eyes on his future farm than he dropped down dead. Perhaps, reasoned the Norsemen, Ketill had not been so foolish after all.

Religion plays a big part in the rest of Kirkjubaejarklaustur's history. In 1186, Benedictine nuns set up a convent here (*klaustur* means cloister), which was closed in the 16th century Reformation. It can't have been a model institution, since two of the nuns were burned at the stake: one for sleeping with the devil, the other for maligning the Pope.

Later, during the 1783 Laki eruptions, a wall of lava looked like wiping the town out when the local curate, Jón Steingrímsson, herded everyone into the wooden church. There he delivered the ultimate fire-and-brimstone sermon whose effect, with great chunks of ash

smashing down just outside the window, can only be imagined. When the sermon had finished, the congregation stumbled outside to find that the lava had been diverted and the town saved. The modern **Steingrímsson memorial chapel** has been built on the old church's site to commemorate this neat piece of divine intervention.

Today Kirkjubaejarklaustur is a pretty but somnolent outpost of 300 people, with the waterfall **Systrafoss** spraying down from steep cliffs as its backdrop. The 1783 lava fields, dotted with pseudo-craters, can still be seen just south of town, en route to the curious **Kirkjugólf** – the name means "church floor," since Viking settlers assumed it was part of a stone floor built by the curse-happy Irish monks. It is, however, a natural formation, with the tops of hexagonal basalt columns fitting together as perfectly as tiles.

Most people stay in Kirkjubaejarklaustur as a jumping-off point to the infamous **Laki craters**, responsible for the 1783 eruptions. Over a period of 10

creeping masfells- ull glacier r Skaftafell ional Park.

months, 30 billion tons of lava and three times as much sulphuric acid belched forth from the so-called "Skaftafell fires." Not only were whole communities wiped out by the flow, but Laki sent up a cloud of noxious gas that began the "Haze Famine" and killed a fifth of Iceland's population and half its livestock – a toll so dramatic that plans were made to evacuate the island completely.

Today Laki is extinct, but the craters at its base are still steaming. There are some fantastic views to be had from the peak. Laki can only be reached by a four-wheel drive road; tours run from Kirkubaejarklaustur daily in summer.

The Ring Road east of Kirkubaejarklaustur runs to the attractive farm of Foss, named for the thin waterfall flowing from the cliffs on the property, followed by the basalt columns of **Dverghamrar**. A sunken plain of moss-covered lava – once again created by Laki – must be crossed before finding the farm of **Núpsstadur**, at the base of the imposing 770-metre (2,500-ft) cliff called **Lómagnúpur** ("loon peak"). Run by two elderly bachelor brothers, Núpsstadur has one of Iceland's most charming 17th-century churches and a still-working antique harmonium.

At this point begins **Skeidarársandur,** the biggest of the southern *sandurs* – great wastelands of black sand and glacial debris carried out by volcanic eruptions from underneath the icecap Vatnajökull. Before the Ring Road was built, the only way across here was on horseback, accompanied by one of the farmers from Núpsstadur who had spent their lives learning to navigate the treacherous terrain. Today, this is the stretch of road most dreaded by cyclists in Iceland: not only is it completely monotonous, but regular sandstorms make any open-air activity a complete misery.

Long bridges and flood barriers have been built to counteract any further glacial flows created by eruptions of **Grímsvötn** – although located under Vatnajökull, the most active and potentially lethal of Iceland's many volcanic craters. Dominating the view on the left

A farmer in the South East.

MORSÁRS-JÖKULL

Skar 839

Kristínartíndar ▲ 1126

706 ▲

▲ 979

Fremrihvaukur ▲ 610

542 ▲

724 ▲

Gláma ▲ 650

Skerhóll ▲ 526

SKAFTAFELL JÖKULL

318

SKAFTAFELLSHEIDI

Sjónarsker

Sjónarnipa

Svartifoss

SKAFTAFELL

Haedir (Sel)

Bölti

Bjónustúmidstöd (store and café) ■ (Information/Service)

CAMPING GROUND

Skaftafel National Park

1200 m / 0.75 miles

is the glacier **Skeidarárjökull**, its flanks scarred black with the volcanic material it has gathered on its path.

The great outdoors: Approached from the west, **Skaftafell National Park** is announced by views over its rugged peaks and the three glaciers that have worked their way between them: from the left, **Morsárjökull**, **Skaftafellsjökull** and **Svínafellsjökull**. The twin glaciers of **Virkisjökull** and **Falljökull** can also be seen further on. Finally, seen from the park, these are all dwarfed by **Oraefajökull** to the east, whose peak, **Hvannadaslshnúkur**, is 2,120 metres (6,700 ft) high. All are fingers of the icecap **Vatnajökull** – which, like other icecaps in Iceland, is believed to have been formed not during the Ice Age but in another cold period 2,500 years ago.

The National Park was established in 1967 and expanded in 1984 to take up some 1,600 sq. km (580 sq. miles). Settlers first came here in the Saga Age, and there are still two farms in the park, one of which now operates as a guesthouse. The park service operates an information centre next to a parking area and large camping ground. On summer weekends, this becomes a cross between a particularly raucous Reykjavík pub and a refugee camp, so anyone interested in communing with nature should come on a weekday. There is also a supermarket and snack bar, which overflows with card-playing backpackers in rainy weather.

All walks into the park depart from this point. The easiest is to the snout of the glacier Skaftafellsjökull, less than half an hour away. Covered in volcanic refuse, the ice is actually a shiny grey, like graphite. You can climb onto the glacier, but be careful. It's slippery – and a fall would dunk you straight into a near-freezing meltwater stream that soon disappears underground.

The most photographed attraction in Skaftafell is **Svartifoss** waterfall, a short walk along the road up to the **Bölti** farm/guesthouse west of the camping ground (theoretically, only farm guests can actually take cars up here, but the only sign is in Icelandic and nobody will

e 18th-
ntury
apel at
psstadir.

challenge you if you'd rather drive). Svartifoss is surrounded on both sides by basalt columns, giving it a grand organ-pipe effect.

The path continues on to the peak of **Sjónarsker**, with a view disk, and then further into the mountains: the more energetic can make a day trip to include views of Morsárjökull and Skaftafellsjökull – twin seas of ice, but no more than mere appendages of the great icecap Vatnajökull, which in parts is 1,000 metres (3,300 ft) thick.

The information office can give instructions for other day trips into the park. Nature lovers can spot over 200 species of plants in the park and Iceland's usual plethora of birds, including the largest breeding colonies of great and arctic skuas in the northern hemisphere.

The lake of ice: East of Skaftafell along the Ring Road is the farm **Svínafell**, which was the home of Flosi Thordarson, the murderer of Njáll and his family in *Njáls Saga*, followed by **Hof**, which offers picturesque farmhouse accommodation and has a small turf church. It is near here that the First Settler, Ingólfur Arnarson, lived before moving to Reykjavík – the promontory of **Ingólfshöfdi** marks the site. In the farm of **Kvisker**, three self-educated elderly brothers have each become specialists of note in different fields, a common occurrence in this part of Iceland.

Immediately after a suspension bridge over the Jökulsá River is one of Iceland's most photographed sights: the iceberg-filled lake of **Jökulsárlón**. The ice has calved from the glacier **Breidamerkujökull**, which runs into the lake, burying its snout underwater. The lake was formed only when the passage to the sea was blocked by land movements this century: geologists suggest it could easily come unblocked in the near future, draining the lake.

Boat cruises operate around Jökulsárlon several times daily in summer. An amphibian craft clears the icebergs away from the dock, then a small boat weaves amongst the glistening ice formations. James Bond fans might get a

Skimming across the glacial lake Jökulsárlón

sense of *déjà vu* – the opening scenes of the film *A View to A Kill* were shot here.

Excursions on the ice cap: East of Jökulsárlon, a turnoff to the left advertises trips to **Jökulferdir** at the top of Vatnajökull and snow-catting on the ice cap. The road itself is passable only by four-wheel drive vehicles, but those without such transport can meet the bus from Höfn on the so-called "Glacier Tour" every morning at 10am for the ride up. A small chalet has been built at the edge of the ice cap, and hire of snowcats can be arranged. It's not entirely environmentally sound – so much noise and the first touches of air pollution on the pristine ice cap – but such considerations are usually forgotten in the excitement of riding the snow. On a clear day, you can see for miles across the white sea of Vatnajökull, and trips usually include a stop at a ravine.

The river valleys along this part of the Ring Road are beautiful but thinly populated, while the flatlands of **Mýrar** are excellent for birdwatching. On one farm here, **Bjarnarnes**, a troll woman named

Ketillaug is said to have been seen taking a kettle of gold up into the multicoloured alluvial mountain **Ketillaugarfjall**. There is one day of the year when humans can try and take the kettle from her, but those that attempt it are subject to hallucinations – typically of the farm below catching fire – and always run back to give the alarm.

The South East's administrative centre, with a population of 1,600, is **Höfn** – the name literally means "harbour", boasting one of the few in the South East. The town's fortunes have improved rapidly with the completion of the Ring Road in the 1970s, turning it from a one-horse town to its present, ungainly concrete self. But what it lacks in aesthetic appeal is made up for by its setting on **Hornafjördur** fjord, almost completely cut off from the sea by spits to form a tranquil lake. There is a **museum** in town, and plenty of fish factories, but the real reason most visitors stay here is to join the summer "Glacier Tour," which includes snow-catting and a visit to Jökusárlon in a single, easy trip.

amatic
astline
ar Höfn.

SNAEFELLSNES AND THE WEST

Icelanders, in their more lyrical moments, are apt to dub their homeland the *Saga Isle*. This description is particularly apt for the Snaefellsnes peninsula and the West, where some of the most dramatic events of the sagas took place. Names of farms, villages and towns conjure up the presence of historical characters like the warrior-poet Egill Skallagrímsson and the chieftain and scholar Snorri Sturluson. Along these shores, constantly swept by the wind and the rain, occurred the terrifying hauntings of *Eybryggja Saga* and the tragic romance of *Laxdaela Saga*.

Mysteries of the glacier: Though the West echoes with historic and literary associations, the jewel in its crown is the work of nature alone: the **Snaefellsjökull ice cap**, at the western end of the Snaefellsnes peninsula. At 1,446 metres (4,743 ft), the glacier dominates the surrounding countryside. From as far away as Reykjavík, 100 km (60 miles) to the south across Faxaflói bay, Snaefellsjökull can be seen when the weather is clear, shimmering on the northern horizon.

Snaefellsjökull, though at 11 sq. km (4 sq. miles) not one of Iceland's larger glaciers, is one of the most famous. In Jules Verne's *Journey to the Centre of the Earth*, the glacier is featured as the gateway for a subterranean route discovered by an Icelandic explorer named Arne Saknussemm. Far-fetched though this may be, the glacier does indeed rest on top of a volcanic crater, which last erupted about 1,700 years ago to create the present three-peaked mountain.

The glacier plays a mystical role in *Christianity at Glacier*, one of the classic works of Nobel-prizewinning novelist Halldór Laxness. In recent years it has become a place of pilgrimage for New Agers in search of cosmic experiences; they congregate beneath the glacier every summer, to the bemusement of local fisherfolk.

Highlands, lowlands, or the ferry: The glacier-bound traveller setting out from Reykjavík can either follow the coast road to the north, or make the first leg of the journey by sea on the *Akraborg* car ferry to Akranes. Another option is to take the spectacular highland Route F35 from Thingvellir via **Kaldidalur**, which runs between the glaciers **Ok** and **Langjökull** to Reykholt.

Route One, the Ring Road, runs north out of Reykjavík along the coastline. A detour east on Route 36 leads to two famous farms: **Laxness** where the writer Halldór Laxness was born; and **Mossfell**, where saga figure Egill Skallagrímsson died – supposedly after ordering his slaves to bury his treasure, and then slaughtering them to ensure secrecy. Having gone slightly dotty in his old age, Egill had intended to take the money to Thingvellir and fling it in the chieftains' faces, but was prevented from so doing by his family.

The Ring Road leads along the roots of **Mt Esja**, 918 metres (3,011 ft) high before turning into **Hvalfjördur** ("whale fjord"), where Iceland's only whaling station operated until recently. In the mountains at the head of the fjord, about an hour's walk above the road, is Iceland's highest waterfall, **Glymur**, at 198 metres (650 ft) high. The modern church at **Saurbaer** on the northern coast of Hvalfjördur is dedicated to the memory of Iceland's greatest devotional poet, Reverend Hallgrímur Pétursson, who served this parish in the 1600s.

On the peninsula at the northern side of the fjord lies the town of **Akranes** (population 5,500). This is where the Akraborg ferry docks after an hour's cruise from Reykjavík. Akranes offers hotels, guesthouse accommodation and restaurants.

About a kilometre to the east in **Gardur** is an interesting folk museum, with the emphasis on maritime history. In the ancient cemetery is a stone given to Iceland by the Irish government in 1974, to commemorate 1,100 years of settlement: an inscription in Icelandic and Gaelic remembers the role of Irish monks in the island's discovery.

Warrior-poet: The town of **Borgarnes**, near the mouth of Borgarfjördur fjord, has grown close to the very spot, Borg,

:eding
es:
ing into a
ice on
efellsjökull.
, the
ɔour at
anes.

where Egill Skallagrímsson lived in the 10th century. The son of one of the first Norse settlers, Egill was a paradoxical figure: a fierce and often cruel Viking warrior, he was also a great poet in the skaldic tradition of intricate word-play and metaphor. A modern sculpture of the same name by Asmundur Sveinsson (1893–1982) at Borg commemorates Egill and his work.

Egils Saga, which tells his story and preserves his poetry for posterity, was probably recorded by one of his descendants, Snorri Sturluson. Iceland's first historian and a great scholar, Snorri was also a wealthy and powerful warlord in the age of unrest and civil war which preceded Iceland's loss of independence. In 1241 he was ambushed and murdered by his enemies at his home at **Reykholt** – today a tiny hamlet some 36 km (22 miles) east of Borganes on Route 30.

Snorri's farmstead is long gone, of course, but a hot pool at Reykholt may well be the one where the scholar and chieftain once bathed. A tunnel (now partially restored) led from the pool to the farmhouse. A modern statue of Snorri by Norwegian sculptor Gustav Vigeland stands at Reykholt, commemorating Snorri's masterly *Heimskringla* (History of the Norwegian Kings), which saved centuries of Norwegian history from oblivion (see *The Saga of Snorri*, pages 48–49).

Lava caves and waterfalls: The green and rolling country of Borgarfjördur is at its most beautiful up beyond Reykholt. **Hraunfossar** is a multitude of tiny cascades tumbling into the Hvítá river along a 1-km stretch. A footbridge crosses the river at the churning **Barnafoss** waterfall, where the Hvítá flows through a rugged chasm. At nearby **Húsafell**, summerhouses cluster in one of Iceland's largest woods.

Hidden beneath **Hallmundarhraun** lava field lies Iceland's largest lava cave, **Surtshellir**, 1.5 km (1 mile) in length. Signposted from the road, the cave is found by following a marked trail. Good shoes and flashlights are essential for exploring the cave.

<u>Left</u>, in Jul Verne's *Journey to Centre of t Earth*, the descent started at Snaefells- jökull. <u>Bel</u> a new way down?

To the west along Route 54 lies the Snaefellsnes peninsula and its mysterious glacier. The first landmark is **Eldborg**, a crater 100 metres (330 ft) high, formed in a volcanic eruption 5,000 to 8,000 years ago. The crater, which commands magnificent views, is about 40 minutes' walk from the main road.

The **Kerlingarskard pass**, over Route 55 which reaches 311 metres (1,020 ft) above sea level, was once a hazardous trail which claimed many lives in bad weather. Tales of ghostly apparitions have long been attributed to Kerlingarskard, and even today stories are told of travellers who sense the presence of an "extra passenger" in the car as they cross the high pass. Kerlingarskard is a popular ski centre in winter.

Mineral springs: A peculiarity of the Snaefellsnes peninsula is its mineral springs, producing naturally-fizzy water – a rarity elsewhere in the country. Probably the most famous is on **Olkelda** farm (the name, naturally enough, means "mineral spring") near **Stadarstadur** on the south side of the peninsula.

Stadarstadur is believed to have been the residence of Ari the Learned (1068–1148), author of the *Book of Icelanders*, one of the most important sources on the early history of the nation.

At **Lysuhóll**, mineral water is found in a geothermal area: it produces natural hot bubbly water, which is used to heat a swimming pool. **Búdir**, once an important fishing centre, is well known for a pleasant hotel of the same name, offering excellent cuisine in the peace of unspoilt countryside.

Hellnar and **Arnarstapi**, small fishing villages beneath the Snaefellsjökull glacier, are famed for their strange rock coastal formations, and for their bird life. Close to Hellnar is a sea cave, *Badstofa* ("farmhouse loft"), where bizarre effects of light and colour are seen. Natural wonders at Arnarstapi include *Sönghellir* ("song cave"), a cave with remarkable acoustics, and a huge natural stone arch. Sea-birds nest on the cliffs in their thousands.

Scaling the glacier: The focus of the peninsula, the Snaefellsjökull glacier,

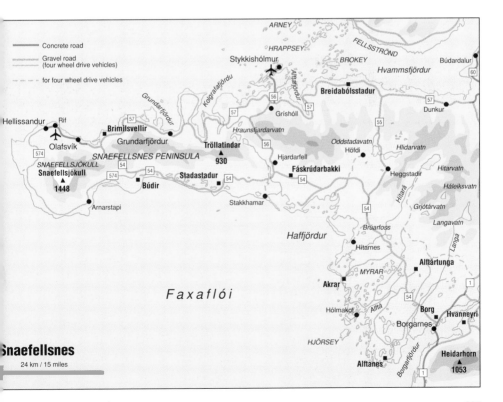

Snaefellsnes

24 km / 15 miles

Ram's Testicles and Rotten Shark

Plenty of traditional Icelandic dishes never make their way to the tables of the fine restaurants of Reykjavík. However, adventurous types in search of authentic food and blessed with a cast-iron gut will relish the midwinter Thorri feast (around February, although many items are available all year). The feast is largely an act of brave and raunchy homage to the old methods of preserving food.

Almost everything a sheep can provide ends up in the Thorri menu, most notoriously *hangikjöt*: the sheep's head, burned to remove the wool and then boiled. This delight is served up at the Thorri feast either in halves or off the bone and pressed into a kind of aspic jelly. Accompanied by mashed turnips, it tastes better than it looks – even, surprisingly, the eyes. All cuts of the sheep's meat and innards are prepared in various ways, with pride of place going to pickled ram's testicles, pressed into a nightmarish cake. Not a dish for the faint of heart, but surprisingly digestible in small quantities.

Guts, blood, fat and a dash of meat for form's sake, nattily sown up in sheep's stomachs, create another dish appropriately called *slátur* (slaughter). *Slátur* is not confined to the midwinter feast; it is eaten regularly in Icelandic homes, and made from scratch in some of them. The dish comes in two forms: *lifrarpylsa*, which means "liver sausage" but isn't, and the darker, fattier *blódmör* or blood pudding, which is like haggis without the spice.

The crowning glory of a midwinter feast, and of many functions around the year, is the ceremonious intake of rotten shark (*hakarl*) and schnapps. After being buried for three months or more, shark becomes acrid and ammoniac, like the most nostril-defying of cheeses. Rubbery and rotten, it is washed down in small lumps with ample quantitites of the Icelandic spirit "black death." A few nips beforehand for courage's sake is not a bad idea!

Icelanders view eating *hakarl* rather like the dark midwinter itself. It strikes an emotional chord deep within the soul, and once over, the joy of having survived makes life seem instantly brighter again.

But not every Icelandic traditional food is quite so stomach-turning. A new favourite amongst travellers is smoked mutton – called in Icelandic *hangikjöt*, which means "hung meat." Served with potatoes, white sauce and peas, *hangikjöt* is a festive dish, obligatory at least once over the Christmas and New Year holidays but eagerly eaten at any time of the year.

Another dish that regularly turns up is puffin. Icelanders have no qualms about eating their national bird in a good sauce – after all, salted or smoked, puffins were one of the dietary staples of centuries past in some coastal communities.

Also well worth a try as a dessert or even for lunch is *skyr*, a rich type of curd. Competition from flavoured yoghurt and ice cream has led dairy producers to create a number of varieties of *skyr* using imported flavours. But the genuine article is still sold unflavoured, mildly sour and served with milk, or, ideally, cream stirred in. A fine topping is wild crowberries, available fresh in late summer and early autumn and eagerly picked on family outings. ■

Medieval meals are still popul, in Iceland today.

can be approached from several directions: the summit is four to five hours' walk from Arnarstapi. From **Olafsvík**, north of the glacier, it is possible to drive part of the way and then walk on – again, a four- to five-hour hike to the summit. While the highest of the three mountain peaks is difficult to scale without special climbing gear, the walk up the glacier itself is fairly easy. In late summer, however, crevasses may open in the ice, so a guided walk is recommended (available from Olafsvík).

Adjacent to Hellnar is the now-deserted farm of **Laugarbakki**, birthplace of Gudrídur Thorbjarnardóttir, one of the heroines of the Norse discovery of America around AD 1000. She emigrated to Greenland as young girl, then later settled with her husband, Thorfinnur Karlsefni, in Vínland, the Norse colony in North America.

Farther down the coast by **Malarrif** stand two lofty pillars of rock, **Lóndrangar**. The taller, 75 metres (248 ft) high, is called "Christian pillar", and the lower "heathen pillar".

While fishing remains the livelihood of the peninsula, some ancient communities have now disappeared, leaving no more than traces of the centuries of fishing seasons: 60 boats used to row out from **Dritvík**, for example, where today there is nothing left but spectacular wilderness – including the great rock formation called *Tröllakirkja* ("church of the trolls").

Test your strength: Those who wish to try out their muscle-power in the true Icelandic tradition should stroll along the shore from Dritvík to **Djúpalón**, where four weighty stones present an age-old test of strength. The aim is to lift them up onto a ledge of rock at about hip height. The largest, *Fullsterkur* ("full strength") weighs in at 155 kg (341 lbs), the second, *Hálfsterkur* ("strong enough"), 140 kg (308 lbs), the third, *Hálfdraettingur* ("half strength"), 49 kg (108 lbs) and the last, *Amlódi* ("weakling"), 23 kg (50 lbs). *Amlódi* , unfortunately, is now broken – presumably after one too many bouts with weaklings. Lifting at least *Hálfsterkur* was a

ural arch
rnarstapi.

requirement for anyone who wanted to join the crew of a boat from Dritvík.

Columbus was here: Now a deserted farm and church just inland from Rif, **Ingjaldshóll** was once a major manor and regional centre. Tradition says that Christopher Columbus spent a winter here in 1477, when he is supposed to have visited Iceland as a merchant – picking up tales of the Norse ventures to the Americas, which would help inspire his 1492 voyage across the Atlantic.

With a population of 1,200, **Olafsvík** is one of the larger communities on the peninsula. It is also Iceland's oldest-established trading town, granted its charter in 1687. Ölafsvík offers a guesthouse and restaurants, as well as a swimming pool and golf course. Skiing is excellent in winter. An old merchant's storehouse dating from 1844 has been restored and houses the local museum.

Stykkishólmur is the principal town on the Snaefellsnes peninsula and the starting point for those who are going to the West Fjords by ferry. Nearby is **Helgafell** (Holy Mountain), a 73-metre (240-ft) hill. According to local folklore, those who climb Helgafell for the first time will have three wishes come true, provided a few conditions are observed: you must not look back or speak on the way; you must make your wishes facing the east; tell no-one what they were; and only benevolent wishes are allowed. Even if your wishes are not fulfilled, Helgafell is worth climbing for the views of Breidafjördur bay.

Helgafell has, in fact, always been considered to have supernatural powers. The first settler here, Thórólfur Mostrarkeggi, built a wooden temple to Thor at its summit. Thórólfur's son, the curiously-named Thorstein Cod-Biter, claimed that on Helgafell he was able to see Valhalla, where dead Norse warriors gorged and drank with the gods.

In the 10th century, Helgafell became a Christian holy mountain with its own church built by Snorri the Priest. According to the *Eyrbyggja Saga,* a long blood feud was sparked off when a certain family group, unmindful of Helgafell's religious significance, used

A sealion lolls on the peninsula's north coast

it as a toilet. To cap this tradition of legends, Helgafell is supposedly also where Gudrún Ösvífursdóttir, heroine of the romantic masterpiece *Laxdaela Saga*, lived out her last years as a hermit, and where she is buried.

In addition to a hotel, Stykkishólmur offers guesthouse and youth hostel accommodation. Jet-skis can be hired to skim over the harbour. The local folk museum is housed in a beautifully-restored timber house dating from 1828. Known simply as **The Norwegian House**, it was imported in kit form from Norway for erection in Iceland, a not-uncommon practice in the 19th century.

Sub-arctic archipelago: The car/passenger ferry *Baldur* plies across **Breidafjördur** bite between Stykkishólmur and Brjánslaekur, the gateway to the West Fjords, calling at **Flatey island**.

Breidafjördur is dotted with islands traditionally regarded as innumerable (although modern counting methods yield a total of approximately 2,700, some scarcely visible). They formerly supported a large population, thanks mainly to the excellent fisheries and the abundant birdlife.

Flatey was the site of a monastery in the 12th century and remained a major cultural centre until the 1800s. One of the greatest treasures of Icelandic literary history, *Flateyjarbók* (the Flatey Book), a medieval illuminated manuscript of sagas, was preserved for centuries on Flatey island before being presented to the Danish king in the 16th century. In 1971 the Flatey Book finally came home to Iceland and is now housed in the Arni Magnússon Manuscript Institute in Reykjavík.

The Flatey islanders gradually deserted their remote homes during the early part of the 20th century, and few remain. Flatey, though, is a delight, a perfectly-preserved example of what an Icelandic village used to be. While the island is all but uninhabited in winter, many families spend their summers there renovating the lovely old timber houses of their ancestors. A recent triumph of painstaking restoration is Iceland's oldest, and smallest, library (4.75 metres by 3.43 metres, or 15 ft 6 in x 11 ft 3 in), built in 1844 to house the book collection of the Flatey Progress Society.

Just east of Stykkishólmur lies the uninhabited island of **Oxney**, which was the home of Eiríkur the Red, discoverer of Greenland, and his son Leifur, known as "the Lucky," who discovered North America in around AD 1000.

Towering up at the eastern end of the Snaefellsnes peninsula are the three pyramids of the aptly-named **Ljósufjöll** (Light Mountains), pale rhyolitic peaks reaching 1,063 metres (3,486ft).

Viking romance: North of the Snaefellsnes peninsula is **Hvammsfjördur** fjord, with the village of **Búdardalur** at its head. Route 59 runs along **Laxárdalur** (Salmon River Valley). This is saga country, and almost every placename strikes a chord for Icelanders.

The farm **Hjardarholt**, for example, just outside Búdardalur, is the birthplace of Kjartan Olafsson (grandson of Egill Skallagrímsson), whose ill-starred love for Gudrún Osvífursdóttir from **Saelingsdalur**, 30 km (18 miles) to the north, is the central theme of *Laxdaela Saga*. Abandoned, as she believed, by Kjartan, Gudrún was persuaded to marry his friend, cousin and blood-brother Bolli Thorleiksson.

Love turned to resentment, and Gudrún incited her husband to kill Kjartan. Bolli in his turn was ambushed and killed by Kjartan's brothers in Saelingsdalur, where overgrown stone ruins still bear the name **Bollatóttir** ("Bolli's ruins"). Widowed, Gudrún left Saelingsdalur, ultimately remarried, and ended her life as a hermit at Helgafell. Gudrún is credited with one of the famous gnomic remarks of the sagas: on her deathbed, her son asks her whom she loved the best. Her reply – "I was worst to the one whom I loved the best" – is justly famous for its ambiguity.

Geothermal springs made Saelingsdalur an important centre in Gudrún Osvífursdóttir's day, when there was a hot bathing pool, of which traces can still be seen, at the farm of **Laugar**. A more modern swimming pool now uses the natural hot water, while a summer hotel operates in the schoolhouse, which also houses a small **folk museum**.

THE WEST FJORDS

Shaped like an outstretched paw, the West Fjords region is one of the least hospitable parts of Iceland. Most of its inhabitants look to the sea for their livelihoods: the area's indented coastline, sheer mountains and deep fjords leave little land suitable for farming but make perfect havens for fishing fleets. By happy coincidence, the confluence offshore of the warm Gulf Stream and icy Greenland Current create ideal spawning grounds for key species of fish.

For centuries, a handful of hardy communities have eked out a living in this remote region against almost insurmountable odds. The mechanisation of the fishing industry in the 20th century has made life more comfortable, but government-imposed fishing quotas in recent years have led to a steady stream of emigrants from the West Fjords to Reykjavík. Meanwhile, many small farms in the area have been abandoned as unprofitable – with more and more farmers giving up as the years go by.

As a result, whole areas of the West Fjords are deserted, creating natural reserves of a beauty and fertility unknown elsewhere in Iceland. Travellers here face a string of serious obstacles, including some of the worst roads in the country, infrequent public transport services and an unbeaten track record of abysmal weather. Yet the region offers Iceland's most dramatic fjords; soaring cliffs host literally millions of breeding sea birds; and some of the best hiking. And, once the proverbial ice is broken, its self-reliant people prove to be among the most hospitable in the land.

Of ice and trolls: Geologically speaking, the West Fjords region is the oldest part of the country, bearing the scars of intense glaciation – so intense, in fact, that the isthmus connecting it to the rest of Iceland is just 12 km (7 miles) wide at one point between the Gilsfjördur and Kollafjördur fjords.

Folklore tells another tale: trolls, it is said, decided to dig a channel at this point, competing over how many is-

lands could be created from the excavated material. The troll in the west fared rather well and in the shallow waters of Breidafjördur built many hundreds of islands. Hindered by deeper waters, the troll in the east was less successful and in rage ripped off a huge chunk of a mountain bordering Steingrimsfjördur, and casting it into the ocean, created the island of Grímsey, some miles offshore (not to be confused with the larger island of Grímsey on the Arctic Circle).

Most visitors start their visits at **Isafjördur**, the focal point of the West Fjords. With a population of 3,500, it is the only town of any size and has recently been connected to nearby towns by a new tunnel. What it lacks in obvious attractions is more than made up for by its dramatic location. The 724-metre (2,375-ft) **Mt Eyrarfjall** rises almost vertically from the cluster of brightly painted houses spread out over Eyri, a sandspit jutting out into the fjord and almost the only flat piece of land in the area. Site of a 9th-century farmstead,

ceding
es: the
magnificent
nbjarg bird
s in the
nstrandir
ure
erve. Left,
elderly
ple in the
st Fjords.
nt, the
granes
y.

Eyri is the oldest part of town, with one of Iceland's best natural harbours.

One of Eyri's more notorious inhabitants was the fanatical 17th-century priest Jón Magnússon, who had two men on a neighbouring farm burnt at the stake for sorcery in a controversial case that was followed by all Icelanders. The oldest buildings in Isafjördur are at the end of the sandspit: four restored timber buildings dating from the 18th century. More by accident than design, these ancient (by Icelandic standards) houses were left standing as fish factories and warehouses sprang up around them.

Oldest of the four is Tjöruhús, built in 1733–42, followed by the adjoining Krambud, dating from 1761 and originally a shop. The meticulously restored Turnhús was built in 1744, once housed a salt-fish plant and now contains the **West Fjords Maritime Museum**. Exhibits trace the development of the town and its fishing industry, displaying all sorts of unusual nautical paraphernalia.

Facing the harbour in what looks like another warehouse is **Sjómannastofan**, a restaurant attached to the seaman's hostel. Forget the ever-present background noise from the television, and enjoy an unpretentious but genuine Icelandic fish dinner with undoubtedly the best harbour view of any restaurant in the country.

Around Isafjördur: Highways 60 and 61 converge at Isafjördur, forming a circular route around the West Fjords that can be driven in about two to three days – although if you include a few detours it is easy to spend a full week on the circuit. Many travellers find it more convenient to make short trips with Isafjördur as a base.

The broad fjord of **Isafjardardjúp**, on which Isafjördur sits, almost severs the West Fjords in two. Situated near its mouth is **Bolungarvík**, the second largest town in the region – a jeep track continues further on, and those seeking solitude will find more than enough at **Skalavík**, farmhouse accommodation in a tiny bay facing the Arctic Sea.

Route 61, which hugs the southern shore of Isafjardardjúp, was completed

only in 1975. **Sudavík** is the only village in these parts, developing from a Norwegian whaling station around the turn of the century. Further along is **Ogur**, an impressive farmstead – built in the 19th century, it was at the time one of the largest in Iceland. At **Mjoifjördur** is a roadside cafeteria, and the only petrol station along this stretch of coast.

Another ancient farm site is at **Vatnsfjördur**, in its heyday a wealthy estate that produced several pastors of note. The village of **Reykjanes**, at the head of Isafjardardjúp, is one of the few places in the West Fjords with plentiful geothermal water, and it is put to good use: a summer hotel, swimming pool and greenhouses are on the site.

The road continues as Route 635 along Isafjardardjúp's northern shore to **Kaldalón**, a sheltered beauty spot. A small glacier here tumbles down from **Drangajökull**, the only large ice-field in the north of Iceland which, like others in the country, has retreated significantly in recent years. Accommodation is available at the farm **Armúli** nearby.

Beyond Kaldalón, the road comes to an abrupt halt at Unadsdalur valley, where the uninviting **Snaefjallaströnd** ("snow mountain coast") begins. The snow line is lower here than anywhere else in the country – even in mid-summer, some snow lies at sea level.

Islands and eider: Islands have traditionally been sought-after farm sites in Iceland, and two of Isafjardardjúp's islands are inhabited: **Vigur**, with colonies of eider and puffins and Iceland's only windmill; and **Adey** ("eider island") which, as the name suggests, also has an impressive bird population. Adey was the scene in 1615 of a brutal massacre by the local sheriff and his henchmen, of shipwrecked Spanish whalers – occurring in the wake of the "Turkish" pirate raids, it was probably a case of mistaken identity or sheer paranoia.

Sub-arctic wilderness: Isafjördur is also the jumping-off point for trips to the uninhabited **Hornstrandir Nature Reserve** to the north. Abandoned by its farming community during the first decades of the 20th century and free from

armigan
arly
ing.

the destructive grazing of sheep, plants and wildlife alike thrive on a scale unknown elsewhere in the country. Here you can wade knee-deep in meadows of wildflowers, fertilised by the guano of countless breeding seabirds, and listen at sundown for the haunting bark of the arctic fox, unpersecuted and tamer here than anywhere else in Iceland.

The Nature Reserve is off limits to all motor traffic, making the only way to explore it by boat or on foot. There is no accommodation and little evidence of the once-flourishing farming community. Traces of bridle paths criss-cross the mountain passes, linking the fjords and inlets.

In summer, the ferry *Fagranes* sails several times a week to the area, bringing day-trippers, long distance hikers and descendants of the original landowners who now use the remaining old farmsteads as summer cottages. On board, take time to talk to the locals – a wealth of knowledge, of fact and folklore, has been passed down through successive generations.

Scheduled stops are at Hornvík, Adalvik and Hesteyri, and by request, at other points along the route. The voyage is an adventure as a day trip, but most hikers choose to disembark and walk between Hesteyri or Adalvik and Hornvik, usually taking 4 to 7 days. Others start at Baeir in Isafjardardjúp and walk over to Jokulfirdir and onwards to Hornstrandir. Twice each summer, the *Fagranes* sails to Reykjafjördur, on the Strandir coast, opening up yet another hiking route.

A solitary life: At **Hesteyri**, a cluster of abandoned houses and a church suggest a once-prosperous settlement, and empty farms are scattered across Hornstrandir. The reserve's sole year-round inhabitant is the lighthouse-keeper at **Latravík**. The longest-serving keeper is said to have found a solitary rubber boot washed up on shore shortly after his arrival, and vowed not to leave until the other one of the pair turned up. It never did and he stayed some 15 years at the post.

Not far from the lighthouse rise the majestic **Hornbjarg bird cliffs**, nesting ground for tens of thousands of pairs of noisy guillemots, Brunnich's guillemots, razorbills, puffins, kittiwakes and fulmars. Not for the fainthearted, **Kálfatindur** peak, the highest point along the cliffs, is a 534-metre (1,760-ft) vertical drop to the Arctic Ocean. From its lofty summit, the noise is deafening and the view simply breathtaking – some claim to have seen the distant Greenland icecap from here

In view of Kálfatindur is attractive **Hornvík Bay**. It boasts a long sandy beach, some impressive waterfalls, a plentiful supply of driftwood and a pleasant camping spot. In a rare bout of clear weather (for some reason, more likely in late summer), the place is nothing short of idyllic and makes an ideal base from which to explore the area. Across the bay is Halavikurbjarg, another impressive bird cliff. Spring still draws daring Icelanders to lower themselves on ropes down the cliff face and collect the prized guillemots' eggs.

South of Isafjördur: Route 60 winds over several high passes to link the fjords south of Isafjördur. In former days the difficulty of each pass was measured by the number of fish-skin shoe soles that were worn through to cross it – a nine-skin pass was not unusual. Nowadays these routes are more a challenge to the nerves of the driver and suspension of the car. A tunnel is planned for Breidadalsheidi, at 610 metres (2,013 ft) the highest pass in the area, which is often blocked, cutting off villages for days, sometimes weeks, at a time. Not surprisingly, air transport is vital in these parts. Extraordinary though it may seem, villages like Flateyri, with populations of only a few hundred, have scheduled flights to Reykjavík.

The village of **Sudureyri**, 17 km (10 miles) off the main road, is buried in the shadow of the steep **Súgandafjördur** fjord. The village's main claim to fame is that it lives without direct sunlight throughout the four winter months, longer than any other village in Iceland. The sun's rays first peek over the high mountains and strike the village on 22 February each year, an occasion celebrated, as everywhere else in the country, with "sun coffee".

ow,
nmer
ours.
ht, the
elavikurb-
g bird cliff,
h view to
vík Bay.

Onundarfjördur, named after its first settler, is unmistakable because of its sandy beach which almost straddles the fjord in a golden arc. On a rare sunny day the shallow waters heat up and locals from nearby Flateyri throng to bathe in sight of the Arctic Sea.

Across the fjord, the historical parsonage of **Holt** was birthplace of the 17th-century bishop Brynjólfur Sveinsson. A collector of Saga Age literary works, he made the Danish king a gift of the priceless *Flateyjarbok* manuscripts, which were only returned to Iceland in 1971 (see *The Arni Magnússon Manuscript Institute*, page 114). The attractive timber church at Holt dates from 1869 and contains artefacts from the time of Bishop Brynjólfur.

Dýrafjördur, the next fjord south, ranks amongst the most scenic in Iceland – sheer mountains seem to rise straight from the shore, leaving little or no lowland for farming. The inhabitants have made do with other resources and the village of **Mýrar** boasts Iceland's largest eider duck colony, with 7,000

pairs. The first settler at the nearby farm **Alvidra** was none other than a son of King Harald Fairhair of Norway. Today it offers accommodation to travellers.

National saints and sinners: Across the fjord, **Thingeyri** (population 450) was the first trading post in the West Fjords. Obscure saga references point to an ancient assembly site here, but the area is better known as the setting for the tragic events of the saga of Gísli Súrsson. Outlawed for a suspected vengeance killing, Gísli, one of the more appealing saga heroes, spent a gruelling 13 years on the run, but was eventually tracked down and slain. Gísli's farms at **Holl** and **Sabol** (8 km/5 miles out along the fjord from Pingeyri) have long since been abandoned.

The village of **Hrafnseyri**, in **Arnarfjördur** fjord, was the birthplace of the nationalist Jón Sigurdsson on 17 June 1811. A small museum is dedicated to his memory.

Further along the fjord, an indistinct route leads up the valley of **Fossdalur** to **Mt Kaldbakur**, the highest summit

in the West Fjords. Although it is officially 998 metres (3,273 ft) high, locals have added an impressive cairn to credit the region with its only 1,000-metre peak. In clear weather the full-day hike is well worth the effort, with stunning views stretching as far away as the icecap of Snaefellsnes.

Dynjandi, the best known waterfall of the region, is located at the head of the northern arm of Arnarfjördur. Also known as Fjallfoss ("mountain falls"), the 100-metre (328-ft) high cascade literally drops off the edge of the mountain, fanning out to a width of 60 metres (197 ft) at its base.

From Dynjandi the road climbs, with views down to **Geirpjofsfjördur**. The saga hero Gísli was slain at head of this uninhabited fjord in 977. His last hiding place is still visible below the road, much as it would have been to his approaching enemies. A poignant silhouette of the outlaw has been carved into a rock, marking the spot where he died.

Europe's most westerly point: Some kilometres beyond here the road splits. If you head west, Route 63 passes the fishing villages of Bildudalur and Tálknafjördur (5 km/3 miles off the main road) and the larger town of **Patreksfjördur**, which has a small guesthouse, although little of real interest to the visitor.

Across the fjord, the small fishing and farming museum at **Hnjótur** is worth a stop and breaks the journey.

The real lure of the area is the **Látrabjarg** bird cliffs, lying at the westernmost point of Iceland – and thus Europe. 14 km (9 miles) long and rising to 444 metres (1,465 ft) at their highest point, the cliffs are home to one of Iceland's greatest concentration of sea birds. Of particular interest are the hundreds of thousands of puffins, which are happy to let visitors approach to within a few feet of their cliff-top perches.

Acknowledging the demand for public transport to this remote and inaccessible peninsula, a weekly bus service now links them with **Breidavík**, which 12 km (7 miles) away offers the nearest accommodation. This only allows a short

Camping or at Hornvík.

stay, however: to reach the highest point of the cliffs involves a long, full-day hike from Breidavík.

The bird cliffs have also been the scene of human dramas. When the British trawler *Dhoon* ran aground below the cliffs in the winter of 1947, a remarkable rescue operation by the local farmers saved all 12 crew members. Lowering themselves down by ropes as if they were collecting eggs, they hauled the exhausted men up the 200-metre (650-ft) cliff face to safety.

South-east of Látrabjarg lies Iceland's most magnificent stretch of golden sand, **Raudisandur**.

Ghost on the coast: At the head of **Patreksfjördur** fjord, Route 62 crosses over to the southern coast of the West Fjords, **Bárdaströnd** – a region that gets more than its share of foul weather. This entire stretch of coast has little over 500 inhabitants, largely because the shallow waters of Breidafjördur Bay do not attract the valuable cod and haddock. Or perhaps it's the ghost of Sveinn Skotti. A 17th-century petty criminal and son of a mass murderer, Svein was hanged on the cliff top road to Vatnsfjördur fjord and is still said to haunt the coast.

This was also where the Viking Hrafna-Flóki made one of the first settlements in Iceland, long before the official First Settler Ingólfur Arnarson. The *Book of Settlements* relates that, so good was the fishing, Flóki neglected to make hay for his livestock and over the winter they perished. In spring he climbed a high mountain and, looking north, saw ice-filled fjords. It was this drift ice, and not the glaciers, that prompted him, disillusioned as he was, to name the land "Iceland" on his eventual return to Norway.

The village of **Brjánslaekur**, at the entrance to Vatnsfjördur, is the terminal for the Breidafjördur ferry, which connects twice daily with Stykkishólmur on the Snaefellsnes peninsula – a route that cuts out the long and less scenic drive south around the fjords.

Route 60 continues south around the fjords, a long and winding drive usually plagued with bad weather. There is a chance of spotting the rare white-tailed sea eagle here, though only 30 or 40 pairs of this now protected species remain after centuries of hunting by farmers. The main settlement here is **Bjarkalundur**, the unofficial gateway to the West Fjords, boasting a hotel with camping facilities within sight of the twin peaks of Vadalfjoll.

The Strandir coast: The rugged eastern flank of the West Fjords is one of the least visited parts of Iceland. The population of the area has been steadily declining over the years, and now the only town of any size is **Holmavik**, which has basic facilities and little else. Farming is hard and good harbours few: **Djupavík**, for example, a once-bustling herring station, is now virtually abandoned, but has a wonderfully situated summer hotel.

The village of **Nordurfjördur** is the end of the road. Beyond here, a hiking trail follows the coast to Hornstrandir. Allow between 10 and 14 days, expect fog and foul weather, take double the normal rations – and don't count on meeting another soul.

rched at
brink,
rnbjarg
d cliff.

HUNAFLOI AND SKAGAFJÖRDUR

Jutting into the icy Arctic Ocean, the Skagi peninsula divides the northern coast of Iceland into the Húnaflói bight and Skagafjördur fjord. This rugged region of mountains and waterfalls has been largely forgotten by tourism – few turn off the Ring Road to find the coast's remoter attractions. But those with the time can follow narrow dirt roads, often little more than graded tracks, into a windswept wilderness of basalt cliffs crowded with nesting sea birds, black volcanic sand spits and beaches inhabited only by seals.

Rural Backwater: The Ring Road runs through some rich agricultural land here, its alluvial soil weathered from some of Iceland's oldest rocks. The entry point to the area is **Brú** ("bridge") – a tiny hamlet which is really little more than a petrol station. It is dominated by the huge bulk of **Tröllakirkja**, a hill that stands over 1,000 metres (3,300 ft) from the flat surrounding farmland. Brú is at the head of the narrow **Hrútafjördur** fjord formed by the extensive glacial moraines (deposits) which dominate the area. The land in this region is rich in minerals and, coupled with the high rainfall, encourages the establishment of many rare alpine and arctic plants, particularly gentians.

The farmstead of **Osar** lies 18 km (12 miles) north along Route 711 on the **Vatnsnes** promontory. From here are superb views across the **Húnafjördur Bay** to **Blönduós**. In the foreground is the moraine-dammed inlet of **Sigridastadavatn**, with the **Hóp** lagoon beyond. Grey seals bask on the sand spits at low tide while eider duck and terns nest amongst the lymegrass. A short distance along the shore, below Osar, are several basalt stacks eroded and awash with the ocean swell. The first, Hvitserkur, has a hole through its base. White guano flecks the ledges of the black rock like icing. According to folklore this 15-metre (49-ft) high stack was a troll turned to stone by the sun.

Shaggy sheep rest in the rain.

Hóp is the largest saltwater lagoon in Iceland. It is virtually cut in half by a narrow sand spit and almost isolated from the sea by **Thingeyransandur**, a low-lying, black sand dune with great swards of lymegrass on its seaward side. This was used in the darker ages of Iceland's history as a seed crop to mill for flour. Over the centuries, the dune has expanded seaward as more sand has been deposited on the beach by the ocean. Tundra plants have then colonised the older dunes to provide great flashes of colour: purple thyme, yellow lady's bedstraw, white northern orchid, gentians in deep blue, as well as beds of parnassus grass and silverweed.

Overhead, arctic skuas wheel about attacking arctic terns; down below, running free across the sands, are groups of Icelandic horses, which are particularly common in this part of the country. They are frequently seen being ridden across the luxuriant green fields, with their unique running gait.

Medieval centre of learning: On the way to the dunes, the dirt track (Route 721) passes one of Iceland's greatest historical places, **Thingeyrar**. The local bishop Jón Ogmundarson built Iceland's first Benedictine monastery here in the year 1112. It quickly became one of the country's literary hotspots, with monks working fulltime transcribing both the Bible and the sagas. The name reflects the original function of the site as a *thing* or district assembly. All that remains today is a solitary church erected a little over 100 years ago.

Near to where Route 721 meets the Ring Road is **Pristapar**, the hilly site of Iceland's last execution which occurred in 1830. Across the road is the **Vatnsdalur** valley, a geologist's dream dotted with steep mounds of ground moraine – the refuse left behind when glaciers receded after the Ice Age.

Just as striking is evidence of the largest known landslip in Iceland that occurred here in October 1720. The side of the huge ridge, **Vatnsdalsfjall** (800 metres/2,624 ft high), collapsed and dammed the river below to created a new lake – **Flodid**.

salt rocks
ar
gurviti.

With a population just over 1,000 the town of **Blönduós** is the best base for exploration. Situated where the **River Blandaá** enters the Húnaflói, it is an important fishing community. The town's bright houses contrast with the local green fields and grey screes.

One of the best views of the settlement and its environs is from the nearby hill, **Hnjúkar**, topped by a radio antenna. There is a steep track up to the 205-metre (672-ft) high summit, which gives an uninterrupted view stretching beyond the Húnaflói to the sheer cliffs on the northwest peninsula.

The Ring Road crosses a bridge that spans the River Blandaá (where salmon fishing can cost up to US$1,300 a day) and there is a short turnoff to the heart of Blönduós, with a large modern hospital, garage and hotel. Near to the bridge is the high school, which has a swimming pool and an open-air jacuzzi in the grounds. All smell distinctly sulphuric due to the natural hot spring water.

In the middle of the river, to the east of Blönduós, the island of **Hrutey** has been declared a nature reserve. It can be visited by crossing a small footbridge from the north bank. There is a circular path through the tundra scrubland and it is a good place for birdwatching, both for land and water species. The river torrent slows as it passes into the tidal stretches of Blönduós, where various rare ducks and divers congregate. From Blönduós, the Ring Road runs directly to Akureyri, passing eventually through the **Oxnadalur** valley, considered the finest scenery on the highway from Reykjavík. Alternatively, Akureyri can be reached following the rougher roads along the wild northern coast.

Remote wilderness: The **Skagi peninsula** lies to the north east of Blönduós. The dirt highway that hugs its western edge passes through a narrow band of agricultural land overshadowed by the mountains behind. **Skagaströnd**, with a population of less than 1,000, is the only settlement of any size. It was established as an important trading port during the 16th century but today is a quiet fishing centre. The town is built on a

The bishop of Hólar, once northe Iceland's religious centre.

rocky outcrop that is joined to the peninsula by good alluvial soil. Brightly coloured wooden houses are scattered along the edge of a sweeping bay with the snow-splashed mountain peaks of **Spákonufell** as the towering backdrop. North of Skagaströnd sand dunes and shingle bays gradually give way to cliffs. The ever deteriorating road climbs upwards and across the top of the **Króksbjarg** and **Bakkar** cliffs – home to a large number of sea birds. Rows of sandstone outcrops contrast with the black basalt lava, usually hexagonal in section. Thousands of kittiwakes vie for nesting space on ledges whilst fulmars nest on the tops of the columns. Near to where the **River Fossá** cascades over the cliff there is a small grassy headland that is almost completely undermined by the sea – an excellent place from which to observe the sea birds.

Beyond Bakkar there is a temporary respite in the high cliffs. **Vogurviti** is an unusual outcrop of basalt rock, formed in a series of extensive hexagonal lava steps. An unmanned lighthouse looks over the small lakes and lagoons, sand spits and rocky shores that provide the habitat for countless coastal birds.

Birds and bandits: Within the **Skagafjördur** fjord lie several small islands which are rich in birdlife. The most famous of these is **Drangey**. In the past, this island was a hideout for outlaws, including the legendary saga figure Grettir the Strong.

The islands can be reached from **Saudárkrókur**, the region's administrative centre at the head of the fjord. First settled by Scotsmen from the Hebrides, Saudárkrókur was visited by the English poet W. H. Auden during his travels in 1937. He was unimpressed, noting that the town "might have been built by Seventh Day Adventists who expected to go to heaven in a few months, so why bother anyway?" Today Saudárkrókur has a population of over 2,500, making it larger than Blönduós and second only to Akureyri in size on Iceland's north coast. As a result, it has many amenities including swimming pool, cinema and even a gliding club at the airstrip. Thermal springs supply hot

water to the town's inhabitants and a number of natural baths can be visited just to the north, at **Reykir**. Another mountain track (Route 744) with superb views of the area runs over Thverarfjall into moorlands of cottongrass.

The eastern flank of the fjord is lined with steep mountains with cascading scree slopes barring all roads through to the interior beyond. This region can be penetrated only by backpackers: those willing to walk to the altitude of 1,300 metres (4,265 ft) can see the remnants of an ancient icecap, consisting today of three main glaciers. Accessible by car is the ancient bishopric of **Hólar**, founded in 1106 and for over 600 years the religious centre of the North. The high-towered church, dating from 1763, is charming. The altarpiece dates back to the 16th century, donated by the last Catholic bishop of the area who was put to death during the Reformation.

A difficult hike, from Hólar to the **Urdir valley** and **Dalvík**, crosses the snow fields of **Heljardalsheidi** through some of the finest scenery in north Iceland. South of Saudárkrókur, at **Glaumbaer**, is a finely maintained turf house museum. The several wood-fronted buildings have thick turf walls and roofs whilst the dark interiors are carefully laid out with furniture.

Visitors driving north around Skagafjördur towards Siglufjördur, will find their eyes are drawn constantly to the island of **Málmey** offshore. This concave-shaped outcrop of lava is 4 km (2½ miles) long and rises at either end into sea-bird cliffs.

The town of **Siglufjördur** is out on a limb at the end of its own road, set in an exquisite fjord. Amidst a range of glaciated mountains, the town's current population of 2,000 is its lowest in recent history. A generation ago this was the centre of the herring industry, with fishing fleets and large processing factories. In recent years there has been a steady decline in fishing off the north coast. Some increase in tourism has helped the economy, particularly the growing popularity of winter skiing, but Siglufjördur remains a shadow of its former self.

AKUREYRI AND SURROUNDINGS

By Icelandic standards, Akureyri is a thriving metropolis: with a population of only 15,000, it is the country's largest town outside of the Greater Reykjavík area. Sitting squarely on the Ring Road, a hub for bus and air transport, it has grown in recent years into the undisputed centre of the North. Everything that comes in or out of the region, from cod shipments to touring rock groups, must pass through Akureyri first.

Luckily, Akureyri is amongst the most pleasant of Iceland's urban centres. Despite being only 100 km (60 miles) from the Arctic Circle, it enjoys some of the warmest weather in the country. In summer, it is not unusual to see day after day of 20°C (68°F) temperatures and clear skies, bringing flowers into the streets and turning Akureyri into Iceland's version of the tropics.

Even the setting is spectacular: located at the base of **Eyjafjördur** fjord,

ceding ges: the urch at ufás looks over afjördur rd. Left, mmer ing at the utinn taurant in ureyri.

Akureyri has a backdrop of sheer granite mountains that are tipped with snow all year round (in winter, an even layer of snow usually makes this Iceland's premier skiing spot). Good roads run on both side of the fjord, making the town an ideal base for day trips to some of Iceland's most photographed attractions. And, while Akureyri's modern architecture leaves a lot to be desired (you can't have everything!), there are enough older wooden buildings scattered around town to give it a certain amount of provincial charm.

Gateway to the North: The first settler to claim the Eyjafjördur region was the Norwegian Helgi the Lean (he got his name from a stint on the Orkneys as a child, when he was poorly fed by some foster parents). Helgi was a man with indiscriminate religious habits: in traditional pagan fashion, he tossed the high-seat pillars from his longship into the sea, allowing the god Thor to choose the location of his new home. But when they washed up 7 km (4 miles) south of modern-day Akureyri, Helgi named his new farm Kristnes (Christ's Peninsula), just in case.

The Viking farmers who ended up around Eyjafjördur were a relatively peaceful bunch, to judge from their low profiles in the great medieval sagas. A notable exception was a certain Víga-Glúmur. A morose and gangly youth regarded as a buffoon by his peers, Víga-Glúmur surprised everyone on a journey to Norway by slaughtering a berserk warrior in combat. He became a worshipper of the god Odin and returned to Iceland to make the lives of his former tormentor a lives a misery, and he soon becoming chieftain of the Eyjafjördur region by trickery and mafia-style intimidation.

Víga-Glúmur's mistake was to offend the goddess Freyr by butchering one of his in-laws in the goddess's sacred cornfield, It took 40 years, but the goddess had her revenge. In old age, Víga-Glúmur lost Odin's protection and was forced to abandon his estates. He died blind and alone, if unrepentant.

The profit motive: The town of Akureyri itself did not come into existence until

Around Akureyri
24 km / 15 miles

FLATEY

Skjálfandi

Húsavík

Ólafsfjördur

Dalvík   Hrísey

Hauganes

Kaldbakur
▲
1167

Grenivík

Hnjúkar
▲
1201

Kambur
▲
1210

Laufás

Sealufjall
▲
1321

Graenihnjúkur
▲
961

yjafjallshnjúkur
▲
1421

Svalbard

Akureyri

Ljósavatn

Godafoss

Háafell
▲
918

Tröllafjall
▲
1471

Kerling
▲
1538

Concrete road

Gravel road
(four wheel drive vehicles)

Gloppufjall
▲
1181

for four wheel drive vehicles

some time in the 16th century, when a trading post was set up as a meeting place for local farmers. In the 1770s, the first permanent house was built, and in 1862, with a grand total of 286 inhabitants, Akureyri was made a municipality. An excellent harbour soon made this the centre of the new cooperative movement amongst Icelandic farmers.

By the turn of this century, grandiose wooden mansions had filled the southern part of Akureyri. The spit at the northern part of town, **Oddeyri**, became the port and warehouse area, and it remains so to this day (the name Akureyri is a blend of *Akur*, meaning field, and *eyri*, spit, after the land that projects into the fjord). Today Akureyri has one of Iceland's most active fishing fleets, its largest canning factory, and accounts for some 30 percent of the country's manufacturing output.

Along with this economic growth has come a university and a modest local flourishing of the arts, with Akureyri boasting several theatre groups, plus a number of nightspots and cinemas.

Small-town vices: Perhaps because of their business success, the residents of Akureyri have a mixed reputation in the rest of Iceland. The town is seen as the bastion of middle-class values and, despite the good weather the town enjoys, its people considered closed, traditional and even somewhat dour.

Icelanders joke that you can't get to know the people of Akureyri unless you are born and raised there – being conceived in the town while your parents were on holidays doesn't count. And even being raised there may not be good enough: tales are told of Akureyri neighbours who accidentally meet in Reykjavík and have long, friendly conversations, only to act like virtual strangers again once they return home.

Whatever the truth of this, Icelanders seem to have no qualms about flocking to Akureyri, especially on weekends: flights from Reykjavík are packed with holidaymakers, while people from every corner of the North drive in to their figurative "big smoke" for a taste of the action. In fact, it is extremely difficult to

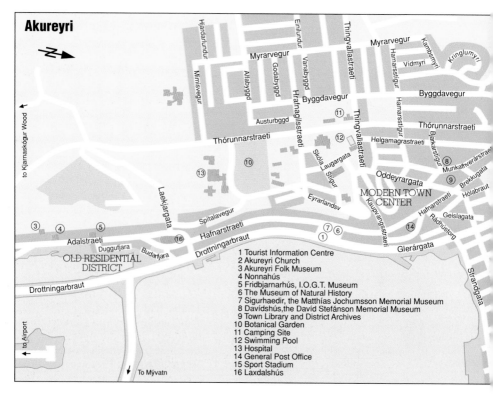

Akureyri

1 Tourist Information Centre
2 Akureyri Church
3 Akureyri Folk Museum
4 Nonnahús
5 Fridbjarnarhús, I.O.G.T. Museum
6 The Museum of Natural History
7 Sigurhaedir, the Matthías Jochumsson Memorial Museum
8 Davídshús,the David Stefánson Memorial Museum
9 Town Library and District Archives
10 Botanical Garden
11 Camping Site
12 Swimming Pool
13 Hospital
14 General Post Office
15 Sport Stadium
16 Laxdalshús

get a hotel reservation at all on summer weekends: foreign travellers should make bookings at least a week in advance. (Better still, say locals, plan to visit Akureyri on weekdays).

Exploring the town: Akureyri is compact enough to explore on foot, and the most logical place to start is the pedestrian mall of **Hafnarstraeti**. This is the *de facto* commercial centre of the town, if not its most attractive point: the buildings are the classic, characterless slabs typical of modern Icelandic towns, and, to top it off, loud piped music echoes through it on summer shopping days. The one saving grace of this part of town is an Akureyri institution, the **Bautinn** restaurant, across the road from Hafnarstraeti at Kaupvangsstraeti. Famed as one of the most reasonably priced eating spots in the whole of Iceland, it has justly been elevated to one of Akureyri's tourist attractions – ask to eat in the glassed-in pergola, which catches the sun (when it is shining).

The fjord **waterfront** is only a short hop from the mall, usually with a few picturesque trawlers sitting in port. From here, there is a good view of the basalt **Akureyri church** that has dominated the town since its construction in 1940. Designed by the architect Gudjón Samúelsson, the church can look distressingly unattractive in most lights. Even so, it is Akureyri's pride and joy, and worth the five-minute walk uphill for a visit.

Inside the church, the stained-glass windows show scenes from Icelandic history and the life of Christ in a style that can only be described as cartoon-book. There is an organ with 3,200 pipes, while the centre window in the chancel was donated by England's Coventry Cathedral – it was one of the only parts that survived the bombing during World War II. Most curious is the model ship hanging from the ceiling, a tradition in Iceland and the Faroe Islands to protect the parish's fishermen at sea.

A climb up Eyrarlandsvegur leads to the **Botanical Garden**, famed throughout Iceland for its 2,000 species of local and foreign flowers blooming without

the need of a greenhouse in Akureyri's warm microclimate. The park was set up by a local women's association in 1912, then taken over by the town in the 1950s – two of the voluntary managers are commemorated by statues (in case you were wondering who they are). With plenty of benches and well-kept lawns, the gardens make a perfect place to wind down on a sunny afternoon. On the way back to town on Eyrarlands-vegur, keep an eye out for Einar Jónsson's sculpture *The Outlaw*, depicting a saga figure named Gísli whose tale was recently turned into a film.

Historical tour: Starting back down in the pedestrian mall, a stroll south along Hafnaestraeti follows the waterline through the oldest part of Akureyri. The town boasts a plethora of small museums, although most are the homes of local literary lions and so not always of interest to many foreigners.

First comes the **Natural History Museum**, where the main attraction is a stuffed bird that is put together from various odd bird species to resemble the extinct great auk. A few doors along is the **Matthías Jochumsson Memorial Museum** (Sigurhaedir), the restored home of one of Iceland's most revered poets and dramatists. Amongst other works, Jochumsson penned the lyrics for Iceland's national anthem, *Iceland's 1,000 Years*, in 1874.

Continuing on past the combined **Tourist Information Office** and **Bus Terminal**, Hafnaerstraeti runs into Akureyri's old business district. The area still boasts many fine mansions in the so-called Icelandic frame house tradition – to the uninitiated, they look rather like Swiss chalets. The last was built in 1911, when some other styles came into vogue, including the use of metal sidings pressed into a brick pattern and painted over to look like stone and mortar.

Located near the intersection with Laekjargata is Akureyri's oldest house, **Laxdalshús**. Built in 1795, this tiny wooden building was occupied until 1978, much of the time as home to some 30 people from three or four families. It

The pedestrian mall of Hafnarstrae Akureyri.

262

has recently been restored and turned into a café – although the interior has been redesigned in sauna-style pinewood, with no concessions to history. They do have some unusual prints of old Akureyri, and show a videotape on the town's history and architecture (available in English and German).

South along the waterfront following Adalstraeti is **Fridbjarnarhús**, the museum of the International Organisation of Good Templars (a chapter opened in Akureyri in 1884), then the decidedly more appealing **Nonnahús**. This is the restored home of Reverend Jón Sveinsson, author of the Nonni series of children's books that are still well loved in Iceland and continental Europe. The house was built in 1850 and has been carefully maintained in its original form – even the kitchen still has its old implements – making this the most interesting of Akureyri's old homes, and worth visiting even if you've never heard of young Nonni and his antics.

Finally, the **Akureyri Folk Museum** (Minjasafn) has an exhaustive collec-tion of local memorabilia, from old farming tools to milk cartons, as well as some excellent 19th-century photographs. Outside, a small church, which was moved from Svalbard across the fjord, sits beside Iceland's first nursery.

Anyone still not sated by museums can head back into town and find **Davídshús** on Bjardarstigur, the 1944 home of poet Davíd Stefánsson left as it was when he died. A short walk away, located on a rock between Glerargata and Thorunnarstraeti, is a statue of Helgi the Lean, with an impressive view over Eyjafjördur.

Short excursions: Pleasant as strolling around Akureyri can be, the real attraction is the surrounding area.

A few short trips are very close to town. Only an hour on foot or 10 minutes' drive south is **Kjarnaskógur** forest, one of Iceland's few spots with trees and a popular picnic place.

Hikers can head for the symmetrical, Fuji-like **Mt Sulur**, visible on clear days from Akureyri. Drive west on Suluvegar (past the garbage dump) to the

ew paint
.

small creek – look out for a wooden ladder over the barbed wire, then follow the yellow markers. Allow several hours of hard (and not very inspiring) walking to reach the 1,144-metre (3,750-ft) summit looking out over the **Glera valley**.

In winter, skiing fans head for the **Skidastadir Lodge** at **Hlidarfjall**, offering the best slopes in the area only a 10-minute drive from town. Many non-skiers also head there for the view of the Vindhimajökull glacier.

Exploring the fjord: Perhaps the most popular day trip from Akureyri – and one that can be driven alone or organised through the tourist office – is along the western flank of Eyjafjördur fjord. The well-paved Route 82 offers sweeping views over the rich farming land of the area, bounded in by glacier-formed mountains to the west (although their peaks are often buried behind a steady line of grey cloud) and steely blue waters to the east.

The district here is known as **Arkógsströnd**. As in the rest of the north, the fields are dotted in summer with hundreds of gigantic white plastic balls containing hay to be stored for the winter – a high-tech innovation that has quickly replaced the more poetic but inefficient methods of traditional hay-gathering in Iceland. Cows, sheep and geese wander at will, and it is not at all unusual for traffic to be stopped while a five-year-old boy leads a line of cattle across the road to pasture.

Although Route 28 can be followed directly north, a turnoff at Route 816 leads to a ruined port area from earlier this century at Gaesabaer, while another short side road (Route 813) leads to the farm **Mödruvellir**, birthplace of the writer Jón Sveinsson (whose house has been turned into the Nonnahús museum in Akureyri).

There is a much-photographed farmhouse at **Staerri-Arskogur**, flush against a steep mountain backdrop.

Dalvík (population 1,500) is the dominant town on this side of the fjord. A prosperous fishing village today, Dalvík's claim to fame in Iceland is the memory of a 1934 earthquake measur-

Boarding th ferry at Hrísey isla

ing 6.3 on the Richter scale that brought rocks crashing down from the nearby mountainside and destroyed about half the town's homes. These days, travellers call in at Dalvík mainly to catch the ferry over to **Hrísey island** – the second largest island off Iceland's coast, giving Eyjafjördur ("island fjord") its name.

On a fine day, the 20-minute trip to Hrísey is well worthwhile – on weekends, there are usually some well-dressed folk from Akureyri making the excursion solely to dine on the island's speciality, Galloway beef, served up at the Brekka restaurant (this is the only place in Iceland that Galloway cattle are raised, and it is prohibited by law to remove them to the mainland).

There is a small village here with a church for the 300 or so inhabitants, which during World War II was the billet for five British servicemen. In what sounds like ideal material for a one-act play, the soldiers' job was to check up on all trawlers entering the fjord, with only a broken machine gun to back them up.

Much of Hrísey is a nature reserve and so off-limits to hikers, but there are still plenty of trails across the flat moorlands, covered in purple heather and full of birdlife. On a clear day, the towering mountains of the eastern fjord seem to be only a stone's throw away.

Back on the mainland, a popular side trip from Dalvík is into **Svarfadardalur** valley, entering on Route 805 and returning along Route 807. From the end of Route 805, hikers and horseback riders can head into the wilderness of **Heljardalsheidi** for camping journeys in what many consider some of the finest mountain country in Iceland.

North of Dalvík, a nerve-wracking and treacherous gravel road winding along the steep coastline was made more bearable by the opening in 1991 of a 3.4-km (2.1-mile) tunnel. A spectacular feat of engineering, this one-lane passage through the mountainside has become something of a tourist attraction in itself, although claustrophobes might prefer to risk the old road around the headland of **Olafsfjardamúli** – which,

e
**untains of
afjördur
m on
sey's
rizon.**

incidentally, is a good place to see the midnight sun in July, offering views on a clear day as far as Grímsey island, on the Arctic Circle.

Olafsfördur is a fishing village of 1,200 people nestled amongst a ring of snow-capped, 1,200-metre (3,900-ft) high peaks. But, despite the setting, it has little more of interest than fishing boats and factories, and so makes a good point to turn back to Akureyri.

Points south: Heading south from Akureyri, Route 821 runs along the **Eyjafjardará** river valley.

The pretty farm **Kristnes**, built on the site where Helgi the Lean first settled, is located 7 km (4 miles) along on a hill with a strategic view of the fjord. A few minutes further south is another farm, **Grund**, with one of the most unusual churches in Iceland – with its several Romanesque spires, it looks transplanted from St Petersburg. The farmer Magnús Sigurdsson built it to his own design in 1906 to serve the whole river valley. Apart from its unusual Russian look, the church broke a nearly millennium-old tradition by being built on a north-south axis instead of east-west.

A good example of a more traditional church, made of turf and stone, is at the farm of **Saubaer**, 27 km (17 miles) south of Akureyri on Route 821. The quaint interior is open to visitors. At this point, the road continues to the farm of **Tortufell** (with farmhouse accommodation), or across the river valley to return to Akureyri on Route 829. En route is the historic farm of **Munkathverá**. Originally known as Thverá, this was the birthplace in the 10th century of the notorious Odin-worshipping Viking Víga-Glúmur, and all around this part of the valley is the backdrop for *Víga-Glúms Saga*. In the 12th century, a Benedictine monastery was built on the site, although none of it remains.

Finally, at **Ytri-holl**, keep an eye out for a classic turf house that is still in use: the tiny chimney poking out from the grassy roof only makes it look even more like a hobbit's house.

Eyjafjördur's eastern shore: The Ring Road runs east of Akureyri – giving

The farmhouse at Grund.

some of the best views of the town – before running north and heading into the **Grýtubakkahreppur district.**

Turn off at Route 83 for **Laufás**, a beautifully-situated farm looking out over Eyjafjördur with a small white church and 19th-century turf farmhouse **museum**. Built in the 1860s, the dirt-floored building was a vicarage and upper-crust home, and is now crowded with antiques. A famous touch is the carved woman's face and duck placed like a masthead over the middle segment of the farmhouse.

Just 22 km (14 miles) from the Ring Road turnoff is the picturesque but somnolent fishing town of **Grenivík** (population 300). Only founded in 1910, Grenivík is at the edge of the rugged **Fjördur peninsula**, which has been uninhabited since World War II. Horseback expeditions into this remote area are offered by Polar Horses at the farm **Grýtubakki II**, 4 km (2½ miles) south of Grenivík.

The Ring Road continues east towards Lake Mývatn, but first passes the small Lake **Ljesavatn** ("lightwater") and turnoff to the farm of the same name. Although there is no evidence of it now, this was the Saga Age farm of the great chieftain Thorgeir Thorkelsson, who was Law Speaker in the Althing in AD 1000 and was forced to decide whether Iceland should be pagan or Christian. As the *Kristni Saga* tells it, Thorgeir spent 24 hours under his cloak before deciding for the Christians. Riding back from Thingvellir to his home at Ljesavatn, he passed a giant waterfall and decided to toss all his carved images of pagan gods into its waters.

This powerful waterfall, **Godafoss** ("fall of the gods"), is virtually sitting beneath the Ring Road a few kilometres further on, and is the easiest of Iceland's major falls to visit. Most cars and buses en route to Mývatn make a stop here at the small petrol station/store at **Fosshall**.

The surrounding area of the **Bardardalur** valley is a 7,000-year-old lava flow, through which the **Skalfandafljot** river has cut a path to form the waterfall of the gods.

ICELANDIC HAUNTINGS

Ohne in every 500 inhabitants of Iceland is a ghost. According to *Vae Hartal*, the spiritual *Who's Who* of Iceland by folklore historian Arni Björnsson, more than 500 ghouls, trolls, and paranormal beings haunt the island, making a substantial – or perhaps insubstantial – addition to its quarter of a million population. This high ghost quotient is not unexpected, as Iceland is the perfect home for any spook, with long periods of darkness in winter and an abundance of grotesque rock and lava formations providing perfect camouflage for monsters and ogres.

Flesh-and-blood Icelanders, it seems, enjoy excellent relations with their neighbours from the other world. In a survey on the supernatural in Western Europe, Icelanders topped the league for ghostly experiences, with 41 percent claiming contact with the dead, compared to the European average of 20 percent.

Traditionally, however, ghosts were not harmless visitations from the dear departed. They usually took the form of an *afturganga*, a dead man turned zombie, and were capable of killing people or (worse) taking them to hell. Only the spiritual powers of a priest or the physical prowess of a strongman could exorcise such a nightmarish spook.

A very uncomfortable characteristic of the *afturganga* is his tendency to walk again before anyone knows he has died. One such was the Deacon of Dark River, who drowned on his way to pick up his girlfriend to take her to a dance. Nonetheless, he turned up, just a little late, and the unsuspecting girl got on the back of his horse. As they rode through the night, she overheard him muttering:

the moon hides, as death rides,
do you not see the white mark
on my brow, Garun, Garun.

Fortunately, this ditty held two clues to his true nature: firstly, ghosts always repeat things, and secondly they cannot say "God." The girl's name was Gudrún, and Gud is "God" in Icelandic. The terrified Gudrún managed to jump off – seconds before the ghostly rider and horse disappeared into an open grave leading straight to hell. She was never the same again, and some say she lost her mind completely.

Other forms of ghost are the *fylgja* or familiar spirit, and its close relations the *mori* or the *skotta*. These are shadowy, malevolent spirits, and when they are ill-wished onto a man, they will follow him and his descendants unto the ninth generation.

Then there are the trolls – elemental beings who, fortunately, turn into stone if they are caught outside in daylight. All of Iceland is dotted with trolls who stayed out just that little bit too long – including the great stone troll-cow, Hvítserkur, caught having a drink of sea-water just off the north-west coast of Iceland.

All things considered, Icelanders probably prefer their more attractive other-worldly neighbours, the elves. Like Hollywood filmstars, they look like humans – but are richer, more glamourous and usually completely amoral.

According to one legend, the elves were the children that Eve hadn't finished washing when God came to visit – they were not fit to be seen, so she had to hide

Elf-maiden rising from her grotto.

268

them. Thus, they are also known as the Hidden People, and with good reason – only 5 percent of Icelanders have actually met one. Nevertheless, elves are held in the highest regard, with 53 percent of the population either believing in, or not denying, their existence.

In legend, those who visit the elves and survive the experience return to the human world laden with riches but often strangely changed. In nearly all cases, the elves decide when and where they will be seen by humans. Usually it is when they need their assistance. Human women, it is said, are sometimes fetched by distraught elfen husbands to act as mid-wives to elf-mothers who are having difficulties in childbirth.

One 20th-century figure to have had an encounter with the Hidden People was trade-union leader Tryggvi Einarsson, who, as a young man, was saved from death by an elf-maiden after he had fallen down a gully. Her beauty, he said, haunted him the rest of his life. Elf-women have been known to have even more intimate physical relations with human men, and are obviously more liberated than their human counterparts, often leaving their lovers holding the baby, as it were.

It is of some consolation that these semi-supernatural offspring are usually highly talented and handsome. Elf-men, on the other hand, make conscientious and kind lovers, according to tales of the few women who have been lucky enough to have tried one out.

The elves of Iceland are treated with great respect. The rocks and hills in which they make their homes are diligently preserved, for great harm traditionally comes to those that tamper with these elusive neighbours. Roads skirt round well-known elf-hills. One such is the road that runs from Reykjavík to the suburb of Kópa-vogur, which is actually called Alfholsvegur, or Elf-Hill Road. On the main street of the town of Grundarfjördur, a rock stands between the houses numbered 82 and 86 – the elves live at number 84.

Despite these superstitious gestures, Dr Árni Björnsson says that true believers in elves and ghosts are only a small minority in Iceland. "Most of us do not actively believe in these things, but on the other hand we are reluctant to deny their existence," he says. "It is really a form of scepticism. We live in a land which is highly unpredictable – what is grass and meadow today could be lava and ash tomorrow. So we have learnt not to rely too much on the factual evidence of our senses."

And of course the existence of elves is such a nice idea. "People think it would be fun if they did exist, so they pretend to believe in them. Unlike other nations, we aren't in the least ashamed of it. In fact, we are rather proud of our elves."

"Iceland is a big country for such a small population," he adds. "We've plenty of room for neighbours of all kinds."

Indeed, this laissez-faire attitude is ensconced in folk tradition and the sagas. The medieval bishop, Gudmundur the Good, once set off to consecrate Drangey, to drive away the multitude of ghouls, fiends and devils that haunted this island. As he went about his holy work, a voice rang out from the rocks. "Consecrate no more, Gudmundur," it cried. "The wicked need some place to be." The bishop sensibly took the point and went back to the shore, where his boat was waiting. ■

rowdy trio f trolls.

GRÍMSEY

The folk on the remote, weather-beaten island of Grímsey tell the tale of a local minister who discovered that the Arctic Circle ran right through his house. He decided that it not only bisected his bedroom, it bisected his bed: the minister slept on one side of the Arctic Circle, his wife on the other, and rarely did either cross the great divide.

The apocryphal story is told and re-told in various forms (sometimes it's a minister, sometimes an old magistrate), but it sums up the tongue-in-cheek attitude the Grímsey islanders have to the Arctic Circle – an imaginary line which, to the outside world, puts Grímsey on the map. They can only regard with some bemusement anyone who makes the pilgrimage all the way to their remote polar outpost just to say that they've walked across a geographical abstraction. "How did it feel?" someone might ask with good-natured concern. "Have your feet turned blue yet?"

But, although its location on latitude 66°30' N may still be Grímsey's claim to fame, a steady stream of travellers are finding out that the island has more concrete attractions to offer. The sheer isolation of this tiny piece of land, with a population of only just over 100, has its own peculiarly Icelandic appeal: the scenery is wild and beautiful, the birdlife extraordinary, while the people remain beguilingly eccentric. And Grímsey has one of the strangest histories in Iceland, settled by chess-playing Vikings and supported by a 19th-century American millionaire. (And, frankly, it *is* quite fun to know that you're standing on the Arctic Circle.)

Island of chess-players: Grímsey was first settled in the 10th century by a Viking named Grímur (hence the name Grím's island), whose descendants took the Icelandic obsession with chess to new extremes. Tradition has it that long summers and longer winters were spent

Preceding pages, fish-drying, the tradition-al way. **Right**, Grímsey is a remote place.

devoted to the game, with some players spending weeks confined to their beds devising new stratagems. Chess was more important than life itself: it was not unknown for a player to fling himself into the sea rather than bear the shame of defeat.

Perhaps not surprisingly, Grímsey did not prosper as a fishing port. On one occasion in the 18th century, the entire male population except for the minister was lost in a single fishing accident (perhaps they were exhausted from playing chess). According to folklore, the minister took responsibility for re-populating the island himself.

Then, in the late 19th century, the island's eccentric reputation was brought to the attention of a wealthy North American named Daniel Willard Fiske – prominent journalist, Old Icelandic scholar, friend of both the Icelandic independence hero Jón Sigurdsson and the writer Mark Twain, and, in 1857, chess champion of the United States. Although Willard Fiske only ever glimpsed the shores of Grímsey as he passed it in a steamship, the island fired his vivid imagination and he decided to take its local population under his wing.

First Fiske sent the essentials: a gift of 11 marble chess sets to each of the farms on the island. These were followed by masses of firewood and a bequest to finance the island's first school and library. Finally, on his death in 1904, Fiske left the inhabitants of Grímsey $12,000 – at that time the most money anyone had ever given to Iceland.

Today, Fiske is still revered on Grímsey as a sort of secular saint. His birthday on 11 November is celebrated every year with a meeting and coffee in the community hall. Fiske's portrait still hangs in the library, while a large number of male islanders sport the decidedly un-Icelandic name of Willard.

Unfortunately, Grímsey hasn't kept up the love of chess. Hardly anybody plays it – these days, the favourite game is bridge.

Last stop before the Pole: Until the 1930s, the only way to reach Grímsey was on the mail ship that left Akureyri

A portrait o
Willard Fis
still hangs
the library
(left), wher
the last of l
donated
marble che
sets is also
kept (below

once every six months (you could return six months later, provided bad weather didn't prevent the ship from running).

Today, there is a twice-weekly ship service in summer, taking about six hours each way from Akureyri, while daily light aircraft flights take only 25 minutes to cover the 41 km (25 miles). Both allow travellers to return from the island on the same day – which, until 1991 when a new guest house opened, was just as well, since the only accommodation was on the floor of the community centre. (Camping is permitted if you site your tent discreetly.)

Getting acquainted with the island is not difficult. It is only 4 km (2.4 miles) by 2 km (1.2 miles) in size, and can be entirely walked around in about 5 hours. There are 10 old farms on the island, but most of the inhabitants live in the "village" of Sandvík – the name for the 15 houses lined up along the harbour.

At the end of World War II, Grímsey still didn't have electricity, there was little fresh water and the occasional case of scurvy was reported amongst the islanders. Modern fishing techniques have brought Iceland's new affluence even to remote Grímsey, and, although the township has a rather scruffy look, the houses are modern, there are radio dishes to pick up television, and greenhouses to grow vegetables. A large indoor swimming pool has been completed, and although there is only one road on Grímsey – and that only 3 km (2 miles) long – the island boasts 10 private cars and a dozen tractors.

The Grímsey **community centre** can be identified by the mural on its walls. Built on the site of the old school financed by Fiske, it still contains the library, original photographs of the benefactor and the only one of the 11 marble chess sets still in existence. Nobody seems to know where the rest have disappeared to.

A short walk west of the village is the whitewashed, turn-of-the-century wooden **church**. Above the altar is a replica of Leonardo da Vinci's famous *Last Supper*, painted by a mainland artist, Arngrímur Gíslason. The nearby

tic terns
k around
island,
in
nmer
ebomb
sersby.

parsonage, which was built in 1909, is now run by a layman – Grímsey pays for a minister to come every three months from Akureyri (if he wants to come more often, he has to pay for the journey himself). With an average age of 28, the community more readily coughs up US$2,000 a time to fly rock bands out from the mainland for concerts.

Along the coast are the traditional fish-drying racks. There are four fish processing plants on the island, concentrating on salted fish and dried cod-heads (which are sold to Nigeria). Sheep used to wander the island until 1988, when an outbreak of scrapie, a stock disease, forced them all to be put down.

In 1973, an unexpected addition to the island's wildlife collection appeared in the form of a polar bear that had floated over from Greenland on an iceberg. It was promptly hunted down and dispatched with a bullet in the head, and it is now stuffed in the museum in Húsavík on the coast.

Dive-bombers of the Arctic Circle: Heading back to the eastern end of the island, the road runs straight into the bitumen runway of the **airport** (where the new **Basar guesthouse**, offering the island's only formal accommodation, is also to be found). The runway is carpeted by resting sea birds – before some landings or takeoffs, a car is driven up and down in an attempt to shoo away these potential hazards to aircraft.

Usually that's the end of the matter. Should you be visiting in June or July, however, the scene is more like something from Alfred Hitchcock's *The Birds*. That's when the arctic terns are nesting all over the island, and anyone coming near a bird's young is fair game for a divebomb attack. The screeching call *kría*! *kría*! *kría*! (which is actually the bird's name in Icelandic) is the prelude to a possible peck on the back of the head – which is why, in this season, everyone wears a thick hat (a leather glove under a beany or beret is recommended) and carries a big stick (the Basar guesthouse will lend a plastic rod for self-defence).

On the northern side of the runway is the Grímsey **road sign**, theoretically marking the location of the Arctic Circle. Arrows point to various world highlights: (New York: 4,448 km/2,763 miles; Sydney: 16,137 km/10,027 miles; London: 1,972 km/1,225 miles), although for some reason the North Pole doesn't get a mention.

A path leads away from the airport towards 100-metre (320-ft) cliff faces, which can be followed completely around the island. Soon the trail disappears beneath a bed of thick, matted grass, which seems to glow green against the blue of the sea. The polka-dot of yellow weeds finishes off the colourful effect (there are some 100 species of flowering plant on Grímsey).

The cliffs on the north and east of the island are also where the most spectacular birdlife can be found, creating a din that is little short of cacophonous. Thirty-six species of bird nest on the island, including 11 different types of sea bird. There is a large puffin community, and it is quite possible to come within a few metres of these birds (but don't walk too close to the edge of the cliffs, since underground puffin nests can be accidentally crushed). There are fulmars, kittiwakes, gulls and arctic terns, and Grímsey is the last place in Iceland where the little auk breeds (only two or three pairs are left, the rest all staying closer to the Pole).

Although it is placed on the Arctic Circle, Grímsey's summers and winters are never as extreme as one would imagine: the June midnight is bright but never blinding, and there are about four hours of vague light in December (provided the weather isn't very cloudy, that is, in which case it stays dark).

Even so, life on the island is still tough, and it says something of the islanders' spirit that they have kept their numbers hovering at over 110 while other tiny Icelandic islands have lost their wealth and population. Schoolchildren, who spend their last three years studying on the mainland, almost always come home to Grímsey. Even though not many play chess here now, the island still shows the eccentric, indomitable spirit that inspired the old benefactor Daniel Willard Fiske.

The glow o the midnig sun.

LAKE MÝVATN

Sitting just to the west of the Mid-Atlantic ridge that is slowly tearing Iceland apart, the Lake Mývatn district is one of the most volcanically active regions on earth. In the mid-1970s, earthquakes centred here were felt in the entire north of the country, with lava erupting from nearby Mt Krafla over several years to spectacular effect. Activity continued through the early 1980s and today there are almost daily subterranean rumblings (although they are mostly too small to be noticed except by scientific instruments). Nowhere else in Iceland can you see the same combination of craters, fresh lava fields, hot springs, geysers and bubbling mud pools.

Meanwhile, the lake's natural beauty and role as a wildlife breeding ground led to it being set aside as a national conservation area in 1974 – a status that actually gives it more protection than a National Park. The lake is a veritable oasis on the fringes of Iceland's bleak northern deserts, supporting, amongst other things, the world's largest population of breeding ducks. As a result, Mývatn has established itself as Iceland's number one tourist attraction outside of the "Golden Circle" and a place that has been known to keep nature lovers occupied for weeks.

In search of sulphur: Although the winters are long and cold, covering the lake with ice for seven months of the year, Mývatn enjoys more sunshine and receives less rain than almost anywhere else in the country. As a result, it has been popular with settlers from the Saga Age onwards: in 1908, archaeologists dug up a Norse long house whose wall was over 40 metres (130 ft) long, and may have contained a temple of Thor.

Dating their ancestry back to those days are the Reykjahlíd family, whose farm covers the whole surrounding area – at some 6,000 sq. km (2,300 sq. miles) in size, it is the biggest in Iceland and

Preceding pages: Route 87 from Húsavík to Lake Myvatn. **Left**, Myvatn at dusk.

more than twice the size of Luxembourg. The family's days glory were in the 14th century, when sulphur was mined from Námaskard on their land and sent to Europe to be made into gunpowder. This remote corner of Iceland helped keep the world's wars rolling until the 19th century, when other sulphur sources were found.

Farming in the area also prospered despite the devastating eruption of the Leirhnjúkur crater (10 km/6 miles northeast of Reykjahlíd). The "Mývatn fires" lasted for five years, from 1724 to 1729, wiped out three farms and wrecked Reykjahlíd's buildings – but created some of the bizarre lava formations which now make the area so interesting.

Today the farm is still working, although the owners have invested in the tourist business and allow visitors access to almost every part of the property. Travellers started arriving in numbers earlier this century, and the family built the first hotel, the Hotel Reykjahlíd, in the 1940s – it has since housed everyone from Prince Harald of Norway to a steady stream of backpackers. In 1968, a diatomite plant was opened at Mývatn, and a small village, **Reykjahlíd**, sprang up around the hotel to become the service centre of the area.

With hotels, camping grounds, supermarkets and snack bars, Reykjalíd is a functional if characterless base for travellers. It does boast the local **church** – although it was rebuilt in 1972, it is on the site of the original church that was in the path of the lava flow in 1729 and seemed certain to be destroyed. Miraculously, the lava parted literally at the church door and flowed on either side of the wooden building, an event that the devout naturally ascribed to divine intervention.

Circuit around the Lake: A mostly dirt road circles Lake Mývatn connecting points of interest. The lake itself is 37 sq. km (14 sq. miles) in area, making it the fourth-largest in Iceland, but unusually shallow – the average depth is only 2 metres (7 ft), with the deepest point only 4.5 metres (15 ft). This shallowness allows the sun's rays to reach the

The crater Hverfjall, overshadow Reykjavík.

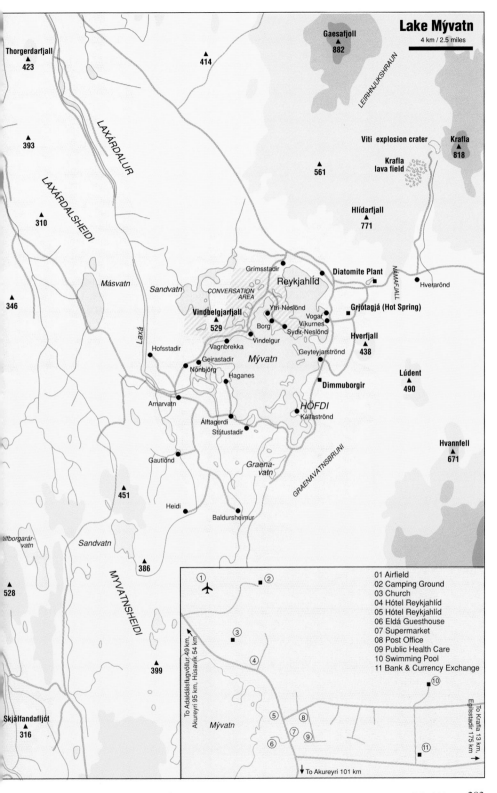

Lake Mývatn

4 km / 2.5 miles

Thorgerdarfjall ▲ 423

Gaesafjoll ▲ 882

▲ 414

LEIRHNJÚKSHRAUN

LAXÁRDALUR

▲ 393

▲ 310

LAXÁRDALSHEIDI

Viti explosion crater

Krafla ▲ 818

▲ 561

Krafla lava field

Hlídarfjall ▲ 771

Másvatn

Sandvatn

▲ 346

Grimsstadir

Reykjahlíd

Diatomite Plant

NÁMAFJALL

Hverarönd

CONVERSATION AREA

Vindbelgjarfjall ▲ 529

Ytri-Neslönd

Vogar
Vikurnes
Sydri-Neslönd

Grjótagjá (Hot Spring)

Borg

Laxá

Hofsstadir

Vagnbrekka

Vindelgur

Hverfjall ▲ 438

Geirastadir

Mývatn

Geyteyjarströnd

Nónbjörg

Haganes

Lúdent ▲ 490

Dimmuborgir

Arnarvatn

HÖFDI

Kálfaströnd

Álftagerdi

Stútustadir

Hvannfell ▲ 671

Gautlönd

Graena-vatn

GRAENAVATNSBRUNI

▲ 451

Heidi

Baldursheimur

álfborgarár-vatn

Sandvatn

▲ 528

MYVATNSHEIDI

▲ 386

①

②

✈

③

④

⑤ ⑧
⑦ ⑨
⑥

⑩

⑪

399

Skjálfandafljót ▲ 316

To Adaldalsflugvöllur 49 km,
Akureyri 95 km, Húsavík 54 km

Mývatn

To Akureyri 101 km

To Krafla 13 km,
Egilsstadir 175 km

01 Airfield
02 Camping Ground
03 Church
04 Hótel Reykjahlíd
05 Hótel Reykjahlíd
06 Eldá Guesthouse
07 Supermarket
08 Post Office
09 Public Health Care
10 Swimming Pool
11 Bank & Currency Exchange

bottom to create a thriving growth of algae and plankton. There are 50 islets.

The name Mývatn actually means "midge lake" and, for long stretches of the summer, clouds of these tiny flying insects can make any visit a misery. Literally billions usually emerge in June and August to dive into eyes, noses and ears with relentless energy. They are often joined by biting blackflies, so make sure you bring some insect repellent. It is cold comfort to learn that the midges are crucial to the lake's ecosystem: their corpses fertilise the lakeside and larvae are a staple for birds and fish.

The surfeit of midges to dine on has also made the River Laxá, which flows through Mývatn, the source of Iceland's biggest salmon (they spawn in the lower part of the lake). Mývatn offers the best trout fishing in the country, and in winter local farmers still cut holes through the ice to lower their hooks – part of a ritual dating back to the Middle Ages, when fish were the only winter food and could mean the difference between life and death.

The fields of fire: Heading north from Reykjahlíd, Route 87 crosses the lava flow from the 1720s that dominates the topography of the village and the northern landscape of the lake. Called **Eldhraun** ("fire lava"), this barren landscape gives a glimpse of the desert that Route 87 runs into – so devoid of life that NASA sent its Apollo 11 crew for training missions here in the late 1960s. Keep an eye out on the left for a giant bubble of dried lava, where the surface layer has been cracked like a huge egg.

Turning left onto Route 848, the landscape becomes much greener and quickly enters the marshes of the **Conservation Area**. This is the main breeding ground for the lake's birds, and during the nesting season (15 May to 20 July) its shoreline is off-limits. Fifteen species of duck have been recorded on the lake, and up to 100,000 birds can be gathered here at once. Amongst other species, almost the entire European population of Barrow's goldeneye birds breed here. The view overlooking the bird-dotted lake from **Neslangatangi**

The bizarre lava formations a Dimmubórg

peninsula, which almost cuts the lake in two, is particularly serene at dusk.

South of the conservation area, the 530-metre (1,750-ft) peak of **Vindbelg-jarfjall**, seen to the right, can be climbed in a couple of hours for views of the lake. Beyond that, another smaller lake, **Sandvatn**, is probably the best place to see gyrfalcons.

South of here, the road now runs into the Ring Road. Devotees swear that the bridge over the Laxá river here is Iceland's premier location, bar none, for spotting birds. On the southern shore of the lake is Mývatn's secondary service centre of **Skútustadir**, with a petrol station, church and snack shop.

From here, there is an easy hour-long path around the **Skútustadagígar** pseudo-craters. These were formed when water was trapped beneath flowing lava, boiled and burst up through the surface, creating what looks like volcanic cones. Some were formed so recently that their sides are still charred.

Picnic promontory: One of the most sheltered and relaxing spots on the lakeside is **Höfdi**, a forested promontory that has been turned into a reserve, with a small admission fee. There is a vaguely fairy-tale atmosphere to the place, with paths running through flower-covered lava outcrops and forests of birch trees. Large rocks by the lakeside rocks also provide ideal picnic hideaways.

A turnoff to the right leads to **Dimmu-bórgir** ("black castles"), a vast, 2,000-year-old field of contorted volcanic pillars, some as tall as 20 metres (65 ft). There is a viewing platform over the expanse, and visitors can wander about amongst the haunting arches, caves and natural tunnels. The most famous formation is Kirkjan (the Church), which looks like the interior of a Gothic cathedral, and a 3-metre (16-ft) hole that provides an amusing opportunity to take a photograph.

Further along the same road is the looming crater of **Hverfjall**, formed in an eruption 2,500 years ago and these days likened to a giant football stadium. A steep path runs up the side of the

crater which is made entirely of loose volcanic rubble, or tephra. Hverfjall's rim provides one of the most sweeping views of the Mývatn area. Inside the 1,000-metre (3,280-ft) wide crater, hikers have written messages in huge letters of light-coloured stone.

En route back to Reykjahlíd, by the left side of the road is **Grjótagjá**, an underground hot spring made by a buckle in the earth (the site is unmarked but a space for parking has been cleared beside it). The green waters feel tepid to the touch but below the surface can be scalding, so swimming is forbidden.

Volcanologists' paradise: The Ring Road running east of Reykjahlíd immediately leads to a completely different landscape, a desolate, sandy plain of mixed orange and brown hues known as **Bjarnarflag**. On the left is Mývatn's **diatomite plant**, processing the microscopic fossils called diatoms that are taken from the lake's floor; on the right is a brick factory, putting the local excess of tephra to practical use. These are the only survivors of a long string of entrepreneurial failures here this century, including attempts to mine sulphur and harness geothermal energy. Easily visible is a huge spraying vent of steam from a bore hole dug 2 km (1¼ miles) down into the earth, the result of a test for a proposed geothermal plant.

Mývatn's contribution to Icelandic cuisine, the sweet, sticky bread called *hverabraud*, is baked in the ground here (metal lids can be spotted in between the brick factory and the highway). The finished product can be bought at the supermarket.

An overwhelming stench of sulphur greets travellers as the road climbs over the ridge of **Namafjall**, whose series of cracks – the largest appeared as recently as 1975 – betray its location plumb on the Mid-Atlantic Ridge. At the pass is a parking area with views over the lake, and, stretching out on the other side is the famous boiling mud pit of **Hverarönd** – perhaps one of Iceland's most infernal and fascinating sights. Walkways run across the multi-coloured clay of the area, through dozens of bubbling

The bubbling mud pools Hverarönd.

pits and steaming vents. The surface here is particularly thin, and at some places likely to crumble, so to avoid being boiled alive in a mud pot, keep well within the marked paths.

Man-made disaster: A rough dirt road leads 7 km (4 miles) north to the **Krafla** area, source of the most recent volcanic activity. Pipes from the **Krafla geothermal power plant** form a metal doorway to the region, which is strangely appropriate: the construction of the plant in 1973, with its many bore holes into the earth's crust, are considered responsible for the eruptions that began here in 1975 – the first since the 1700s.

The activity began with a dramatic spurt of molten lava that lit up Reykjalíd by night. Some 15 eruptions followed in the next decade, but luckily the lava all flowed away from the small village and no major damage was done. Even so, the earth's thin crust has regularly risen and fallen several centimetres at a time as magma moves through underground chambers, and volcanologists are expecting Krafla to blow again any time.

A stern warning sign (VOLCANIC HAZARD ZONE – DO NOT ENTER) at the first parking area here was put up in the 1980s to keep tourists away, but had the opposite effect: hundreds gathered here to see what would happen. It seems to serve the same purpose today, directing a stream of visitors out to the black, still-warm lava field of **Kröfluöskjunni** that was spat up from the earth during the 1970s and 1980s, and the crater of **Leirhnjúkur** (formed during the explosions of the 1720s). If you can forget the disconcerting possibility of being blown to kingdom come, this whole lifeless, primeval area gives as good a glimpse of the freshly-formed earth as anyone is likely to get.

Further on, a second parking area sits at the base of **Viti**, a colourful explosion crater whose name is Icelandic for "hell" and which was the initial source of the 1725 eruptions. This is close to Mt Krafla, which, far from being a classic volcanic cone, is the rim of a larger caldera that has been worn and exploded almost beyond recognition.

crater, r Mt fla.

THE NORTH EAST

Bypassed by the Ring Road and its stream of regular traffic, the North East is one of Iceland's most isolated areas. Only the growing fame of the Jökulsárgljúfur National Park usually brings travellers here, with very few continuing on to explore the rugged coastline – largely because of poor transport services, bad roads and few good hotels.

Yet the coastal route has a number of attractions for those with their own transport and an interest in finding out what lies off the beaten track. Dozens of atmospheric fishing towns cling precariously to this shore just south of the Arctic Circle. Exploring these quiet, conservative outposts and the wilderness areas around them reveals the harsh seafaring world that is in many ways Iceland's backbone.

Gateway to the North-East: The transport artery of the region, following the whole coastline, is Route 85. Approaching from either Akureyri or Lake Mývatn, this road runs through the **Adaldalur** valley to the shoreline of **Skjálfandi** ("shivering fjord"), an expanse of sand dotted by small lakes with an impressive wall of mountains as a backdrop.

Rows of picturesque fish-drying racks by the roadside fittingly announce the main town in the region, **Húsavík** (population 2,500). The name "house bay" was given by the Swedish Viking Gardar Svavarsson, who journeyed to Iceland in AD 850 after his mother had seen it in a dream.

Long before the official First Settler, Ingólfur Arnarson, set foot on the island, Gardar spent a winter at Húsavík – and, when he left, an unfortunate fellow named Náttafari was left behind with two slaves. The trio settled down permanently across the bay from Húsavík (the site can be seen from town), but have been disqualified from being considered Iceland's first settlers because their presence was involuntary.

<u>Left</u>, the canyon Asbyrgi in Jökulságláfur National Park.

Húsavík today is a tidy and agreeable town set above the first-rate **harbour** that provides for its existence: nearly everyone who lives here is involved with fishing or fish processing. The view of the colourful trawlers, murky black waters and snow-spattered granite mountains across the bay is particularly impressive. Near the docks is the headquarters of the Thingeyjarsýsla Cooperative Society, established in 1882, the first of its kind in Iceland and a landmark in Húsavík's growth.

Dominating the town is an unusual cross-shaped **church**, with a 26-metre (85-ft) spire and some typically grotesque modern sculptures in the garden. The local **museum** (Safnahusid) is the best in the North East: prize exhibits include a replica of the 1584 Gudbrandur's Bible (the first translation of the Old and New Testaments into Icelandic, still considered the most ambitious publishing project ever undertaken in Iceland); and the polar bear that floated from Greenland to Grímsey island in 1973 only to be greeted by a bullet in the skull and then stuffed.

Arctic vista: For a panoramic view over the whole Húsavík area, drive a kilometre north of town to the unmarked yellow gate on the right, then continue as far as your car can take you (only a four-wheel drive should attempt the full distance on this dangerously slippery road). There is a **viewfinder** at the top, from which you can spot two small islands in the bay: **Flatey** had over 100 inhabitants 50 years ago but has now been abandoned, while **Lundey** is crowded only with puffins.

From this point onwards, the roads become dustier and road signs fewer. Lying north along Route 85 is the squat peninsula of **Tjörnes**, whose 60-metre (200-ft) cliff faces are renowned among geologists for their ancient fossils and easily visible geological strata. Non-geologists can get an idea of what is going on at a well-known but difficult to find site by the seashore, turning off on a dirt road to the left at the **Ytri-tunga** farmhouse (the farm is unmarked but the road is before the **Hallbjarnarstadir** farm, and crosses an electric fence).

The road reaches the coast, then steeply descends the alarming cliff face at **Hallbjarnarstadakambur Crest**, a dip on either side of the river where the layers of geological deposits are obvious to the naked eye and fossils of molluscs can be picked out of the earth. At the shore, look out for a large greenish slab of rock that is not native to Iceland, and is thought to have arrived from Greenland on sea-ice.

East of Tjörnes, the plain of **Kelduhverfi** is made up of sandy glacial wash (similar to the larger *sandur* in the South), and is at the northern point where the two halves of Iceland are splitting apart. Volcanic activity in the 1970s here was related to the eruptions at Krafla near Lake Mývatn, with fissures appearing that are still visible. The whole area is at the mouth of the **Oxafjördur** fjord. To the north of the highway is **Lake Vingavatn**, and two farms of the same name: the newer offers farmhouse accommodation, while the older has been occupied by descendants of the same family since the 1700s.

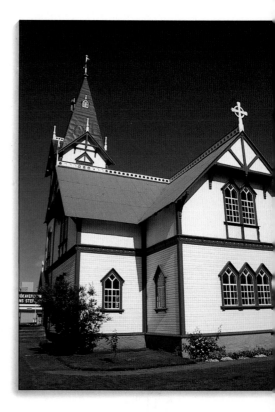

The Húsavík church.

Giant hoof print: The great attraction of the North East, and one that has become increasingly popular in recent years, is the **Jökulsárgljúfur National Park** (the full name is nearly unpronounceable to non-Icelanders, but can be referred to as Jökulsá Canyon – pronounced *yer-kool-sar*). Once private property within the huge As estate, the park was formed in 1973 and extended later to cover 150 sq. km (370 acres).

The park's focus is the great canyon of **Asbyrgi**, located almost immediately at the turnoff from Route 85. It's not hard to see why the first Viking settlers decided that the canyon had been formed by Slaettur, the god Odin's flying horse, crashing a giant hoof into the earth. A 100-metre (328-ft) cliff face makes a smooth, 1 km-wide ring around a profuse carpet of greenery, while a smaller outcropping of cliffs (suitably called **Eyjan** or "island") rises in the middle.

Geologists believe that the canyon was formed relatively recently by a gigantic *hlaup* or glacial flow from an eruption under the faraway icecap of Vatnajökull. The best view is from the furthest part of the canyon, which can be reached after a 100-metre (330-ft) walk west from the parking area. Turning east from the car park leads to a natural spring for drinking water, while taking the trail straight ahead ends up at a small lake full of ducks – their quacks echo around the natural amphitheatre.

Camping is permitted in the canyon near its entrance, where a park ranger keeps an information office and sells small brochures on walks in the park (food can be bought at the Asbyrgi petrol station/supermarket at the Asbyrgi farm outside the park, the only place selling supplies within about 25 km/15 miles). From here, a path also leads to the top of the cliffs, climbing the canyon at its easiest point (although a rope is provided to help in the ascent). Once up, walkers can follow the cliffs, with excellent views over the whole canyon, or even take the trail as far south as Dettifoss – two days' walk away.

No matter whether you walk for an hour or a day, this is one of the most

e view
m Húsavík
oss
álfandi
.

pleasant hikes in Iceland, and if you get tired, just lie on the heather and eat some of the wild berries that grow abundantly in the canyon's summery climate.

Towards Dettifoss: The rest of the park follows the powerful **Jökulsá á Fjollum**, Iceland's second longest river. Two roads run down the length of the park, one on either side of the river: the western road runs across some classic highland heather to **Vesturdalur** ("west valley") walking trails and the mysterious natural columns of **Hljódaklettar**, which form a sort of ghostly stone forest that can be explored for hours. Further on, the road heads to **Hólmatungur**, a lush stretch along the river canyon, before crossing a suddenly barren desert landscape to Dettifoss.

Unfortunately, the western road is deeply corrugated and, while two-wheel drives can make the journey, they need to crawl along at a gruelling 15 kph (10 mph). The eastern road is far better, but only goes to Dettifoss.

Either way, it's worth the effort: **Dettifoss** is Europe's largest waterfall, and the effort needed to reach it only seems to add to the excitement. There is nothing contained or artificial about Dettifoss, no wooden boardwalks or viewing balconies installed to detract from Nature. Clouds of spray can first be seen several kilometres away; from the car parks, visitors scramble over square blocks of grey lava, hearing the thunderous drumming before getting a glimpse of the falls. Some 500 cubic metres of water spill over its ledges every second: although it is just 44 metres (145 ft) tall, the sheer hypnotic volume of the flow makes this arguably Iceland's most awesome sight.

For those who want to see more falls, **Hafragilsfoss** is located 2 km (1½ miles) downstream, and **Selfoss** about the same distance upstream. A four-wheel drive road heads from Dettifoss south to Lake Mývatn, but other cars will have to track back to Route 28.

Cod coast: Heading north from the entrance of the National Park leads to Iceland's least visited area. Tourist officials say that even the uninhabited centre

THE MOST USEFUL SERVANT

One of the incidental advantages of Iceland's almost total isolation through the centuries is that the Icelandic horse, the stocky breed introduced with the first Nordic settlers, has survived almost unchanged for over 1,000 years. Today, it is protected by strict regulations which forbid the import of horses into Iceland, and an Icelandic horse sent out of the country can never return to Iceland, for fear of importing diseases to which the local breed has no immunity.

"Elegant" is not an adjective which springs to mind to describe the Icelandic horse. These chunky, thick-set, muscular animals bear little resemblance to their leggier mainland relatives, though they can put on a fine turn of speed. They have adapted to the cool climate by growing a warm and shaggy overcoat to keep them warm in winter, which is shed in the spring. In summer, their coats can be groomed to shining smoothness.

In spite of their relatively small stature (13 hands on average), Icelandic horses are famed for their strength and stamina. They have played a vital role in Iceland's history, for centuries a roadless, bridgeless land. Known affectionately as *tharfasti thjónninn* ("the most useful servant"), the horse was the sole form of overland transport in Iceland until the 19th century.

In many remote regions, the horse's supremacy has continued, and even today has a vital role to play during the autumn round-up when sheep must be herded from remote mountain pastures.

Surefooted, intelligent, affectionate, home-loving and sometimes headstrong, the horse is also known for its five gaits. In addition to the conventional walk, trot and gallop, it has two additional steps in its repertoire: the *tölt* or running walk, and the *skeid* or pace. Some can't manage the *skeid*; these are known as four-gaiters. The *tölt*, almost unknown in other breeds of horse, is a smooth run, which (unlike the trot) does not shake the rider about in the saddle and is understandably very popular for overland travel, particularly for those who are not used to horseback travel.

Horse-riding is now Iceland's number-one leisure activity. Riding clubs flourish all over the country, and various competitions, races, shows and meets are held throughout the summer months. Iceland's equine population numbers in the region of 50,000 animals. Horse breeding and trading, while on a relatively modest scale compared to many other countries, is becoming an important business.

Fifteen national organisations in Europe and north America are affiliated to the International Iceland-horse federation FEIF (Föderation Internationale der Islandpferde Vereine), and international Iceland-horse championships are held annually.

Iceland always sends a team of horses and riders to the world championships, and invariably that team carries off many of the prizes – although, frustratingly, the *crème de la crème* of local-bred Icelandic horses can never be sent to the international contests. Since horses taken overseas are not re-admitted, no devoted rider would think of taking their best horse to compete in Europe only to leave the poor creature behind. ∎

The shaggy-haired Icelandic horse.

of Iceland attracts more travellers than the North East coast.

The first village, **Kópasker**, with a population of 150 souls almost all involved in the fishing of shrimp, can seem like a ghost town on most days. Like the other villages of the area, Kópasker thrived on the herring boom this century until overfishing decimated the population in the late 1960s.

Beyond Kópasker is the flat, exposed peninsula of **Melrakkaslétta** ("fox plain"), where winds howl straight from the North Pole in winter and, on a bad day, summer can seem almost as dismal. The northernmost point of mainland Iceland (and, incidentally, the spot where the saga character Thorgeir Harvarsson was finally brought down after he had slaughtered 14 attackers), **Hraunhafnartangi**, is marked by a lighthouse – unfortunately, instead of windswept charm, it looks like a Third World apartment block.

Even so, the remoteness of the barren plain, which can support very little agriculture, is perversely appealing. The coastline is covered with driftwood from as far away as Siberia and supports a good deal of bird life.

Although **Raufarhöfn** made the transition from herring to cod fishing in the 1970s, it has never recaptured the great days when thousands of seasonal workers came to its factories. Today there are many more buildings and jetties than the population of 450 can use, and Raufarhöfn is losing more young people to the cities. Trying to keep people in this economically important area, the Icelandic government recently built an airstrip (during long winters, the town had been completely cut off except by sea). Even so, the isolation of this town – which does not even have a local doctor – is extreme.

Lying south of Raufarhöfn is the **Langanes peninsula**, whose marshy, cliff-bound expanses are the last word in Icelandic remoteness – it can really only be visited with a four-wheel drive or on foot. At the peninsula's tip is a monument to some shipwrecked English sailors who managed to climb the

Below, trekking to the Jökulsá canyon. Far right, poetic waterfall in Juokulsárgl júfur Nation Park.

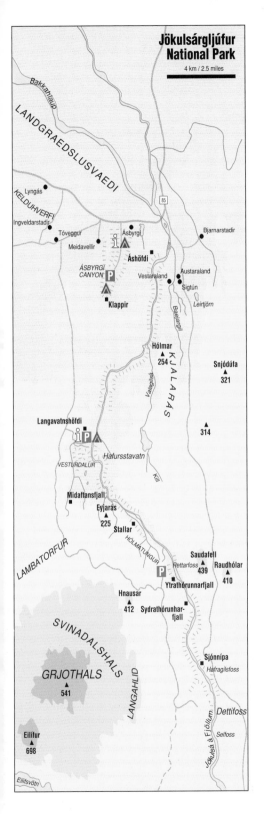

Jökulsárgljúfur National Park

4 km / 2.5 miles

Bakkahlaup
LANDGRAEDSLUSVAEDI
Lyngás
KELDUHVERFI
Ingveldarstadir
Tóveggur
Meidavellir
Ásbyrgi
85
Bjarnarstadir
Áshöfdi
ÁSBYRGÍ CANYON
Vestaraland
Austaraland
Sigtún
Klappir
Leirtjörn
Baejargil
Hólmar
254
KJALARÁS
Snjódúfa
321
314
Langavatnshöfdi
Hafursstavatn
VESTURDALUR
Kíli
Midaftansfjall
Eyjarás
225
Stallar
HÓLMATUNGUR
LAMBATORFUR
Saudafell
Rettarfoss 439
Raudhólar
410
Ytrathórunnarfjall
Hnausar
412
Sydrathórunhar-fjall
SVINADALSHALS
Sjónnípa
Hafragilsfoss
GRJOTHALS
541
LANGAHLID
Dettifoss
Jökulsá á Fjöllum
Eilífur
698
Selfoss
Eilifsvötn

100-metre (330-ft cliffs) only to subsequently die of exposure.

Heading south, the villages of **Thorshöfn** and **Bakkafjördur** fit the nondescript pattern of the north-eastern landscape, but **Vopnafjördur** (population 850) is in a surprisingly picturesque setting. The snow-capped mountains behind the town seem to trail down into huge rocks broken into the sea, complemented by the granite range across the fjord. Here the weather is better and the atmosphere more optimistic – the feeling is closer to the East Fjords than the North East. To top it off, Vopnafjördur had its 15 minutes of fame in 1988, when local girl Linda Petursdóttir became Miss World.

From Vopnafjördur, the highway runs away from the coast, passing **Bustafell**, an excellent folk museum in a 19th-century farmhouse. The road now climbs into the north-eastern desert, passing a viewing platform over **Lake Nykurvatn**, before eventually rejoining the Ring Road in some of the most barren landscape Iceland has to offer.

THE EAST FJORDS

For travellers arriving from mainland Europe and the Faroe Islands by ferry, the jagged, snow-capped profile of the East Fjords provides the first glimpse of Iceland. It's a breathtaking sight as the boat edges into Seydisfjördur fjord towards the town's ornate wooden buildings strung out along the seaboard. But not many stay to see what else this region has to offer. Iceland's eastern coast has a reputation of a place to be passed through quickly en route to somewhere else.

This is a pity, and not just because the East enjoys the sunniest weather in the country. The rugged coastline and dry interior here are full of wilderness areas rarely visited by foreigners, although they are well known amongst Icelanders. And along the way are remote farms and fishing villages that, unusually for Iceland, have still hung on to a degree of old-world charm.

Hub of the East: Whether arriving by ferry, car or bus, travellers use as an orientation point the East's most important urban crossroad, **Egilsstadir** (population 1,400). The first houses were built here less than 50 years ago, and Egilsstadir still has an unfortunately prefabricated feel: like many smaller towns in this part of Iceland, its social and economic life seems to hinge around the Esso petrol station. Flanking the station are the camping ground, tourist information office and a huge supermarket – a place that can turn into an elbows-only feeding frenzy on days that the ferry arrives in nearby Seydisfjördur.

Still, Egilsstadir also has a number of hotels and makes a convenient base. Its sister-settlement, the tiny village of **Fellabaer** (population 50) lies across a long bridge and has a more picturesque setting: try for lakeside accommodation in huts on the Skipulaekur farm, although they are often booked up months in advance.

The port of **Seydisfjördur**, where the ferry from Europe docks, lies directly east along the mostly paved highway

Route 93. The journey is worth making even for those not taking the boat: in complete contrast to Egalsstadir, Seydisfjördur is full of Scandinavian character, a town that approximates to one's mental image, so rarely fulfilled, of an Icelandic fishing town. Set on the fjord of the same name and surrounded by sheer mountains, it was founded in the 1830s and soon became the largest and wealthiest town in the East – resulting in the construction of many wooden homes in an elegant Norwegian style.

Most of Seydisfjördur's 1,000 inhabitants are involved in fishing, and the arrival every autumn of herring schools in the shallow waters of the nearby fjords is still a cause for mass mobilisation, bringing everyone from schoolchildren to the aged out to the fish factories. (The autumn herring catch is from different stock to the summer catch, which from the 1930s to 1960s turned Iceland's north-eastern outposts into Klondike-style boom towns, before overfishing wiped out the population). In summer, the ferry traffic keeps much

eding
s: the
ng village
larfjördur.

isfjördur,
e the ferry
Europe
s. Right, a
len cross
Is off
ts on the
to
afjördur-
i.

of Seydisfjördur busy, and on Wednesday evenings and Thursday mornings an arts and crafts market is held here to coincide with arrivals and departures.

There is a spectacular view of the town and fjord from the highway, which winds up past small waterfalls into the looming **Fjardarheidi** mountains. The best spot for photos is a columnar basalt **monument** to the first postman of the region, who regularly made this journey on horseback when it was decidedly more dangerous than it is today.

Haunted highway: Another spectacular excursion from Egilsstadir is to Borgafjördur-Eystri, following Route 94 north. The highway passes the Edda Hotel at **Eidar** before entering an expanse of marshland bordered to the north by the **Jökulsá á Brú** river. The whole area is crowded with birdlife.

Over a high pass, **Dyrföll**, one of Iceland's most dramatic mountain ranges, comes into view. Watch out on the left for the bridge of a fishing trawler sitting in a field – it was dragged there on truck-back by a local Fitzcarraldo, who wanted to piece together a boat in Borgafjördur. He gave up half way, leaving a surreal vision for passersby.

This is an unnerving stretch of highway, with dramatic drops down into the sea and graphic evidence of recent landslides. A **wooden cross** records that the road was once said to be haunted. Fatal accidents were so common here in the Middle Ages that they were attributed to a ghost named Naddi, supposed to live in a particular scree called Naddagil. In the early 1300s, a priest was dragged out here to perform an exorcism, and just to make sure locals erected a cross in 1306. The cross has been replaced innumerable times, but all of them bear the Latin inscription, *Effigiem Christi: qui transis pronus honora* – "You who are hurrying past should honour the image of Christ."

The town of **Borgafjördur-Eystri** (East Borgafjodur, to distinguish it from the bigger Borgafjördur in West Iceland) is also known as **Baakkagerdi**. It is tinged by dramatic mountains: the ochre range to the east, past the black

A dusk bike ride near Valthjófssta

sand beach, is made from an acidic form of lava called rhyolite. This black rock is polished into everything from paperweights to gravestones at the **Alfasteinn stone and mineral works**, along with pieces of jasper and agate that turn up in the mountains.

Ask at the shop for the key to the local **church**, with an altarpiece painted by the renowned artist Johannes Kjarval, who was born in Borgafjördur. Kjarval made the Borgafjördur region famous in his paintings, and has been said by one critic to have "taught the Icelanders to experience the beauty of their own landscape." Across the street is a colourful turf house that is still inhabited and, towards the beach, a stone hillock called **Alfaborg** ("elf hill"), held to be inhabited by the hidden people.

Eastern isolation: A second road north of Egilsstadir (Route 925, via the Ring Road) leads to **Húsey**, a farm that has earned a measure of fame, especially in Germany, for its remoteness and serenity – representing, as one traveller put it, "the real Iceland."

Lying in the flatlands just south of the Jökulsá á Brú river, in the shadow of the Dyrfjöll mountains, Húsey's gaily-painted corrugated-iron buildings date from the 1930s. The farm is still operational, and is one of the few in Iceland that still engage in sealing. Sealskins are left drying in the courtyard amongst the whale bone and reindeer antlers, detracting from the charm for those who find sealing objectionable. Seal meat is also for sale, along with salmon and trout, although a baby seal is kept as a pet in a nearby pond.

Walks can be made across the heather to the black sand beach nearby, where gyrfalcons hover menacingly overhead, or horseback trips may be made into the surrounding wilderness. Húsey's utter peacefulness is seductive, and many visitors find themselves staying much longer than planned. The old-style accommodation offered is simple but comfortable, and lying in bed at night listening to the howling wind, one gets a vivid idea of just how isolated Icelandic farmers have always been.

andoned

Heading inland from Húsey, the Ring Road follows the Jökulsá á Brú river valley before hitting the central deserts en route to Lake Mývatn. The bridge across the Jökulsá á Brú was held to be haunted by a fearsome monster who would occasionally dine on unsuspecting travellers.

Farmhouse accommodation is available at a space-age concrete building at **Brúarás**. Further west, keep an eye out for the rise of **Godanes** overlooking the river south of the highway: this was supposedly once a temple of Thor, and sacrifices were held nearby. Today there are ruins below the hill, of indeterminate age.

The rough Route 923 heading south of the Ring Road along the Jökulsá á Brú heads for the farm of **Adalból** and country related to the much-beloved *Hrafnkels Saga*. The story tells of Hrafnkell Hallfredarson, an unsavoury chieftain who lived at Adalból and worshipped Freyr, the Norse god of war. Hrafnkell swore to Freyr that he would kill anyone who rode his favourite horse,

Freyfaxi, and when one of his shepherds innocently did so, felt obliged to hunt him down and chop open the poor fellow's skull. A blood feud resulted in Hrafnkell being outlawed at the Althing and ambushed by the victim's cousin, Sámur – who, rather than killing Hrafnkell, maimed him horribly by stringing him up with a rope through the Achilles tendon and seizing his lands. The horse that had caused all the trouble was flung into a pond and drowned.

At this stage, Hrafnkell decided that Freyr was little practical use as a deity and abandoned his worship. Appearing to turn over a new leaf, he slowly rebuilt his fortune at a nearby farm. Of course, Hrafnkell was only biding his time: six years later, he took his revenge, descending on Sámur with a band of warriors and driving him from the East. According to the Saga, Hrafknell then lived happily ever after.

Some ruins from Viking times have been found at the farm Adalból, but fans of the sagas will mostly have to use their imaginations.

A lone tra⋯ plies an eastern fjo⋯

The great Icelandic forest: South of Egilsstadir stretches the pencil-shaped lake of **Lögurinn**, famed throughout Iceland for the country's largest wooded area, **Hallormsstadarskógur**. Although foreigners are unlikely to get excited, the reforestation programme here (using tough plants from Alaska and Siberia amongst others) has created optimism that other parts of Iceland might return to their pre-Viking state of being "covered by woods from mountain to shore." For those who wish to know more, there is a **Tree Museum** here.

On the lake, **Hallormsstadur** is a popular spot for Icelandic vacationers (there is a camping ground and an Edda hotel). At the southern end of the lake, **Valthjófsstadur** farm is where the famous carved wooden church door, dating back to AD 1200 and on display in the National Museum of Reykjavík, was found. The box-like modern church now on the site sports a shiny new replica. North of Lögurinn, a steep hour-long walk leads to the "hanging falls" of **Hengifoss**, 120 metres (393 ft) high.

nping out the banks .ögurinn.

A difficult four-wheel drive road runs south of Lögurinn to **Mt Snaefell**, the 1,833-metre (6,013-ft) peak that dominates the valley. Further on are the **Kverkfjoll mountains** at the northern edge of the Vatnajökull icecap.

Following the fjords: The Ring Road runs directly south of Egilsstadir, although many prefer to take the slower but better-paved and more scenic route hugging the coast. The road runs through a steep river valley lined by pencil waterfalls at regular intervals – any one of which would be a marvel in other countries but in Iceland just forms part of the backdrop. **Reydarfjördur** is the first of many quiet fishing villages along this part of the coast, magnificently situated at the base of the steepest fjord in the East. The town's old streets give it an unusually authentic, human feel: small plants are neatly lined up in the windows of corrugated-iron buildings and, on a fine afternoon, old fishermen promenade along the split-level streets.

Route 92 runs north along the coast to **Eskifjördur** (population 1,100), noted for its **Maritime Museum** with exhibits on fishing and whaling dating back to the 18th century. **Neskaupstadir**, with a population of 1,700, is the largest town in East Iceland, despite its remote position at the end of the narrow, winding highway. Most travellers will bypass it and head south along the fjords, following the road squeezed between the choppy North Atlantic and steep mountains – their twisted peaks are usually shrouded in a haunting mist, making this look like troll country.

The small villages of **Fáskrúdsfjördur**, **Stödvarfjördur**, **Breiddalsvík** and **Djúpovingur** all pass in quick succession, lonely outposts in this thinly-populated corner of Iceland. Many more sheep traverse the highways than cars, and occasionally reindeer might be seen. The uninhabited island of **Papey** is visible out to sea from Djúpovingur, named after Irish monks. A short distance south of Djúpovingur is the farm of **Stafafell**, which offers accommodation to travellers and has become a popular base for hikers making day trips into the surrounding river valleys.

THE INTERIOR

During the Age of Settlement few Viking colonists braved the wild desolation of the interior. Only outlaws, banished from their society and the fertile coast, took refuge in its chilly expanses. By the 13th century, some paths had been created through the Central Highlands for short cuts from north to south, but today, nearly 800 years later, the vast region of the interior is still totally uninhabited.

Despite this – or rather, because of it – the interior is Iceland's premier attraction for adventurous travellers. Nowhere else in Europe is so remote from civilisation, or offers such a range of scenery, the most dramatic Iceland has to offer: broad icecaps which split their sides into great glacial tongues; volcanoes of every size with extensive fields of block lava and pumice; freezing deserts and endless out-wash plains of black sand.

Challenge of the wild: There are serious logistical problems to be overcome before visiting the interior. Roads are reduced to mere tracks, most only passable in four-wheel-drive vehicles. Many of the interior routes are only open in the middle of summer and even then snowfalls and blizzards can still occur. There are years when some tracks never open due to the severe weather.

The weather is unpredictable and camping is the only real form of accommodation. There are exceptions in the form of a few huts operated by the Icelandic Touring Club (Ferdafélag Islands). Located in key areas, like the Sprengisandur and Kjölur, they cannot be booked and preference is given to members of the club. Facilities are very basic but useful in emergencies. The larger huts have wardens, while at others a payment is left in an honesty box upon departure.

Modes of transport through the interior vary from the latest high-tech 4x4 or beaten-up Land-Rover, to mountain bikes and walking. Whichever way is chosen, extreme care is required in preparation. Because of the dangers, many travellers opt to embark with one of the adventure tour operators based in Reykjavík. These use short wheelbase, four-wheel-drive coaches, for tours ranging from day excursions to longer-term camping trips. For the latter, the vehicles are heavily modified, often to include a kitchen and a full complement of picnic tables and chairs. A popular alternative form of adventure tour is traversing the interior on horseback.

Independent travellers will first need a four-wheel drive vehicle. Hiring cars is expensive and insurance, for the interior, difficult to obtain. Needless to say, the vehicle must be in good order as the terrain can be very punishing. The more difficult tracks require experience in off-road driving and are not for the novice – fatalities have occurred when vehicles overturned while crossing fast-flowing glacial rivers.

The most common problem, however, occurs when inexperienced drivers stall their cars in rivers or become bogged down. It is recommended that

Preceding pages: lunging by a natural jacuzzi at Landmannalaugar; a biker braves a storm in the interior in winter. Left, the basalt gorge that leads to cross Eldgjá, with Ófaerufoss in the background. Right, patterns formed by molten lava.

two vehicles travel together, to tow one another should difficulties occur. **Careful preparations:** Every requirement for a trip must be obtained beforehand. Sufficient food should be taken and water is not always available, particularly in the cold desert region of the Odádahraun. Even when water is found, it may have to be filtered first to remove the fine particles of rock found in the glacial rivers (made up of rock flour eroded away over centuries by the glaciers and incorporated into the ice). Prior route planning is essential to determine fuel requirements: petrol consumption is heavy on the interior's bad roads and extra fuel needs to be carried.

In case of difficulties, rescue is often difficult. Wardened huts and most Icelandic vehicles have radio communications and can summon help in an emergency. It is wise for independent travellers to take out insurance that covers emergency rescue, which although efficient, can be very expensive.

One of the nearest areas to Reykjavík for a beginner to experience a taste of the interior is the easily traversed **Kaldidalur** route between **Thingvellir** and **Húsafell**. The rocky track that picks its way northwards from Thingvellir usually opens during July when the snows melt around the Langjökull icecap. Shield volcanoes dominate the skyline while, on the ground, colourful tundra flowers stud ancient lava flows. River crossings are straightforward and the track runs very close to the hanging glaciers of the icecap.

There are two main routes through the interior. The first, the Kjölur route, is comparatively straightforward to drive and passes between the **Langjökull** and Hofsjökull icecaps. The second route passes to the north and west of Vatnajökull, the Odádahraun and Sprengisandur regions.

Wherever the traveller goes, it is essential that vehicles keep to the specified tracks. Leaving these tracks is not only against the law but will quickly destroy the delicate balance of the tundra environment. Tearing away those few plants that hold the interior topsoil

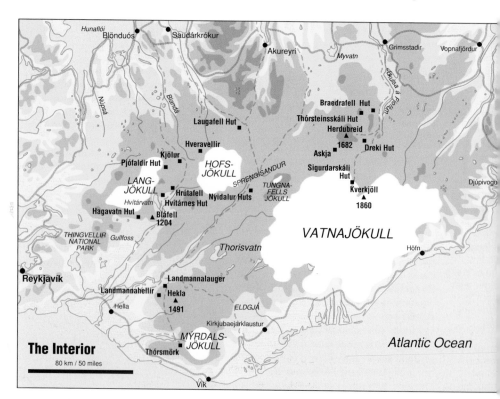

The Interior

80 km / 50 miles

together can begin a cycle of erosion that is basically irreversible.

Kjölur and the Central Highlands: Close to Reykjavík and comparatively short, the Kjölur route through the Central Highlands is the most popular venture into the interior for most travellers. A 4x4 is advisable but other vehicles are seen on the main track that begins at the majestic waterfall of Gullfoss and runs northwards to Blönduós on the coast.

The track is based on an ancient byway that was in use during the Saga Age as a north-south crossing of the interior. The first part of the journey, to the famous hot springs of Hveravellir, is on a road of gravel, stones and rock, the occasional small river to be forded. Beyond Hveravellir, the route deteriorates as the track becomes muddy and has several extended river crossings. In comparison with other routes across the Icelandic tundra plateaux, the Kjölur is relatively busy during the summer and could be tackled in a day.

Leaving Gullfoss, the grassland on the plain above the falls soon changes to lichen-dotted stones. There is a steady drop in temperature as the landscape looks increasingly bleak and uninviting. On the skyline the only relief is the snow-sprinkled mass of **Bläfell** mountain (1,160 metres/3,800 ft).

Before Bläfell there is a ford across the **River Sandá** and a track branching off to the left. This detour from the main route, taking several hours as a round trip, goes to **Hagavatn** and the icecap of **Landjökull.** As the track winds and bumps its way towards the edge of the ice, it crosses a once volcanically active fissure several miles in length. All that remains today is a high ridge of black rock with a narrow break that allows access through to the edge of the glaciers. The final approaches to the icecap are very steep due to huge deposits of glacial moraine, and vehicles should be left below. Water gushes out from the top of the moraine where a large glacial lake has formed. Standing on the edge of the moraine, buffeted by the cold wind, there is a view of the lake, edged in ice, and way below the sweeping

ur-wheel ve across interior.

plains of black sand that are blown southward and enrich the agricultural land beyond Gullfoss.

The main Kjölur route leads to a second, even larger glacial lake, **Hvítárvatn**. Skirting around the bulk of Mount Bläfell, the track begins to descend to the **River Hvítá**, plunging through four or five tributary streams and small rivers. A spectacular view opens up across desolate dark tundra towards the distant blue glaciers of the icecap and waters of Hvítárvatn.

On the horizon lies another icecap, **Hofsjökull**: the conflicting winds from the two icecaps create swirling dust clouds in between. From the bridge over the Hvítá, there is a clear view to the lake with a dramatic glacier towering above it. Small icebergs can usually be seen in the water, and on the far shore, the outlet glacier from which they originated. A good base for a more extended exploration of the area is the Touring Club hut at **Hvítárnes**.

Beyond here, the brown dusty plain gives way to expanses of gravel and then great black stretches of volcanic clinker, with mountains and glaciers always on the horizon.

The track soon crosses the southern stony slopes of the small mountain, **Innriskule**. As well as affording a panoramic view over the **Jökulfall** river valley to the Hofsjökull icecap and the Kerlingarfjöll mountains, the slopes are particularly rich in tundra plants. Most are no more than tiny specks which eke out an existence sheltered between the rocks. Small pink cushions of moss campion compete with white mountain avens and other alpines for space. In common with other tundra life, such plants have to be able to cope with long and severe winters, followed by short and relatively warm summers. This ensures that any growth is very stunted. Woolly willows grow barely centimetres above the ground and as soon as they do so they become bent over by the constant wind.

The track detour to **Kerlingarfjöll** is well signposted as it dips down into the Jökulfall river valley. The fjord here can

A fresh lav; field near I Askja.

312

FLOWERS AMONGST THE LAVA

Most unfairly, Iceland is often called a "barren" country. True enough, it's hardly a riot of flowers, fields and forests from coast to coast – in fact, well over half the country's area is wasteland. Visitors arriving at Keflavík Airport often think they could be on the moon when they look out on the treeless lava fields and the dark mountain slopes that lie beyond.

This impression is, however, misleading. While Iceland has next to no trees (a waggish visitor once remarked, "if you're lost in an Icelandic forest, stand up"), there is plenty of compensation. Mosses, lichens and many flowering plants flourish all over the country. And even in the barest sections of the highlands, an occasional bloom takes root.

Birch, Iceland's most widespread tree, generally takes the form of a relatively low-growing shrub, often in dense copses and thickets. In the rare locations where it can grow straight and tall, the birch may reach a height of 10 to 12 metres (30–35 ft). Afforestation efforts have introduced many foreign tree species, mostly evergreens of various kinds. Some have flourished in their new environment, so mixed glades and woods are seen in many parts of the country today. Iceland's largest forest is at Hallormsstadur, in the east.

Botanists believe that half of Iceland's plant species are survivors of the Ice Age, while around 20 percent have been introduced, deliberately or by chance, since mankind's arrival in the 9th century.

The local vegetation has been characterised as oceanic sub-arctic in character. About one-third of the plant species are of the arctic-alpine type. Many species of sedges and rushes are found in marshes and bogs; cottongrass (common and Schewchzer's), which flourishes in wetlands all over the country, was formerly used to provide wicks for the fish-oil lamps which were the main form of lighting.

In addition to its 470 vascular plants (30 of them rare enough to be protected by law), Iceland has no fewer than 500 different mosses and liverworts. Mosses are generally the first plants to take root on lava fields, preparing the ground for later colonisation by grasses, ferns and later trees. One of the most interesting species among Iceland's flora is the mis-named *Bryoxiphium norvegicum*, sword moss. Though named "norvegicum," sword moss has never been found in Norway, and was first identified at Lake Kleifarvatn in 1928. While found in the US, Mexico and parts of Asia, it is unknown elsewhere in Europe.

About 450 lichens and 250 fungi are known in Iceland. Very few of Iceland's mushroom species are harmful to eat (though some do not taste very nice), and none is deadly poisonous, so mushroom picking is a popular autumn pastime. Courses in mushroom identification are held from time to time, generally culminating in field trips to gather mushrooms under expert supervision.

Berry-bearing plants like the crowberry and bog whortleberry are common on heathlands, and after a good summer they provide abundant berries for jam-making. Families often take a day or two in the autumn to travel out into the country in search of the biggest, juiciest berries. ∎

Reindeer horns at Húsey farm (East Fjords).

become a raging torrent when it rains, making it difficult to cross. Nearby is a small airstrip. These are dotted throughout the interior for emergency use but this one also allows access to the summer ski school of **Arskardur**.

The Kerlingarfjöll region is an excellent climbing area with superb views of Hofsjökull, many deep ravines and well vegetated slopes. The mountain peaks, rising to 1,400 metres (4,600 ft), are made of rhyolite, making a stark contrast to the dark plains of Kjölur. In a succession of small gorges, sulphur and boiling water vent to the surface – which looks particularly eerie when there is a mild drizzle in the air and great clouds of steam rise out of the myriad small fissures in the ground. Boiling pools have splashed mineral-laden waters across rocks, colouring them green, red and yellow.

These mountains can be a very cold place to camp and there are occasional snowfalls even in August. At the end of the track, near to the ski school, is a touring hut which operates a small café in season. It makes a delightful refuge, even if only for a brief coffee!

Hveravellir, 100 km (60 miles) from Gullfoss, is an oasis within the cold desert. The hot springs here are very different from those at Kerlingarfjöll. Deep pools of brilliant, near-boiling blue water, are lined with white silica; all around are small mud pools of black, brown and red minerals. Hissing jets of steam emerge from tall rocky cones, while a number of springs cascade water which runs gently down the slopes. The deposits of silica and sulphur cover the ground like great sheets of glass with fine traces of yellow.

Some of the blue pools are as close as the natural world comes to a jacuzzi. With the air temperature near freezing, bathing is possible in one of the outlet pools located by the car park. Hveravellir is close to being classified as the interior's only settlement due to the presence of a touring hut, campsite and weather station.

North from Hveravellir runs 70 km (43 miles) of rough track before a hard

Camping or in Land- mannalaug

road is reached. The winding **River Seydisá** has several fording places which frequently change: great care is needed when crossing. The shallower parts attract water birds, such as phalaropes, which churn the bottom up by walking round in circles to dislodge small animals for food. Much of the water comes from the two icecaps and on a clear day there are magnificent views.

From Lake Myvatn to Askja: Other tracks through the interior are more difficult than the Central Highlands excursion described above. Two-wheel drive vehicles should not attempt these routes, and even four-wheel drives are sorely put to the test. It is worth noting that this region is one of the most ecologically sensitive in Iceland. Vehicles must stay on the designated tracks as tyre marks carved into the landscape may remain for hundreds of years. Most tracks are marked by yellow poles or cairns of stones and, with reference to good maps, navigation is fairly straightforward.

The track that leads off Route 1 to the east of **Lake Mývatn** is marked by several makeshift signs warning against two-wheel drive vehicles attempting to go any further. The track travels for some 64 km (39 miles), following close to the glacial river **Jölkulsá á Fjollum**, before reaching the mountain of **Herdubreid**. To begin with, the view across the **Odádahraun** plain is quite intimidating. A flat expanse of black gravel and pebbles (called *grjot* in Icelandic), which is made up from the country's largest lava flow, stretches almost to the horizon.

The going is hard due to the severe corrugations in the track. A small range of black hills has to be negotiated, giving from the summit a spectacular view of the Jökulsá – a vast braided glacial river. Patches of black sand become more frequent with pockets of stabilising lyme grass.

In this desert, few plants survive. The ancient and twisted frames of dwarf willow are testimony to the harshness of the environment. Amongst the dark gravel lie balls of primordial-looking grey lichens. Under stones protected

e Land-
annalaugar
t springs.

from the wind sit small brown moths, barely moving, the only visible sign of animal life.

The track twists and turns eventually towards the edge of the **River Lindaá**, a tributary of the Jökulsá. This is the first major river crossing and along the river banks are great carpets of the pink-flowered arctic river beauty, contrasting against the black sand.

The track undulates considerably for the next 20 km (12 miles) as it climbs and descends an extensive lava field. The bare rock is covered at times with patches of sand and pumice. The mountain of **Herdubreid** gradually comes to dominate the view as it rises some 1,060 metres (3,500 ft) above the surrounding plain. The name Herdubreid aptly means "broad-shouldered": it is a great flat-topped block of sheer-sided palagonite rock thrusting up out of a skirt of vast scree slopes. On a cloudy day the upper reaches of Herdubreid are often hidden from view, which only adds to the mountain's gloomy splendour.

The Jökulsá á Fjöllum nearby becomes a violent glacial torrent, creamy brown with rock flour and running between banks of dark lava.

The journey from Herdubreid to **Askja** is another 35 km (21 miles), much of which is across the yellow pumice fields of **Vikursandar**. The soft honeycombed segments of pumice, originally produced by the eruption of Víti in 1875, have become blown by the wind into small yellow dunes, contrasting with the dark block lava beneath. Storms in this area can make travelling very hazardous.

At both Herdubreid and Askja there are basic tourist huts as well as camp-sites. The latter are very primitive and expensive, with wardens present for six weeks in the middle of summer – tents have to be pegged into the pumice and the only flattened area doubles as an airstrip.

Mt Askja itself is not the neat cone that it appears on the horizon. Seen from closer up, it is a 45 sq. km (16 sq. mile) caldera of black lava, cream pumice screes and white snow. Low cloud often clings around the summit, which is lo-cated amidst the sprawling **Dyngjufjöll** massif. A narrow track winds around the base of Askja, through the **Oskjuop pass** to a small parking area. A walk leads through the outer walls of Askja into the huge crater, where the great jagged **Vikraborgir** lava field was created as recently as 1961. A deep inner crater is partially flooded with steaming water and marks the site of the 1875 eruption. Oskjuvatn, a lake several kilometres across, is the deepest in Iceland at 217 metres (715 ft).

To the north lies the centre of the vast Odádahraun lava field which, at over 3,000 sq. km (1,080 sq. miles), is the largest in the world.

For most travellers, Askja marks the end of the interior route and all organised tours return the same way they came. But for the most adventurous independent travellers, the track does continue. There is a hazardous south-west track from Askja, **the Gaesa-vatnaleid route**, which passes very close to **Vatnajökull**, the largest icecap in Iceland. This 120-km (72-mile) route from Askja to **Tomasarhagi** in the Sprengisandur was immortalised in Desmond Bagley's thriller *Running Blind*. The route that the book's hero Alan Stewart drove in his Land-Rover has changed little except for the bridging of the **River Tungná** at the end. It may be difficult, but at least you're unlikely to have a hail of bullets at your back, as Stewart had.

Spring meltwater brings a flood from the Vatnajökull icecap and, with it, black volcanic sand. This outwash plain runs for many kilometres towards Askja and offers the first major obstacle on the track. Marked at intervals with yellow poles, the track reaches the icecap at the black glacier of **Dyngjyjökull**. Close inspection reveals ice covered in black volcanic ash.

Navigation becomes more treacherous as the route crosses the difficult boulder-strewn sides of the shield volcano **Trölladyngja**. The weather here is inevitably cold and wretched, and blizzards are commonplace in summer. Yet the solitude of this wilderness is awe-inspiring.

After hours of slow driving across block lava spewed out by a succession of volcanic craters, the track emerges above a ridge of cairns high on the edge of the Mid Atlantic Ridge that runs through Iceland. Below lies the **Sprengisandur**, a vast gravel plain sandwiched between the icecaps of **Hofsjökull** and Vatnajökull. This is also where the meltwater from the icecaps collect in a succession of rivers, many of which are bisected by the track.

Routes through the Sprengisandur Plain:
The Sprengisandur can be reached more easily, although a 4x4 is still necessary, from the north via **Godafoss**. A scraped road soon degrades into a rough track, which climbs past the beautiful waterfall of **Aldeyjarfoss** with its tall basalt columns. On clear days there are spectacular views across the Odádahraun towards Askja.

The shield volcano of Trölladyngja, part of the Gaesavatnaleid route, is clear on the horizon. Near the turn westwards to **Laugafell** (where there is a tourist hut) the Sprengisandur truly begins with

magnificent vistas to Vatnajökull and the smaller icecap of **Tungnafell**. A number of river crossings later, the blue tongues of glaciers come into view. A track forking to the east leads off the gravel plain to **Gaesavotn**, a small yellow-green oasis and crystal-clear lake amidst the dark dramatic landscape. Beyond lie the Gaesavatnaleid and Askja. **Tomasarhagi** is a junction of braided rivers beneath Tungnafell.

At **Nýidalur**, in the centre of Iceland, stand several huts – invariably a welcome sight. There is a small campsite on the only patch of green in the area, but even in the middle of summer high winds and near-freezing temperatures make camping a desperate option. The better choice is to stay in the huts which offer both warmth and hospitality. Wardened during the summer months, they can be cut off for periods by snow and bad weather. But, whatever the climate outside, the atmosphere inside these huts is always congenial, with travellers habitually swapping tales and sharing food.

The dusty track south to **Thorisvatn** (Iceland's second largest lake) continues the landscape of glaciers and black gravel plains. Just beyond the lake and close to the main track is the tiny settlement of **Sigalda**, important only for its petrol station. With the development of new hydroelectric schemes several lakes, not shown on all maps, can be seen close to the fork in the main track to **Landmannalaugar**. This is a part of the Fjallabak Nature Reserve and has become a popular centre for tourists.

After a relative absence of vehicles, there is a steady increase in traffic south of Sigalda. The greatest change here is in the colour of the scenery. Instead of the dark Sprengisandur gravel, gaudy green mosses now coat the ancient rhyolytic rocks. The hills are bright yellow, green and red, dotted with deep blue lakes, creamy brown outwash plains and snow patches lying on grey Rhacometrium mosses. Hot springs form the nucleus of Landmannalaugar, and steam rises from every corner of the valley. There are several camping areas but in midsummer the main site near to the hot pools, used for swimming, tends to become crowded.

Travellers are faced with several routes from here. Perhaps the most dramatic is south east to **Bläfjell** and eventually the coast. Although improved, the track still provides adventure in the form of numerous river crossings, many of which require long periods of wading down the rivers to check their depth.

Before Bläfjell there is a track off to the gorge and waterfall of **Eldgjá** (the "fire gorge"). The gorge is the most extensive explosion fissure in the world and cascading into it is the famous waterfall of **Ofaerufoss**. It used to have a much-photographed arch of basaltic rock with a footpath over the lower cascades. The arch, which featured in the Icelandic film *In the Shadow of the Raven*, has since collapsed. The hilly region around Bläfjell is a popular walking area. Ancient lava flows are carpeted with mosses and lichens, while streams and small waterfalls pour out of rocky fissures only to disappear under broken lava and cushions of moss.

Walking rules: Deep crevasses, jagged lava flows and huge expanses of desert – not to mention the weather – don't exactly make Iceland the ideal place for a walking holiday. Moreover, all these features are doubly dangerous in the interior – which is perhaps why hardened hikers are attracted here.

If you are going to venture off the beaten track, you should have already had wilderness experience. Watch the weather carefully: glacial rivers can flood after heavy rainfall or a hot summer day. When crossing (choose the widest point), face upstream and link arms with other members of your party. Make sure that you are more than adequately provisioned – and remember that the water may need filtration before drinking. Wherever, possible seek advice of the wardens and leave details of your intended route with people you trust (don't forget to inform them of your safe return). Many cross-Iceland bus companies will take hikers into remote areas and, if pre-arranged, will pick up again further along the route.

Left, a rainbow ove Landmanna laugur. **Rig** a bus cross the interior, using a rive bank as a r

INSIGHT GUIDES
Travel Tips

Your vacation.

Your vacation after losing your hard-earned vacation money.

 Lose your cash and it's lost forever. Lose American Express®
Travelers Cheques and get them replaced. They can mean
the difference between the vacation of your dreams and
your worst nightmare. And, they are accepted like cash
worldwide. Available at participating banks, credit unions, AAA offices
and American Express Travel locations. *Don't take chances. Take American Express
Travelers Cheques.*

do more

**Travelers
Cheques**

For information, call 1-800-321-0882. © 1997 American Express Travel Related Services Company, Inc. All rights reserved.

Getting Acquainted

The Place

Area: 103,000 sq. km (39,750 sq. miles), Europe's second largest island.

Capital: Reykjavík.

Largest Geographical Feature: Vatnajökull, a plateau icecap is 8,300 sq. km (3,200 sq. miles) in area, equivalent to all of continental Europe's glaciers combined.

Population: 268,000, of which 104,000 reside in Reykjavík.

Language: Icelandic, a very pure descendant of Old Norse.

Religion: 91.5 percent of Icelanders belong to the Lutheran Church.

Time Zone: Iceland stays on Greenwich Mean Time, GMT. In winter: same time as London, 5 hours ahead of New York. In summer: 1 hour behind London, 4 hours ahead of New York.

Currency: the Icelandic króna (Ikr), approximately 100 to the pound sterling and 67 to the US dollar.

Weights and measures: metric.

Electricity: 220 volts alternating at 50 cycles. Visitors from the US will need a transformer. Two pin plugs are the norm, so take a universal adapter.

International dialling codes: to call Iceland from overseas dial +354 then the seven-digit telephone number without area code. To call overseas from Iceland dial 00 for an international line or 115 for the international operator.

Climate

Influenced by the warm Gulf Stream and prevailing south-westerly winds, Iceland's temperate oceanic climate is surprising mild for the latitude (63–66°N). Reykjavík's average January temperature is similar to that of Milan, –0.5°C (31°F), though the July average is a cool 11°C (52°F). Because the Gulf Stream influences the south and west of the country, there are marked regional differences in climate. This is due also to the prevailing winds and

the position of mountain ranges. The north and east of the country experience colder winter temperatures but warmer summers, and markedly less precipitation. The south side of Vatnajökull can get up to 10 times the annual 400 mm (16 inches) of those areas north of it. This is quite evident in the vegetation cover on lava flows. In the Northeast, lava dating back thousands of years is still bare, whilst in the south of the country a 200-year-old flow is covered with a thick layer of spongy moss.

Whatever the weather, you are likely to experience Iceland's most frequent natural element – wind. The Icelandic language allows for at least eight different degrees of wind, from *logn* (calm) to *rok* (strong gale) and you can expect to encounter most of them during your stay. Finding shelter is not generally a problem in the settled lowlands but for the hiker or cyclist, a storm in the central highland deserts or glacial outwash plains of the south may mean hours, even days, of unimaginable misery. The sand and soil whipped up by such winds can blot out the sun, enveloping the land in a brown haze.

Not surprisingly, Icelanders take their weather seriously. The Icelandic Meteorological Office provides recorded bulletins in English, tel: 902-0600, then choose extension 44 on a touch-tone phone.

When to Visit

Summer in Iceland is a brief affair. By June the lowlands are snow free and the land bursts into colour. Between mid-May and the end of July there is almost perpetual daylight. July signals the opening of the highland routes and Icelanders and visitors alike take to their vehicles in a frenzy of activity. By mid-August the nights are cooler, the long hours of daylight tail off and the tourist season draws to a rapid close.

Mid-June to mid-August is the high tourist season and experiences the warmest, though not necessarily the best weather. Most people choose to visit within this period and as a result accommodation is hard to find and some of the more popular campsites get very busy. However, if you travel off the beaten track – and this is not hard to do in Iceland – you will still find

plenty of open space and wilderness.

The first half of June and last two weeks in August see less tourist traffic and often have fine weather, though nights can be chilly.

For birds and flowers the first half of summer is undoubtedly better, but if you want to be sure of getting into the highlands don't travel before mid-July. You can catch the midnight sun in June up in the north of Iceland but it is not until late-August that the northern lights start to appear, as the nights get cooler and darker. Most campsites, summer hotels, tours and excursions only operate from June to the end of August. The first of September signals the end of summer and many tourist operations ground to a definitive halt. This is due, not to a sudden change in weather but to the fact that the school year starts the first week in September. Many teachers and students take summer jobs in the travel business and the Edda chain of summer hotels are boarding schools and must revert to their normal rates.

However, farms and other hotels will welcome business and if you have brought a tent, camping presents no problems. Many of the highland routes are passable with care throughout September – the added dimension of autumn colours and a dusting of snow on the mountain ranges making this one of the most beautiful months for photography.

Reykjavík is increasingly gaining popularity as a winter break destination, and a number of tour operators offer bargain packages out of season. Hotels, most museums and some excursions operate all year round in Reykjavík. If you are prepared to take a chance with the weather, Iceland in winter has its own rewards for the independent traveller. Some bus routes and all flights operate all year round but schedules can be severely disrupted by weather. If you plan to hire a vehicle in winter, a four-wheel drive is a must, but as car rental companies and hotels have special winter rates, it need not cost the earth.

Some tour operators offer winter activity holidays with travel by jeep, skidoo or on cross-country skis (*see Tour Operators*).

Economy

Iceland's economy is heavily dependent on fish, its principal export. Although employing only 12 percent of the workforce, fish and fish products make up over three quarters of export earnings of goods. A national fleet of some 900 vessels, ranging from small boats to the most modern of stern trawlers, brings in the annual catch of around 1.5 million tonnes. Cod is the most valuable catch for export followed by redfish and capelin, though prawns are set to account for an increasing share. Other species include haddock, saithe and lobster.

In a country lacking natural resources, diversification of exports is difficult. Iceland does, however, have huge tapped and untapped potential for hydro-electric power generation. A number of viable schemes have been developed and the government aims to attract power-intensive industry from abroad. Two such industries, a large aluminium plant and ferro-silicon works, were built in the seventies, just outside Reykjavík, with others in the pipeline. Other significant exports are equipment for the fishing industry and diatomite. Although unable to compete on the export market, Iceland is self-sufficient in meat and dairy produce. Woollen goods, skins and leather garments are the principal contribution to exports from the farming sector. A growing industry, which holds promise for the future, is salmon and trout farming, and there are good incentives for farmers to diversify away from sheep-rearing.

Government

Since proclaiming full independence from Denmark in 1944, Iceland has been an independent republic with a parliamentary government. The Icelandic parliament or Althing has 63 members, elected for a term of four years and drawn from eight constituencies on a system of proportional representation. The voting age is 18. For purposes of local government, the country is divided into 23 districts, roughly in line with the administrative division of Iceland into counties (*syslur*). In addition there are 23 municipalities (*kaupstadir*) and 200 rural districts (*hreppar*). Since 1944, no political party has attained an absolute majority in parliament and with few exceptions all of Iceland's governments have been coalitions of the major and sometimes minor parties.

In the centre of the political spectrum is the Independence Party (Sjálfstaedisflokkur), with a fusion of conservative and liberal ideals, and the Progressive Party (Framsóknarflokkur), rooted in the co-operative movement and farming communities. With roughly 38 percent and 19 percent of the vote respectively, these are the largest parties. Left of centre are the Social Democratic Party (Althyduflokkur) and socialist People's Alliance (Althydubandalag) with about 15 percent of the vote each.

Recent developments on the political front have seen the rise of the Women's Party – of much interest to the outside world and taking 8 percent of the vote. Attracting huge publicity and electoral success in the early years, the party has suffered from a real lack of cohesive policies on all but social issues, as its members are drawn from both ends of the political spectrum.

Iceland's head of state is a democratically elected president, serving a four year term of office. Unless opposed, a president is normally re-elected for another term. President Vigdís Finnbogadóttir, elected in 1980, ended her fourth term in 1996, upon which Dr. Ólafur Ragnar Grímsson was elected to office.

Geography

Though often considered an Arctic country, mainland Iceland lies entirely below the Arctic Circle. With an area of 103,000 sq. km (39,750 sq. miles), it is Europe's second largest island. Greenland lies 290 km (180 miles) to the west, whilst to the east almost 1,000 km (600 miles) of ocean separate Iceland from Norway.

Geology

Straddling the mid-Atlantic Ridge on what geologists term a constructive plate boundary, Iceland is one of the so-called "hot spots" and has been built up over some 20 million years, in successive bouts of volcanic activity. The present-day volcanic zone cuts through the centre of the country in a line running roughly south-west to north-east, and it is here that the processes of rifting continue at a rate that has been calculated at 2 cm (a little less than an inch) every year. Around 18 volcanic systems are thought to have been active in historical times resulting in eruptions at some 30–40 different locations, an eruption occurring on average every five years.

Vegetation

Roughly 10 percent of Iceland is covered by post-glacial lava. Some 1,500 sq. km (600 sq. miles) of land have gone under lava or 1.5 percent of the total land mass. Icecaps cover 11 percent of the country, lakes 3 percent, glacial outwash plains a further 4 percent and a staggering 75 percent of Iceland is devoid of vegetation.

Over half the country lies above 400 metres (1,300 ft), and at this northerly latitude the growing season is short. It is therefore not surprising that only one quarter of the country has vegetation cover and a minute 1 percent is forested. Over half the vegetation cover has eroded in the 1,100 years since the settlement.

Icecaps

The 11 percent of the country under ice includes nearly all types of glacier, from small cirque glaciers to extensive plateau icecaps. The largest of these, Vatnajökull, is 8,300 sq. km (3,200 sq. miles) in area, equivalent to all of continental Europe's glaciers combined. On its southern edge Vatnajökull descends to sea level and its maximum depth is thought to be over 1000 metres (3,280 ft). Other large icecaps are Langjökull (1025 sq. km/395 sq. miles), Hofsjökull (953 sq. km/367 sq. miles) and Myrdalsjökull (700 sq. km/270 sq. miles). All the major icecaps are located in the centre and south of the country except for Drangajökull (160 sq. km/61 sq. miles) in the northwest. Contrary to what might be expected, Iceland's icecaps are not from the ice age, but were formed during the last 3,000 years. Since the turn of the century the glaciers have greatly retreated and in some cases almost disappeared.

Lakes

Representing 3 percent of its surface area, lakes of all shapes, sizes and origin are found in Iceland. The largest, Thingvallavatn and Thórisvatn, are of tectonic origin, whilst Lögurinn, in the east, filled a glacially eroded valley. Jökulsárlon in the south was only formed this century, its waters filling the depression scoured by a now-retreating glacier tongue. Lake Myvatn, formed when lava dammed a river course, is one of the shallowest of the lakes, only 4.5 metres (14 ft) at its deepest point. Öskjuvatn, which fills the sunken Askja caldera, is one of many crater lakes, and with a depth of 217 metres (712 ft), is Iceland's deepest lake. Many lakes, large and small, offer excellent trout and char fishing.

Rivers

With high rainfall and abundant glacial melt-water, Iceland is well endowed with rivers. The powerful, debris-laden glacial rivers have an extremely variable discharge with a maximum flow occurring usually in July and August. The longest of these, Thjorsá (237 km/147 miles) and Jökulsá a Fjöllum (206 km/128 miles) can easily treble in volume after prolonged rainfall. Direct run-off rivers drain the older basalt areas, whilst spring-fed rivers are found in areas of post-ice age lava. Most rivers are unnavigable and until quite recently many were formidable obstacles to travel.

Flora

Essentially North European in character, 97 percent of Iceland's vascular plants are also found in Norway, 87 percent in Britain, but only 60 percent in Greenland. The relative paucity of vascular plant species, only 470, is due to the country's isolation and the effects of the ice age. Of the species found today, 50 percent are considered glacial survivors, the remainder have colonised over the last 10,000 years. Typical of northern areas are the high percentage of moncotyledons including sedges and grasses and the huge number of species of lichens. Though many plants are found in most parts of the country, some have a distinct regional distribution and others are limited to a particular valley or slope. By law, a number of species are protected and within national parks and conservation areas all disturbance of vegetation is prohibited. The best time of year for flowers is June

and July. The most widespread tree is the dwarf birch. In most places it rarely exceeds 1 or 2 metres in height, but in sheltered spots can grow to 10 metres (32 ft). Also commonly found are various willows, again mostly stunted, and less frequently a solitary rowan. The only native conifer is juniper, but the Sitka spruce and others thrive in forestry plantations around the country.

People

With a quarter of a million inhabitants, Iceland ranks among the least densely populated nations in the world. Around half of the population live in Reykjavík and surrounding area; the remainder are scattered around the country in smaller towns (the largest, Akureyri, has only 15,000 inhabitants), villages and farms. The principal farming districts are the lowland plains of the south and west, the valleys of the north and the area around Egilsstadir in the east. The steep-sided mountains of the fjord country offer little level land for farming but have excellent sheltered harbours supporting many of Iceland's fishing villages.

Icelanders are the least Nordic of the Scandinavian peoples. Research has shown a stronger Celtic element than was once believed, but the exact percentage has yet to be established. Immigration is strictly controlled and foreigners are encouraged to integrate. Population growth is steady, at around 1½ percent per annum, and migration from the country districts and villages to Reykjavík continues at a rate of 3 percent.

Etiquette

Shyness towards visitors may be mistaken for coldness, but Icelanders are by nature hospitable and innately curious of foreigners and their ways. Family ties are strong yet they are great socialisers and many a tale is told around the coffee table. Within such a small, closeknit society Icelanders find invariably that they are all related, albeit distantly, to one another and are quick to establish connections when introduced, by delving into the respective family trees.

If you are invited to an Icelander's home, it will most likely be for coffee, often accompanied by copious quanti-

ties of cakes and biscuits. It is customary to shake hands, when greeting and leaving, and Icelanders always remove shoes before entering their home.

Iceland uses the old system of patronymics, once common throughout Scandinavia. It raises eyebrows when an Icelandic family checks into a hotel abroad – mother, father son and daughter will all have different last names. Very few Icelanders have surnames. Instead a child takes his father's first name, to which is added son or dóttir (son or daughter) as the case may be. Thus, if a father named Magnus has a son, Jón and a daughter, Kristín, their full names will be Jón Magnússon and Kristín Magnúsdóttir. And as Icelandic women never change their names on marriage, their mother too will have a different name.

A child may also take the mother's name by law, though this is less common. If the identity of the father is not established the child may take the mother's or grandfather's name.

Icelanders always use first names and visitors will be expected to follow suit. The concept of titles, except for ministers of religion, is unknown. The exception to this is on formal letters when Herra Magnús Jónsson or Frú Kristín Jensdóttir would be a correct form of address on the envelope.

In the telephone directory, all entries are listed under first names and if the prospect of sifting through pages and pages of Jón Jónsson is daunting, many entries also give the person's profession (in Icelandic) as well as the address.

Planning the Trip

What to Bring

Iceland is expensive and a hefty 24½ percent VAT on most goods means that many items are double the price you would pay abroad. Bring everything you are likely to need during your stay in the way of clothing and equipment. If you plan to back-pack around the country it is well worth bringing in your duty-free food allowance (3 kg/6.6 lb, up to Ikr 4,000 in value) in the form of dried foods. Freeze-dried products are very expensive and virtually unavailable outside specialist shops in Reykjavík.

Iceland's freak wind gusts have been known to wreak havoc at campgrounds – if you bring your own tent, make sure you are able to repair bent poles, broken guy ropes and holes in canvas. Bring heavy-duty tent pegs; lightweight aluminium pegs may not be enough.

What to Wear

In summer, light woollens and a wind- and rain-proof jacket or coat are essential, together with something for warmer days (wearing a number of layers works best in Iceland's changeable summer weather). If you plan to travel around the country, getting out and about on foot or venture into the uninhabited interior, you must dress accordingly. Your best investment for Iceland will be a quality rain/wind jacket and leggings together with a thick sweater, scarf, hat and gloves. For footwear, bring a thick-soled pair of walking shoes or trainers. Even if you don't plan to do any serious hiking, a pair of lightweight hiking boots is a good idea – many of Iceland's most visited sights are reached on foot and paths that are often uneven and rocky.

Bring swim-wear – even the most confirmed non-swimmers will enjoy Iceland's geothermal bathing pools.

Icelanders are very clothes-conscious, reflected in the range of styles in Reykjavík's fashion shops. If you plan to eat out at one of the city's better restaurants, you should dress up. Although most pubs are casual, for a night out at a club it's a jacket and tie for men and no jeans or trainers for either men or women. The bouncers are generally relentless in their determination to keep to the rules.

For travel in Iceland between October and May conditions can be severe. Although prolonged cold spells are rare, thanks to the warming effects of the Gulf stream, temperatures as low as −20°C (−6°F) can occur and with the wind chill factor, can be much colder. So, any visitor planning to travel outside the Reykjavík area in winter must be well kitted out.

Film

Crystal-clear air and long hours of daylight create ideal conditions for photography and camera enthusiasts will go through more film than they anticipate. All photographic equipment, film and film processing is very expensive in Iceland, so bring your own; think of a number and double it. You may be able to pass on any unused film to other travellers who have run out. If you do have to buy film in Iceland, bear in mind that outside Reykjavík slide film, in particular, may be hard to obtain.

Entry Regulations

The normal entry stamp in your passport is valid for a stay of up to three months. If you wish to extend your stay after arrival, this can be done at the main police station in Reykjavík, at Hverfisgata 115, or at police stations around the country. You may be asked to produce evidence of funds to support yourself and an air or ferry ticket out of the country.

Drink and Tobacco Allowances

Visitors aged 20 and over are allowed to bring in 1 litre of spirits up to 47 percent alcohol content and 1 litre of wine up to 21 percent alcohol content. Six litres of foreign beer or 8 litres of domestic beer may be brought in instead of either the wine or spirit allowance. Visitors aged 16 and over may bring in 200 cigarettes or 250 grams of tobacco. As alcoholic drinks are very expensive in Iceland it is worth bringing your full allowance. If you do not use it yourself, it will make a very welcome gift.

Other Regulations

You may bring in 3 kg of food up to the value of Ikr 4,000 free of duty, but import of uncooked eggs, raw milk products, and uncooked meat, including salami, bacon and uncooked ham, is prohibited.

Angling gear that has been used outside Iceland, including boots and waders, must be disinfected by a vet before bringing it into the country. You may be asked to produce a certificate stating that this has been done. Your equipment can be disinfected on arrival at your own expense.

It is forbidden to introduce any animal into Iceland without permission from the Ministry of Agriculture. A lengthy period of quarantine is invariably required.

Money

The Icelandic króna, divided into 100 aurar, is the monetary unit. Notes are in denominations of 5,000 Ikr, 2,000 Ikr, 1,000 Ikr and 500 Ikr. Coins are in denominations of 100 Ikr, 50 Ikr, 10 Ikr, 5 Ikr, 1 Ikr and 50 and 10 aurar.

You can bring in unlimited foreign currency in the form of traveller's cheques or bank notes and up to Ikr 14,000 in Icelandic currency. It is generally not worth purchasing large amounts of Icelandic króna abroad as a poorer rate of exchange is given. Similarly you should make sure to change back all unused króna before leaving Iceland (this can be done at the airport departure lounge) and you may need to produce receipts of exchange transactions from foreign currency or traveller cheques to króna.

In Iceland most town banks will change foreign currency or travellers cheques and are open from 9.15am–4pm. In country districts banks have much more limited opening hours. US dollars, sterling and other major European and Scandinavian currencies are easily exchanged. Many hotels, local shops, even roadside restaurants and taxi drivers will accept payment in foreign currency. Hotels will usually exchange travellers cheques and banknotes to guests, at a rate slightly below the bank rate, depending on the availability of cash in the till.

Outside normal banking hours **exchange facilities** are available on arrival at Keflavík Airport before passing through immigration (hours: 6.30am–6.30pm), but note that amounts in excess of Ikr 10,000 are not accepted 6.30–9am and 5–6.30pm weekdays, nor on weekends.

In Reykjavík you can change money at Hotel Loftleidir's branch of Landsbanki (weekdays 8.15am–4pm and 5–7.15pm, Saturdays 8.15am–7.15pm), at the Tourist Information Centre in Bankastraeti (June–August weekdays 8.30am-8pm and Saturdays 9am–1pm), and at McDonald's, Austurstræti, Reykjavík, 9.00am-11pm daily.

Credit cards are widely accepted by hotels, restaurants, bars, shops and supermarkets and car rental firms. They cannot be used to pay for petrol at service stations.

Cash advances are available from all banks, savings banks and post offices on Visa and MasterCard/Eurocard and from branches of Islandsbanki on Diners Card. In case of loss here is where to cancel your credit card: **Visa** at Álfabakki 16, tel: 525-2000; **MasterCard/Eurocard** at Armuli 28, tel: 568-5499; **American Express** at Úrval-Útsyn-Travel, Lagmuli 4, tel: 568-2050, emergency cancellation at 800-8111; **Diners Club** at Engjateigur 9, tel: 588-0050.

Health

Life expectancy in Iceland is amongst the highest in the world, attributed to a low infant mortality rate, fish-based diet and excellent health care.

All visitors should have adequate medical insurance, though an agreement exists between Iceland and the member states of the European Economic Area for limited health insurance coverage of its residents. No vaccinations are required unless you are arriving from an infected area.

Public Holidays and Festivals

Public holidays

New Year's Day (*Nyarsdagurinn*) – 1 January
Maundy Thursday, Good Friday, Easter Sunday and **Easter Monday**
First Day of Summer (*Sumardagurinn fyrsti* – Third Thursday in April)
Labour Day – 1 May
Ascension Day – May, June
Whitsunday and **Whitmonday** – May, June
Independence Day – 17 June
August Public Holiday (*Verslunnarmannahelgi*) – the first weekend in August; nearly all shops and businesses close from Friday afternoon/evening to Tuesday morning.
Christmas Eve afternoon, Christmas Day and **Boxing Day**
New Year's Eve afternoon.

Festivals

Dark Music Days: Every other year in January. A festival organised by the Composers' Society, with emphasis on new Icelandic music.
Reykjavík Arts Festival: First held in 1970, this takes place every other year for three weeks in June. The festival features music, theatre, visual arts, opera and ballet and attracts national and international artists and performers.
Festival of Church Arts: Held annually in Reykjavík, around Pentecost and in Akureyri in early summer, it focuses on large-scale oratorios.
International Film Festival: Held every other year in October.
Reykjavík Cathedral Music Days: An annual November festival featuring organ and choral music, with a guest composer or organist.
Christmas: Celebrated in much the same way as elsewhere, Christmas is essentially a family occasion but for the visitor is a time of frustration as most restaurants, pubs, museums and shops are closed. Traditionally Icelanders exchange gifts and eat their festive meal, often ptarmigan or smoked lamb, on Christmas Eve. Icelanders have not one but 13 father Christmas characters, arriving from the mountains where they live with their much feared mother Gryla, one by one on the 13 days before Christmas. Each has its own character but they are all mischievous.
New Year: New Year's Eve is another great family occasion which culminates at midnight with a spectacular display of fireworks. Many communities hold bonfire parties.
Thorrablót: There is no fixed day for Thorrablót, but most communities celebrate it in February. Essentially an occasion to eat, drink and be merry, Thorrablot has its roots in a long forgotten pagan ritual. A feast of Icelandic delicacies, including the dreaded rotten shark (*hákarl*) and singed sheep's heads, is washed down with Brennivin and plenty of song and dance. If you are in Iceland in February it is well worth enquiring if there is a Thorrablót scheduled. Many are private affairs but those in the smaller villages are open to all, though must usually be booked in advance.
Bolludagur, Sprengidagur and Öskudagur: The Monday before Shrove Tuesday everyone bakes *bollur*, a kind of pastry eclair filled with cream, hence *Bolludagur*. Shrove Tuesday is called Sprengidagur (Explosion Day) and traditionally a hearty meal of salted lamb and split peas is served. On Ash Wednesday children collect money, for sweets and delight in pinning small cloth bags, in the old days containing ashes, to the backs of unwary strangers.
Sun Coffee: For many of the remote fishing villages situated in steep sided fjords, real winter starts when the sun ceases to rise above the mountains and even in fine weather the village is in perpetual shadow. It is often absent for several months but when its first rays hit the village again, everyone celebrates with sun coffee.
First Day of Summer: In a country where winter seems to drag on interminably, celebrating the first day of summer in April (usually the third Thursday) seems a little premature. Even so, there are big festivities in Reykjavík.
Sjómannadagur (Seafarer's Day): The first Sunday in June is the greatest celebration of the year in many fishing villages. Often a holiday for the whole village and always for seamen, there are rowing and swimming races and a chance for the young and not so young to test their skill and strength in contests from tugs of war to sea rescue. A fun filled and lighthearted occasion with lots going on.
Independence Day (17 June): Iceland's national day is celebrated on 17 June, the day in 1944 when the country declared full independence from Denmark and also the birthday of Jón Sigurdsson who contributed more than any other Icelander to the struggle. The greatest celebrations are in Reykjavík, with parades, street theatres and music, side shows and dancing, but throughout the country the day is a festive occasion.
Harbour Days: During four days at the end of June, the old Reykjavík harbour is a beautiful background to the fishmarket and maritime exhibition. Also with entertainment programme and a fairground.
Verslunarmannahelgi: The first weekend in August is a long weekend throughout Iceland and everything is shut on the Monday. Icelanders by the thousands take to their cars and head out of town to camp in the wilds or join in one of the organised events that are held throughout the country. These range from teetotalling family festivities to loud rock festivals. Most visitors will probably want to avoid popular destinations for Icelanders (invariably

those where there are trees, like Thórsmörk) at this time. On the same weekend, Heimaey on the Vestmannaeyjar (Westman islands), celebrates its own private festival commemorating the day in 1874 when Iceland got its constitution. Bad weather prevented the islanders from reaching the mainland so they celebrated independently and have done ever since. The occasion draws Icelanders from all corners of the country to a huge outdoor camp for a weekend of music, song and dance and a fair amount of drinking. At Brekkubaer, near Arnastapi, the weekend festival is centred on the mystical powers of Snaefellsjökull and attracts visitors from all over the world.

Réttir: During the month of September farmers set off on horseback to gather up their sheep that have grazed freely in the highlands over the summer. When the sheep are brought down to the lowlands they are herded into pens and sorted. The end of this major event in the farming calendar is celebrated with singing dancing and general festivities. If you are in Iceland around this time it is well worth checking out where *réttir* is scheduled to take place. The Tourist Information Centre in Reykjavík will be able to assist further.

Getting There
By Air

Icelandair is the main carrier operating regular scheduled flights from Europe and North America to Keflavík, 50 km (31 miles) from Reykjavík. The building was opened in 1987 and is regarded as one of the most modern airports in Europe. Airport tax is due on all flights. After every flight arrival a transfer bus connects with the city centre. There are plans for a regular air link to Akureyri, in the north of Iceland, and Egilsstadir in the East. Icelandair offers one- and three-month PEX tickets, a standby youth fare and discounts for seamen. Often the cheapest way to fly to Iceland is to buy a package through one of the tour operators that includes a bus or air pass.

ICELANDAIR OFFICES

Iceland: Reservations, tel: 50 50 100. Ticket Offices, Laugavegur 7; Hotel Esja; Kringlan (Mall); tel: 50 50 300.

Domestic Services: Tel: 50 50 200.
UK: 172 Tottenham Court Road, 3rd floor, London W1P 0LY, tel: (0171) 388-5599.
US: 610B Fifth Avenue, Rockefeller Center, New York, NY 10020, tel: (212) 967-8888.

By Sea

Smyril Line, based in the Faroe Islands, offers a weekly car ferry service mid-June to late-August, linking the port of Seydisfjördur in East Iceland with Tórshavn (Faroe Islands), Lerwick (Shetland Islands, UK), Bergen (Norway) and Esbjerg (Denmark). From the UK the service links with P&O sailings between Aberdeen and Lerwick. If travelling from Denmark, you should allow plenty of time as the return journey takes seven days. From the end of May to the beginning of September, the *MS Norröna* links Esbjerg and Seydisfjördur once a week. Details from tour operators and travel agents or through the Smyril Line offices.
Faroes: PO Box 370, 3800 Tórshavn, tel: (298) 15707.
Shetland (UK): 780 European Ferries, Holmsgarth Terminal, Lerwick, tel: (0595) 4848.
Iceland: Norraena Travel, Laugavegur 3, 101 Reykjavík, tel: 562-6362.

Eimskip, the Iceland Steamship Company, operates a once-weekly cargo service with limited passenger accommodation. Sailings operate year round on the following: Reykjavík – Thorshavn (The Faroe Islands) – Hamburg – Copenhagen – Aarhus – Helsingburg – Gothenburg – Fredrikstadt. Vehicles can be taken, accompanied or on a freight basis. Cabin space is limited and early reservations are essential for sailings between June and September. In Germany and Holland bookings are through Eimskip offices.
Iceland: Úrval/Útsyn Travel, Lágmúli 4, 105 Reykjavík, tel: 569-9300.

Tour Operators

An excellent range of travel packages are offered by tour operators both in Iceland and abroad. These include comfortable hotel or farmhouse accommodation coach tours, camping tours or activity holidays including hiking, river rafting, snowcatting and mountain biking. For those who prefer

a roof over their heads but do not mind roughing it a bit there are sleeping-bag-accommodation holidays. For the energetic, there are backpacking holidays. Winter packages offer cross-country skiing, snowcatting and jeep touring.

For most people it makes sense to buy a package through a tour operator abroad because it will include flights and tour operators are able to get favourable rates from airlines to make the holiday cheaper. The packages offered by the operators listed below are also offered by tour operators abroad. Some operators offer a special service for school and university groups.

Tour Operators In Iceland

Félag Leidsögumanna (The Iceland Travel Guides Association), Mörkinni 6, 108 Reykjavík, tel: 588-8670, has a list of all registered Tour Guides working in the country. A private guide can be hired in conjunction with other travel arrangements.
Atlantic Tours, Kringlan 4, Reykjavík, tel: 588-9880. Package tours.
Austurlands Travel, Stangarhyl 3a, Reykjavík, tel: 567-8545. Mostly camping and sleeping-bag-accommodation tours.
BSI Travel, BSI Bus Terminal, Vatnsmyrarvegur 10, Reykjavík, tel: 552-2300. Mostly bus travel but some inclusive packages.
Icelandic Farm Holidays, Hafnarstraeti 1, Reykjavík, tel: 562-3640. Farm holidays specialist.
Gudmundur Jónasson Travel, Borgartún 34, Reykjavík, tel: 511-1515. Mostly camping tours.
Iceland Safari Travel, Borgartún 22, Reykjavík, tel: 562-4222. Trekking, hiking, camping, snowshoe and cross-country ski excursions, mostly in small groups.
Iceland Tourist Bureau, Skógarhlíd 18, Reykjavík, tel: 562-3300. Mostly hotel tours.
Iceland Travel Service, Engjateigur 17-19, tel: 588-6770. Various types of group and individual touring arrangements, including incentive travel.
Reykjavík Excursions, Bankastraeti 2, Reykjavík, tel: 562-4422.
Samvinn Travel, Austurstraeti 12, Reykjavík, tel: 569-1010. Hotel, sleeping-bag accommodation and camping tours. Incentive tours and conferences also available.
Two local outdoor organisations offer

backpacking tours and day walks and take bookings for the mountain huts. **Ferdafelag Islands** (Touring Club of Iceland), Mörkinni 6, 108 Reykjavík, tel: 568-2533.
Útivist, Hallveigarstígur I, Reykjavík, tel: 561-4330.

UK Tour Operators

Arctic Experience Ltd, 29 Nork Way, Banstead, Surrey, tel: (01737) 362321, fax: (01737) 362321, and The Flatt Lodge, Bewcastle, near Carlisle, Cumbria, tel: (016978) 356, fax: (016978) 327. A comprehensive travel and information service for Iceland. Hotel tours, camping and sleeping-bag-accommodation tours, activity holidays including mountain biking, hiking, river rafting and skidooing, fly drive and independent travel arrangements, bus and air passes. Winter activity holidays. Book and map service. Special arrangements for school and university groups.
Dick Phillips, Whitehall House, Nenthead, Alston, Cumbria, tel: (01498) 81440. Backpacking and coach tours and independent arrangements. Information and book and map service. Special arrangements for school and university groups.
Scanscape Holidays, Hillgate House, 13 Hillgate Street, London W8 7SP, tel: (0171) 221-3244, fax: (0171) 792-3142. Hotel and camping tours, independent travel, fly drive, bus and air passes, information service.

North American Tour Operators

Icelandair/Europak, 21 Pen Plaza, 360 West 31st Street, New York NY10001, tel: (212) 330-1470 ,fax: (212) 330-1456.
Víking Travel, 77 4th Avenue, Box 1080 Gimli, Manitoba ROC 1BQ, tel: (204) 642-5114, fax: (204) 642-8457.

Accommodation

Accommodation in Iceland is expensive but facilities are generally good and the overall standard is high. Guesthouses offer only limited facilities. Most accommodation outside Reykjavík and other towns is only open in the summer months, from June–September. Especially in July and August reservations are essential for all but dormitory sleeping-bag accommodation and campsites. Even Youth Hos-

tels are often full at this time.
All accommodation, except the campsite, can be booked through tour operators abroad and better rates can often be obtained this way. Hotels accept credit cards but payment for guesthouses, farms, hostels and campsites is usually cash.

Hotels

International-style hotels with a full range of facilities are only found in the Reykjavík and Akureyri area. Elsewhere they are only few and far between. Prices range from Ikr 10,000 for a twin room or Ikr 6,500 for a single in a luxury hotel, ensuite shower or bath and breakfast included. Eleven top quality hotels have formed the rainbow chain and offer a special rate: a minimum of four nights with ensuite shower and breakfast costs about Ikr 6,500 for a double and Ikr 5,300 for a single room. The membership pass can be obtained in any participating hotel or travel agency. Tourist-class hotels offer less facilities but most have rooms with private shower/bath and a restaurant. They are to be found in Reykjavík and in towns around the country and are open all year round. Prices are usually somewhat less than those of the international style hotels. In summer Iceland's country boarding schools open as "summer hotels", most operating under the Hotel Edda chain. They offer comfortable accommodation, generally in rooms with basin but not private shower/wc and prices range from Ikr 7,100 for a twin with ensuite bath and Ikr 4,800 for a single with no ensuite bath. Most summer hotels have their own restaurant.

Guesthouses

These are usually small , often family run, which offer basic bed and breakfast accommodation. Prices with breakfast range from Ikr 2,000 for a single room and Ikr 2,600 for twin. Prices can be higher in central Reykjavík.

Private Homes

Because of the shortage of hotel space during the height of the summer, a number of families offer bed and breakfast accommodation in their own homes, mostly in the Reykjavík area. Bookings can be made through local tour operators (see Tour Opera-

tors). Private lodgings in Reykjavík can be booked via tourist information, Bankastreati 2, tel: 562-3045. Prices are similar to those given for guesthouses.

Farm Guesthouses

Over-dependent on sheep-farming, many farmers have been encouraged to move into other areas of economic activity, such as tourism. A network of farms around the country offers a variety of services to visitors from bed and breakfast and sleeping-bag accommodation to self-catering holiday cottages (or summer houses as they are known locally), rented on a weekly basis. Excursions on horseback, fishing and other activities can be arranged. Not all are working farms.

farming guesthouses are listed in the *Icelandic Farm Holidays* booklet, available through tour operators, which also handle bookings, or direct from Icelandic Farm Holidays, Hafnarstraeti 1, Reykjavík, tel: 562-3045. The booklet is also available at tourism offices.

Prices start at around Ikr 1,000 per person for sleeping-bag accommodation, Ikr 2,000 per person in a twin (an extra Ikr 650 with breakfast) and around Ikr 3,000 for a single. Cottages cost Ikr 25,000–35,000 per week.

Travelling via farmhouses can be recommended highly for anyone interested in really getting to know Iceland. Many of the farms are in unique locations, and staying on working farms gives an insight into the country's ancient rural lifestyle.

Booklets of 10 pre-paid nights at farms can be bought either in Reykjavík or from tour operators, giving some discount. Note that anyone interested in saving money should carry a sleeping bag. Staying in "sleeping-bag accommodation" often means you get your own room, although not all farms provide this service. Many farms offer kitchen facilities for cooking, and almost all will cook guests meals for around Ikr 1,300– home cooking, and the ingredients couldn't be fresher.

Each of the farms has its own character and range of services, so careful perusal of the Icelandic Farmhouse Holiday booklet is recommended. They range from the rustic simplicity at Húsey (in the East) to the luxurious accommodation at Hraunbaer in the North. Reservations at the individual farms can be made by telephone, or you can simply drop in at any farm where the IFH sign is displayed.

Holiday Homes

Iceland Travel Service, Engjateigur 17-19. Reykjavík, tel: 588-6770 has 20 selfcatering holiday homes spread all over the country. They cost IKr 35,000-45,000 and provide beds for 4-8 people. They are equipped with shower, toilet, electricity and complete kitchen. Some can only be rented during the summer months.

Youth Hostels

There are 32 Youth Hostels around Iceland, situated in towns, villages and farming districts. Offering dormitory sleeping-bag accommodation with cooking facilities, many hostels also provide meals. Some prohibit sleeping bags, providing a duvet or blankets, but you will need to hire or use your own sheet lining. Hostels are open to people of all ages and in Iceland you do not have to be a member of the IYHF (International Youth Hostels Federation) though prices are slightly lower for members. In July and August it is advisable to pre-book hostels through tour operators or direct with Icelandic Youth Hostels Association, Sundlaugavegur 34, PO Box 1045, 121 Reykjavík, from which can be obtained a booklet, listing hostels and the facilities they offer. It costs Ikr 1,200 per person per night at the hostels, Ikr 1,000 for members.

Mountain Huts

Marked on maps by a triangle, you find mountain huts in uninhabited areas.

Touring Club Huts are owned and maintained by: Ferdafelag Islands, Mörkinni 6, 108 Reykjavík, tel: 568-2533; the Touring Club of Iceland based in Reykjavík; and Ferdafelag Akureyrar, Strandgata 23, Akureyri, tel: 462-2720. Some huts are accessible by road but others are intended solely for hikers. Some are small, sleeping six to eight persons and have no facilities – others sleep over 100 and offer cooking facilities and flushing toilets. It is always advisable to pre-book the huts, as some are kept locked and have no resident warden. For these a key is obtained from the Touring Club's office. All huts are uncatered, so please bring your own supplies. Non-

members are charged a small fee of about Ikr 400.

Sheep Round-Up Huts

These are generally rather basic huts, owned by farming communities and used during the annual sheep round-up in September. Often marked on maps as *Kofi*, many will be kept locked at other times of the year and are not intended for use by tourists.

Emergency Huts

Located on mountain passes, remote stretches of road and along uninhabited coast, these orange painted huts are stocked with blankets, stove, food and a radio. They are, by law, intended only for emergency use.

Campgrounds

Camping is allowed most places in Iceland, but on private or farming land it is usual to ask the owner's permission. Within national parks and nature conservation areas camping is only permitted at designated areas.

Official campsites are found in most towns and villages, at national parks, nature conservation areas, places of natural beauty and at some farms and community centres. The standard and facilities of campgrounds, though not the price, varies. Expect to pay Ikr 330-550 per person per night for anything from a layer of pumice and an earth closet to soft turf and hot showers. A leaflet listing campgrounds is published by the Iceland Tourist Board.

Camping equipment can be hired from Sportleigan, Laufásvegur 74, Reykjavík, tel: 551-9800.

On Departure

The Fly Bus leaves Hotel Loftleidir two hours before flights leave Keflavík. Arrange pick up at reception desks in major hotels. Many people flying out of Iceland combine the journey to Keflavík with a visit to the "Blue Lagoon". Most tours to the Reykjanes peninsula allow you to get off at the airport for afternoon flights (*see Tour Operators page 327*).

(*see Tour Operators page 327*).

If you have purchased tax-free goods (*see Shopping*), you will need to present your receipt, together with the unopened goods and a customs declaration, at customs before departure.

The only exceptions are woollen goods, which you can pack into your suitcase. Don't forget to keep the paperwork available. You are advised to change back any unused króna at the bank in the departure lounge as you will receive a poor rate abroad. Again you will need to produce receipt of previous exchange transactions.

Useful Addresses

Tourist Information In Iceland

Reykjavík: Tourist Information Centre, Bankastraeti 2, 101 Reykjavík, tel: 562-3045. June–August Monday–Friday 9am–6pm, Saturday 9am–4pm, Sunday 10am–2pm; September–May Monday–Friday 10am–4pm, Saturday 10am–2pm, Sunday closed.

Akureyri: Tourist Information Centre, Hafnarstraeti 82, 600 Akureyri, tel: 462-7733. Open: in summer, weekdays 7.30am–8pm, Saturday and Sunday 7.30am–10am and 1pm-6.30pm; in winter Monday–Friday 8.30am–5pm.

Tourist Information Outside Iceland

UK: 172 Tottenham Court Road, 3rd floor, London W1P 0LY, tel: (0171) 388-5599.

US: Iceland Tourist Board, 655 Third Avenue, New York, NY 10017, tel: (212) 949-2333.

EMBASSIES IN REYKJAVÍK

UK: Laufasvegur 31, tel: 550-5100.
US: Laufasvegur 21, tel: 562-9100.

ICELANDIC EMBASSIES ABROAD

UK: 1 Eaton Terrace, London SW1W 8EY, tel: (071) 730-5131.
US: 2022 Connecticut Avenue, NW Washington DC 20008, tel: (202) 265-6653.

Practical Tips

Banks are open Monday–Friday 9.15am–4pm, but country branches may have limited opening hours.

Post Offices are open Monday–Friday 8.30am–4.30pm. Late opening on Thursdays to 6pm at the central Post Office in Reykjavík, Posthusstraeti 5; and Monday–Friday to 7.30pm, Saturdays 8.30am–3pm at the BSI Bus Terminal, Vatnsmyrarvegur 10, Reykjavík.

Most **shops** are open Monday–Friday 9am–6pm, Friday 9am–7pm and Saturday 10am–4pm. Some shops in Reykjavík do not open on Saturday, others open only in the morning. Especially the case in summer. Kringlan shopping mall in Reykjavík is open 10am–4pm and many shops are also open for a few hours on Sunday. Many corner shops, selling confectionery and basic groceries, stay open until 10pm. Out in the country, some supermarkets in the Kaupfélag (Co-op) chain, particularly those attached to petrol stations, may stay open until 8 or 10pm. In the evenings basic groceries, snacks and confectionery are sold at a *Sjoppa* (kiosk). **Office hours** are generally 9am–5pm.

Petrol stations open daily 7.30am–8pm. Sunday opening hours June–September are 9am–8pm. After-hours petrol can be bought at station pumps labelled "Sjálfsali" (self service).

Doing Business

Iceland may be isolated but it has never been insular. From its early days of settlement the nation has relied on trade survival. Iceland continues to trade avidly and there is as much enthusiasm for imports as there is energy in establishing markets abroad for its many excellent products.

To establish business contacts, the following addresses may be useful:
Iceland Chamber of Commerce, Kringlan 7, 103 Reykjavík, tel: 588-6666, fax: 568-6564.

Association of Icelandic Importer, Exporters and Wholesale Traders, Kringlan 7, 103 Reykjavík, tel: 588-8910, fax: 568-8441.
Central Bank of Iceland, Kalkofnsvegur 1, 150 Reykjavík, tel: (91) 699 600.
Trade Council of Iceland, Hallveigarstígur 1, Reykjavík, tel: 511-4111, fax 511-4040.

Doing business in Iceland is generally informal and always on first name terms. Though smart dress will not go amiss, it is really only essential if you plan to eat out at one of the better restaurants or visit one of Reykjavík's less casual nightspots. In business, most Icelanders dress smart casual.

If you are invited to a business associate's family home, a gift of flowers would be most appropriate, or a bottle of whisky. But a word of warning – some Icelanders drink but others never touch a drop.

Just over 91 percent of Icelanders belong to the Lutheran Church, about 1 percent are Roman Catholics and various denominations account for the remaining 7 or so percent.

Reykjavík has a number of churches which hold regular services on Sundays and during the week. In central Reykjavík are Hallgrimskirkja, Skolavorduhaed, tel: 510-1000; the cathedral, Dómkirkjan, Kirkjustraeti 16, tel: 551-2113; the Catholic Church, Tungata, tel: 552-5388; the Free Church, Frikirkjan, Frikirkjuvegur 5, tel: 551-4579.

The **Catholic Church** celebrates Holy Mass in English on Sundays at 8pm.

Outside Reykjavík there are Lutheran churches in all towns and villages and on many farms as well though services may not be held every Sunday in rural districts. Akureyri also has a Catholic church at Eyrlandsvegur 26, tel: 462-1119.

With 100 percent adult literacy and more books published per capita than anywhere else in the world, it hardly comes as a surprise that Icelanders read a lot. Nor that they have several national and daily papers, weekly regional press and countless glossy magazines covering every conceivable subject. *Morgunbladid*, the longest established daily, has excellent coverage of foreign affairs, reflecting an isolated nation's desire to keep pace with the world. *DV*, the other major daily, has a more popular appeal but is still based on serious news coverage.

The English language glossy *Iceland Review* is published quarterly and is available from newsagents or by subscription from Iceland Review, Nóatún 17, 105 Reykjavík, tel: 511-5700. They also publish the quarterly *Iceland Business* and offer a free daily news service on the Internet at: http://www.centrum.is/icerev/.

That a nation of 268,000 should have no fewer than four television channels is also astounding, with a number of locally produced programmes. Channel 1 is state run whereas the other three are pay-TV. Both feature a fair number of foreign films, documentaries and serials and these are almost without exception undubbed. As a result, many Icelandic children have a grasp of other languages, English in particular, even before they start on it at school.

On the Internet

http://EyeonIceland.com. A travel newsletter produced in English for Icelandophiles.

Post offices (*Póstur og Sími*) are found in all major towns and villages and some country districts. The postal system is generally efficient with letters taking 3–5 days to reach Europe or North America. Compared to prices in general, postage is a bargain. Air mail letters or postcards to Europe cost Ikr 45 and overseas Ikr 65. Stamps are obtained from post offices though it is often worth checking at shops selling postcards, as some of them also stock stamps. The Central Post Office, Posthusstraeti, Reykjavík has a philatelic section but stamp collections are also sold at souvenir shops. Icelandic stamps often depict birds, flowers and natural phenomena and many are of low value, making an unusual and affordable gift to take home.

Poste Restante is available at post offices throughout the country – letters should be clearly marked with the surname in capitals or underlined.

Telephone, Telex and Fax

The Icelandic word for telephone is *Simi*. Public telephone kiosks are something of a rarity in Iceland so making a telephone call demands ingenuity and perseverance. Restaurants, roadside service stations and hotels often have coin box telephones, taking 10 and sometimes 50 króna coins and as calling abroad is expensive you will need a plentiful supply. Calls made after 8pm are charged at a reduced rate. Post offices also offer a public telephone service and this is the cheapest and most efficient way of calling abroad. Opening hours are usually 9am–7pm. Try to avoid calling from your hotel room – hotels often charge three times the official rate.

Direct dialling is available to most countries – to call internationally, dial 00 followed by the country code. International dialling procedure in English and country codes are listed in the telephone directory, which in itself makes interesting reading. All listings are under first names followed in many cases by the subscriber's profession. In June 1995 Iceland adopted a digital dialling system which did away with the old regional area codes; instead all numbers were changed to seven digits, the first two of those determining the region. When dialling Iceland from abroad the country code is 354, followed by the seven-digit telephone number. Dial 114 to enquire about the correct country code and 115 for the international operator.

Public telex and fax services are available from post offices around the country and many hotels also offer telefax service to guests and sometimes non-residents.

Emergencies
Security and Crime

Iceland is one of the world's safest countries. Violent crime is virtually non-existent, bar the odd domestic dispute and drunken brawl. However, on Friday night the city's youth takes to the streets of central Reykjavík on a good-humoured drunken spree with a fair amount of bottle-slinging. The centre is best avoided after midnight.

Though Icelanders are relaxed when it comes to locking up, for the visitor all normal precautions apply. Petty theft does occur and places to watch out for in particular are swimming pool changing rooms (always leave valuables at the pay desk) and bars and nightclubs. In the event of theft or loss, immediately contact the nearest police station, where you will be required to fill in a statement. A copy of the statement is invariably required if you plan to claim on insurance.

Medical Services

If you need medical treatment outside normal hours the health centre (Heilsuverndastödin), Baronsstígur 47, Reykjavík, tel: 552-1230, runs an emergency service (Laeknarvaktin) 5pm–8am weekdays and 24 hours on weekends and public holidays. The same centre is open during normal hours, tel: 552-2400. A nominal charge is made. **Emergencies** are treated at the casualty ward (Slysadeild) of Borgarspítalinn, Reykjavík's city hospital, tel: 525-1000. Open 24 hours. Around the country hospitals or health centres in major towns and many small villages give emergency treatment. Emergency numbers are in the phone book.

Dental treatment in Iceland is costly. In an emergency it can be arranged throughout the country and in Reykjavík a 24-hour emergency service is available, tel: 568-1041.

Left Luggage

Hotels, guesthouses and hostels will often store luggage free of charge for guests. The BSÍ Bus Terminal at Vatnsmyrarvegur 10, Reykjavík, has left luggage facilities. Open: Monday–Friday 7.30am–9.30pm, Saturday 7.30am–2.30pm, and Sunday (summer only) 5–7pm.

Special Groups
Children

In Iceland, children are greeted with enthusiasm and welcomed at hotels, restaurants and homes. Most restaurants provide baby chairs and children's portions. Tourist Menus give free meals to children of five and under and a 50 percent discount to those aged 6–12. Hotels, if notified in advance, will provide a cot but families travelling with a baby would be advised to bring their own carry cot. Children aged four and under will often stay free if not occupying a separate bed, but where this is required a reduction for the child is usually given. The Iceland Farm Holidays network offers free accommodation to under fours and half price to those aged 4–11.

Gays

For information and advice contact: Samtökin '78, Lindargata 49, 101 Reykjavík, tel: 552-8539. Open: Monday-Friday 11-12am; telephone help line also on Monday and Thursday 8–11pm.

22, Laugavegur 22, Reykjavík, tel: 551-3628. The city's unofficial gay bar and a popular spot with punters of all persuasions.

Disabled

Wheelchair access is available at most of the major hotels. The terrain and the lack of developed facilities mean wheelchair access to Iceland's natural wonders is rare. There are paved paths in the Geysir area and Thingvellir National Park. For information on vehicles for hire suitable for disabled persons, contact one of the tour operators. Highland buses for wheelchair users are available on request.

The following organisation may be able to assist with information:

Landsamband fatladra, Hátún 10, 105 Reykjavík, tel: 551-2512.

Students

Student discounts are rarely, if ever, advertised. It is worth asking at museums. Icelandair offers a standby youth fare which may help students planning on spending longer than the standard one and three month PEX tickets.

Getting Around

For the independent traveller, a first visit to Iceland can seem a somewhat daunting prospect. Prices are among the highest in Europe; getting to Iceland, both by air and ferry is a major expense; car hire is expensive and four-wheel drive is even more costly and necessity for the highland routes; buses are the cheapest mode of transport but connections are often difficult; air travel is relatively expensive and though services are frequent they are limited to towns and villages and miss out on areas of scenic interest; hitchhiking is unreliable and for the walker distances are enormous. No wonder many independent travellers opt for a travel package. Tour operators offer a wide range of options from a simple fly drive or flight and bus or air pass deal to a week in Reykjavík or a full board hotel, farmhouse or camping tour. It often works out cheaper to take a package of some sort.

On Arrival

Most travellers arrive in Iceland at Keflavík Airport. Some Greenland flights land at Reykjavík Airport and the odd international flight lands at Akureyri, in the north of Iceland. Arriving by sea you will dock either at Seydisfjördur, in the east of the country, or Reykjavík. On arrival you may be asked to produce evidence of sufficient funds to support yourself during your intended stay and an air or ferry ticket out of the country. Icelandair offices abroad are not allowed to sell one way tickets to non-residents unless in conjunction with a return ferry ticket. If you intend to work in Iceland, you will need a pre-arranged job and a residence and work permit which your prospective employer applies for before you enter the country.

The "Fly Bus" transfer coach meets all incoming flights and takes roughly 45 minutes, (50 km/31 miles) by road from Reykjavík to the air terminal at Hotel Loftleidir in Reykjavík. From here an onward transfer service can be arranged to major hotels or you can ring for a taxi on one of the free phones. Bus No. 17 goes at 30-minute intervals during the day and evening to the centre of town.

Maps

Map stockists abroad seem to draw a blank when it comes to Iceland. Some tour operators run a book and map service. Iceland tourist offices abroad may stock the useful (and free) tourist map of the country and city plan of Reykjavík which is adequate for general planning purposes and orientation but not for actual touring. The same maps can be picked up at tourist information centres, airports, bus terminals and accommodation throughout Reykjavík and Iceland.

In Iceland, maps can be bought from bookshops but the best choice by far is direct from the Iceland Geodetic Survey, **Landmaelingar Islands** shop at Laugavegur 178, PO Box 5060, 125 Reykjavík, Iceland. For general touring purposes the 1:500,000 touring map Ferdakort is excellent. Greater detail is on the nine sectional maps in the 1:250,000 series but for most visitors the cost precludes the purchase of a full set. Large-scale 1:100,000, 1:50,000 and 1:25,000 maps of areas of particular interest to visitors, such as Thórsmörk/Landmannalaugar, Myvatn, Skaftafell, Hekla, Vestmannaeyjar and Hornstrandir are also sold there. But a word of warning – the accuracy of such maps, especially when marking footpaths and cliff faces, falls far short of maps in other countries. A general map series on the same scales also covers all areas of the country but some sheets are still under preparation or out of print. Highly recommended is the excellent geological map 1:500,000, with a key in English and Icelandic. A full catalogue is available from Landmaelingar Islands, *see* address above.

Reykjavík

By Bus

Reykjavík's city centre is tiny in comparison to its sprawling suburbs. You can easily wander around on foot through the narrow streets clustered around the harbour and lake and cover most points of interest in a morning. But since most hotels, guesthouses, the main youth hostel and camping site are all outside the centre, it makes sense to use the excellent public bus system run by the Reykjavík bus company SVR. Most services operate 6am–midnight weekdays and Saturdays with a reduced service on Sundays. At peak times buses run at 20- or 30-minute intervals but less frequently in the evenings and at weekends. Bus stops are marked SVR and a flat fare is charged with no change given. If you need to change buses, ask for a transfer ticket (*Skiptimidi*), which is valid for 45 minutes. If you plan to use the buses a lot, it is worth buying pre-paid tickets, which give a small discount, available along with a route map from the two terminals at Laekjargata and Hlemmur.

By Taxi

Reykjavík taxis are one of Iceland's pleasant surprises cost-wise and are certainly preferable to wrestling with luggage on the public buses. Hailing taxis on the street is a hit and miss affair. It is easier to go to one of the taxi ranks around town or ring the stations direct. The five main ones are Hreyfill, tel: 588-5522; BSR, tel: 561-0000; Baejarleidir, tel: 553-3500; and Borgarbíll, tel: 552-2440. Most taxis seat four passengers but some seating up to seven are available on request. If you have unusually large or long items of luggage ring Sendibílastödin, tel: 552-5050, and ask for a minibus "Sendibíll". These are often cheaper than a taxi but are only licensed to carry one or two passengers in addition to the luggage. Don't try to tip taxi drivers – you may get a puzzled response if not actually offend. All taxis are metered and if you require a receipt ask for a *Nóta*. Most drivers speak some English or Scandinavian languages. The busiest time for taxis is after midnight on Friday and Saturday nights when it can be virtually impossible to find one.

Iceland

By Bus

Bus travel around Iceland is time consuming and can be frustrating – many connections involve overnight stays –

but it is nevertheless the cheapest way of getting around. Long distance buses all depart from the BSI Bus Terminal at Vatnsmyrarvegur 10, Reykjavík. In summer, buses depart daily for destinations around the Ring Road and elsewhere. On some routes, brief stops are made at tourist attractions en route.

Because of road conditions and distances, some destinations, like Egilsstadir in the east, require an overnight stop in Akureyri or Höfn. On other routes, such as to the West Fjords, services are less frequent. From late-June to mid-August it is advisable to book in advance, which can be done through tour operators abroad, or once you arrive in Iceland. BSI also operates scheduled bus tours in summer, some with guide but mostly unguided, to places of interest, such as Thingvellir, Gullfoss and Geysir, Thórsmörk, Landmannalaugar and Eldgjá (all daily) and across the central highlands over the Kjölur and Sprengisandur routes (four times a week).

The scheduled main routes, summer frequency and journey times are detailed below but full details are available in the BSI booklet, published each year, available from tourist offices and tour operators.

Reykjavík–Akureyri: daily (8 hours) lkr 3,850, via a mountain route lkr 7,200
Akureyri–Myvatn–Egilsstadir: daily (6 hours) lkr 3,300
Egilsstadir–Höfn: daily (7 hours) lkr 3,300
Höfn–Reykjavík: daily (9 hours) lkr 4,300
Reykjavík–Isafjördur: 2/3 times weekly (12 hours) lkr 5,300, 5,500 or 6,200, depending on route taken.
Reykjavík–Stykkishólmur: daily (4 hours) lkr 2,000

BSI offers two bus passes that are well worth considering. The Omnibus Pass gives unlimited travel on most routes for a period of one (lkr 14,800), two (lkr 21,400), three (lkr 28,000) or four (lkr 31,300) weeks – a one-week out-of-season ticket costs only lkr 9,500. The Circle Pass (lkr 13,600; lkr 19,900 if the West Fjords are included) allows one full circuit around the Ring Road following the same direction. The Circle Pass is unlimited in time and on both passes you can stop off as often as you like. Both passes also offer discounts on other tourist services within Iceland, such as scheduled tours, accommodation, bike hire and ferries.

Combined bus and air travel tickets, Air/Bus Rover tickets, permit a round trip or circular route including some of the highland bus routes and offer a small discount. You buy them abroad through a tour operator.

By Air

Icelandair, together with several affiliated regional airlines, serves all major towns and many minor ones as well throughout the country. In winter, when many roads are blocked by snow, flying is simply the only way to get around. Needless to say, flight schedules can be severely disrupted by weather, even in summer. Icelandic pilots are reputed to be among the most experienced in the world because of the variety and frequency of extreme conditions they fly in. Reservations are advisable on all routes, especially in the height of summer. Information and reservations at Icelandair, tel: 50 50 200.

The main routes with several flights daily are:
Reykjavík–Akureyri: lkr 6,865
Reykjavík–Höfn: lkr 7,965
Reykjavík–Isafjördur: lkr 6,265
Reykjavík–Vestmannaeyjar: lkr 4,565
Reykjavík–Egilsstadir (one flight daily) : lkr 8,365

The airline Myflug operates a once daily summer service between Reykjavík and Lake Myvatn. Travellers who arrive with Icelandair can purchase various air passes which combine several cheap inland flights (round trips all the year round, unlimited flying for 12 days, the *Vestnorden Discovery Pass* or the *Iceland Air Pass*, the latter having to be booked through tour operators abroad). The *Air Rover Ticket* offers flights to the main cities and a combination of routes with an unlimited number of breaks.

Icelandair also has information on several other carriers (*Islandsflug*, *Flugfélag nordurlands*). Reservations can be made in advance or on the spot.

Stand-by reductions are available on certain flights. It is worth checking before paying for a full price ticket. Full price one-way fares are expensive and better rates can be obtained by booking through tour operators abroad.

By Car

Though road conditions in general fall far below the standard of their European and North American counterparts, Route 1, also known as the Ring Road, which goes around the island, together with minor roads in settled districts, present no major problem to the normal two-wheel drive car in summer. Large sections of Route 1 are now paved, as are some of the minor country roads. Unpaved sections can become pot-holed and rutted, unpleasantly dusty in dry weather and muddy when it rains but are still perfectly passable. Where the surface is loose gravel, vehicles need to slow down for oncoming traffic.

For travelling around the coast, a two-wheel drive is perfectly adequate. Anyone contemplating a trip to the interior is entering a different league. Four-wheel drives are essential, and even then you should travel in teams of two or more cars (note that insurance companies will not cover hire cars taken into the interior).

Almost all rental cars are manuals, which can be a problem for those who have only driven automatics. Rental offices will give basic lessons in their car parks, then you're on your own.

Iceland drives on the right. It is mandatory to drive with headlights on at all times and use of seat belts, both front and rear (where fitted) is compulsory. Drink driving is a serious offence – just one can of lager will take you over the legal limit – the alcohol limit is zero! Priority, unless otherwise indicated, is given to traffic from the right – when in doubt, give way.

From November–May, snow tyres or studded tyres are mandatory and all rental vehicles will be fitted with them.

For jeep enthusiast Iceland is a playground of unbounded delights, its many rugged mountain tracks and unbridged rivers a challenge for even the most experienced. Travel through the uninhabited highlands also requires extreme caution and year after year unwary visitors (and Icelanders) undergo the unpleasant and sometimes fatal experience of their vehicle overturning in a seemingly innocuous river or the less serious but nevertheless frequent occurrence of getting stuck in sand. Fording rivers requires the utmost care.

Highland routes generally open the first week in July and close at the end of August, but this varies from year to year and route to route. A map is published every summer showing which highland routes are open and is constantly updated throughout the season. It is forbidden to attempt these routes before they are opened.

By law, driving off marked roads and tracks is prohibited. The high latitude and cool climate means the growing season is very short: four months in the lowlands but only two months in the highlands. As a result damaged vegetation takes years, sometimes decades, to recover. Particularly at risk are marshlands and mossy areas where deep ruts caused by vehicles leave huge scars. The very fine, loose soil is vulnerable to erosion and damage is likely to accelerate the process.

Speed limits are 50 kph (30 mph) in urban areas and 30 kph (20 mph) in residential areas with narrow streets. On gravel roads outside urban areas the limit is 80 kph (50 mph) and 90 kph (60 mph) on paved roads.

Petrol is expensive in Iceland, but regulated to be the same price everywhere: about Ikr 76 per litre (Ikr 310 per US gallon). Regular, super and unleaded petrol and diesel fuel are available in towns, villages and even in remote country districts, but not always at frequent intervals. Before leaving a town or village it is always a good idea to check how far it is to the next fill-up station. In uninhabited areas there is no petrol available and you will need to take spare fuel tanks with you. Petrol stations also stock basic spare parts and most have toilets and a cafeteria or restaurant.

The Ministry of Tourism publishes a brochure on travels in the Iceland Highlands which is available free in many travel agencies or tourist information centres. Or write to: Ferdamálaráð Islands, Laekjargata 3, 101 Reykjavík.

BRINGING YOUR VEHICLE

See Getting There for information on car ferries to Iceland.

Given the high cost of hiring vehicles in Iceland, it may seem an obvious choice for Europeans to bring their own vehicle. However, remember that road conditions are not good and unless you drive constantly at low speed your suspension may suffer and flying stones from passing vehicles are likely to damage your paintwork, whatever speed you drive. The constant vibrations from rutted and potholed roads may also damage your vehicle, not to mention the copious quantities of dust that will enter every nook and cranny. Nevertheless many visitors do bring their own cars to Iceland, year after year, without suffering major damage.

On arrival in Iceland your vehicle may be inspected to ensure that it is roadworthy. You will need to produce the following documentation: a passport, driving licence, car registration document and a green card. A temporary importation permit will then be issued for the duration of your stay, which may not exceed three months.

Fuel may only be imported in the vehicle's fuel tank. If your vehicle uses diesel, it will be subject to a special tax on arrival in Iceland. This is because diesel fuel is very much cheaper than petrol and normally this tax is built into the purchase price of the vehicle. The amount will depend on the make of vehicle and intended length of stay. Full details can be obtained from Icelandic embassies abroad.

Use of mudguards is compulsory to minimise stones being thrown onto oncoming vehicles on gravel roads. It is advisable to buy a grille for the front of the car to protect headlights from damage. Before leaving home try to make your vehicle is completely dustproof and ensure that any luggage stored on the roof is adequately protected against both dust and water.

Before taking a car over a mountain road you should find out whether it is open, tel: 563-1400.

HIRING A VEHICLE

You can hire anything from a Fiat Uno to a 40-seater coach in Iceland, depending on your requirements and group size, but at a very high price. Cars are only hired out to people over the age of 23. It is without exception better to arrange vehicle hire with one of the tour operators abroad who offer a package including flights and car hire. When arranging your rental check what the rates include. Many hire companies do not offer unlimited mileage and do not include the hefty 24½ percent VAT or the highly recommended fully comprehensive insurance in their daily rental price.

For those who prefer to hire locally the following companies offer a full range of vehicles:

ALP, Skemmuvegur 20, Kopavogur, tel: 567-0722 and at the BSI bus terminal, Vatnsm†rarvegur 10, Reykjavík, tel: 551-7570.

Avis, Sigtun 5, Reykjavík, tel: 562-4433 or at Keflavík Airport tel: 562-4423.

Budget/Gullfoss, Dalvegur 20, Kopavogur, tel: 588-0880.

Europcar/Inter Rent, Skeifan 9, Reykjavík, tel: 568-6915.

Geysir, Dugguvogur 10, Reykjavík, tel: 568-8888.

Hertz/Icelandair, Reykjavík Airport, 101 Reykjavík, tel: 50 50 600.

Some rental firms offer pick-up and drop-off at Keflavík Airport and at other places around Iceland. There is often a charge for this. Provided you stick to roads designated for the category of vehicle, assistance will be provided in the event of breakdown. Hire nothing but a four-wheel drive vehicle for a tour across the highlands. It is worthwhile going over your intended route with the rental company to check what roads are permitted for your type of vehicle. Rental charges include basic third party insurance but collision damage waiver is never included and always payable locally.

For groups of 15 or over it is often worth considering hiring a bus and driver. Favourable rates can be obtained through tour operators abroad.

On Foot

Lacking a well established network of long distance trails and with formidable obstacles such as huge expanses of desert, jagged lava flows, deeply crevassed glaciers and swift glacial rivers, not to mention the weather, Iceland is not the obvious choice for a walking holiday.

Yet these challenges are what draw the hiker, and for walking off the beaten track and variety of scenery Iceland is unsurpassed. All safety rules apply and doubly so when hiking in uninhabited areas or crossing rivers.

Venturing off the beaten track is only for properly equipped hikers with considerable wilderness experience. Wherever possible seek the advice of local people at farms, mountain huts and national park wardens' offices and leave details of your intended route.

Remember to inform people when you have arrived back safely. Many of the BSI and other highland bus services will take hikers into remote areas and if pre-arranged, will pick up again further along the route, several days later. Along uninhabited stretches of coastline, spaced at regular intervals, are emergency huts for shipwrecked seamen. These huts are equipped with radios and are not for hikers' use except in a genuine emergency.

The most popular marked long distance trail runs from Landmannalaugar south to the coast at Skógar and takes four to five days. There are huts along the way, owned by Ferdafélag Islands, from whom a key can be obtained in Reykjavík to gain entry, but it is advisable to take a tent as well. This is a very popular route, known to the locals as Laugavegur, also the name of Reykjavík's main shopping street. Scenically, the route is quite stunning but well trodden, though venturing off the track you are unlikely to encounter another soul.

In the Jökulsá Canyon National Park a two-day walk follows the length of the spectacular gorge from Asbyrgi to Dettifoss, with camp sites en route. Within the two other national parks of Thingvellir and Skaftafell and protected areas such as Myvatn, there are marked paths suitable for day hikes.

Another area which is attracting growing numbers of backpackers is Hornstrandir, in the extreme northwest of the country. Abandoned by its farming community over the last decades, flora and fauna alike thrive on a scale unknown elsewhere in Iceland. A series of indistinct and for the most part unmarked trails link the fjords and bays of this rugged area. Completely uninhabited, Hornstrandir is linked to Isafjördur by a scheduled boat service.

The East Fjords district from Borgarfjördur Eystri southwards and Lónsöraefi in the southeast also offer challenging wilderness hiking.

For some the ultimate challenge is to traverse Iceland's interior following one of the highland tracks that run north to south. In clear weather the views are stunning, but much of the route is over bare sand and stone desert with little variation in terrain or scenery. Far more interesting hiking is often to be found in the areas immediately bordering the settled districts.

National parks and some nature conservation areas produce leaflets, including maps and hiking times. These are often more accurate and up to date than the general map series. Maps of Hornstrandir, Landmannalaugar and Thórsmörk areas mark paths but should be used with caution – the Hornstrandir map, for example, does not mark cliff faces. These maps should only be used in conjunction with the general map series.

Crossing Rivers

Many rivers, particularly if glacial, can vary enormously in flow. Heavy rainfall or a hot sunny day can treble their flow in hours. Generally speaking, in hot weather, the flow is highest in late afternoon and lowest in early morning.

If the river looks deeper than knee height, stop before crossing and look for the best place to ford, checking the flow in several places. With sediment-laden glacial rivers it is difficult to judge the depth. Narrow crossings are the deepest, wider crossings will be shallower, especially on straight stretches. On bends, the deepest water is usually on the outside. Where there is an obvious fording place, where the water enters a calm phase forming a pool, the water will be shallower on the downstream side.

By car: Watch out for large boulders, swept down into the fording place by strong flow, or sand – both should be avoided. If necessary, and safe to do so, wade first, using a safety rope. And most important of all – if in doubt, do not cross. Wait for another vehicle, get a second opinion, and help each other through. Keep in your lowest gear, in low ratio if available, and drive slowly and steadily without stopping. If there is a strong current, try to cross by heading downstream, so as to avoid fighting against the current.

On foot: Face upstream when crossing and link arms with other members of the party to steady yourself, forming a wedge shape. Glacial rivers can flood after heavy rainfall or a hot summer day. They can be very dangerous and it is always best to wait until the flood subsides, often in only 12 hours.

Hitchhiking

If you have unlimited time and patience and are prepared to carry a tent and plenty of food, walking where necessary, then hitchhiking will get you round the Ring Road and on some of the more travelled minor roads. But bear in mind that the sparse traffic on Icelandic roads often consists of visitors and locals on holiday, with little space to spare in their vehicles. There is little in the way of long distance commercial traffic and you may find that most rides are from locals on a trip to the nearest shop. Hitchhiking is safe, and though quite reserved, most Icelanders do speak some English. Once the ice is broken they may go out of their way to help and provide fascinating snippets of information about their country. If you plan to hitch on the highland routes be prepared for a long wait – on some routes you may only see one or two vehicles a day.

Cycling

For the mountain bike enthusiast, Iceland might seem an obvious choice. There are miles and miles of rugged mountain track empty of traffic, and even the main roads can hardly be called busy. But there are snags: accommodation and shops are far apart and virtually non-existent in the highlands, so carrying a heavy load is unavoidable; high winds, sandstorms and driving rain can make the cyclist's life a misery; if you damage your bike, you may have to resort to a bus to get you to a repair shop. It is fair to say that most Icelanders regard foreign bicyclists as clinically insane.

But Iceland is however growing in popularity for cyclists, and a number of tour operators offer biking holidays with support vehicle back-up.

Airlines will carry your bike free, providing it forms part of your basic 20 kg (45 lb) luggage allowance. When booking, make sure you specify that you are taking a bike and preferably pack it in the box it came in when you bought it. Around Iceland you can transport your bike on the buses if there is space available, but you may be asked to remove pedals and wheels. Iceland does not have many specialist cycle shops, but for repairs most villages have a *verkstaedi* (workshop).

BIKE SHOPS IN REYKJAVÍK

Fálkinn, Sudurlandsbraut 8, tel: 581-4670.
Örninn, Skeifunni 11, tel: 588-9890.

REPAIRS IN REYKJAVÍK

Gamla Verkstaedid, Sudurlandsbraut 8, tel: 568-5642.
Reidhjólaverkstaedid, Borgarhjol, Hverfisgata 50, tel: 551-5653.

MOUNTAIN BIKE HIRE

BSI Travel, at the main bus terminal, tel: 552-2300. Bookings through tour operators abroad who offer a package including bike hire and flights.

BIKE HIRE AROUND ICELAND

Many places around Iceland hire out normal bikes, enquire at hotels and campsites. Akureyri Bus Station and Lake Myvatn by Hotel Reynihlíd, have a reasonable selection.

Ferries

Iceland has lots of small offshore islands dotted around its highly indented coastline. Many are inhabited because in past centuries they offered easy defence against enemies as well as good fishing. Sea birds too were an important supplement to the diet and their droppings fertilised the grassy islands, making them ideal for farming. Scheduled ferry services link these islands with the mainland.

The schedules given are for May–September only. In winter, a reduced service operates on most routes but the Hornstrandir, Jökulfirdir and Grímsey ferries do not operate at all.

THORLÁKSHÖFN–HEIMAEY

Heimaey (Vestmannaeyjar), the largest group of islands, is reached by a daily ferry service from the south-coast port of Thorlákshöfn. The summer schedule (1 May–17 September) for Herjolfur, tel: 483-3413, is as follows:

Daily except Sunday, 8.15am from Heimaey, 12 noon from Thorlákshöfn. Sundays 2pm from Heimaey, 6pm from Thorlákshöfn. Extra service on Fridays: 3.30pm from Heimaey, 7pm from Thorlákshöfn.

The journey takes 2½ hours each way and there are bus connections to Reykjavík for each sailing. Price one way: Ikr 1,300 for adults, Ikr 650 for children 6-11 years, Ikr 1,300 per car.

ARSKOGSSANDUR–HRÍSEY

The island of Hrísey, in Eyjafjördur, is reached by ferry from Arskógssandur, near Dalvík. Saevar sails daily every two hours each way 9.30am–11.30pm in summer. The journey takes 15 minutes. Price: Ikr 500 each way. Return 9am–11pm. Info and bookings: Nonni Travel Agency, Akureyri, tel: 461-1841.

DALVÍK–GRÍMSEY

The island of Grímsey, the only part of Iceland to touch the Arctic Circle, is reached by ferry from Dalvík. It sails Monday and Thursday, leaving Dalvík at 11am, arriving in Grímsey 3½ hours later and departs from there at 5.30pm.

There is a special bus service from Akureyri, leaving at 10am and picking passengers up when the ferry docks on its return. Price one way: ferry only, Ikr 2,800; with bus: 3,200. Info and bookings: Nonni Travel Agency, Akureyri, tel: 461-1841.

STYKKISHÓLMUR–FLATEY–BRJÁNSLAEKUR

The island of Flatey in Breidafjördur Bay is linked by a scheduled car ferry from Stykkishólmur on Snaefellsnes to Brjánslaekur in the West Fjords, tel: 438-1120. It sails from Stykkishólmur Sunday, Monday and Thursday at 1.30pm, returning at 4.30pm; Tuesday, Wednesday, Friday and Saturday at 10am, returning at 2.30pm.

The journey takes 2½ hours and all sailings call at Flatey Island. If you wish you can stop over in Flatey and catch a later sailing. Price: Ikr 1,300 each way, Ikr 650 for children 6–11. Cars up to 5 metres long pay Ikr 1,300 each way.

Connecting buses to/from Reykjavík run 24 June to 31 August, from Reykjavík at 7am and Stykkishólmur at 4pm.

REYKJAVÍK–AKRANES

A useful car ferry service to avoid the long drive around Hvalfjördur. Reykjavík tel: 551-6050 and Akranes tel: 431-2275. Departs year round at:

Akranes	Reykjavík
8am*	9.30am*
11am	12.30pm
2pm	3.30pm
5pm	6.30pm
8pm#	9.30pm#

* Not on Sunday October–March.
\# Only on Sunday April–September and Friday June–August.

Price: Ikr 700 each way; children 6-11 years Ikr 350.

ISAFJARDARDJÚP JOKULFIRDIR & HORNSTRANDIR

From Isafjördur the ferry *Fagranes* sails to this part of the West Fjords during the summer.

The ferry has regular scheduled sailings on Tuesdays and Fridays on Ísafjardardjúp bay. It stops at the islands Vigur, Aedey and Baeir. Departs Ísafjördur at 8am, returns at 12.30pm. Cost: Ikr 1,800. On Thursdays it leaves at 8pm for Hornstrandir and docks in Adalvik (Ikr 2,300). On Saturdays it sails for Hornstrandir at 10am and docks briefly in Adalvík, Fljótavík, Hlöduvík and Hornvík (Ikr 3,300).

Where to Stay

Reykjavík Hotels

Expensive
(Ikr 12,500 and up for double)

Grand Hótel Reykjavík, Sigtún 38, tel: 568-9000. Modern and comfortable; close to centre of town. All rooms with bath and shower. Children 12 years and younger stay free when sharing with their parents. Restaurant.

Hotel Borg, Posthusstraeti, tel: 551-1440. Historic building in the old town centre, renovated in art deco style.

Hotel Holt, Bergstadastraeti 37, tel: 552-5700. The best address in Iceland. Beautiful art collection and historic library in the public area. Breakfast not included.

Hotel Island, Armúli 9, tel: 568-8999. Brand new, comfortable hotel; 5 minutes by bus from centre of town. Nightclub and café. Largest disco in the country. Location leaves something to be desired.

Hotel Loftleidir, Reykjavíkflugvöllur, tel: 552-2322. Very near the national airport. Restaurant, indoor swimming pool, car hire.

Hotel Odinsve, Odinstorg 11, tel: 552-5224. Modern hotel, Scandinavian style. Exquisite restaurant.

Hotel Saga, Hagatorg, tel: 552-9900. Modern; 20-minutes walk from town centre. Large rooms, some with private steam bath. Nightclub, restaurant, sauna, jacuzzi, conservatory.

Moderate
(Ikr 7,500–12,000 double)

Hotel Leifur Eiríksson, Skólavördursígur 45, tel: 562-0800. Opposite Hallgrímskirkja. Modern, inexpensive restaurant.

Hotel Lind, Raudararstigur 18, tel: 562-3350. Modern; just outside the old centre, smallish rooms. Restaurant.

Hotel City, Ranargata 4a, tel: 551-8650. Quiet location near town centre, small rooms.

Hotel Hjá Dóru, Laugavegur 140, tel: 562-3204. Located in the main shopping street. Large double rooms.

Hotel Reykjavík, Raudarárstígur 37, tel: 562-6250. New hotel, 20 minutes from pedestrian precinct.

Reykjavík Guesthouses

There are scores of guesthouses and private homes offering bed and breakfast in Reykjavík. Some are only open in summer. The tourist information centre and local tour operators have a full list and can help with reservations locally, but in the high season it is best to book through tour operators abroad.

Moderate
(Ikr 5,500–7,500 double)

Baldursbrá, Laufásvegur 41, tel: 552-6646. Rooms with telephone.

Fjölskylduhúsi, Flókagata 5, Reykjavík, tel: 551-9828. Located near Hallgrímskirkja church in the centre of the city.

Gudmundur Jónasson, Borgartún 34, tel: 511-1515. Very modern rooms with shower.

Hjálpraedisherrin (Salvation Army), Kirkjustraeti 2, tel: 561-3203. Rooms for 1–4 people. Near town centre. Cheapest place in Reykjavík.

Isafold, Bárugata 11, tel: 561-2294. Old house in quiet location. Small, cosy, family-run.

Svala, Sakólavördustígur, tel: 562-3544. Near the town centre.

Reykjavík-Area Youth Hostels

Sundlaugavegur 34, tel: 553-8110. Thirty minutes walk from town centre, by the main swimming pool and campsite. About Ikr 1,300 a night.

Arahús, Strandgata 21, Hafnarfjördur, tel: 555-0795. Located in the picturesque town of Hafnarfjördur, near Reykjavík. Accessible by bus.

Reykjavík Campsites

Laugardalur, Sundlaugavegur, tel: 568-6944. Cooking and laundry facilities, hot showers. Busy in summer. Prebook for groups.

Around Iceland

Accommodation is listed by location, alphabetically. Outside of urban areas, establishments are listed by name, or where appropriate by their location. Not all hotels offer rooms with private shower and toilet.

South Iceland
Blue Lagoon

Hotel Blue Lagoon, tel: 426-8650.

Fljótshlíd Valley
(near Hvolsvöllur)

Farm Guesthouse Smaratun, tel: 487-8471. Sleeping-bag accommodation.

Farm Guesthouse Eyvindarmúli, tel: 487-8492. Made up beds and sleeping-bag accommodation.

Youth Hostel Fljotsdalur, tel: 487-8498. Open 15 April to 15 October.

Fludir

Hotel Flúdir, tel: 486-6630.

Guesthouse Ferdamidstödin, tel: 486-6756.

Gullfoss / Geysir

Farm Guesthouse Brattholt, tel: 486-8941. Sleeping-bag accommodation and camping. A short walk from Gullfoss.

Hótel Geysir, by Geysir in Haukadalur, tel: 486-8915.

Guesthouse Geysir, tel: 486-8916.

Hella

Guesthouse Mosfell, Thrudvangur 6, tel: 487-5828.

Camping by the river, also pretty wooden houses for 4–8 people.

Hveragerdi

Hotel Örk, Breidamörk 1c, tel: 483-4700. Good hotel with swimming pool and folklore show.

Guesthouse Sólbakki, Hveramörk 17, tel: 483-4212.

Youth Hostel, Hveramork 14, tel: 483-4588.

Camping by the swimming pool and school.

Hvolsvöllur

Hotel Hvolsvöllur, Hlidarvegur 7, tel: 487-8187.

Guesthouse Asgardur, near Hvolsvollur, tel: 487-8367. Sleeping-bag accommodation at the school (tel: 487-8384).

Camping at Austurvegur, tel: 487-8781.

Kirkubaejarklaustur

Hotel Edda, tel: 487-4799. Also offers sleeping-bag accommodation.

Farm Guesthouse Geirland, near Kirkjubaejarklaustur, tel: 487-4677.

Camping at Kleifar outside the village.

Laugarvatn

Hotel Edda Laugarvatn, (2 hotels), tel: 486-1118/1154 (summer only). Sleeping-bag accommodation at Hotel Edda. Campsite: tel: 486-1155. Swimming pool and steam bath.

Leirubakki

Farm Guesthouse and Youth Hostel, near Mt Hekla, tel: 487-6591. Also camping.

Selfoss

Hotel Selfoss, Eyrarvegur 2, tel: 482-2500.

Farm Guesthouse Hjardabol, just outside Selfoss, tel: 483-4178.

Heimagisting Guesthouse, Heidmörk 2a, tel: 482-1471. Bed with linen, sleeping-bag accomodation, big breakfast and packed lunch available. Discounts for three or more nights.

Seljavellir (near Skógar)

Attractive camping ground and open air swimming pool, tel: 487-8810.

Skógar

Hotel Edda, Skógar, tel: 487-8870 (summer only). Also offers sleeping-bag accommodation.

Farm Guesthouse Sólheimahjáleiga, between Skógar and Vík, tel: 487-1320. Also offers sleeping-bag accommodation.

Camping by the waterfall.

Vík

Farm Guesthouse Höfdabrekka, near Vík, tel: 487-1208. One of the most beautiful farm stays in the country. Horse riding and jeep tours.
Hotel Vík, Klettsvegur, tel: 487-1480.
Reynisbrekka Youth Hostel, near Vík., tel: 487-1243.

Thingvellir

Hotel Valhöll, tel: 482-2622 (summer only).

Thórsmörk

Sleeping-bag accommodation in three huts at different locations. Also three camping grounds.

South-East Iceland

Fagurhólsmyri

Hof Farm Guesthouse, tel: 478-1669. Sleeping-bag accommodation.

Höfn

Hotel Höfn, Víkurbraut, tel: 478-1240. Hotel annex has cheaper rooms.
Hotel Edda Nesjaskóli, near Höfn, tel: 478-1470 summer only. Also offers sleeping-bag accommodation.
Youth Hostel Nyibaer, Hafnarbraut 8, tel: 478-1736.

Hrollaugstadur

Farm Guesthouse, between Skaftafell and Höfn, tel: 478-1057. Also offers sleeping-bag accommodation.

Skaftafell

Freysnes Guesthouse, just outside the National Park, tel: 478-1845. All rooms with shower and toilet en-suite.
Farm Guesthouse Bolti, tel: 478-1626. Also offers sleeping-bag accommodation.
Youth Hostel, Campsite and Farm Guesthouse Stafafell, tel: 478-1717.
Camping at Skaftafell National Park.

East Iceland

Borgarfjördur eystri

Guesthouse Borg, tel: 472-9870. Sleeping-bag accommodation and camping at Stapi, tel: 472-9983 and at Alfaborg.

Breiddalsvík

Hotel Bláfell, Solvellir 17, tel: 475-6770.

Djúpivogur

Hotel Framtid, by the harbour, tel: 478-8887.
Camping just outside the village.

Egilsstadir

Hotel Valaskjálf, Skógarlond, tel: 471-1500.
Summer Hotel Menntaskóli, tel: 471-1505.
Farm Midhús, ½ mile east of Egisstadir, tel: 471-1365. Sixteen beds in two summer houses with shower, woodcarving workshop.
Farm Guesthouse Skipalaekur, tel: 471-1324. Also offers sleeping-bag accommodation and cottages for rent.
Campsite with hot showers in the centre of town.

Eidar
(north of Egilsstadir)

Hotel Edda, tel: 471-3803. Also offers sleeping-bag accommodation.

Eskifjördur

Hotel Askja, Holsvegur 4, tel: 476-1261.
Camping at Byggdarholt, just outside the town.
Farm Guesthouse, between Djúpivogur and Breiddalsvík, tel: 478-8971. Only sleeping-bag accommodation and camping.

Faskrudsfjördur

Hotel Bjarg, Skolavegur 49, tel: 475-1466.
Camping in the centre of the village.

Fell (Bakkafjördur)

Farm Guesthouse, between Bakkafjördur and Thorshöfn, tel: 473-1696. Only sleeping-bag accommodation and camping.

Fell (Breiddalur)

Farm Guesthouse, near Breiddalsvík, tel: 475-6679. Also offers sleeping-bag accommodation.

Hallormsstadur
(south of Egilsstadir)

Hotel Edda, tel: 471-1705 (summer only). Also offers sleeping-bag accommodation.
Campsite at Atlavík by the lake; crowded at weekends.

Húsey

Húsey Youth Hostel, tel: 471-3010. Off the beaten track, north of Egilsstadir.

Neskaupstadur

Hotel Egilsbúd, Egilsbraut 1, tel: 477-1321.
Camping just outside the town.

Seydisfjördur

Always book well in advance.
Hotel Snaefell, Austurvegur 3, tel: 472-1460.
Thórsmörk Farm Guesthouse, tel: 472-1324.
Youth Hostel Hafaldan, tel: 472-1410.
Stóra Sandfell, tel: 471-1785. Between Egilsstadir and Breiddalsvík. Pleasant campsite and horseriding in wooded surroundings.

Vopnafjördur

Hotel Tangi, tel: 473-1224.
Farm Guesthouse Sydri Vík, tel: 473-1449. Eight kilometres from Vopnafjördur. Also offers sleeping-bag accommodation.

North-East Iceland

Ásbyrgi

Excellent **campsite** in the National Park.

Hraunbaer
(between Húsavík and Myvatn)

Thinghusid Farm Guesthouse, tel: 464-3595/3695. Beautifully renovated house.

Húsavík

Hotel Húsavík, Ketilsbraut 22, tel: 464-1220.
Guesthouse and Youth Hostel Arból, Asgardsvegur 2, tel: 464-2220.
Camping east of the village.

Jökulsá Canyon

Camping at Hljódaklettar (Vesturdalur) with basic facilities and Dettifoss, no facilities.
Summer Hotel Laugar, tel: 464-3120. Hotel which also offers sleeping-bag accommodation.

Lundur (near Ásbyrgi)

Summer Hotel Lundur, tel: 465-2247. Also camping and sleeping-bag accommodation.

Myvatn

Hotel Reynihlíd, Reykjahlíd, tel: 464-4170.
Guesthouse Hraunbrún, Reykjahlíd, tel: 464-4305. Also offers sleeping-bag accommodation.
Private **family accommodation** through Elda Travel, Reykjahlíd, tel: 464-4220.
Skjólbrekka Community Centre, Skutustadir, tel: 464-4202. Sleeping-bag accommodation.
Skútustadir School Guesthouse, Skutustadir, tel: 464-4279.
Farm Guesthouse Skútustadir, tel: 464-4212. Also offers sleeping-bag accommodation.
Camping sites: behind Hotel Reynihlíd, hot showers; Bjarg, by the lake in Reykjahlíd, limited facilities; Skutustadir by the school, limited facilities.
Gistihúsid Kópasker, Bakkagata, Kópasker, tel: 465-2121.
Hotel Nordurljós, Adalbraut, Raufarhöfn, tel: 465-1233. Tourist information, fishing.
Farm Víkingavatn, tel: 465-2293. Twelve miles west of Ásbyrgi at lake Víkingavatn, fishing, boat hire.

North Iceland

Akureyri

Hotel Odal, Hafnarstraeti 67, tel: 461-1900. A new hotel which overlooks the harbour.
Hotel Nordurland, Geislagata 7, tel: 462-2600. Newly renovated in a central location. Restaurant.
Edda-Hotel, Grammar School, tel: 461-1434 .
KEA, Hafnarstraeti 87-89, tel: 462-2200. First in the North, but on a very busy road.
Stúdíó-Ibúdir, Strandgata 13, tel: 461-2035. Elegant private apartments for 2–3 people as an alternative to hotel accommodation.
Guesthouse Ás, Hafnarstraeti 77 (opposite the bus station), tel: 461-2249. Made-up beds and self-catering. Rooms for 1–3 persons.
Guesthouse Sólgardar, Brekkugata 6, tel: 461-1133. Located in town centre.
Youth Hostel, Storholt 1, tel: 462-3657. There is another hostel at Lonsa, further out, tel: 462-5037.
Campsite by the swimming pool, with laundry and hot water but no showers.

Near Akureyri

Hotel Edda, Thelamörk, tel: 462-1772.
Hotel Harpa, Kjarnalundur, tel: 461-1014. Summer hotel in woodland setting just south of Akureyri.
Farm Guesthouse Petursborg, just off route 1, north of Akureyri, tel: 462-5925.
Farm Guesthouse Ytri Vík, Arskogsstrond, between Akureyri and Dalvík, tel: 466-1982. Also offers sleeping-bag accommodation.

Blönduós

Hotel Sveitasetrid, Adalgata 6, tel: 452-4126. Campsite in the village.

Dalvik

Gisthúsid Saeluhúsid, Hafnarbraut 14, tel: 466-1488.

Fossholl

Near Godafoss, tel: 464-3108. Sleeping-bag accommodation and camping.

Grímsey Island

Hotel Básar, at the airport, tel: 467-3103.
Múli Community Centre, tel: 467-3138. Also has a restaurant.

Hnausar

Farm Guesthouse, south of Blöndúos, tel: 452-4484. Also sleeping-bag accommodation and cottages.

Hrísey island

Guesthouse Brekka, tel: 466-1751.
Camping in the village.

Olafsfjördur

Hotel Olafsfjördur, Bylgjubyggd 2, tel: 466-2400.
Camping by the swimming pool.

Saudarkrokur

Hotel Aning, Adalgata 21, tel: 453-6717.
Guesthouse Maelifell, Adalgata 7, tel: 453-5265.
Camping by the swimming pool.
Farm Fagranes, tel: 453-6503. North of Sandarkrokur, boat trips to Drangey.

Siglufjördur

Hotel Laekur, Laekjargata 10, tel: 467-1514.

Varmahlid

Hotel Varmahlid, Laugavegur, tel: 453-8170. Past tourist information centre.
Summer Hotel Varmahlidarskóli, tel: 453-8130.

North-West Iceland

Facilities in the North West are limited and official camping sites are few.

Alvidra, Dyrafjördur

Farm Guesthouse, Alvidra, tel: 456-8229. Also offers sleeping-bag accommodation.

Armuli, Kaldalon, Isafjardardjup

Farm Guesthouse Armuli, tel: 456-8801. Also offers sleeping-bag accommodation.

Bjarkalundur (in Reykholasveit)

Hotel Bjarkalundur, tel: 434-7762 (summer only). Also sleeping-bag accommodation and camping.

Breidavík (near Latrabjarg bird cliffs)

Guesthouse and Youth Hostel, tel: 456-1575. Set on a beautiful cove on the westernmost tip of the peninsula.

Brjanslaekur

Camping near the ferry terminal.

Djupavík

Hotel Djupavík, tel: 451-4037. Also offers sleeping-bag accommodation.

Flateyri

Guesthouse Vagninn, Hafnarstraeti 19, tel: 456-7751.

Flokalundur, Vatnsfjördur

Hotel Edda, Flokalundur, tel: 456-2011 (summer only).

Holmavík

Hotel Matthildur, Hofdagata 1, tel: 451-3185.
Farm Guesthouse Baer, Drangsnes (west of Holmavík), tel: 451-3241.

Isafjördur

Hotel Isafjördur, Silfurtorg 2, tel: 456-4111.
Isafjördur Summer Hotel, tel: 456-4485.
Guesthouse, Austurvegur 7, tel: 456-3868. Also offers sleeping-bag accommodation.
Camping by the summer hotel or outside town.

Laugarhöll, Bjarnafjördur

School guesthouse, tel: 451-3380. Has sleeping-bag accommodation and camping.

Patreksfjördur

Guesthouse Erla, Brunnar 4, tel: 456-1227.
Youth Hostel Alfahús, Adalstraeti 65, tel: 456-1280.

Reykjanes (Isafjardardjup)

Hotel Edda, Reykjanes, tel: 456-4842/4844 (summer only).

Skalavík (north of Bolungarvík)

Cottage for rent in a remote bay overlooking Arctic Ocean, tel: 456-7193.

West Iceland

Akranes

Hotel Osk, Vogabraut 4, tel: 431-3314.
Guesthouse Barbró, Kurkjubraut 11, tel: 431-4240.

Arnastapi (Snaefellsnes)

Arnafell Guesthouse, tel: 435-6783. Also camping and an attractive turf roofed restaurant.

Bifrost

Hotel Bifrost, tel: 435-0000/0005 (summer only).

Borgarnes

Hotel Borgarnes, Egilsgata 14–16, tel: 437-1119/1219.
Camping by the main road into town.
Youth Hostel Hamar, tel: 437-1663. Two-and-a-half miles north of Borganes in the club near the golf course.

Búdir (Snaefellsnes)

Hotel Budir, tel: 435-6700 (summer only). Restaurant and an attractive camping site in the area.

Gardar (Snaefellsnes)

Farm Guesthouse Gardar, tel: 435-6719. Also offers sleeping-bag accommodation and camp site.

Grundarfjördur

Guesthouse Asafell, Grundargata 54, tel: 438-6988.
Farm Kverná, tel: 438-6813. Half a mile east of Grundarfjördur. Ideal location for fishing, walking, horseriding.

Fljotstunga (Borgarfjördur near Húsafell)

Farm Guesthouse, Fljotstunga, tel: 435-1198. Also offers sleeping-bag accommodation.

Hellissandur

Guesthouse Gimli, Keflavíkurgata 4, tel: 436-6825 (summer only).
Camping in the village.

Húsafell (Borgarfjördur)

Campsite and **cottages** for rent, tel: 435-1378.

Island Flatey

Vogar, tel: 438-1413. Sleeping-bag accommodation and food in the blue house at the port.

Laugar, Dalasysla (north of Budardalur)

Hotel Edda, tel: 434-1265 (summer only). Also sleeping-bag accommodation and camping site.

Lysuhóll (Snaefellsnes)

Guesthouse, tel: 435-6716. Also sleeping-bag accommodation.

Midhraun (Snaefellsnes near Vegamot)

Farm Guesthouse Midhraun, tel: 435-6675. Also offers sleeping-bag accommodation.

Olafsvík

Guesthouse Hofdi, tel: 436-1650.
Camping just outside the village.

Reykholt

Hotel Edda, Reykholt, tel: 435-1260.
Farm Guesthouse Breidabolsstadur, tel: 435-1132.

Stykkishólmur

Guesthouse Egilshús, Adalgata 2, tel: 438-1450.
Hotel Stykkishólmur, tel: 438-1330.
Hotel Eyjaferdir, Adalgata 8, tel: 438-1450.
Sjonarholl Youth Hostel, Hofdagata 1, tel: 438-1095. Also camping site by the sports field.

Varmaland

Varmaland Youth Hostel and Guesthouse, tel: 435-1301. Also offers camping.

Eating Out

What to Eat

Traditional Icelandic food is based on fish and lamb, the two ingredients most readily available. Throughout the centuries they have been boiled fresh, and smoked, salted, pickled or dried to store for the winter months. Many of these traditional foods have survived to this day and are as popular as they have been for centuries. Nothing is wasted, and you will find cod's cheeks and roe alongside salmon and prawns on the fish counter. Blood pudding, singed sheep's head and pickled ram's testicles can be tried at Thorrablót, a traditional feast that takes place each February. For the really adventurous, how about rotted shark or sheep's head jelly? Many of these specialities will not feature on the restaurant menu but can be bought at supermarkets.

For the more conventional palate, try Icelandic smoked lamb, often served in the home with pickled red cabbage and sugar-browned potatoes. Lamb in any form is delicious in Iceland. Haddock and halibut are often boiled or grilled and served with a prawn sauce or simply with butter.

Seabirds, particularly puffin and guillemot were an important supplement to the diet in days of old but are now something of a delicacy.

Salmon and trout are served fresh or smoked – traditionally using dung. Thin slices of smoked fish are served with hot spring-baked rye bread. Try herring, smoked, pickled or the tinned variety in mustard or paprika sauce.

Icelandic dairy produce is excellent. *Skyr*, a skimmed-milk curd preparation is whipped with milk and eaten with generous lashings of cream. High in calcium and low in calories (without the cream) there is nothing quite like it outside Iceland. *Súrmjólk*, soured milk, is eaten at breakfast and with brown sugar. (If you want normal milk, pick out the *nymjólk* from the plethora of choices.) *Mysingur*, a sweet spread made from whey is popular with children. At the baker's, try rye bread in its many forms and the excellent *flatkökur*, rye pancakes.

Where to Eat

Eating out in Iceland is expensive and the portions tend to be small. The quality of ingredients and preparation is, however, excellent. Many restaurants offer lower prices at lunchtime. Nearly all restaurants accept Visa and Mastercard and many will take American Express and Diners cards. All restaurants displaying the sign **Tourist Menu** offer a set menu during the summer months with a soup or starter followed by a fish or meat main course and coffee, for a fixed price. Prices are lower at lunch ranging from Ikr 750–1300 per person with Ikr 1,200–2,000 for the evening meal. Meals are generally good value and children under 6 eat free and 6–12 year olds pay half price. Most restaurants are open for lunch 11.30am–2.30pm and evening meals 6–11.30pm. In Reykjavík it is advisable to book in advance for evening meals at weekends.

A la carte prices for a three-course meal (without drinks) range from **Expensive** (Ikr 3,500–5,000), to **Moderate** (Ikr 2,500–3,500) and **Good Value** (Ikr 1,500–2,500).

Outside of Reykjavík and Akureyri restaurants are generally in hotels. On the road, many service stations serve snacks and light meals. These tend to be fast food, such as burgers and hot dogs and not really good value for money. The good news is that coffee is almost always a bottomless cup.

The following list covers only Reykjavík. Outside the capital there is little choice and, as mentioned above, most restaurants are in hotels.

Expensive
Perlan, Öskjuhlid, Reykjavík, tel: 562-0200. An unmistakable landmark, built on top of the geothermal hot water storage tanks on Öskjuhlid hill, Perlan offers fine views over the city to the mountains beyond. Inside the glass dome are a cafeteria, cake shop and ice cream parlour. On the revolving top floor, a restaurant.
Hotel Holt, Bergstadastraeti 37, Reykjavík, tel: 552-5700. International cuisine, with a strong Icelandic ele-

ment, Hotel Holt's restaurant doubles as an art gallery, with fine works of some of the country's best artists.
Hotel Loftleidir Floral, Reykjavík Airport, tel: 552-2321. Fish and lamb specialities. Pleasant atmosphere and good service.
Videyjarstofa, Videy Island, tel: 552-8470. Fine Icelandic cuisine in a unique setting on this island just off the coast of Reykjavík. The ferry leaves from Sundahöfn.

Moderate
Café Opera, Laekjargata 2, tel: 552-9499. Cosy café and restaurant with chunky steaks. Tourist menu.
Jónatan Livingstone Mávur, Tryggvagata 4–6, tel: 551-5520. Very good fish restaurant, Icelandic cuisine and home cooking near the harbour.
Laekjarbrekka, Bankastraeti 2, tel: 551-4430. Restored wooden building in the town centre. Tourist menu.
Marhaba, Hotel Reykjavík, Raudarar-stígur 37, tel: 562-6766. What used to be the first brewery in Iceland is now a Mediterranean restaurant. Lebanese cuisine and belly dancing included.
Naust, Vesturgata 6, tel: 551-7759. Icelandic menu and buffet during the summer. Interior decorated like a ship.
Pasta Basta Café, Klapparstígur 38, tel: 561-3131. Inexpensive pasta buffet at noon. Lamb and fish recommended in the evening.
Vid Tjörnina, Templarasund 3, tel: 551-8666. *Fruits de Mer* by one of the country's best chefs. Wine and dine in a grand mansion of bygone days. Private rooms for groups.
Thrir frakkar hjá Ulfari, Baldursgata 14, tel: 552-3939. Small restaurant in the old town living quarters. Fish à la Iceland, delicious.

Good Value
Caruso, Thingholtsstraeti 1, tel: 562-7335. Italian restaurant, inexpensive seafood and pasta buffet in the evening.
Pizza 67, Tryggvagata 26, tel: 561-9900. At the harbour with good pizza and pasta dishes.
Potturinn og Pannan, Brautarholt 22, tel: 551-1690. Outside the town centre. Inexpensive fish dishes and a self-service salad bar.

Vegetarian
Until recently, authentic vegetarian restaurants were as rare as white elephants in Iceland. Happily, the situation has improved.
A naestu grösum, Laugavegur 26, Reykjavík (entrance from Klapparstígur), tel: 552-8410. The city's first – and for years the *only* – vegetarian restaurant. Limited opening hours (daily 11.30am–2pm and 6–8pm). Organic wines and beers.
Graenn kostur, Skólavördustígur 8, tel: 552-2028. Reasonably-priced. Offers meals for candida sufferers. Eat in or take out.
Vaent og Graent, Veltusund 1, tel: 551-5543. Newest addition to the vegetarian scene, smokeless and overlooking Ingólfstorg Square.

Drinking
Like elsewhere in Scandinavia, Iceland has strict rules about buying and drinking alcohol. Visitors should bring in their full duty free allowance because all alcohol drinks is very expensive in Iceland. Wines, spirits and beers over 2.25 percent alcohol are only sold at state controlled outlets, ATVR shops in Reykjavík, Hafnarfjördur, Keflavík, Selfoss, Egilsstadir, Höfn, Seydisfjördur, Húsavík, Akureyri and Isafjördur. Light beer can be bought in supermarkets.

In restaurants wines are expensive starting at Ikr 1,800 and the sky is the limit. In pubs a half-litre of draught lager costs around Ikr 500. Penalties for drink-driving are heavy, and the permitted blood-alcohol level is zero.

Iceland's local home-produced drink is Brennivin, a caraway seed flavoured spirit, drunk icy cold. It is generally referred to as "Black Death", to give you an idea of its strength. Most Icelanders drink beer, vodka, whisky, wine, water or coffee. The water is considered to be the cleanest in Europe and can be consumed straight from almost any river or stream. Coffee is very cheap. You pay once and drink as much as you like.

Pubs
In the last decade Reykjavík at night has been transformed from a sleepy provincial city to one of the hottest nightspots in Scandinavia, with as lively a pub culture as you will find any-

where. But most pubs don't even start getting lively until 11pm. Many are closed in the day, and up to 10pm they only admit guests who are also eating. If you are intent on serious drinking come prepared – a half litre of draught beer costs Ikr 500–600 in most places. And pubs come, pubs go; names change and so do the clientele; and nowhere more than in Reykjavík. Outside of Reykjavík, few towns have a pub and the only place for a drink will be the local hotel.

In most pubs, the clientele is young and dress is casual. For upmarket Reykjavík establishments you have to dress up, as for night clubs. Most pubs are open Sunday to Thursday 6pm–1am and Friday to Saturday 6pm–2.30am. Some open at lunch, some stay open until 3am on Friday and Saturday. In Iceland you have to be 20 to buy alcohol and you may be asked to show proof of your age.

REYKJAVÍK PUBS

Cafe List, Klapparstígur 26, Reykjavík, tel: 562-5059. Small but very popular Spanish-style pub. Favourite hang-out of artists, writers, actors and other trendy types. Serves tapas.

Café Romance, Laekjargata 2, tel: 562-4045. Up market pub in the heart of Reykjavík with piano bar and open fireplace. Cosy and chic. Over 30's, smart dress required.

Fógetinn, Adalstraeti 10, tel: 551-6323. An English-style pub in one of Reykjavík's oldest buildings. Live music on some nights, often Icelandic tunes. Mixed age group.

Gaukur á Stöng, Tryggvagata 22, tel: 551-1556. Reykjavík's first pub, often crowded at weekends. Good live rock music at weekends. Under 30s.

Glaumbar, Tryggvagata 20, tel: 552-6868. A lively, American style bar in central Reykjavík. Clientele mostly young. Many athletes – some professional. Dress and music – the louder the better. Very loud at weekends.

Hard Rock Café, Kringlan Centre, tel: 568-9888. Much the same as others in the chain around the world, but many travellers visit only to buy the T-shirt. Don't miss the little bar on the second floor.

Kaffibarinn, Bergstadastraeti 1, tel: 551-1588. Small with decor which calls forth images of Amsterdam coffee shops. Owned in part by hip indi-

viduals from the artistic community. Tends to be very busy at weekends.

Kringlukrain, Kringlan 4 (next to the shopping mall), tel: 568-0878. English-style sing along pub often with live music. Over 30s.

Sólon Islandus, Bankastraeti 7, Reykjavík, tel: 551-2666. European-style cafe by day, popular bar by night. Huge windows make for great people-watching.

Tunglid, Laekjargata 4, Reykjavík, tel: 551-6313. Hot disco, techno-crowd.

Ölver, Alfheimar 74, Glaesibaer, tel: 568-6220. Iceland's first karaoke bar. Big-screen satellite TV which draws a crowd for watching sports events.

Attractions

Culture

That a country with a population of 250,000 has four professional theatre companies, a thriving film industry, a national ballet, opera, symphony orchestra and hosts an international arts festival every other year is itself remarkable. Add to this a dozen or so museums and galleries in Reykjavík and over 50 throughout the rest of the country, an opera singer of international acclaim, a jazz band that made it in the UK charts, a rock group with a cult following abroad, and a world-class female pop star – can anywhere else in the world match Iceland for variety and intensity of cultural activity within such a small community?

Museums and Galleries
Reykjavík

Many museums and galleries are closed on Monday and throughout the winter. Some will open at special times for groups, by arrangement. Entrance fees, where charged, are usually modest, Ikr 100–300 with reductions for children and sometimes students. An offer worth noting is the Reykjavík Tourist Card which entitles its holders to free fares on buses, as well as free admission to swimming pools and

some museums. One, two or three-day cards available, costing Ikr. 600, 800 and 1,000 respectively. Available from Tourist Information centres.

Arbaer Open-Air Museum, Arbaer, tel: 577-1111. Ikr 300, free for children younger than 16 and for holders of Reykjavík Tourist Card, 50 percent discount for students and groups. A collection of turf and timber buildings moved to the site of Arbaer farm from various locations in Reykjavík and around Iceland. As well as housing permanent displays of household items and furnishings used through the centuries, the museum puts on special exhibitions, demonstrations of traditional skills and a variety of activities during the summer. Open: June–August daily except Mondays 10am–6pm; at other times, open by arrangement. Buses: 10 from Hlemmur terminal and 110 from Laekjartorg.

Asgrimur Jónsson's Collection, Bergstadastraeti 74 (city centre), tel: 551-3644. Permanent display by one of the country's best artists. Open: June–August daily 1.30–4pm except Monday; September–November and February–May Saturday and Sunday 1.30–4pm only.

Asmundur Sveinsson Museum, Sigtun, tel: 553-2155. Ikr. 200, free for holders of Reykjavík Tourist Card. An outdoor display of works by one of Iceland's greatest sculptors and an indoor museum collection. Asmundur Sveinsson drew inspiration from saga events, folklore and everyday life. His works are also on display at locations around Reykjavík. Open: May 1–Sept. 30, 10am–6pm, daily except Monday; during winter on Saturday and Sunday only 1pm–4pm. (sculpture garden open at all hours). Bus: 5 eastbound from Laekjartorg.

Arni Magnússon Institute, Sudurgata (on the university campus), tel: 525-4010. A research institute which also displays to the public some of Iceland's treasured early manuscripts of sagas and other works. Open June–August, 1–5pm daily. **Einar Jónsson Museum**, Njardargata (near Hallgrímskirkja, in the city centre), tel: 551-3797 (free for children under 12). Ikr 200. A collection of works by one of Iceland's great sculptors. Many of his works combine a classical human form with symbols drawn from Norse, Greek and Oriental mythology. Open: June 1–

September 15 daily 1.30am–4pm; October–November and February–May Saturday and Sunday, 1.30–4pm. Sculpture garden open all year.

Hafnarborg, Strandgata 34, Hafnarfjördur, tel: 555-0080. The Hafnarfjördur municipal arts centre with exhibitions by Icelandic and foreign artists. Open daily (except Tuesday) 12–6pm, Thursday until 9pm. Hafnarfjördur bus from Laekjargata, Reykjavík.

Kjarvalsstadir, Flókagata, Reykjavík, tel: 552-6131/6188. Ikr. 300, children under 16 free, seniors, disabled, students (with card) and holders of Reykjavík Tourist Card. Reykjavík's municipal art gallery hosts exhibitions of works of Icelandic and foreign artists and dedicates a whole room to a permanent display of the works of renowned painter, Jóhannes S. Kjarval, noted for his textured landscapes of moss, rock and earth as well as some fine portraits. Open daily 10am–6pm. Buses: 1 and 3 from Laekjartorg or 15 minutes walk from city centre.

Maritime Museum, Vesturgata 8, Hafnarfjördur, tel: 565-4242. Exhibition tracing the development of the fishing industry. Hafnarfjördur Folk Museum is next door. Ikr 200 (free for students, seniors and children under 17). Both open: June–September 1–5pm daily; October–May Saturday and Sunday 1–5pm. Hafnarfjördur bus from Laekjargata, Reykjavík.

National Gallery of Iceland, Frikirkjuvegur 7 (by the lake), tel: 562-1000. The most comprehensive collection of Icelandic art in the country on permanent display, with special exhibitions. Open: daily except Monday noon–6pm.

National Museum of Iceland, Sudurgata (by the university campus), tel: 552-8888. Ikr 200, children free. Founded in 1863 the museum covers settlement to the early 20th century. Mid-May to mid-September daily 11am–5pm, except Monday. Otherwise Sunday, Tuesday, Thursday and Saturday noon–5pm.

Natural History Museum, Hlemmurtorg, (by Hlemmur bus terminal, 10 minutes walk from the city centre), tel: 562-9822. An exhibition of Icelandic geological, botanical and zoological specimens. Open Sunday, Tuesday, Thursday and Saturday 1.30–6pm. Admission free.

Nordic House, Saemundargarta (by the university campus), tel: 551-7030.

Established to maintain cultural links between Iceland and other Nordic countries, the centre hosts exhibitions throughout the year and has a library and cafeteria open daily. Open: 2–7pm during exhibitions.

Sigurjón Olafsson Museum, Laugarnestangi 70, tel: 553-2906. Ikr 200, children free. A permanent display, indoors and outdoors, of works by one the country's best known modern sculptors. Seaside cafe with one of the most impressive views in the city. June–August Tuesday night concerts at 8.30pm. Open: June–August 2pm–5pm daily. Bus: 4 from Laekjargata, eastbound.

SMALL GALLERIES

The following galleries are mostly small and privately owned. For those interested in buying a work of art, many exhibits are on sale.

Bjarni, Skólavördustígur 44, Reykjavík, tel: 552-5128. Open: 10am–6pm daily.

Galleri Borg, Austurstraeti 6, Reykjavík, tel: 552-4211. Open: Monday–Friday noon–6pm, Saturday and Sunday 2–6pm.

Galleri Fold, Laugavegur 118d (entrance from Raudarárstígur), Reykjavík, tel: 551-0400. Hours: Monday–Friday, 10am–6pm, Saturday 10am–4pm, Sunday 2pm–5pm. (Closed Sunday in July and August).

Galleri Kobold, Laugarvegur 55b, Reykjavík, tel: 552-6080. Open: Tuesday–Friday noon–5pm, Saturday and Monday at irregular intervals.

Galleri List, Skipholt 50b, Reykjavík, tel: 581-4020. Open: Monday–Friday 11am–6pm, Saturday 11am–2pm.

Akureyri

Botanical Gardens, Eyrlandsvegur. An almost complete collection of Icelandic flora makes this a must for anyone interested in botany. The sheltered and beautifully laid out gardens thrive in Akureyri's warmer summer climate. Open: daily 8am–10pm except Sunday 9am–10pm from June to the end of September.

Folk Museum, Adalstraeti 58, tel: 462-4162. A collection of items pertaining to everyday life in past times, gathered from all over the Eyjafjördur area. The turf church outside the museum dates from 1846 and was moved here from the nearby village of

Svalbard. Open: daily June to mid-September, 11am–5pm; at other times of year open Sunday 2–4pm.

Nonnahús, Adalstraeti 54, tel: 462-3555. The house where the writer Jón Sveinsson spent part of his youth, now open to the public. With its rustic furnishings it is a good example of a simple 19th-century family home. Open: daily June–August 10am–5pm.

Sigurhaedir, Eyrlandsvegur 3, tel: 462-1030. The home of priest, poet and writer, Matthias Jochumsson (1857–1920). Contains his works, furniture and personal effects. Daily mid-June to mid-September 3–5pm.

Laxdalshús, Hafnarstraeti 11, tel: 462-4490. The oldest house in town shows pictures and videos of bygone days in Akureyri as well as the town history. The restaurant is recommended. Open: 11am–5pm daily.

Around Iceland

Most country museums are either Folk or Maritime Museums. Folk Museums are often in turf farm buildings and contain furnishings and farm and household implements used in the past. Maritime Museums are concerned with life at sea and many have well preserved examples of boats and fishing equipment and photographs that document the hardships of life in these remote communities.

WEST ICELAND

Dalamanna Folk Museum, Hotel Edda, tel: 434-1265. A folk museum, stone collection and photographic archives at the birthplace of Gudrún Osvífursdóttir, heroine of Laxdaela Saga.

Hnjótur Folk Museum, (near Patreksfjördur), tel: 456-1590. A small museum displaying implements used in fishing and agriculture with a stone collection and fine old photographs. Open: June to mid-September, 10am–5pm. At other times by arrangement.

Jón Sigurdsson Museum, Hrafnseyri, Arnarfjördur, tel: 456-8260. A small museum and chapel dedicated to Jón Sigurdsson, a key figure in the 19th-century struggle for independence. Jón Sigurdsson was born at Hrafnseyri on 17 June 1811. Each year Iceland celebrates Independence Day on 17 June. Open: daily 1–8pm during the summer.

NORTH ICELAND

Glaumbaer Folk Museum, (in Skagafjördur), tel: 453-6173. One of the country's best and most visited folk museums, housed in original turf farm buildings from the 18th and 19th centuries. The church dates from 1865 and contains a 17th-century pulpit. The rowan tree behind it dates from the same year, planted on the grave of his parents by the builder and is one of the oldest trees in Iceland. Open 1 June to 30 September, 9am–6pm.

Grenjadarstadur Folk Museum, Grenjadarstadur, Adaldalur, tel: 464-3545. A 19th-century turf farm museum and an interesting gravestone in the nearby church with runic inscriptions. Open: daily June–August, 10am–6pm.

Laufás Folk Museum, Laufás (in Eyiafjördur), tel: 463-3106. A renovated mid-19th century turf parsonage and farm. Less visited than others and well worth a look. Open: 1 June–15 September, daily except Monday 10am–6pm.

Reykir Folk Museum, Hrutafjördur, tel: 451-0040. Shows the reconstructed interior of a 19th-century farmhouse, an old shark-fishing boat and household and farm implements from past days. July–August 10am–noon and 1–6pm, at other times by arrangement.

Saurbaer Turf Church, Saurbaer (near Akureyri). The church, built in 1838, is a protected building open to the public. If closed, ask for the key at the farm.

Vídimyri Turf Church, Varmahlid, tel: 453-8167. The church is open daily 9am–6pm, if closed the key can be obtained from the farm nearby.

EAST ICELAND

Burstafell Folk Museum, (near Vopnafjördur), tel: 473-1466. One of the finest preserved turf farms in the country, off the beaten track and little visited. Open: daily mid-June to mid-September, 10am–7pm.

SOUTH ICELAND

Keldur, (near Hella), tel: 487-8458. This historical turf farm dates in part from the 12th century, making it the oldest building in Iceland. A hidden underground passage provided an escape route at times of siege. June to mid-September, 10am–6pm, at other times by arrangement with the farm.

Nupsstadur Turf Church, Nupsstadur (between Kirkjubaejarklaustur and Skaftafell). A beautiful turf church, dating in part from the 17th century and maintained by the National Museum. Open: daily throughout the year.

Skógar Folk Museum, Skógar, tel: 487-8845. Several turf farm buildings and an attached museum containing one of the finest collections of household and farming implements in the country. The knowledgable curator delights in showing visitors around. Daily May–September, 9am–6pm.

Reconstructed Medieval Farm in Thjorsadalur (near Burfell power station), tel: 487-7713. A reconstruction of an 11th-century farm, based on the remains uncovered by the excavations at nearby Stöng. The excavation site at Stöng is also open to visitors. Open: during the summer daily 1–5pm.

Concerts

Regular venues in Reykjavík include the following:

The Nordic House, Hringbraut (by the university campus), tel: 551-7030.

The Sigurjon Olafsson Museum, Laugarnestangi, tel: 553-2906. Tuesday evenings.

University Concert Hall, Hagatorg (opposite Hotel Saga), tel: 562-2255. Home of the Iceland Symphony Orchestra.

Instrumental and choral music concerts often take place in Reykjavík's churches. These are advertised in *What's on in Reykjavík* and in the national press.

Summer concerts are held in the church at Skálholt, focusing on baroque chamber music, tel: 486-8860. Each year an Icelandic "Composer in Residence" is featured. Concerts are held every weekend throughout July and August and are free. In the north of Iceland regular summer concerts take place in the churches at Myvatn (Reykjahlíd) and Akureyri. Enquire at tourist offices for details.

Theatre, Ballet & Opera

For information on current productions contact the Tourist Information Centre.

Reykjavík

The City Theatre (Reykjavík Theatre Company), Listabraut 8, tel: 568-8000.

The National Theatre, Hverfisgata 19, tel: 551-1200.

The National Ballet Company, Engjateigur 1, tel: 588-9188.

The Icelandic Opera, Ingolfsstraeti, tel: 551-1475.

Light Nights, Tjarnabio, Tjarnagata 12, (by the lake in the city centre), tel: 551-9181. A unique theatrical presentation in English of scenes from Iceland's history and literature. Performing mid-June to the end of August, nightly except Sunday at 9pm. A synopsis of the show is available at the door in French, German, Norwegian and Icelandic.

Akureyri

The **Akureyri Theatre Company**, Hafnarstraeti 57, tel: 462-1400. Open September–June.

Cinema

Icelanders are avid cinema-goers and Reykjavík has an amazing number of screens considering its size. Most films are from the US though a certain number of Icelandic and European films are shown as well. All films are advertised in the daily press and shown with the original soundtrack, sub-titled in Icelandic. Occasionally there are special film festivals which are advertised in the press and in *What's on in Reykjavík*.

The Volcano Show, Hellusund 6a, (opposite Hotel Holt), tel: 551-3230. A 2-hour film programme, presented by the film maker Vilhjalmur Knudsen, documenting volcanic eruptions in recent years in Iceland. There are daily showings in summer in English (10am, 3pm, 8pm) and other languages, including German at 5.30pm. Essential viewing for anyone interested in Iceland's natural history.

Other towns throughout Iceland have cinemas and smaller villages will show films once or twice a week.

Architecture

No houses from the settlement or medieval times remain, but excavations and early documents suggest that houses at that time resembled the long houses of Atlantic Norway and Northern Britain. Excavations at Stöng (Thjorsá Valley), destroyed by an eruption of Hekla in 1104, led to the reconstruction of an 11th-century house which is open to the public.

These large buildings were not

suited to Iceland, needing lengths of timber unavailable in the country and having huge rooms that dwindling supplies of firewood could not heat. By the 16th century significant changes had taken place, the predominant design becoming that of the 'passage house', which contained a number of small rooms leading off from a central corridor. With increasing shortage of fuel supplies and worsening climate, the main living and eventually sleeping quarters of the house transferred to one room, the *badstofa*, a room which had orginally been a sauna. This design of house built mostly of turf and stone, with timber used only for the gable ends, survived with modifications, until the end of the last century. Timber was either imported or washed up as driftwood from as far as Siberia.

There are some fine examples of traditional turf buildings, which have been renovated and are open to the public (*see under Regional Museums*). But sadly most of them, particularly the houses of the common people, have disappeared without trace. With the coming of concrete as a building material, few thought to preserve what for centuries had provided miserable living conditions.

The oldest buildings in Iceland date from the mid-18th century and are the above mentioned turf farms along with churches, trading posts and administrative buildings. They were mostly in the hands of Danish merchants and consisted of timber buildings in the 18th- and 19th-century Danish style. Historical stone buildings are notably absent, the local stone, entirely of volcanic origin, being mostly unsuitable and difficult to work with. Exceptions are the parliament building and Stjórnarrád in Reykjavík, the manor house on Videy Island and the stone churches at Thingeyrar and Hólar.

At the end of the last century a number of Norwegian timber houses were imported into Iceland to become the homes of wealthy town-dwellers. Many of these fine houses still stand, though like most other timber dwellings they are clad on the outside with corrugated iron offering protection against the elements. There are fine examples of such houses in Seydisfjördur, Akureyrì and Reykjavík.

Most modern public buildings prior to 1950 were designed by (then) State Architect, Gudjón Samúelsson. The more interesting examples of his work include the church in Akureyri and Hallgrímskirkja in Reykjavík.

Nightlife

When Icelanders go out for the night they do it in style. They dress up and, leaving all inhibitions at home, go out for a good time. And they get it. At weekends, Reykjavík's nightclubs and discos buzz 'til the early hours, with pure enjoyment liberally dosed with alcohol. Where to go – ask an Icelander, places come and go, as does the clientele.

Astro, Austurstraeti 22, tel: 552-9222. A very popular restaurant/pub with dancing upstairs. Owned by a rock star, a top chef and a star entrepreneur, it has a unique decor that in itself is almost worth the visit.

Hotel Island, Armuli 9, tel: 568-7111. Iceland's largest club. Shows at the weekend (musicals, cabaret etc.) Consult the paper *Morgunbladid*.

Leikhúskjallarinn, Hverfisgata 19, Reykjavík, tel: 551-9636. A perennially popular club located in the basement of the National Theatre.

Further Attractions
Reykjavík

If you base yourself in Reykjavík for a few days, there is much to enjoy. Get a copy of the two free English leaflets *What's on in Reykjavík* and *Around Reykjavík*, from tourist information centre, hotels, guesthouses, the bus station and the airport. These invaluable publications list all current events and are packed with up to date information, including maps of the streets and bus routes.

The old centre: Reykjavík's city centre is clustered around the lake and harbour area. From a town of only a few thousand inhabitants at the turn of the century it has grown at a staggering rate to a modern city of 104,000. Its sprawling suburbs, for the most part architecturally uninspiring, extend for miles inland and around the coast but thankfully the old centre has avoided much of the space-saving high rise developments of other capitals.

The old residential quarter, around the lake, has many fine examples of restored houses, dating from around the turn of the century. Public buildings of note include the parliament house or Althing (1880), the cathedral (1796) the grammar school (1846) and Stjórnarrádid (1764) originally built as a prison but now the offices of the prime minister and president. New government offices are being built. Adalstraeti (Main Street) is the oldest in Reykjavík, dating back to the mid-18th century. Here the first attempt at industry was set up in the form of small workshops. The oldest house in Reykjavík, now the pub Fógetinn in Adalstraeti, is from this period.

Tjörnin (the lake): Iceland's first official settler Ingólfur Arnarson established his home near the lake where the centre of Reykjavík now lies. Today, the lake and its surrounding gardens serve as one of the city's recreational areas. Curiously, it is still a natural bird habitat and an excellent place to observe a number of species.

Hallgrímskirkja: The imposing church which dominates Reykjavík's skyline offers the best view over the city and its surroundings. A lift (open Tuesday–Sunday 10am–6pm) takes you up the bell tower. Admission: adults Ikr 200; children Ikr 100. Designed over 50 years ago, the church has only recently been completed.

The fishing harbour: Reykjavík is Iceland's major fishing centre and its harbour is home to dozens of brightly painted small vessels, packed in alongside the larger stern trawlers. On a working day you can watch as the catch is unloaded and sent for processing direct to the freezing plants. A café on the waterfront attracts fishermen off the boats and factory workers.

The swimming pool: If there is one thing that Icelanders have perfected, it must surely be the design and running of its swimming pools. Reykjavík's main pool is next to the Youth Hostel and campsite in Laugárdalur, literally "Hot spring valley".

In the old days local women would bring their laundry here, following Laugavegur (Hot Spring Road), now the principal shopping street in the capital. Now the springs are tapped and along with several deep boreholes water is extracted to heat the city's housing and its wonderful open air swimming pools. The Laugardalur complex is the largest with two main swimming areas, an open air jacuzzi and several steaming "hot pots". The entrance fee (Ikr 150) covers all of these; water slide, sauna and solarium are extra. You can also hire a swimsuit and towel.

The pool is open during the summer Monday–Friday 7am–9.30pm and Saturday–Sunday 8am–7.30pm; during the winter Monday–Friday 7am–8.30pm and Saturday–Sunday 8am–5.30pm. Swimming is a mandatory school subject in Iceland so the pools are often busy. For reasons of hygiene all bathers must shower before entering the pool, without a swim suit on, using soap and shampoo.

Ellidaá: Reykjavík can safely boast that it is the only capital city with its own salmon fishing river. Ellidaá flows through the outer suburbs and its wooded (by Icelandic standards!) valley is a recreational area with walking and cycling trails. The big attractions are the salmon which, particularly in July and August can be seen leaping clear of the water as they make their way upstream. A half-day permit for Ellidaá costs Ikr 6,800 from the Angling Club of Reykjavík (see Sports). Advance booking is necessary.

Videy Island: Reached by ferry from Sundahöfn, Reykjavík's container port, the tiny island of Videy makes an unusual evening excursion. Ferries depart at half-hourly intervals in summer, 6–8pm, returning half hourly 10pm–midnight, the schedule linked to the opening hours of the island's restaurant. At other times tel: 892-0099 for the schedule. Videy's history dates back to settlement times for it was part of Ingólfur Arnarson's land claim. Later it became the site of a monastery which, like all others in Iceland, was sacked and disbanded in the Reformation. No trace of these early residents remains but in 1755 an imposing manor house was built as the residence of the then national treasurer, Skúli Magnússon, the first Icelander to hold this office under the then Danish administration. The restored house, a fine example of Danish colonial architecture, is one of Iceland's oldest buildings. It is now an unusual, if expensive, restaurant, tel: 552-8470.

Seltjarnanes: On a clear evening the end of the Seltjarnanes peninsula is a great place to watch the sun go down over distant Snaefellsnes. Bus no. 3 from the city centre will take you most of the way there and you can continue on foot out along the shore. There's a fair amount of bird life, including waders, ducks and arctic terns.

The "Golden Circle" Tour: Iceland's classic day tour runs from Reykjavík every morning in summer and is operated by all tourist companies. Buses run to Hveragerdi, the Kerid crater, Skálholt, Gullfoss, Geysir and Thingvellir – a whirlwind itinerary of some of Iceland's most spectacular sights. It can seem too much, too fast, but the tour is the easiest way to visit these places in a short time. For details on the places themselves, see the South West chapter page 195.

TOURS OF REYKJAVÍK

The following companies offer city and area sightseeing:

Reykjavík Excursions, Hotel Loftleidir, Reykjavík, tel: 562-1011. The largest operator of day excursions. Excursions also include:

Reykjanes and Blue Lagoon (dropoff at Keflavík airport possible).

Grindavík and Krisuvík Hot Springs.

Borgarfjördur and Kaldidalur mountain route.

South Shore including Skógafoss, Solheimajökull Glacier and Dyrholaey bird cliffs.

Akranes.

BSI Travel, BSI Bus Terminal, Vatnsmyrarvegur, tel: 552-2300. Bus excursions some guided, offering transportation only across Iceland including:

Thórsmörk.

Kjölur and Sprengisandur (through the interior to Akureyri).

Veidivotn.

Gullfoss and Geysir.

Landmannalaugar and Eldgjá to Skaftafell

BSI Excursions by air include Akureyri, Myvatn, the Westmann Islands and East Greenland and can be booked through the local tour operator. Book in advance for Greenland.

Some of Reykjavík's taxi companies offer sightseeing **by taxi**. For three or more people this can work out cheaper than a bus excursion.

Hiking tours for several days are a good opportunity to meet the locals. Contact **Ferdafeélag Islands**, Mörkinn 6, 108 Reykjavík, tel: 568-2533.

Mountain bikers can get information from: **Islenski Fjallakjálaklubburinn** (Icelandic Mountain Bike Association),

PO Box 5193, 125 Reykjavík, tel: 562-0099.

Around Iceland

Nearly all towns and villages around the country offer some kind of accommodation for visitors, but organised tourism with specific attractions and activities, other than those provided by nature, are limited. Any additional services for the visitor are usually arranged by the accommodation establishments and it is always worth asking your hotel what is available.

Most towns and villages have swimming pools and many have golf courses (you will need to bring your own clubs). Boat trips and sea angling are available from a number of fishing villages; enquire at hotels.

The following towns and villages are listed alphabetically. The list includes cultural attractions, such as local museums, boat and fishing trips and excursions where available.

AKRANES

Akranes is an important fishing town, linked to Reykjavík via a ferry service (see Ferries) and makes an unusual day excursion from the capital. The local folk museum at Gardar, on the outskirts of the town is open daily in summer from 10.30am–noon and 1.30–4.30pm, tel: 431-1255. The tourist office at Skólabraut 31, tel: 431-3327, offers bike hire.

AKUREYRI

The main urban centre of north Iceland, Akureyri's cultural attractions are listed under Culture page 342. **Nonni Travel**, Brekkugata 3, tel: 461-1841 or Úrval–Úts‡n, Radhustorg 3, tel: 462-5000, offers trips around Akureyri and surrounding area, including Lake Myvatn (daily in summer) and Grímsey Island, by boat or air.

DJÚPIVOGUR

Hotel Framtid, tel: 478-8887. This hotel runs boat trips to the offshore island of Papey, believed to have been inhabited by Irish monks prior to the Norse settlement. The islands teem with seabirds, though there are no traces of the Irish settlement. The hotel arranges bike hire and sea angling trips and can suggest suitable routes for walking in the area. It also serves one of the best fish soups ever tasted.

EGILSSTADIR

The main commercial centre for the east of Iceland. Though the town is of limited interest there is much to see in the surrounding area.

East Iceland Travel Centre, Skógarlönd 3, tel: 471-2000 organizes group and individual tours around the area.

Fljótsdalshérad Touring Club offers guided local hikes, details can be had from the Egilsstadir camping site info centre, tel: 471-2320.

Húsey Youth Hostel in Hróarstunga, tel: 471-3010, offers horse-riding tours to Borgarfjördur eystri (8 days) and to Stóraud, Dyrfjöll (4 days).

Flugfélag Austurlands (East-Iceland Air), Egilsstadir airport, tel: 471-1122. Aerial sightseeing Egilsstadir-Snaefell-Kverkfjöll-Askja-Herdubreid-Egilsstadir. Also plane charter.

Tanninn, Strandgata 14 in Eskifjördur, tel: 476-1399. Trips from Egilsstadir to Vatnajökull glacier in summer; also 5-8 day jeep safaris from Egilsstadir.

ESKIFJÖRDUR

Eskifjördur has the East's maritime museum housed in a 19th-century storehouse and containing items relating to the development of the fishing and whaling industry in the area, tel: 476-1179. The museum is open daily 2–5pm, from mid-June to late August, entrance fee: Ikr 200. Just outside the town is the mine, Helgustadanama, once of the world's chief sources of Iceland spar.

FASKRÚDSFJÖRDUR

A fishing village with strong links with the French, who made Faskrudsfjördur their base for fishing operations at the end of the last century. Boat trips to the offshore island of Skrúdur, a gannet colony and scene of a tragic shipwreck some years ago, may be arranged through Vattnes Farm, tel: 475-1397. Cruises along the shore can be arranged through Hotel Bjarg, Skólavegur 49, tel: 475-1466.

HÖFN

The company Jöklaferdir, tel: 478-1701 operates most of the services for visitors from the Hotel Höfn, including the campsite and tourist information centre. It offers a number of package tours onto Vatnajökull glacier starting at Ikr 6,400 and ending at Ikr 42,000 (for a 3-day all-inclusive trip, including helicopter transport and overnight stays atop the glacier). Those who have tried snowcatting there claim that it is an exhilarating experience not to be missed. Many of the tours stop at Jökulsárlon on the way back, a beautiful glacial lagoon where a boat trip takes participants out among the icebergs. That trip may also be taken separately, takes 20–30 minutes and costs Ikr 1,200.

For independent travellers, an hour on a snowcat costs Ikr 4,900, or for Ikr 16,000 you can traverse the icecap for a whole day.

HÚSAVÍK

This commercial and fishing centre houses the regional museum, which has a stuffed polar bear that was shot on the island of Grímsey in 1973. The museum is open daily in summer 10am-5pm.

The tour company Björn Sigurdsson Húsavík arranges a three-day Ice and Fire Expedition which goes to Vatnajökull glacier, Kverkfjöll, (on the northern edge of Vatnajökull) and the volcanic caldera Askja. The tour departs from Akureyri on Mondays and Fridays at 8.15am, and picks up at Húsavík at 10am and Reynihlíd at 11am. On the second day a guided walking tour on Vatnajökull and around the hot spring area at Kverkfjöll is offered. You can camp there or stay in the hut and you will need to take all your own food. The basic cost price of Ikr 12,800 is for transportation and the guided tour only. The tour must be pre-booked. Húsavík's wooden church is one of the largest in the country. Try and find out when the church choir practices – they are one of the best in the country.

HVERAGERDI

See if you can get to look around one of the real greenhouses, it is fascinating to enter a sub-tropical world in the sub-arctic. Failing that, the tourist complex of Eden has examples of many tropical plants on show but they are rather overshadowed by the huge cafeteria, noisy games machines and expensive gift shop.

ISAFJÖRDUR

The main town in the West Fjords is way off the beaten track but it is the jumping-off point for trips to the uninhabited Hornstrandir Peninsula to the north. During the summer bus and flight connections to Ísafjördur are quite frequent with Icelandair flying there three times daily and Íslandsflug offering 1–2 flights per day from Reykjavík and 6 flights per week from Akureyri. Buses run from Reykjavík 4–6 days a week, passing through both Brjánslaekur and Hólmavík.

Fagranes, Bliki and Kjölur boat services run regular services to the Hornstrandir area (see Ferries), which can also be used as day excursions. The sea is usually pretty calm but if you don't like sea travel the Hornvík trip is best avoided on a windy day. All trips can be arranged through the tourist office, West Tours, Adalstraeti 7, tel: 456-5111 or through Hotel Ísafjördur, Silfurtorg 2, tel: 456-4111.

The tourist office also offers a 3-hour sightseeing tour of Ísafjördur and neighbouring Bolungarvík daily in summer at 8.30am (Ikr. 2,800). Other tours include a daily 4-hour trip to the bird island of Vigur (Ikr 3,000) and a day's hike with guide to the nature reserve Hornstrandir (Ikr 6,500).

Isafjördur's museum is its main cultural attraction, situated in a cluster of four beautifully restored buildings, originally warehouses, a shop and residence of the shop manager. This is the best-preserved example in the country of a traditional 18th-century trading post. The museum contains a fascinating array of old photographs, and items pertaining to the development of Isafjördur and its fishing industry. It is open daily in July and August from 10am–7pm and from 1–5pm in May-June. At other times tel: 456-4418, entrance fee: Ikr 200.

KIRKJUBAEJARKLAUSTUR

A convenient stopping off place along the south coast and formerly the site of a convent. North of the petrol station lies the aptly named Kirkjugolfid, a basalt formation created by a glacier. Daily tours from mid-July to late-August along a rugged mountain track to the spectacular Laki craters, source of the 1783 eruption that laid waste to Iceland. Austurleid coach service offers daily trips to Lakagígar craters, Eldgjá and Landmannalaugar and sightseeing tours to Skaftafell, Vatnajökull glacier and Jökulsárlon glacial lagoon and Núpsstadarskógar woods. For information contact the tourist information centre, tel: 487-4620.

LAKE MYVATN

The most popular destination for visitors in the north of Iceland, Myvatn has natural wonders and more organised tourist facilities than most parts of the country.

There are a number of options available for those who wish to take sightseeing tours in the area.

Eldá Travel Service, tel: 464-4220, offers the daily "Grand Myvatn Tour"; also tours to Gjástykki and Dettifoss.

Hlíd Travel Service, Hraunbrún by Hotel Reynihlíd, tel: 464-4103, has mountain-bike tours to places of interest east of Lake Myvatn.

Jón Árni Sigfússon, Birkihraun 11, Reykjahlíd, tel: 464-4285, has tours during the summer to Askja and Herdubreidarlindir on Monday, Wednesday and Friday and to Dettifoss–Ásbyrgi–Hljódklettar on Tuesday, Thursday and Saturday and Mt. Lúdent daily.

BSH, tel: 464-2200, offers 3-day trips to Vatnajökull–Kverkfjöll–Askja in July and August.

Myvatn is famed for its birdlife, particularly ducks, of which there are around 10,000 breeding pairs. The principal breeding areas for the ducks are on the western shore of the lake in among the countless tiny ponds dotted around. During the nesting season, the breeding area is closed to visitors (you can drive through but not get out and about on foot) from 15 May–20 July. Many of the birds are quite shy but in a good summer they can be observed, once the chicks are fledged, all over the lake, but less so from the northern shore.

The air charter company Myflug offers sightseeing flights from the airfield behind the campsite. On a clear day the 20-minute flight over the lake is well worth the Ikr 3,700. They also fly over Krafla, the Jökulsá Canyon, and over the central highlands to Askja and Kverkfjöll. There is usually a minimum participation of four persons to operate the flight. Tel: 464-4107 or just turn up at the airport and enquire.

OLAFSVÍK

Helgi Pétursson coach service, tel: 552-2300. Coach tours circling Snaefellssjökull glacier. For hiking, contact Guesthouse Höfdi, tel: 436-1650.

SAUDÁRKRÓKUR

A local regional centre and jumping off point for boat trips to Drangey. The steep cliffs of the island made it an easily defended refuge for the outlaw Grettir, though he was eventually slain through sorcery. Traces of what may have been his shelter are visible. The island also has prolific birdlife. The price of the boat trip is negotiable, according to numbers, and can be arranged through Hotel Aning, Saemundarhlíd, tel: 453-6717. The path is steep and not for sufferers of vertigo.

STÖDVARFJÖRDUR

One of the smaller villages on the east coast. The chief attraction is the private rock and mineral collection of Petra Sveinsdóttir, Fjardarbraut 21, tel: 475-8834. The collection is open to visitors all year, by arrangement, and contains fine examples of zeolites, quartz, calcedony, jasper and calcite, for which the East Fjords are renowned.

STYKKISHÓLMUR

Boat trips to the Breidafjördur Islands, including Flatey, are run by Eyjaferdir, tel: 438-1450. The village has a museum, open daily, houses in Norska Húsid, the Norwegian House.

VESTMANNAEYJAR (HEIMAEY)

The 1973 catastrophic eruption on the island of Heimaey focused attention worldwide on the plight of this fishing community. In the wake of the eruption visitors have been drawn here to witness the evidence of man's daring battle with natural forces. A film, documenting the salvage operations following the eruption, is shown twice daily in summer at the community centre in Heidarvegur. Also shown is a documentary on one Icelander's remarkable feat of survival after shipwreck in icy seas, 8 km (5 miles) off the coast of the Westmann Islands.

Ferdathjónusta Vestmannaeyja, tel: 481-1515, offers daily sightseeing tours on land and sea. Gísli Magnússon, Breakastígur 11a, tel: 481-1909, has group and sightseeing tours, and aerial sightseeing can be arranged through Flugfélag Vestmannaeyja (Valur Andersen), tel: 481-3255/852-2643. The aquarium and natural history museum is worth a

visit, open daily in summer 11am–5pm, tel: 481-1997 or by special arrangement with the caretaker, tel: 481-2426.

VOPNAFJÖRDUR

Some of the best and most expensive salmon fishing in Iceland is to be found in this area. The Hofsa River permits cost up to Ikr 40,000 for a day but need to be arranged months, even years in advance. Hotel Tangi can arrange sea angling and boat trips and can advise on any opportunities for salmon fishing. Tel: 473-1224.

Sport & Leisure

Participant Sports

Horseback Riding

The sturdy Icelandic horse is a pure and unique breed, descended from stock brought over by the first settlers from Norway in the 9th century. No horses have been imported for 800 years so the breed has remained pure. It has adapted to the demands of harsh weather and rough terrain and is ideally suited to local conditions.

Small but strong and sure-footed, the Icelandic horse was until early this century the only alternative to walking in a country where glacial rivers, mountains and icecaps were formidable obstacles. In contrast to most other breeds, the Icelandic horse has a fifth gait, the *tolt*, a fast smooth trot that lets the rider sits fast in the saddle. Long distances can be covered comfortably by *tolt*.

Nowadays it still plays a vital role in the autumn round-up, when farmers from all over the country set off for the highlands on horseback to gather their sheep. Mostly, however, horses are used for recreational purposes and riding is a popular sport among Icelanders. Increasingly, visitors to Iceland have enjoyed excursions on horseback and many farms throughout the country offer anything from a one hour ride to a seven-day trek. Most of these farms are listed in the *Icelandic Farm Holidays* booklet, (*see Tour Operators*). Below are listed some of the farms that offer longer guided treks, which must be booked in advance. Most of these can be booked through tour operators abroad, (*see Tour Operators*).

Prices start at Ikr 1,500 for an hour's ride. On long treks food and lodging is included; price per day Ikr 6,000–10,000. Information on stables from Ferdathjónusta Baenda, Hafnarstraeti 1, Reykjavík, tel: 562-3640, fax: 562-3644.

Austvadsholt, Landssveit, 851 Hella (South Iceland), tel: 487-6598. Longer treks to the Hekla and Landmannalaugar areas. Special excursions out of season, accompanying the farmers at lambing time and for the autumn roundup.

Brekkulaekur, Midfjördur, 531 Hvammstangi (North Iceland), tel: 451-2938. Longer treks through the uninhabited Arnavatnsheidi region. Pick up and return to Reykjavík is included.

Hestaleiga, Reykjakot, Hveragerdi, tel: 483-4462. Riding sessions of 1–4 hours and day trips.

Ishestar, Baejarhraun 2, 220 Hafnarfjördur, tel: 565-3044. Anything from 1-hour rides to seven-day day treks through the central highlands. Departs from various points throughout the country; for longer treks a transfer service is included from Reykjavík.

Pólar Hestar, Grytubakki II, Sudur-Thingeyrarsysla (near Grenivík, North Iceland), tel: 463-3179, fax 463-3144. Treks lasting from one hour up to 12 days.

Stora-Sandfell, Skridudalur, 701 Egilsstadir (East Iceland), tel: 471-1785. Short rides or seven-day treks into the spectacular region around Mt Snaefell.

Laxnes Farm, just outside Reykjavík, tel: 566-6179/562-1011. Offers 3-hour treks leaving at 10am and 2pm; arranges pick up from Reykjavík. Also operates a horse-rental service on Videy Island, off the coast of Reykjavík; 1-hour treks available.

Angling

Unlike many other countries, Iceland has clean water and salmon runs have not been disturbed by sea fishing. Salmon stocks are on the increase, they doubled in the last decade, so excellent fishing is available but at a price beyond most visitors. Permits per day cost Ikr 6,300–21,000 and the sky is the limit. The other snag is that most rivers have to be booked months if not years in advance. The Angling Club of Reykjavík, Haaleitisbraut 68, Reykjavík, tel: 568-6050, offers advice and arranges permits.

Trout fishing can often be arranged on the spot and at a reasonable price. Many of the farms in the *Icelandic Farm Holidays* booklet (*see Tour Operators*) offer trout fishing. An open voucher system is available for some of the farms in this network.

Sea angling can be arranged from many fishing villages and coastal farms and can be combined with a boat trip to offshore islands. This is usually best arranged direct with hotels and farms.

Iceland's waters are disease free, so all equipment including waders and boots must be disinfected (immersion for 10 minutes in a 2-percent formaldehyde solution). A certificate from a vet may be required on entering Iceland. Disinfection can be carried out on entry but a fee will be charged.

Snowcatting

Snowcatting (skidooing), is an exhilarating sport that has to be experienced. An essential means of communication on remote farms in winter, snowcats are increasingly used for recreation. In summer, trips run daily from Höfn to the Vatnajökull icecap, from where you can join a one- or two-hour guided excursion by snowcat.

A full day trip is also possible but must be booked in advance through Jöklaferdir, PO Box 66, 780 Höfn, tel: 478-1503. Price per hour: Ikr 4,900 or Ikr 16,000 for the full day. If you have a four-wheel-drive jeep you can drive the track up to the glacier (off from the Ring Road at Smyrlabjarg) an experience in itself.

Other agents also offer skidoo trips on Myrdalsjökull glacier, tel: 568-8888 for more information.

Arctic Experience (*see Tour Operators*) run snowcatting holidays in Iceland in winter and spring.

Ice Climbing

In summer guided day walks on the glaciers can be arranged from Skaftafell National Park, through the park warden's office. For more ambi-tious expeditions contact: Iceland Alpine Club, Islenski Alpaklubburinn, Mörkinni 6, Reykjavík, tel: 581-1700.

River Rafting

A half-day trip down the gorge of the River Hvítá below the waterfall Gullfoss is offered for groups by Bátafólkid, Háagerdi 41, Reykjavík, tel: 588-2900. The trip can also be booked through Reykjavík Excursions.

Downhill Skiing

Facilities and conditions for skiing in Iceland fall far short of the Alps or North America. Snow cover is most consistent in the north. In the south, foul weather, even lack of snow, often closes the slopes for days on end. On a clear, calm weekend the whole of Reykjavík seems to head out of town and there can often be long queues for the lifts. Skiing is one of Iceland's bargains – a day ticket costs around Ikr 1,000 and children pay half price. The best facilities are in Reykjavík and Akureyri but other towns also have skiing areas and shorter drag lifts.

REYKJAVÍK

The best facilities are at Bláfjöll, about half an hour's drive from Reykjavík. Buses depart from the BSI bus terminal in Reykjavík at 10am and 1.30pm at weekends; Monday and Friday at 2pm and 5pm; Tuesday, Wednesday and Thursday at 2pm, 4pm and 5pm. The track to the ski slopes is open to private four-wheel-drive vehicles.

The lifts are open 10am–6pm daily and until 10pm on Tuesday, Wednesday and Thursday, when the slopes are floodlit. There is one chairlift and several drag lifts and boot and ski hire is available. There is no overnight accommodation but a cafeteria serves snacks and drinks. For up-to-date information (recorded message in Icelandic) on conditions and opening times. Tel: 580-1111.

AKUREYRI

There is more reliable snow and similar facilities at Hlídarfjall, just above Akureyri, which has one chair lift and three drag lifts. Buses depart from the city bus terminal three times a day and the slopes are open 1–6.45pm, until 8.45pm on Tuesday, Wednesday and Thursday, and 10am–5pm at weekends. There is a cafeteria and overnight sleeping-bag accommodation. For information, tel: 562-7733.

Cross Country Skiing

Both Bláfjöll and Hlídarfjall have marked cross country ski trails but most people will probably want to head off on their own. This is quite safe in the farmed lowlands but venturing into uninhabited areas is only for the properly equipped and fit.

Summer Skiing

The Kerlingarfjöll Mountains, just off the Kjölur route through the central highlands, offer summer skiing. The season starts as soon as the track opens and goes on as long as the snow lasts (mid-June to late-August). There are drag lifts, a camp site and sleeping-bag accommodation available. Buses to Kerlingarfjöll are operated through BSI (*see Tour Operators*); up-to-date information on departures can be obtained from them. A full weekend package, including transportation, food and lodging, instruction and lift pass costs Ikr 15,900. Book through BSI, Vatnsmⴕrarvegur 10, Reykjavík, tel: 562-3320.

Golf

Golf is thriving in Iceland with over 50 courses, mostly 9 hole. Eighteen-hole courses are at Reykjavík, Hafnarfjördur, Gardabaer, Hella, Keflavík, the Westmann Islands and Akureyri. For information contact: Golfsamband Islands, Engjavegur 6, Reykjavík, tel: 568-6686.

The major golfing event in Iceland is the Arctic Open, which takes place in June each year and is open to professional and amateur golfers alike. Hosts to the event are the Akureyri Golf Club, PO Box 896, 602 Akureyri, tel: 462-2974. A complete package including flights, accommodation and entrance fees can be booked through tour operators abroad.

Watersports

With sea and lake temperatures so low, it is a wonder that anyone would contemplate water sports in Iceland. Luckily most places offering water sports also rent out wetsuits which makes the prospect of water skiing or wind surfing a little less daunting.

Akureyri: Jet skiing in the harbour.

Egilsstadir: Jet skiing on the lake

Logurinn from Skipalaekur farm, tel: 471-1324.

Grimsnes: Jet skiing and waterskiing on Lake Svínavatn, near Laugarvatn, tel: 486-4500.

Laugarvatn: Windsurfing and boat rental at Lake Laugarvatn, tel: 486-1151.

Spectator Sports

Icelanders are avid sports fans and **handball**, **football** and **basketball** are all popular. Football is a summer sport, whilst handball and basketball being indoor sports are played year round. In all three sports Iceland has excellent players under contract to well-known teams abroad. Most international matches take place in Reykjavík and international and national games are advertised in the press. For more information contact: the Iceland Sports Association, Iprottasamband Islands, Iprottamidstodin, Laugardalur, Reykjavík, tel: 581-3377.

Boxing is banned in Iceland, but Glima, a form of **wrestling** from settlement times, is still practised. Information from Glímusamband Islands at the Iceland Sports Association.

Possibly Iceland's best known spectator event is **chess** and the country has produced several grand masters in recent years. International chess tournaments are regularly held in Iceland, and Reykjavík was the venue for the Fischer-Spassky match in 1972.

Riding clubs hold races and other events throughout the summer.

The Reykjavík **Marathon** takes place in August each year and includes the marathon, half marathon and a 7.5 km (4.6 miles) fun run. For information and registration contact Úrval/Útsyn Travel, Lágmúli 4, Reykjavík, tel: 569-9300 or the Athletics Federation of Iceland, Laugardalur Sports Centre, tel: 581-3377.

Shopping

What to Buy

Woollen goods: The Icelandic sheep is an almost pure breed descended from the animals brought over by the first settlers. Its fleece is of an exceptional quality in that the outer hairs are long and coarse, containing natural oils to keep water out, whilst the inner wool is soft and insulates well against the cold. The two types spun together, create a wool that is durable and naturally water resistant, yet soft and warm. It is this wool which is used to produce the beautiful handknitted sweaters with traditional patterns around the yoke. A simple cottage industry has grown to be one of the country's major agricultural export, and though the traditional sweaters are still handknitted, the bulk of the woollen goods are now machine made. For a handknitted sweater expect to pay Ikr 6,000–9,000 but if you buy the wool, circular needles and pattern (available in a number of foreign languages) you can knit yourself one for under Ikr 3,500.

Sheepskin goods: These are expensive but the quality is good. Hats, slippers and gloves sell for around Ikr 1,500–3,000.

Books: There are many fine and expensive books on Iceland intended for the visitor. Most are available in English. Many of these books can be bought abroad for the same price through tour operators who also run a book and map service (*see Tour Operators*). Books published outside Iceland will be cheaper to buy abroad.

Fine art cards: There are some very attractive yet inexpensive cards depicting the works of some of Iceland's finest painters such as Johannes Kjarval and Asgrimur Jónsson. These are available at the National Gallery in Reykjavík and at bookshops.

Slides: If bad weather was a feature of your holiday, excellent slides can be bought to supplement your own, there are also good slides of volcanic eruptions. At souvenir and book shops.

Ceramics: If the rather garish lava ceramics are not to your taste, shop around. Pottery in Iceland is art rather than functional, so expect to pay accordingly. There are some fine potters producing unusual pieces.

Food: If you can protect your luggage against the smell take back some dried fish. It weighs nothing, keeps for ever and may amuse your friends. Eat it with lashings of butter. Smoked trout and salmon also keep quite well. If you like *skyr*, take some home, you can make your own culture in the same way as yoghurt and it freezes well. A wide range of Icelandic foods are sold at the duty free shop at Keflavík Airport for departing passengers.

Where to Shop

The best selection of woollen goods, books and crafts is in Reykjavík. Most of the shops are in the city centre, which makes shopping quick and painless (apart from the bill that is). Reykjavík has two main shopping areas; in the centre, most of the tourist shops are in and around Hafnarstraeti and Austurstraeti, though Laugavegur, leading out of the centre, has most of the fashion shops. The other main shopping area is Kringlan mall, out of the town centre but easily reached by bus. The woollen goods and souvenir shop Rammagerdin has a branch here, there is a Hagkaup supermarket if you need to stock up on food at a reasonable price, and there are many attractive but pricey boutiques.

For handknitted sweaters it is worth trying at some of the establishments in the Icelandic Farm Holidays network. They are usually cheaper than in the shops and will be home- as well as hand-knitted.

In Reykjavík try the following shops for a variety of gifts woollens, ceramics, crafts and jewellery:

Alafoss, Pósthússtraeti 13, Reykjavík.
The Icelandic Handicrafts Centre, Hafnarstraeti 3, Reykjavík.
Islandia, Kringlan shopping mall.

Rammagerdin, Hafnarstraeti 19, Reykjavík and in the Kringlan mall.
Thorvaldsen's Basar, Austurstraeti 4, Reykjavík. (Proceeds to charity.)
Prices are fairly standard but shops sometimes have special offers.

For books: Eymundsson, Austurstraeti 18, Reykjavík and Mál og Menning, Laugavegur 18, Reykjavík.

ceramics, jewellery and hand-crafted gifts: Hladvarpinn, Vesturgata 3, Reykjavík, Kirsuberjatréd, Vesturgata 4, (across the street), or the various other shops or ateliers in that area.

food: Hagkaup in Kringlan mall.

photographic equipment: Hans Petersen, Bankastraeti 4, Reykjavík and in the Kringlan mall.

Most shops will accept payment by credit card, travellers cheques or Eurocheque. Some offer discounts for cash and it is always worth asking.

Tax-Free Shopping

All non-residents (other than Icelandic citizens) are entitled to a VAT refund on goods purchased in Iceland if their value exceeds ISK 5,000 in one shop.

You pay the full amount, VAT included, in the shop. Ask for your VAT-refund and the shop assistant will fill out a special "Tax-Refund Cheque" which you then take along with your purchased articles. The refund (less about 5 percent handling charge) will amount to approximately 15 percent of the purchase price.

Departure from Keflavík Airport: If the refund amount is less than ISK 5,000 you go directly to Landsbanki Íslands (agent for Europe Tax-Free Shopping) in the transit area. Present the purchased goods for inspection and collect your refund in the currency of your choice.

If the refund amount is more than ISK 5,000 you contact the Customs Authorities Office prior to check-in and have them stamp your "Tax-Refund Cheque". Please make sure that you are able to present the purchased articles, on request. Refunds are paid out at Landsbanki Íslands in the transit area. Please note that you do not have to present woollen goods for inspection due to their bulk.

Departures outside Keflavík Airport: When leaving Iceland from other departure points than Keflavík Airport you can have your "Tax-Refund Cheque"

stamped by customs officials. Please make sure that you are able to present the purchased articles (other than woollens), on request. Refunds are paid out at Landsbanki Íslands outlets at points of departure in the currency of your choice.

Alternately you can cash your "Tax-Refund Cheque" at any one of 3,000 refund points in Europe, or you can have the refund sent to your home address or paid to your credit card account. Write to: Europe Tax-Free Shopping AB, Kontinentgatan 2, P.O.Box 128, 231 22 Trelleborg, Sweden.

Language

About Icelandic

Icelandic is one of the Nordic family of languages and most closely resembles Norwegian and Faroese. Remarkably, the Icelandic spoken today has not changed that greatly from the language of the early Norse settlers. In fact modern Icelanders can read, without difficulty, the sagas written in the 13th century.

The *Landnámabók* (Book of Settlements), compiled probably in the 12th and 13th centuries, tells of a number of settlers from the British Isles, some of whom may actually have been themselves descendants of Norwegians. The exact numbers will never be known but of significance is the virtual absence of words of Celtic origin in the language. These are limited to a few place names, such as Papey and Dimon and personal names such as Kjartan and Njáll.

For the foreigner, Icelandic is daunting. The good news is that most Icelanders, particularly the younger generations, speak English fluently, as well as Danish, Swedish or Norwegian. German and French are less widely spoken, but also taught at school. Icelanders are by nature quite reticent with foreigners. Don't mistake their shyness for rudeness or lack of interest – it may take a while to draw them into conversation but it will be worth it. Similarly if you are able to pick up a few phrases of Icelandic, it will be much appreciated.

The Sounds

Stress, in Icelandic, falls naturally on the first syllable of a word. The following examples of pronunciation are for guidance only – many Icelandic sounds simply do not exist in English.

Vowels and Consonants

a as in *hard*
á as in *how*
e as in *get*
é as in *yet*
i or y as in *thin*
í or y as in *been*
o as in *ought*
ó as in *gold*
ö as in *first*
u as in *hook*
ú as in *fool*

ae as in *fight*
au between the sounds in *fate* and *oil*, as in the French *feuille*
ey/ei as in *day*

∂ is th as in *the*
π is th as in *thing*
fn is pn as in *open*
g when followed by i (except at the start of a word) is *y* as in *yet*
hv is *kf* as in *thankful*
j is *y* as in *yet*
ll is *tl* as in *bottle*
r is always lightly rolled
rn is *tn* as in *button*
rl is *rtl* as in *heartless*
tn and **fn** when at the end of words are almost silent.

Geographical Features

The following lists show common elements in place names, an example, and an English translation.
Á (river) *Hvítá* (white river)
Borg (rocky crag)
    Dimmuborgir (dark crags)
Breidur (broad)
    Breidafjördur (broad fjord)
Brekka (slope)
    Brekkulaekur (slope stream)
Dalur (valley)
    Fljótsdalur (river valley)
Drangur (column)

Drangajökull (rock column/glacier)
Eldur (fire)
    Eldfell (fire mountain)
Eyja (island)   *Flatey* (flat island)
Eyri (sand spit)
    Thingeyri (assembly sand spit)
Fell (mountain)
    Snaefell (snow mountain)
Fjall (mountain)
    Bláfjöll (blue mountains)
Fjördur (fjord)
    Hafnarfjördur (harbour fjord)
Fljót (large River)
    Markarfljót (wood river)
Foss (waterfall) *Gullfoss* (gold falls)
Gígur (crater)
    Lakagígar (cow's stomach craters)
Gil (ravine)
    Jökulgil (glacier ravine)
Gjá (fissure)
    Grjótagjá (rock fissure)
Heidi (heath)
    Hellisheidi (cave heath)
Hellir (cave)
    Sönghellir (song caves)
Hlid (hillside)
    Reykjahlíd (steamy hillside)
Hóll (hill/hillock)
    Vatnsdalsholar (lake valley hills)
Holt (hill)
    Brattholt (steep hill)
Hraun (lava)
    Odádahraun (ill deeds lava)
Höfdi (cape)
    Höfdabrekka (cape slope)
Höfn (harbour)
    Thórshöfn (Thor's harbour)
Jökull (glacier)
    Vatnajökull (lake glacier)
Kvísl (river)
    Jökulgilskvísl (glacier ravine river)
Laekur (stream)
    Varmilaekur (warm stream)
Laug (hot spring)
    Laugarvatn (hot spring lake)
Lind (spring)
    Hvannalindir (angelica springs)
Lón (lagoon)
    ökulsárlón (glacier river lagoon)
Myri (marsh)
    Myrdalsjökull (marsh valley glacier)
Nes (peninsula)
    Snaefellnes (snow mountain glacier)
Reykur (steam)
    Reykjanes (steam peninsula)
Sandur (sand)

    Myrdalssandur (marsh valley sand)
Skard (pass)
    Kerlingarskard (troll wife's pass)
Skógur (wood)
    Skógafoss (wood falls)
Stadur (place)
    Egilsstadir (Egil's place)
Strönd (coast/Beach)
    Hornstrandir (horn peak coast)
Tindur (peak)
    Tindfjöll (peak mountains)
Tjörn (pond)
    Störu-tjarnir (big ponds)
Vatn (lake)
    Hvítarvatn (white river lake)
Vík (small bay)
    Reykjavík (steam bay)
Vogur (inlet)
    Kópavogur (seal pup inlet)
Völlur (plain)
    Thingvellir (assembly plains)

Numbers

Einn	One
Tveir	Two
Thrir	Three
Fjorir	Four
Fimm	Five
Sex	Six
Sjö	Seven
Atta	Eight
Níu	Nine
Tíu	Ten
Ellefu	Eleven
Tólf	Twelve
Threttán	Thirteen
Fjórtán	Fourteen
Fimmtán	Fifteen
Sextán	Sixteen
Sautján	Seventeen
Atján	Eighteen
Nítján	Nineteen
Tuttugu	Twenty
Tuttugu og einn	Twenty one
Thrjátíu	Thirty
Fjörtíu	Forty
Fimmtíu	Fifty
Sextíu	Sixty
Sjötíu	Seventy
Attatíu	Eighty
Níutíu	Ninety
Hundrad	Hundred
Thúsund	Thousand
Miljon	Million

At the Restaurant

Most restaurant staff speak some English or other Scandinavian languages. The list below will help you order from simpler menus.

Eg aetla ad fá... – I would like...
Attu til...? – Have you got any...?
Meira... – More...
Ekki meira takk – No more thank you
Mjög gott – Very good

Matsedill – Menu
Forréttir – Starters
Fiskréttir – Fish dishes
Fiskur – Fish
Kjötréttir – Meat dishes
Kjöt – Meat
Eftirréttir – Desserts
Drykkir – Drinks

Lambakjöt – Lamb
Nautakjöt – Beef
Svínakjöt – Pork
Kjúklingur – Chicken
Hangikjöt – Smoked lamb
Ysa – Haddock
Lúda – Halibut
Raekjur – Prawns
Lax – Salmon
Silungur/Bleikja – Trout
Graenmeti – Vegetables
Kartüflur – Potatoes
Franskar – Chips
Blómkál – Cauliflower
Graenar baunir – Peas
Raudkál – Red cabbage
Sveppir – Mushrooms
Gulraetur – Carrots
Rófur – Turnips

Salat – Salad
Sósa – Sauce
Súpa – Soup
Is – Icecream
Kaka/Terta – Cake

Braud – Bread
Smjör – Butter
Te – Tea
Kaffi – Coffee
Mjólk – Milk
Sykur – Sugar

Appelsínusafi – Orange juice
Björ – Beer
Pilsner – Low alcohol beer
Hvítvín – White wine
Raudvín – Red wine
Vatn – Water

Useful Words and Phrases

Please: Icelandic does not have an equivalent to *please*. The phrase *Gerdu svo vel* is used to invite a person into a house or to the table. It also translates to *here you are* when giving something to somebody. On a public notice *please* is *vinsamlegast*. For example, *please take your shoes off*, a common request when entering a home or changing room, is *vinsamlegast farid ur skonum*. When leaving the table or saying goodbye after a meal or drinks it is customary to thank the host by saying *Takk fyrir mig*.

Hello/good morning – *Gódan dag*
Good evening – *Gott kvöld*
Goodnight – *Góda nótt*
How are you? – *Hvad segirdu gott?*
Fine, and you? – *Allt fint, en Thú?*
Fine – *Allt fínt*
Alright – *Allt i lagi*
Goodbye – *Bless*
Yes – *Já*
No – *Nei*
Thanks – *Takk*
Thank you very much – *Takk fyrir*
Yes please – *Já takk*
No thank you – *Nei takk*
I would like... – *Eg aetla ad fá...*
May I have... – *Ma eg fá...*
When? – *Hvenaer?*
Today – *I dag*
Tomorrow – *A morgun*
Yesterday – *I gaer*
In the morning – *Fyrir hádegi*
In the afternoon – *Eftir hádegi*
Cheers! – *Skál!*
How much does this cost? – *Hvad kostar Thetta?*
Come! – *Komdu!*

Signs

Toilet – *Snyrting*
Gents – *Karlar*
Ladies – *Konur*
Open – *Opid*
Closed – *Lokad*
Danger – *Haetta*
Forbidden – *Bannad*
Campsite – *Tjaldstaedi*
Entry – *Inngangur*
Exit – *Utgangur*
Parking – *Bílastaedi*
Schedule – *Aaetlun*
Airport – *Flugvöllur*
Blind summit (road sign) – *Blindhaed*
Jeep track – *Jeppavegur*

Police – *Lögreglan*
Hospital – *Sjúkrahús*
Health Centre – *Heilsugaeslastöd*
Doctor – *Laeknir*
Dentist – *Tannlaeknir*
Bank – *Banki*
Post Office – *Póstur og Simi*
Chemist – *Apotek*
Co-op store – *Kaupfelag*
Swimming pool – *Sundlaug*
Mechanic/garage – *Verkstaedi*

Further Reading

Where to buy Books

Iceland Review, Nóatún 17, 105 Reykjavík, tel: 511-5700, publishes a large selection of books on Iceland, listed in a catalogue. Due to the relative difficulty in obtaining books on Iceland abroad, many tour operators stock books for visitors.

Carwardine, Mark. *Iceland: Nature's Meeting Place.* Iceland Review, Reykjavík, 1986. A guide to Iceland's wildlife and wild places.

Escritt, Tony. *Iceland: The Traveller's Guide.* The Iceland Information Centre, Harrow, Middlesex, (UK) 1990. For group expeditions and backcountry travellers.

Kristinsson, Hördur. *A guide to the Flowering Plants and Ferns of Iceland.* Orn & Orlygur, Reykjavík, 1987.

Magnússon, Magnús. *Iceland Saga.* The Bodley Head, London, 1987. An invaluable introduction to Iceland's early history and literature.

Magnússon, Sigurdur A. *The Icelanders.* Reykjavík, Forskot Publishing Company, 1990. A study of the people, their culture and its roots.

Perkins, John W. *Iceland: A Geological Field Guidebook.* Department of Extra-Mural Studies, University College Cardiff (UK) 1983. On Iceland's geology.

Sagas

Many of Iceland's Sagas have been translated into English and other languages; particularly readable are *Egills Saga*, *Laxdaela Saga* and *Njáls Saga*. Nobel prize winning author Halldor Laxness has also been translated. Recommended are *Independent People*, *Under the Glacier* and *Salka Valka*.

Art/Photo Credits

Photography by
Georges Athias 306/307
Mick Barnard/Nor-Ice 148, 194, 236R, 239, 240, 247
Bodo Bondzio 22, 131, 171, 182, 188, 227, 233, 234, 280/281, 293
Julian Cremona 50, 74, 152, 294L, 282, 311
Bragi Gudmundsson 24, 75, 95, 96, 219
Hrafn Gunnlaugsson 36, 37, 40/41, 45
Catherine Harlow 7, 142, 143, 145, 156/157, 175R, 210, 224/225, 229, 232/233, 242/243, 245, 249R, 250, 251, 254, 285, 294, 295, 303, 304/305, 312, 318
Bob Krist 12/13, 14/15, 21, 72, 73, 77, 78, 79, 82/83, 90, 91, 92, 95, 98/99, 103, 104, 107, 108/109, 110, 112, 113, 114, 117, 119, 120/121, 122/123, 125, 126, 127, 128/129, 130, 132, 133, 134, 135, 139, 149, 158/159, 162/163, 164, 170, 177, 180, 186, 189, 199, 206/207, 217, 220, 223, 244, 246, 261, 263, 277, 286, 308, 314, 317, 319
Nikos Photography 16/17, 200, 309
Tony Perrottet 1, 18/19, 25R, 26, 34, 42, 44, 46, 47, 56, 58/59, 62, 63L, 63R, 70/71, 80/81, 86, 89, 93, 94, 100, 102, 105, 115, 136, 137, 138, 144, 146/147, 160/161, 168/169, 175L, 176, 178, 181, 183, 192/193, 195, 197, 202/203, 208, 211, 212, 214, 216, 218, 221, 222, 228L, 230, 256/257, 258, 262, 264, 265, 266, 267, 270/271, 272/273, 274, 275, 276, 284, 287, 288/289, 290, 291, 292, 296/297, 298, 299, 300, 301, 302, 320
Andy Price 174, 187, 196
Barbro Schröder 76
Hasse Schröder 27, 28/29, 48, 49, 65, 84/85, 88, 124, 140/141, 155, 179, 184/185, 198, 201, 226, 252, 278/279, 313, 315

Maps Berndtson & Berndtson

Visual Consultant V. Barl

Index

A
B
C
D
E
F
G
H
I
J
a
b
c
d
e
f
g
h
i
j
k
l